Mac®
OS 9.1
Black Book

CORIOLIS™

President and CEO
Keith Weiskamp

Publisher
Steve Sayre

Acquisitions Editor
Charlotte Carpentier

Product Marketing Manager
Tracy Rooney

Project Editor
Toni Zuccarini Ackley

Technical Reviewer
Gordon Larson

Production Coordinator
Laura Wellander

Cover Designer
Jody Winkler

Layout Designer
April Nielsen

CD-ROM Developer
Chris Nusbaum

Mac® OS 9.1 Black Book

Limits of Liability and Disclaimer of Warranty

The author and publisher of this book have used their best efforts in preparing the book and the programs contained in it. These efforts include the development, research, and testing of the theories and programs to determine their effectiveness. The author and publisher make no warranty of any kind, expressed or implied, with regard to these programs or the documentation contained in this book.

The author and publisher shall not be liable in the event of incidental or consequential damages in connection with, or arising out of, the furnishing, performance, or use of the programs, associated instructions, and/or claims of productivity gains.

Trademarks

Trademarked names appear throughout this book. Rather than list the names and entities that own the trademarks or insert a trademark symbol with each mention of the trademarked name, the publisher states that it is using the names for editorial purposes only and to the benefit of the trademark owner, with no intention of infringing upon that trademark.

The Coriolis Group, LLC
14455 N. Hayden Road
Suite 220
Scottsdale, Arizona 85260

(480) 483-0192
FAX (480) 483-0193
www.coriolis.com

Library of Congress Cataloging-in-Publication Data
Bell, Mark R.
    Mac OS 9.1 black book / by Mark R. Bell and Debrah Suggs.
        p.   cm.
    Includes index.
    ISBN 1-57610-929-1
    1. Mac OS.   2. Operating systems (Computers).   3. Macintosh
(Computer)--Programming.   I. Suggs, Debrah D.   II. Title.
QA76.76.O63 B4496   2000
005.4'469--dc21   00-047552
                                                                                              CIP

Printed in the United States of America ——
10   9   8   7   6   5   4   3   2   1

CORIOLIS™

The Coriolis Group, LLC • 14455 North Hayden Road, Suite 220 • Scottsdale, Arizona 85260

Dear Reader:

Coriolis Technology Press was founded to create a very elite group of books: the ones you keep closest to your machine. Sure, everyone would like to have the Library of Congress at arm's reach, but in the real world, you have to choose the books you rely on every day *very* carefully.

To win a place for our books on that coveted shelf beside your PC, we guarantee several important qualities in every book we publish. These qualities are:

- *Technical accuracy*—It's no good if it doesn't work. Every Coriolis Technology Press book is reviewed by technical experts in the topic field, and is sent through several editing and proofreading passes in order to create the piece of work you now hold in your hands.

- *Innovative editorial design*—We've put years of research and refinement into the ways we present information in our books. Our books' editorial approach is uniquely designed to reflect the way people learn new technologies and search for solutions to technology problems.

- *Practical focus*—We put only pertinent information into our books and avoid any fluff. Every fact included between these two covers must serve the mission of the book as a whole.

- *Accessibility*—The information in a book is worthless unless you can find it quickly when you need it. We put a lot of effort into our indexes, and heavily cross-reference our chapters, to make it easy for you to move right to the information you need.

Here at The Coriolis Group we have been publishing and packaging books, technical journals, and training materials since 1989. We're programmers and authors ourselves, and we take an ongoing active role in defining what we publish and how we publish it. We have put a lot of thought into our books; please write to us at **ctp@coriolis.com** and let us know what you think. We hope that you're happy with the book in your hands, and that in the future, when you reach for software development and networking information, you'll turn to one of our books first.

Keith Weiskamp
President and CEO

Jeff Duntemann
VP and Editorial Director

Look for these related books from The Coriolis Group:

The Mac® OS 9 Book
by Mark R. Bell

Windows® 2000 Mac Support Little Black Book
by Gene Steinberg and Pieter Paulson

Illustrator® 9 f/x and Design
by Sherry London

Illustrator® 9 Visual Insight
by T. Michael Clark

Photoshop® Visual Insight
by Ramona and Joshua Pruitt

Also recently published by Coriolis Technology Press:

C++ Black Book
by Steven Holzner

Data Modeling Essentials, 2nd Edition
by Graeme Simsion

Software Project Management: From Concept to Deployment
by Kieron Conway

XHTML Black Book
by Steven Holzner

XML Black Book, 2nd Edition
by Natanya Pitts

To my wife, Virginia: Tar Heel, Blue Devil,
unofficial Ambassador of North Carolina.
—Mark R. Bell

❧

To my mother and father, Marvin and Martha Dodgens,
so they can see their names in print.
—Debrah D. Suggs

❧

About the Authors

Mark R. Bell is a best-selling author of over 22 computer books, articles, and software manuals, including *The Mac Web Server Book, The Mac OS 8 Book, Mac OS 8.5 Black Book, The Mac OS 8.6 Book,* and *The Mac OS 9 Book.* He is also a technical editor, contributing author, and has been known to speak to large groups of people on occasion. Mark lives in Chapel Hill, North Carolina, with his wife, Virginia.

Debrah D. Suggs is the best-selling coauthor of *Mac OS 8.5 Black Book,* contributing author to several Mac books, technical editor, software trainer, and system administrator. She currently serves as the Macintosh Specialist for the Systems Administration group of Duke University Office of Information Technology.

Acknowledgments

Creating computer books is a lot like putting on a play because there are many roles to perform, some of which are more visible than others. A large cast of characters made this book possible, including Charlotte Carpentier (Casting), Toni Zuccarini Ackley (Executive Producer), Virginia D. Smith (Script Editor), Mary Catherine Bunn (Script Proofreader), Gordon Larson (Fact Checker), Laura Wellander (Set Design), as well as a cast of dozens who make us look good and whom we never get to meet. You *are* appreciated!

Next, there are the Macintosh professionals around the world who tolerate our queries for information and provide their software for our CD-ROM. In return, they ask only for a free copy of the book instead of what their time and effort is really worth. Caerwyn Pearce is a consistent contributor of his information on Mac OS error codes, and the very glamorous Rob Terrell can accurately take credit for getting us into the book writing business. Um, thanks, Rob. ;-)

Finally, we receive a huge amount of support (and tolerance) from our family and friends, who push us on to complete our assigned tasks. Virginia, Mary Catherine, Gregg, Marc, Anthony, Bailey, and Ruby all receive credit in this category.

Contents at a Glance

Table of Contents

Chapter 5
Disk and File Systems **131**

Immediate Solutions

Introduction

Thanks for buying the *Mac OS 9.1 Black Book*! As system administrators and managers of large installations of Macs, we noticed an absence of reference-style books for intermediate and advanced Mac users. So, in 1999, we wrote *Mac OS 8.5 Black Book* to meet the needs of power users, network administrators, system technicians, and even programmers and developers. A lot has changed since Mac OS 8.5 and we cover it all in this book, as well as put it into a historical context relating to previous versions of the Mac OS.

Is This Book for You?

The *Mac OS 9.1 Black Book* was written with the intermediate or advanced user in mind. Among the topics that are covered are:

- Comprehensive coverage of all system-level components

- Detailed analysis of Internet and multimedia features

- Historical reference of how the Mac OS has changed in this version

Of course, not everyone who needs this book is a bona fide Mac geek, and not all the geeks who read this book will have new and exciting information revealed on every page. Instead, this book is for most everyone in-between these two poles. If you are not as experienced with the Mac OS, then we suggest you read Mark's best-selling *The Mac OS 9 Book* instead.

How to Use This Book

In this book, each chapter builds on the previous chapter, each of which is divided into two sections:

- A technical section, "In Depth," which covers the main topics found in each chapter and is designed to lay the groundwork for the other two sections or serve as a standalone section that can be reviewed at any time.

- A practical section, which consists of "Immediate Solutions" that cover the steps necessary to administer the Mac OS. This is usually the largest section and may be used as a refresher course to test your skills for a particular topic.

Several appendixes are included as well, covering tips, trick, tools, shortcuts, and even a comprehensive listing of Mac OS error codes from Caerwyn Pearce.

What do you need to use this book most efficiently? First, this book assumes you have significant experience with the Macintosh family of computers, the Internet, and some level of interest in cross-platform connectivity and interoperability. This last point may not seem too relevant for many readers, but let us suggest that we all need to realize that the Mac OS will probably never reach the level of monopoly that the various versions of Microsoft Windows enjoy, and that the best OS is often the one that gets along best with all the others. To this end, we're assuming that you share this view on the state of things and are interested in using the Mac OS to communicate and share data with other operating systems, and that you have some experience with these operating systems.

Next, it assumes that you have a Mac with a PowerPC processor, which is required to run Mac OS 8.6 and higher. Finally, this book assumes that you have experience with, and connectivity to, the Internet. You may have a permanent connection through your computer at work, or you may be one of the lucky ones with Internet access through a cable modem, DSL, ISDN, or frame relay. But even us poor souls with a modem and a PPP connection can still qualify.

The following overview of the book's chapters will help you see how we've organized things; feel free to jump right into the middle if that's what you think you need. Each chapter is self-contained, but the first paragraph or so will make it clear if you need to see a previous chapter in order to proceed with the present chapter:

- **Chapter 1** introduces the latest version of the Mac OS and all of its recent additions. The Immediate Solutions show how to use its most significant features.

- **Chapter 2** covers everything you need to know to successfully launch and quit the Mac OS. The Immediate Solutions provide detailed examples of how to perform these tasks and how to correct the most common problems associated with starting and stopping the OS, such as Extension conflicts.

- **Chapter 3** introduces the main elements of the Mac OS's many user environment options. The Immediate Solutions explain how to make changes to the user environment and correct any problems you might encounter while making such changes.

- **Chapter 4** covers how to install, add, and remove portions of the Mac OS, as well as the default configuration settings. The Immediate Solutions take you through the exact steps required to add, modify, or delete the Mac OS.

- **Chapter 5** provides details on the disk and file systems used by the Mac OS. The Immediate Solutions cover everything you need to know to administer fixed and removable media and how to use the HFS and HFS+ formats of the Mac OS.

- **Chapter 6** explores the memory management capabilities of the Mac OS. The Immediate Solutions provide examples of how to configure and maximize the efficiency of your computer's physical and virtual memory.

- **Chapter 7** covers all the issues of mobile computing for PowerBook and iBook users. The Immediate Solutions show users how to take advantage of the Mac OS's built-in security features and the improved Location Manager.

- **Chapter 8** details the printing capabilities of the Mac OS. The Immediate Solutions show users how to select, configure, and print to a wide variety of local and networked printers.

- **Chapter 9** introduces the Mac OS's built-in multimedia capabilities. The Immediate Solutions describe how to best use the audio and video features on the Mac OS, paying close attention to the latest release of QuickTime.

- **Chapter 10** explores the many ways in which the Mac OS is compatible with the various version of Microsoft Windows. The Immediate Solutions show users how to exchange data with users of Windows 95, 98, NT, and 2000, as well as run these versions of Windows on their own Macs.

- **Chapter 11** covers the many networking capabilities of the Mac OS. The Immediate Solutions show users how to connect to local area networks and the Internet using AppleTalk and TCP/IP using the Mac OS and several popular applications.

- **Chapter 12** explores how to connect the Mac OS to the Internet using TCP/IP. The Immediate Solutions explain how to install the most popular network adapters and modems, as well as configure TCP/IP communication software and Apple Remote Access.

- **Chapter 13** covers the many types of Internet and intranet services that can be provided using the Mac OS. The Immediate Solutions cover how to install and configure software to serve Web, FTP, email, and other services.

- **Chapter 14** covers the built-in scripting abilities of the Mac OS. The Immediate Solutions show how to use AppleScript to perform routine tasks, as well as what other scripting options are available to Mac OS users.

- **Chapter 15** explores the Java capabilities on the Mac OS. The Immediate Solutions explore installing Mac OS runtime for Java, the Apple Applet Runner, and Java security, as well as using applets in HTML documents.

- **Chapter 16** covers all the aspects of system security that are important for single users, network users, and Internet access. The Immediate Solutions explain how to make your Mac as safe as possible.

- **Chapter 17** covers the tools you'll need to monitor your Mac's internal events and system integrity. The Immediate Solutions show users how to use the tools necessary to patrol the state of the OS, its RAM, and network usage.

- **Chapter 18** covers how to troubleshoot the Mac OS. The Immediate Solutions explain how to resolve Extension conflicts, overcome boot problems, fix disk errors, and much more.

- **Appendix A** lists the most popular shortcuts for the Mac OS.

- **Appendix B** lists the best tools to help administer the Mac OS.

- **Appendix C** covers the changes and enhancements to the Mac OS.

- **Appendix D** provides explanations for the most common Mac OS error codes.

- **Appendix E** provides several additional resources for getting help.

The *Black Book* Philosophy

Written by experienced professionals, Coriolis *Black Books* provide immediate solutions to global programming and administrative challenges, helping you complete specific tasks, especially critical ones that are not well documented in other books. The *Black Book*'s unique two-part chapter format—thorough technical overviews followed by practical immediate solutions—is structured to help you use your knowledge, solve problems, and quickly master complex technical issues to become an expert. By breaking down complex topics into easily manageable components, our format helps you quickly find what you're looking for.

We welcome your feedback on this book. You can email us directly at **mbell@MacOSBook.com** and **dsuggs@MacOSBook.com**. Errata, updates, and more are available at **www.MacOSBook.com**.

Chapter 1

Using Mac OS 9.1

In Depth

This chapter introduces the key components of version 9.1 of the Mac OS. Although a number of differences have emerged between 9.1 and previous releases of the Mac OS since version 8.0, the main concepts haven't changed. If you're familiar with previous versions of the Mac OS, you'll be able to use 9.1 with very little difficulty. Veterans and new users alike will be amazed by the speed, stability, and features of the latest version of the Mac OS. This chapter will explain how to utilize the enhancements introduced in version 9.1.

What's New in Mac OS 9.1?

Mac OS 9.1 builds on previous versions of the Mac OS by incorporating welcomed enhancements into an operating system that has long been known as one of the world's easiest to use. What's new in Mac OS 9.1 falls under the following categories:

- Improved Mac OS features
- New Mac OS features
- New applications

Mac OS 9.1's tweaks and new features are far too numerous to describe in detail here. However, the following list captures the most significant changes:

- FireWire and USB support for connecting peripherals and sharing printers
- ColorSync 3.0
- New menu for navigating Finder windows
- Image Capture 1.0 for connecting with digital cameras
- File Exchange 3.0
- Support for multiple users
- Apple File Security with 128-bit encryption
- Rewritten General Controls, Monitors, and Sounds Control Panels
- More PowerPC-native code, including Process Manager, Resource Manager, and Finder
- Virtual memory improvements
- User-interface themes and sounds
- Font smoothing (anti-aliasing)

- Icon proxies
- Multiple scroll bar options
- Sherlock 2 search engine
- Sizable and scriptable Application Switcher, which supports tear-off menus
- More PowerPC-native AppleScript 1.5.5 capabilities, including Folder Actions
- Open Transport 2.7.4, which supports SNMP and improved DHCP
- Control Strip 2.0
- Improved navigational services (Open/Save dialogs)
- OpenGL 1.2 and QuickDraw 3D 1.6
- Mac Help in a new, HTML-like format
- Text encoding and Unicode and European character support
- Desktop printer browser
- Network Browser for file server and TCP/IP services
- Personal Web Server update
- Easier access to List View options
- JPEG files that are dropped onto the System Folder are redirected to the Desktop Pictures folder
- New Get Info window
- Faster Disk cache improvements
- Pervasive zoom recticles
- Date & Time Control Panel includes synchronizing and time server capabilities
- File Exchange Control Panel replaces Mac OS Easy Open and PC Exchange
- File Sharing improvements
- Internet Control Panel integrates Internet Config 2.0 capabilities
- Revised Location Manager Control Panel
- PowerBook/Energy Saver replaces several PB Control Panels
- QuickTime 4.1
- Remote Access Control Panel/Apple Remote Access 3.1 replaces OT/PPP and ARA 2.1

Mac OS Components

The components of the Mac OS (excluding the third-party applications that come bundled with the OS, such as Microsoft Internet Explorer) perform the tasks necessary to allow you to display, input, and store data. These components are typically stored in the System Folder, although some of their associated parts may be located in other folders on your computer's hard drive.

TIP: *Never attempt to store essential OS components on removable media such as floppy disks or Zip cartridges, or on network volumes or file servers.*

The System Folder, shown in Figure 1.1, contains the programs necessary for the operation of the OS as well as many folders (and a few files) that must be properly named in order for the OS to function.

The System Folder on your computer may look a bit different, depending on which OS components you've installed. In addition, it may house files and folders added by other software you have installed.

The Finder and the System suitcase are components that are critical to the booting of the OS (see Figure 1.2). They constitute the kernel of the OS and work in conjunction with Control Panels, Extensions, and System Extensions to provide access to the computer, network services, disks, and files, as well as to printing and other kinds of input and output.

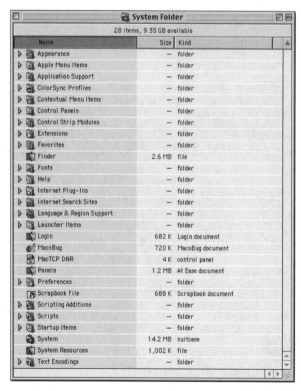

Figure 1.1   The typical System Folder for Mac OS 9.1.

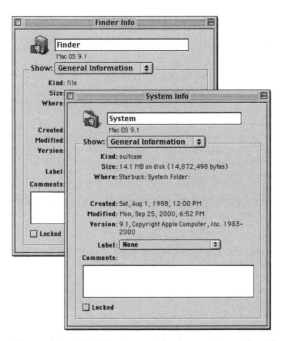

Figure 1.2   The Finder and System suitcase for Mac OS 9.1.

TIP: *For a detailed description of all the components of the System Folder, please see Chapter 2.*

In addition to the OS itself and its associated files and folders, a default installation of Mac OS 9.1 includes over 2,000 files that constitute many additional applications, utilities, and documentation. These files fall into several broad categories:

- Help files, documentation, and Assistants

- Multimedia applications, such as QuickTime

- Internet applications, such as Netscape Navigator and Microsoft Internet Explorer

- Utilities for printing and disk drive repair

A typical installation is shown in Figure 1.3.

Unlike the Finder and System suitcase, which are directly responsible for the low-level operation of your computer. The other components of the Mac OS are usually modular and upgraded by Apple after the initial release of the OS has reached consumers. These components add valuable functionality in areas such as networking and multimedia support. Mac OS 9.1 includes the components listed in Table 1.1.

Figure 1.3   A typical installation of Mac OS 9.1 looks much like this. The appearance of your installation, however, depends on your computer and the options you installed.

Table 1.1   The modular components of Mac OS 9.1 that are not part of the low-level OS and may be easily updated.

Component	Version	Purpose
Appearance Manager	1.1.4	Display of different user interface themes
Apple Remote Access	4.0	Remote access
AppleScript	1.5.5	Scriptability of applications
AppleShare	3.8.8	File sharing services over AppleTalk and TCP/IP
Mac OS Runtime for Java	2.2.2	Java applications to run on a Mac
Open Transport	2.7.4	Networking and SNMP capabilities
Personal Web Sharing	1.5.4	HTTP serving capability
QuickDraw 3D	1.6	Variety of screen drawing routines
QuickTime	4.1.1	Multimedia support
Speech Manager	2.0.2	Speech recognition and playback

User Interface Objectives

Although the objectives of the user interface under Mac OS 9.1 remain much the same as with Mac OS 8, 9.1 brings the interface itself and access to information on the Internet closer to the user. Mac OS 9.1 utilizes the characteristics that have always made the Mac OS extremely easy to use—icons and a mouse instead of a command line interface—to make Internet access via the Mac OS equally straightforward. The Internet Setup Assistant (see Figure 1.4) helps novice users connect more easily to the Internet and a variety of user interface options now offer closer ties to the Internet.

The elements of the Mac OS user interface described in the following section demonstrate just how simple it can be to access the Internet from the Mac OS.

Figure 1.4   The Internet Setup Assistant helps you connect to the Internet without third-party connection software.

Internet Access Tools

Mac OS 9.1 comes with many tools to help you connect to the Internet. For example, Figure 1.5 shows several of the tools that assist in creating or modifying an Internet service provider account.

Sherlock 2 (Search Internet)

The old Find application has undergone a major upgrade. Now known as Sherlock 2, this application allows you to find information by name, by content on an indexed hard drive, or on the Internet. Sherlock 2's new capabilities, shown in Figure 1.6, show exactly how far Apple has extended the reach of the Mac OS. It's now possible to control information beyond the local file system with the same ease that has made the Mac OS famous.

Figure 1.5   Mac OS 9.1 provides several options to access the Internet, including shortcuts to the Internet Setup Assistant and a utility that helps you locate an Internet service provider.

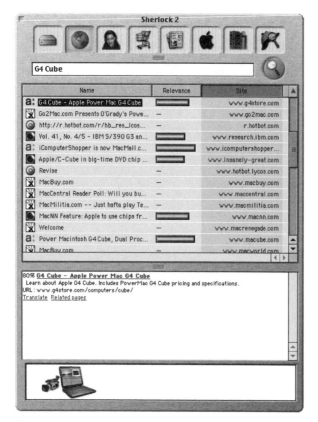

Figure 1.6   You can now search the Internet from the Mac OS itself.

Internet-Style Help

You can now seek help using a Web browser-like interface, thanks to Apple's application of HTML technology to its new Mac Help. The searchable Help Viewer, shown in Figure 1.7, uses frames to display help topics on the left and detailed information on the right. Clickable hyperlinks direct you to additional information on a topic.

Icons and Metaphors

Enhanced icons and listing metaphors for volumes, files, folders, applications, and aliases make it easier to navigate and display the contents of your hard drive. Many of the icons have been updated to make them more appealing and easier to view. Figure 1.8 shows the System Folder with its folders viewed as buttons and as icons.

Translucent file names and the addition of an arrow to the alias icon are two recent improvements to the Mac OS icons. Both of these enhancements are shown

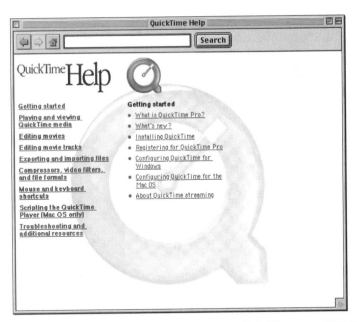

Figure 1.7   The Mac OS now uses the new Help Viewer and HTML technology in place of the AppleGuide.

in Figure 1.9. Translucent file names are much easier to read when viewed against a colored background; they're invisible against a white background. The addition of the arrow to the alias icon helps identify a file as an alias. As in previous versions of the Mac OS, the file name of an alias appears in italicized text. Because italic and regular styles can be hard to distinguish in some listview fonts, the arrow was added to eliminate any confusion.

Pointing, Clicking, Dragging, and Dropping

Mac OS 9.1 supports all the traditional methods of manipulating text and objects (such as files and folders) that have been present in the Mac OS for many years, including:

- Pointing with the mouse
- Clicking and Shift+clicking
- Shift+dragging
- Dragging selections
- Dropping selections

To simplify the copying of a selected object or the creation of an alias of the object, two enhancements originally introduced in Mac OS 8 reappear in Mac OS 9.1.

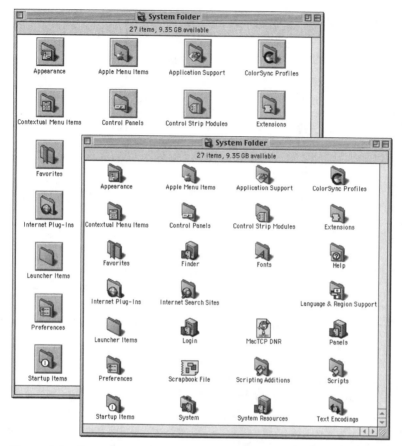

Figure 1.8 Enhanced folder icons make using the Mac OS easier than ever.

Figure 1.9 An example of translucent file names and the alias icon.

While you're in the process of copying or making an alias, the cursor is enhanced with an additional visual clue: a small plus sign indicates copying and a small right arrow indicates aliasing. Figure 1.10 shows the Utilities folder being copied (left) and aliased (right).

Figure 1.10   Visual clues help you manage file copying and alias creation.

Summarizing Text

Mac OS 9.1 includes two great features related to the OS's capability to summarize text. Text clippings are now automatically named using the first 18 characters of text plus the word "clipping," as in Figure 1.11. Not all applications support this capability, however. Applications that are not clipping-aware don't allow you to drop a block of selected text onto the Desktop, nor do they allow the OS to name the clipping file.

Alternatively, a summary of a file may be created and sent to the clipboard by way of the contextual menu. Figure 1.12 shows a SimpleText document that has been summarized.

Windows and Menus

The Appearance Manager, with its capability to display sets of themes (appearance, font, Desktop picture, and pattern preferences), is one of the most popular elements of Mac OS 9.1. Although the Appearance Manager is capable of displaying kaleidoscopic appearances, Mac OS 9.1 installs the Apple Platinum appearance only.

Users of Systems 6 and 7 were stuck with the old "System 7" appearance; then Mac OS 8 introduced the "Platinum" appearance. Now OS 9.1 maintains the framework for third-party software developers to create entirely new appearances (a feature which initially appeared in Mac OS 8.5). Figure 1.13 shows the effects of an appearance called Dimple from Power/Mac (**www.powermac.co.uk**).

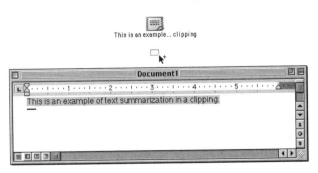

Figure 1.11   A text clipping summary.

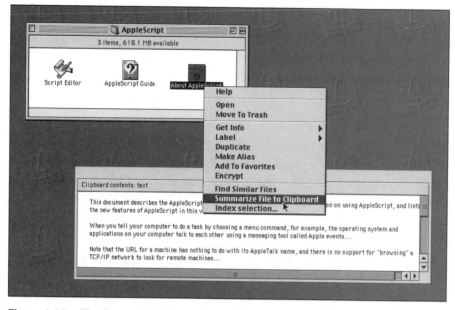

Figure 1.12   The Summarize File To Clipboard command.

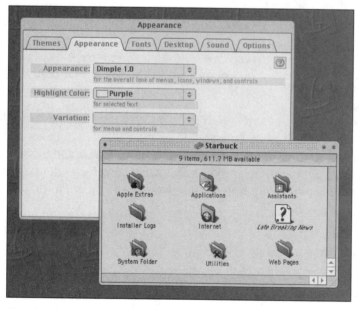

Figure 1.13   A custom appearance.

Apart from the visual aspect of the new appearance, nothing has really changed. Windows, menus, and all mouse actions work the same, regardless of what Appearance Control Panel settings you choose.

NOTE: *For more information on the Appearance Manager and themes, see Chapter 3.*

The Finder and Desktop

The Finder and Desktop views have changed significantly since OS 8.1. These improvements provide a much better user experience compared to previous versions of the OS. They include the following changes:

- New menu items
- More PowerPC-native code for faster performance and stability
- Additional scriptability

New menu items can be found in the File menu (Add To Favorites), the View menu (Reset Column Positions and Standard Views), the Window menu, the Help menu (Help Center and Mac Help), and the Applications menu (this menu has short or long names, and the menu itself can be "torn off" and placed on the Desktop). Figure 1.14 shows how the new menus appear in Mac OS 9.1.

The Preferences and View Options menus have been modified to consolidate several preferences configuration options into a single location. In addition, it's now possible to create a "Standard Views" option for each disk drive or folder; you can then use this option to control the View preferences for all enclosed folders. (This was possible in System 7, but not in Mac OS 8.0 or 8.1.) Figure 1.15 shows the View options for the List view.

This much-needed enhancement also enables you to easily change the options for one or more of the enclosed folders on a folder-by-folder basis while retaining the default view for the others.

NOTE: *For additional information on how to customize your Desktop, file, and folder views, turn to Chapter 3.*

Managing Menus

People who prefer to use a mouse to make menu selections will find the new Window menu helpful when selecting an open window in the Finder. Figure 1.14 includes an example of this new menu. Mac OS 9.1 uses faster routines to draw hierarchical menus on screen, which makes navigating menus seem faster than ever.

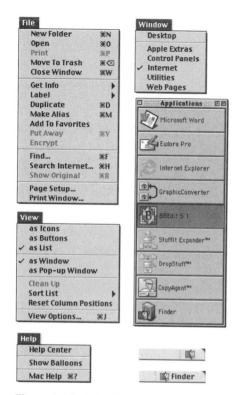

Figure 1.14   The Finder gets a few menu tweaks in Mac OS 9.1.

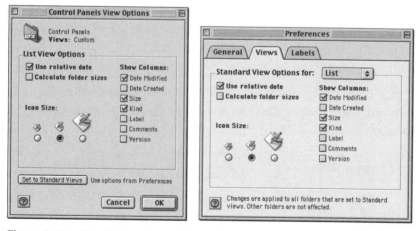

Figure 1.15   New Finder view options give you more control over how you view the contents of your computer.

Users who prefer to use any and all keyboard shortcuts whenever possible will be relieved to know that the menu changes do not affect keyboard equivalents. Figure 1.16 shows one of our favorite keyboard equivalents, throwing a selected item in the Trash by pressing Command+Delete.

Figure 1.16   Keyboard shortcuts like this one can be great time-savers.

Immediate Solutions

Changing Theme Views

You can change the theme view on your computer in at least two different ways: Selecting Appearance from the Control Panels or clicking on the Desktop while holding down the Control key to open the Finder's contextual menu and then selecting Change Desktop Background. Both options launch the Appearance Control Panel.

Although some confusion may exist between the following terms, they essentially control the same thing—how your computer displays windows, menus, and backgrounds:

- *Themes*—A collection of user-defined preferences for your computer's appearance, font, Desktop pattern, sound track, and scroll bar options. You can mix, match, and save elements of each for quick activation as a set.

- *Appearance*—A set of window and menu definitions created by a software programmer for use by the Mac OS, such as Apple Platinum (which ships with Mac OS 9.1), Dimple (seen in Figure 1.13), or others created by third-party developers.

Using the Appearance Control Panel

To change to another theme, or create a new theme, using the Appearance Control Panel:

1. Go to the Apple menu, navigate down to Control Panels, and select Appearance.

2. Select a theme from the Themes panel or an appearance from the Appearance panel, as in Figure 1.17.

Using the Contextual Menu

To change to another theme view using the contextual menu:

1. Click anywhere on the Desktop while holding down the Control key.

2. Choose Change Desktop Background, as shown in Figure 1.18.

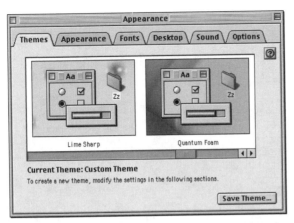

Figure 1.17   Selecting a theme, which is a collection of appearance preferences saved as a set, such as Lime Sharp or Quantum Foam.

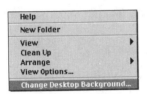

Figure 1.18   Using a contextual menu to change a theme view.

3. Select a theme from the Theme tab of the Appearance Control Panel, such as Roswell, shown in Figure 1.19. The selected theme takes effect immediately without requiring you to quit the Appearance Control Panel or restart the computer.

After you select a theme, any changes to the Fonts, Desktop, Sound, or Options tabs will result in the creation of a new theme. You can save these settings with a new name using the Save Theme command in the File menu.

Related solutions:	Found on page:
Configuring Monitors	68
Configuring the Appearance	78
Changing Finder Window Views	93

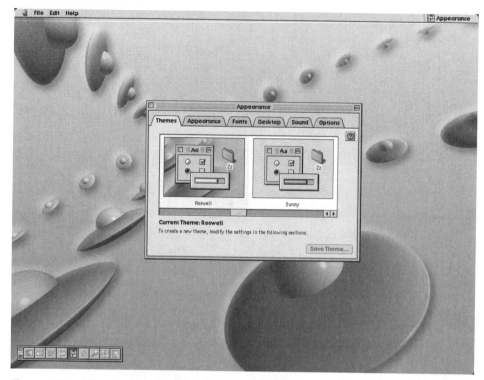

Figure 1.19   When you select an appearance, the change goes into effect immediately.

Changing Desktop Views

In addition to themes and appearances, you can change several elements of the Desktop environment independently of the other Appearance settings. As in previous versions of the OS, Mac OS 9.1 supports Desktop patterns and pictures as well as several ways of viewing icons on the Desktop.

To change the Desktop pattern or to place a picture on the Desktop:

1. Select the Appearance Control Panel from the Apple menu or from a contextual menu, as described previously.

2. Select the Desktop tab, as shown in Figure 1.20.

3. Select a Pattern from the scrolling list on the right to preview how it will look on the Desktop.

4. To activate the pattern, double-click on the preview window or select the Set Desktop button.

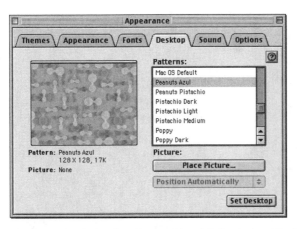

Figure 1.20   Selecting the Desktop tab to change the Desktop pattern or picture.

5. To select a picture instead of a pattern, click on the Place Picture button and select a picture from the scrolling list on the left, as shown in Figure 1.21.

6. Select the Choose button to return to the Desktop tab, then select the Set Desktop button or double-click in the preview area to activate the picture. Figure 1.22 shows how Quantum Foam looks when set as a Desktop picture.

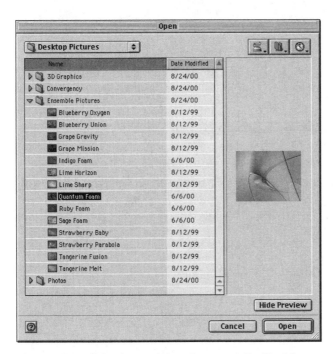

Figure 1.21   Selecting a picture for use on the Desktop.

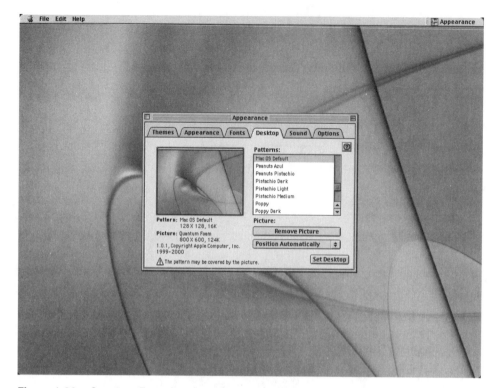

Figure 1.22   Quantum Foam in use as a Desktop picture.

Changing Your Desktop Icons

With Mac OS 9.1, you can view your Desktop icons as icons (large or small) or as buttons (large or small), but not as a list. Buttons can be opened with only a single click; opening icons requires a double click.

To change your Desktop view to icons or buttons:

1. Activate the Desktop in the Finder by clicking anywhere on the Desktop.

2. Select View As Icons or View As Buttons from the View menu.

3. Select View Options from the View menu (or press Command+J) to select a size (small or large) for the icons or buttons.

Figure 1.23 shows a portion of the Desktop viewed as large buttons (left) and large icons (right).

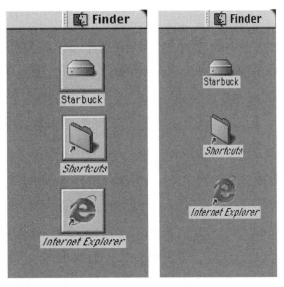

Figure 1.23   Two views of the same Desktop.

Arranging Files and Folders

Mac OS 9.1 allows you to customize how files and folders are viewed through the Finder (the portion of the OS that provides access to the contents of all storage devices). You've already seen how you can view objects on the Desktop as icons or buttons, but not as a list. The list view is available only for folders that reside on your hard drive, removable media, file server volumes, and other storage devices.

Using List View

To change a folder to a list view:

1. Select a folder by single-clicking anywhere in the folder.

2. Select View As List from the View menu.

3. Select View Options from the View menu (or press Command+J), the result of which is illustrated in Figure 1.24.

4. Select the View Options you want to activate, such as Use Relative Date, and which columns you want to show.

5. Click OK to make the changes, or select Set To Standard Views to revert this folder—and all enclosed folders—to the default view settings.

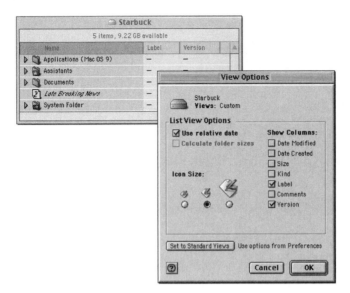

Figure 1.24   Selecting the viewing options for a folder.

Using Standard View

Defining a set of standard configuration options for each of the views—list, icon, and button—enables you to easily revert a disk or folder to that view with just two easy commands. To define a standard view:

1. Select Preferences from the Edit menu, the result of which is shown in Figure 1.25.

2. Make sure the Views tab is selected and then choose one of the view options from the pop-up menu.

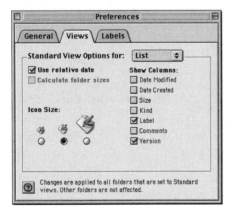

Figure 1.25   Setting the standard view options for list views.

3. Select the desired configuration options and close the Preferences window.

The next time you go to a window's View Options and select Set To Standard Views, these standardized options will be activated in any window of that type (list, icon, or button).

Related solutions:	*Found on page:*
Setting Finder Window Preferences and Views	94
Rearranging and Resizing Window Columns	96

Copying Files and Folders

You can copy files and folders in Mac OS 9.1 in at least three ways: by issuing the Duplicate command (Command+D), by dragging items from one volume to another, and by Option+dragging items from one folder to another on the same or another volume.

To copy a file or folder using the Duplicate command:

1. Select one or more files and/or folders in the Finder.
2. Choose File|Duplicate (or press Command+D).

The items will be duplicated with their original file names followed by the word "copy" if copied in the same folder or on the Desktop.

Copying to Another Volume

To copy items from one volume to another:

1. Select one or more files and/or folders in the Finder.
2. Drag them to another volume.

The items will be copied with no change in file name.

Copying Using the Option+Drag Method

To copy items using the Option+drag method:

1. Select one or more files and/or folders in the Finder.
2. Drag them to the same or another volume while holding the Option key.

The addition of the small plus sign to the file icon is a visual clue that a Copy command has been issued.

Manipulating Windows

The Mac OS has two main types of windows: normal windows, which we're all familiar with, and pop-up windows. Pop-up windows have been around since Mac OS 8 (or earlier, with a little help from certain third-party utilities). They are very easy to use and provide quick access to folders from within the Desktop.

To create a pop-up window, follow these steps:

1. Select any folder or volume in the Finder.

2. Drag it to the bottom of the screen until it turns into a pop-up window, as in Figure 1.26. Alternatively, you can select a window and choose View|As Pop-up Window.

To access the contents of a pop-up window, just click on the window's tab.

Pop-up windows can be resized by dragging the top-left or -right corners. You can still resize normal windows in the usual way, and collapse them by clicking on the WindowShade button (see Figure 1.27).

Figure 1.26   Dragging a folder to the bottom of the Desktop to create a pop-up window.

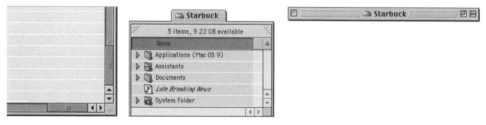

Figure 1.27   Your favorite window-manipulation tools, including scroll bar options, pop-up windows, and the WindowShade feature are present in Mac OS 9.1.

Switching between Open Windows

In the Finder, as in any other application in Mac OS 9.1, you can have many windows open at the same time, but only one can be the frontmost, or active, window. Like many popular applications, such as Microsoft Word or Internet Explorer, Mac OS 9.1 allows you to easily select among its open windows:

1. Select the Finder from the Applications menu.

2. Select an open window or the Desktop from the Window menu, as shown in Figure 1.28.

There are several shortcuts you can use with the new Window menu; refer to Appendix A, "Shortcuts and Tricks," for more information.

Figure 1.28   Mac OS 9.1 now includes a Window menu to help you navigate while using the Finder.

Launching Applications

Customizing the user interface experience to best suit your needs allows you to launch applications in a variety of ways. Mac OS 9.1 makes it possible for you to launch applications by performing any of the following options:

- Double-clicking on an application's icon

- Double-clicking on a file belonging to an application

- Double-clicking on an alias to an application or document

- Selecting an application, alias, or document from the Apple menu, or from the Recent Applications or Recent Documents folder from within the Apple menu

- Selecting an application, alias, or document from the Launcher

- Selecting an application, alias, or document in the Finder and choosing File|Open (or pressing Command+O)

- Dropping a document onto an application icon or alias

Switching among Applications

The Mac OS has long been a multitasking operating system; starting with Mac OS 8, it has been multithreaded as well. These two features enable multiple applications to run at the same time while returning mouse and keyboard control to the user. Now, you can switch among open applications by using any of the following four methods:

- Select an application through the Applications menu (see Figure 1.29)

- Select an application through the tear-off Applications menu (see Figure 1.29)

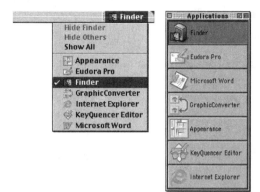

Figure 1.29   Two of the four ways you can switch among running applications.

- Press Command+Tab to cycle through the applications alphabetically
- Click on an application's window

Related solutions:	Found on page:
Using Window Shortcuts	99
Using Default Folder and ACTION Files	102

Running Foreground and Background Processes

Under the Mac OS, most applications can run in the foreground or background. In most cases, however, an application must be in the foreground in order for user input to take place. Some applications, such as the HotSync application for use with the PalmPilot, are designed specifically to run in the background and are referred to as "faceless" applications.

To switch an application between the foreground and background, take these steps:

1. Select an application such as Internet Explorer from the Applications menu.
2. Select Hide Internet Explorer (for example), as shown in Figure 1.30.
3. Select Hide Others to move all but the current application into the background.
4. Select Show All to display all applications that are currently running, leaving the selected application in the foreground.

Only one application at a time can be in the foreground; all others are considered to be in the background, whether or not they are hidden.

Figure 1.30   Selecting an application to hide in the background.

Chapter 2

System Startup and Shutdown

In Depth

The Macintosh computer uses a standard process for booting and for shutting down the system, but you do have some options for controlling how the system loads. You can also determine how system resources are used while the computer is running and try to control the graceful shutdown of your computer so your data is not lost. First though, you have to start the computer.

Startup Options

You have several choices available when starting a Macintosh. The options you use depend on the task or tasks you are attempting to do (or undo). In some cases, you'll be improving system performance; in others, you'll be dealing with a machine that's incapable of running in its current condition and requires intervention on your part—ranging from a simplistic to an heroic effort.

Your first startup option is to boot normally and allow the computer to load all system components. For most users, this procedure is standard. During startup, you should see a small computer icon—named the happy Mac—in the center of the gray screen. This icon indicates that the computer hardware is in working order and that an operating system has been found. The appearance of any other icon indicates problems with the computer. The most common error icon is the floppy disk with a blinking question mark, which indicates that no working operating system has been found. Other icons signal potentially serious problems, probably related to hardware. Older Macintosh computers will also make a very distinctive arpeggio sound when the computer is malfunctioning. Although the maxim "the prettier the startup sound, the sicker the Mac" isn't always true, any change in the starting sound of a Macintosh may be an indication of computer hardware problems. Figure 2.1 shows some of these startup icons.

Turn It On

For years, the vast majority of Macs were turned or powered on by pressing the power button on the keyboard. This convention persisted into the iMac and G4 generation. In July 2000, however, Apple introduced a new keyboard that does not contain a power button. You must use the power button located on the computer itself to start the system. Some systems can also be started from the monitor.

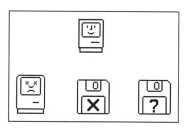

Figure 2.1   Samples of some startup icons.

You are not limited to launching the system installed on the hard drive. By inserting a CD-ROM that contains an operating system, you can run diagnostics on the internal hard drive and make repairs. External hard drives, DVD disks, floppy disks, and CD-ROMs are all capable of booting a Macintosh computer.

After the happy Mac icon appears, proceed to the "Loading the OS" section of this chapter for the rest of the booting process. However, if you know that problems exist within the system, you may opt to change the startup configuration. The most basic way to start up is to load with Extensions off; to do this, hold down the Shift key during startup. The startup screen will display the message "Welcome to Mac OS. Extensions Off." At this point, you may release the Shift key. An Extensions off startup permits only the most basic system components to load. In many cases, a system that hangs during startup has a system component conflict. Booting with the extensions off permits you to begin the Extensions conflict troubleshooting process. Alternatively, you can activate the Extensions Manager Control Panel during startup by holding down the spacebar. This action allows you to choose which Extensions and Control Panels you want to load. Once you successfully boot, you can continue activating Extensions and Control Panels until you determine which files are conflicting.

Several key combinations are available that perform tasks such as modifying the way the OS loads or performing system repairs, such as zapping the PRAM or rebuilding the desktop file. (See Chapter 18 for more information on troubleshooting your computer.) Table 2.1 lists the most common combinations.

Table 2.1   Startup key combinations.

Key Combination	Usage	Function
Shift	Hold until startup screen appears	Disables all Extensions
Spacebar	Hold before Extensions begin loading	Launches the Extensions Manager
Option+Command	Hold until dialog box (Figure 2.2) appears	Rebuilds the Desktop file

(continued)

Table 2.1 Startup key combinations *(continued).*

Key Combination	Usage	Function
Option+Command+P+R	Press and hold down before startup	Zaps the PRAM.
C	If bootable CD-ROM is in the drive, hold until happy Mac appears	Commands the computer to boot from the CD-ROM
Shift+Option+Command+Delete	Press before startup	Boots from an alternate SCSI device
Command	Press before startup	Disables virtual memory

Figure 2.2   The dialog box for rebuilding the Desktop file.

Loading the OS

After an operating system has been located, a startup screen appears. Unless you or another user have changed this screen to reflect personal tastes, you should see the logo for the Mac OS (Figure 2.3) accompanied by a progression bar, indicating what proportion of the system components have loaded. Icons for several of these components appear at the bottom of the screen and, depending on the amount of software installed, may wrap upward several lines. Near the end of the booting process, the various Desktop icons appear, including the hard drive, trash, and all additional drives or files stored on the Desktop.

Figure 2.3   The Mac OS startup screen.

Finally, File Sharing, if you have enabled it, will begin loading. Depending on the size of the hard drive and how many volumes exist on the system, File Sharing may take some time to finish launching. Nevertheless, the system should be useable while File Sharing is loading.

Elements of the System Folder

In addition to housing the brains of the operating system, the System Folder contains many of the components that load by default. These components include System Extensions, Extensions, Control Panels, Preferences, Startup Items, Shutdown Items, and Apple Menu Items. The following sections cover these components.

System Extensions

Although there are not many System Extensions, they are among the first items to load during the booting process. One of the most useful is MacsBug, a valuable tool that can tell you what process caused the system malfunction. When a system crashed or froze in the days before MacsBug, the user's only recourse was to reboot immediately. The user was given no chance to reboot gracefully, or—even more important—to learn exactly what caused the crash. Now that it's routine to run multiple applications simultaneously (especially Internet-based ones that can cause a system crash while running in the background), MacsBug is more valuable than ever. It can identify the culprit behind your problem and even allow you to quit the offending program from the MacsBug command line.

Extensions

Rather than write a new operating system every time a software program is released or a system component is tweaked, developers create Extensions that plug into the system to increase functionality or improve performance. More than any other folder, the Extensions folder has a tendency to get out of control, gathering cryptically named files that eat away at precious system and memory resources.

The files stored in the Extensions folder load after System Extensions. Most Extension icons have the distinct puzzle-like appearance similar to those shown in Figure 2.4 (even the folder sports a puzzle-piece graphic). The most well-known Extensions are printer, peripheral, CD-ROM, video, and network drivers, but there are facetious ones as well, such as singing trashcans.

Occasionally, Extensions or Control Panels fail to load properly and cause the system to hang. This condition is termed an *Extension conflict*, although the problem may be isolated to a Control Panel. Previously, we discussed options for booting the system and one of these options is to boot with Extensions off. For clarification, this actually entails disabling both Extensions and Control Panels.

Figure 2.4   Some sample Extension icons.

Weed out those useless Extensions. If for no other reason than to tighten your system performance, it's one of the best things that you, as a user or administrator, can do. Several Web sites define what these Extensions do and whether you can live without them. The Extensions Manager also can provide some information about these files, such as the creator and version number.

Control Panels

One of the biggest differences between Control Panels and Extensions is that Control Panels have windows or dialog boxes that allow you to change Control Panel settings. Control Panels are among the last of the system components to load. They often deal with the way that the system looks and behaves and include some screen savers, appearance managers, network configuration applications, and monitor settings. Control Panel icons, like Extension icons, also have a distinctive appearance, as shown in Figure 2.5.

If a programmer wants you to have some control over how an application runs within the system, he will write the code as a Control Panel. Otherwise, the code is written as an Extension.

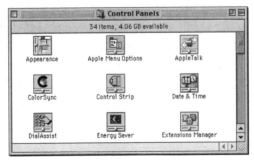

Figure 2.5   Some sample Control Panel icons.

Preferences

Every application that launches on a Macintosh creates a preference file. Even if you used the application only once, decided that it didn't meet your requirements, and dragged it to the Trash, there is still a file in the Preferences folder that indicates how the program should be run in the future.

Information stored in a preference file can include options input by the user, such as preferred email address, custom toolbars, default views, and so on, as well as window positioning of a particular document. Applications that keep a list of recently used documents store this information in a preference file.

Most users do not need to interact with the Preferences folder unless something has stopped working within a particular application. Programs that hang when launching (and those that are not functioning normally) may have a corrupt preference file. In most cases, removing the preference and allowing the program to create a new one will solve the problem. You'll need to input some user preferences again, however. Make sure that important information—such as the IP number assigned to the machine, serial numbers for software, and configuration options—is available or documented, should you have to delete important preferences.

Startup Folder

If you have applications that you use every time you launch the machine (such as Web server software, Internet applications, or client programs), you may want to take advantage of the Startup Items folder. As the OS nears the end of the booting process, it looks to this folder to see if any applications should be launched. Although you can place the actual application in the folder, it's better for system security to use an alias.

You can place multiple items in the Startup Items folder. Because they are launched alphabetically, you can control the launch order by manipulating the first character in the name of an item. For example, adding a space before the first letter of BBEdit will cause it to launch before Adobe PhotoShop; adding a bullet character before the first letter of Fetch will cause it to launch after Outlook Express.

Related solutions:	*Found on page:*
Creating and Using Aliases	156
Resolving Startup Conflicts	527

Shutdown Folder

Just as the Startup Items folder runs the programs within it during the boot process, the Shutdown Items folder runs applications during shutdown. Common applications that run at this time are disk utilities, optimization programs, and virus protection—although any application placed in the Shutdown Items folder will run. You'll find more information on shutting down a little later in the chapter.

Apple Menu Items

The System Folder also is home to the Apple Menu Items folder. This folder contains the applications or aliases that are available under the Apple menu, which is located in the top-left corner of the screen. You can launch applications from the Apple menu simply by selecting them. Figure 2.6 shows the Apple menu under Mac OS 9.1.

Shutting Down

As with any graphical interface, you must exercise care when shutting down the operating system. There are several ways to shut down a Macintosh properly.

The most common method is to select Shut Down from the Special menu, as illustrated in Figure 2.7. The system will begin closing open programs. If you have made changes to any open documents, the system will display a dialog box that asks whether you want to save the changes. When all applications are closed, the system will shut down and turn off the power. Older Macintoshes that have a power button will display a window, indicating that you can now turn off the computer.

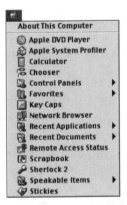

Figure 2.6   The contents of the Apple menu.

Figure 2.7   The Special menu with Shut Down selected.

You can also shut down the computer by pressing the power key. This method is often discovered by accident. The dialog box shown in Figure 2.8 will appear, asking if you're sure you want to shut down the computer and offering you the option to restart, sleep, or cancel the command. Notice that the default shuts down the system. If you press the Return or Enter keys at this point, the system will begin the shutdown process.

Finally, some Macintosh systems have a Shut Down option under the Apple menu. This option will effectively bring down the operating system gracefully. It is not included by default in Mac OS 9.1, but is often found on systems as legacy software.

Should you turn your computer off whenever it's not in use? In most cases, it's perfectly fine to leave a system running. In many workplaces, backup systems run during the night and cannot back up a computer that has been shut down. At home, however, it's better to turn off the system because most home computers have long periods of inactivity. Running them while not in use wastes energy. Keep in mind that restarting a computer also provides useful benefits like freeing up memory and removing hidden temporary files.

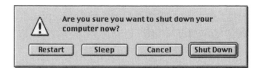

Figure 2.8   The Shut Down Options dialog box.

Immediate Solutions

Starting the Computer

So, you've removed the packing material from the computer. You've got the monitor, keyboard, mouse, and whatever else will fit plugged into the back of the CPU. If you normally use a PC, at this point you may be looking for the power button. However, a Mac is different (of course). To start the computer, take the following steps:

1. Make sure a power cord is plugged into the CPU (not to mention the wall).

2. Locate the power button on the keyboard or CPU. The power button has an arrowhead pointing to the left (pictured in Figure 2.9).

3. Press the power button.

4. You should hear some kind of musical sound. This indicates that the computer has started. Note that the new G4 Cube has no starting sound because the cube does not have internal speakers.

TIP: *A few Macintosh models, such as the Centris 610 and Power Macintosh 6100/66 (we refer to them as "pizza boxes"), actually have a power button that you must push to turn on the computer. If the computer fails to start when you press the power button on the keyboard, try pressing the power button on the CPU. Interestingly, the new Apple keyboards do not have power buttons and you must turn on the computer from the CPU.*

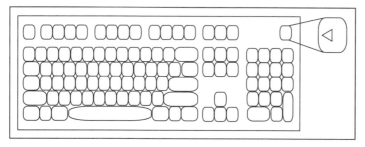

Figure 2.9   The power button on the keyboard.

Monitoring Startup Progress

You've started the computer. Do you have time for a coffee break while the system launches? You can tell by the progress bar, which looks something like a thermometer. It shows you how much of the system has launched. The progress bar also appears during regular functions within the Finder (for example, copying files from one folder or drive to another). As Extensions and Control Panels load, the progress bar will begin to fill. When the bar is full, the window will disappear and the system will begin loading the Desktop. Figure 2.3 earlier in the chapter shows a typical progress bar in action.

Disabling Extensions

If your Mac can't seem to finish the startup process, then you probably have an Extension conflict. Symptoms include freezing immediately on startup, hanging while the Extension and Control Panel icons are flashing across the bottom of the screen, and just plain hanging.

Before you can solve this problem, you have to determine whether the computer will boot at all. Start the computer with Extensions off. Although you won't be able to do much productive work on a Mac in this condition, at least you can determine your next step in the troubleshooting process by taking these steps:

1. Start or restart the Macintosh.

2. Hold down the Shift key.

3. Continue holding down the Shift key until you see the Mac OS startup screen. It should say "Welcome to Mac OS 9.1 Extensions Off." Figure 2.10 shows this screen.

Figure 2.10   The Extensions Off startup screen.

If the computer boots successfully with Extensions off, then you have a conflict with your INIT programs. If it doesn't boot, you may have fundamental problems with your installed system. Refer to Chapter 18 for additional steps you can take to resolve this problem.

Using the Extensions Manager to Load System Extensions Only

In the stone age of conflict diagnosis, you had to create an Extensions backup folder, move all your Extensions into that folder, and then begin the painful process of loading a few Extensions at a time. After multiple (and we mean multiple) restarts, you may or may not have identified the offending application.

Now, thankfully, we have the Extensions Manager. If you've determined that you do indeed have an Extensions conflict, the Extensions Manager is where you should start the process of resolving this problem. Your first step is to load only the Extensions necessary for the system to run. The following instructions are written with the assumption that you've already had to restart your computer with Extensions off:

1. Go to the Apple menu and select Control Panels.

2. Double-click on the Extensions Manager Control Panel.

3. Click on the box with the arrows by the words "Selected Set" to view a pop-up menu. See Figure 2.11 for assistance.

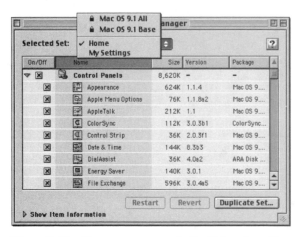

Figure 2.11   The pop-up menu in the Extensions Manager.

4. Select Mac OS 9.1 Base.

5. Restart the computer.

The computer will now boot with a basic Extension set. If you still have trouble booting, then you may have a fundamental problem with one of your system components.

Saving Custom Extension Sets Using the Extensions Manager

In the previous section, we covered loading only necessary Extensions. However, a more powerful use of the Extensions Manager is the capability, based on the situation, to load certain Extensions. This is accomplished by creating Extension sets. For example, you may have a PowerBook that you use at work and at home. You could have two Extension sets—one for work, where you can directly access the Internet, and one for home, where you use a dial-up software program. This is also useful in a teaching lab environment where a class may require different Extensions to be loaded for specialized software.

Follow these steps for saving a custom Extension set:

1. Go to Apple menu|Control Panels and select **Extensions Manager**.

2. Go to the File menu and select **New Set**.

3. Give this set a name (Figure 2.12 shows an Extension set named Home) and click on OK.

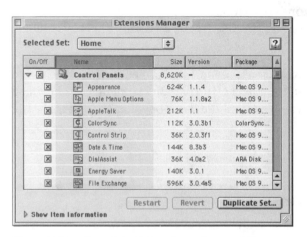

Figure 2.12   A custom Extension set named Home.

4. Turn off or on the desired Control Panels and Extensions. Changes will be saved when you close the Control Panel.

Manipulating Load Order

You've determined that there is an Extension conflict on your system and rein-stalled the software. Nonetheless, the programs are fighting like two sumo wres-tlers, and you still need to run both applications simultaneously. Extensions load alphabetically. Changing the order in which the programs load may resolve an Extension conflict. To make a particular Extension load first, take these steps:

1. Locate the file (it is in the System Folder hierarchy).
2. Click once on the name of the file to put the name in an edit mode.
3. Click at the beginning of the file name and insert a character that will make the file load first (such as a space or a numerical character).

To make an Extension load last, repeat the preceding steps, but insert a tilde (~), bullet (*), or any other character that will force the file to load last.

Disabling Extensions at Startup

Just think of this little gem as a solution to the "uh-oh" situation. An example of an uh-oh situation is realizing—at the moment you slam the car door—that the keys are in the ignition. For Mac users, the uh-oh situation happens when you know you have an Extensions conflict but restart the computer without remem-bering to hold down the Shift key. (In case you've forgotten, this key combination disables Extensions.)

All is not lost. If Extensions haven't begun loading yet, simply hold down the spacebar until the Extensions Manager Control Panel launches, as shown earlier in Figure 2.12. However, if you wait until the icons begin appearing at the bottom of the screen, it's too late.

Using Conflict Catcher

If you have continual Extension conflicts, you may want to invest in Casady & Greene, Inc.'s Conflict Catcher software. Conflict Catcher retails for less than $100 and goes beyond Extensions Manager: It can scan files and locate damaged resources, lock sets so they cannot be modified, and show the program file names during startup. You can also stop or pause the system during startup, as well as restart or shut down while Extensions are being loaded. You can even find out which files are using the most memory and locate damaged files. If you are running or supporting a system that seems to be suffering from extension overload, then you should consider purchasing Conflict Catcher.

You can find more information, including system requirements and latest version information, at **www.casadyg.com**.

Checking for Available Resources by Using About This Computer

You may occasionally sit down at a computer and be unsure of some important information, such as how much memory is installed, how it is allocated, what system is running, and so on. About This Computer is an excellent tool for accessing this information quickly. It's very easy to access—just take these steps:

1. Make sure that you are within the Finder (if not, go to the Applications menu and select Finder).

2. Go to the Apple menu and select About This Computer.

Figure 2.13 shows an About This Computer window that indicates what applications are running and how memory is allocated to each.

Figure 2.13   The About This Computer window.

Using MATM

MATM (pronounced "madam") is an acronym for "More About This Macintosh." This shareware utility builds and expands on the information shown in the section "About This Computer." Figure 2.14 gives a thorough overview of this utility.

In MATM, not only can you see what applications are running, you can also see exactly how the memory is being allocated. For example, in About This Computer, you may only see that the largest unused block of memory is 15MB. MATM, on the other hand, shows you whether this memory is fragmented and what application is causing the break. How many times have you been told by the system that there is not enough memory to launch a particular application and that you must close open programs? MATM can tell you exactly what application to close; in the case of applications that cause memory leaks, MATM can advise you to fix the fragmented memory by restarting the computer. Finally, MATM also includes volume and system information. Although it hasn't been updated since 1998, MATM works with Mac OS 9.1 and can still provide very useful information.

For more information on MATM, visit its Web site at **www.pobox.com/~albtrssp**.

Figure 2.14   The MATM window.

Checking for Available Resources by Using the System Profiler

One of the best tools included in Mac OS 9.1 is the System Profiler. It certainly gives some commercial programs a run for their money.

Figure 2.15 shows an overview of the System Profiler. The System Profile tab presents information about the system, the Finder, and installed and virtual memory. The Devices and Volumes tab includes information about installed devices and their numbers on the SCSI chain. This is very useful when adding external SCSI devices, such as scanners and external drives. The Control Panels tab and Extensions tab show you what's installed in those system components just as the Applications tab tells you what programs are installed on the hard drive. The System Folders tab tells you about active and inactive System Folders on the boot volume. Information in individual fields of the System Profiler can be dragged to the Desktop and saved as clippings.

To launch the System Profiler, do the following:

1. Go to the Apple menu.

2. Select Apple System Profiler.

3. Click on the appropriate tab to retrieve the desired information.

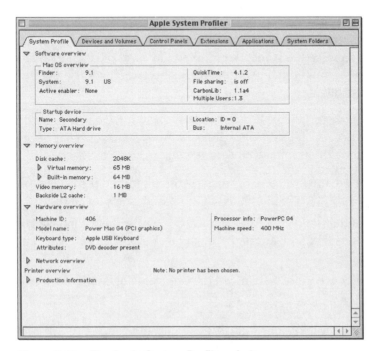

Figure 2.15   The Apple System Profiler window.

Related solution:	Found on page:
Resolving Startup Conflicts	527

Shutting Down Gracefully

There is a right way and a wrong way to shut down a Macintosh. Tight integration between the hardware and the system software makes these procedures necessary.

To properly shut down a Macintosh, choose either of the following options:

- Go to the Special menu and choose Shut Down, as shown earlier in Figure 2.7.

- Press the power button on the keyboard to bring up the Shut Down options menu, as shown earlier in Figure 2.8.

Managing Abnormal Endings (Crashes and Freezes)

Although some users believe that Macintosh computers are perfect machines in-capable of any wrongdoing, those of us in the real world know that it isn't always possible to shut down or restart the machine gracefully. In this section, you'll learn what to do when your Macintosh crashes or freezes.

First, let's define our terms. When we say *crash*, we refer to an occasion when the system no longer functions, but tells you this in the form of an alert dialog. In some cases, you'll be granted mercy in the form of retaining mouse control and being able to restart the Mac—or you may not be so lucky.

A *freeze* is also a system failure, but unlike the crash, a freeze occurs without warning or dialog box. A freeze is also different from a *hang* in that no mouse control remains, and thus you have no recourse but to force a restart.

If you're faced with an unresponsive or frozen screen, a forced restart is probably in order. The following steps explain how to force the computer to restart:

1. Determine whether you must force a restart. If you still have mouse con-trol, go to the next section, entitled "Managing Abnormal Endings (Hanging Applications)."

2. If you must force a restart, hold down the Control+Command+Power keys.

3. You should hear the computer restart.

This keystroke combination resembles the PC three-fingered salute (Ctrl+Alt+Delete). If you support PCs as well, you'll feel right at home with this keyboard shortcut.

Since the debut of the iMac, Macintosh desktop computers have been paired with USB keyboards. Because of this change, the traditional keystroke combination just described will not work. If you have an iMac, G4, or cube, try the following variation to restart the computer.

1. Hold down the Shift+Command+Power keys

2. You should hear the computer restart.

If this keystroke combination fails, then it's time to use the restart button on the computer.

Some Macintosh models have a restart button on the front of the computer. This small button should have a left-pointing triangle similar to the power key on the keyboard. This button will also restart the computer.

NOTE: *The bondi blue and first edition "five flavors" iMacs have a restart button that is modeled after the PowerBook restart switches. You have to insert a paper clip into the small hole on the side of the iMac to restart the machines. Entrepreneurs have seized this opportunity and sell small plastic devices that basically give you the functionality of a button. Check out the iReset at* **www.macsonly.com** *or the iSafe at* **www.quadmation.com/iSafe/** *for ordering information.*

One of the more intimidating warning messages is the "bomb" (see Figure 2.16). The bomb icon most often appears during the initial boot process and indicates that the OS cannot load. In this case, you may need to restart with Extensions off or even boot from another volume to resolve the problem.

Figure 2.16   A system bomb icon.

Managing Abnormal Endings (Hanging Applications)

In the preceding section, we talked about system crashes or freezes. However, occasionally an application will cause the system to stop reacting to mouse clicking and dragging. You can still move the mouse around the screen but can't do much else. Your first impulse may be to do the Macintosh version of the three-fingered salute. However, when an application is hung, you still have an opportunity to gracefully restart your computer.

You need to force the offending application to quit. However, because you don't have mouse control, the following keystroke combination is called for:

1. Hold down the Option key.

2. Press the Command key.

3. Unless you're double-jointed, use your other hand to press the Escape key. (This is one of the few times that you use the Escape key.)

4. The dialog box shown in Figure 2.17 will appear. Choose Force Quit.

WARNING! *The Force Quit dialog box in Figure 2.17 also indicates which application has developed problems. If an application is causing the problem, you have a much better chance of closing down the offending program and gracefully restarting your system. Don't panic if the Finder happens to be the culprit—occasionally a process within the Finder, such as a print command, doesn't respond as it should. You can still force the process to quit and properly restart the computer. Be aware, however, that a Force Quit dialog box can lead to a freeze or crash.*

After forcing an application to quit, your computer may seem to function just fine. Don't ignore the warning in the Force Quit dialog box that reminds you to restart your computer. Restarting will reduce the chance of a system freeze or crash.

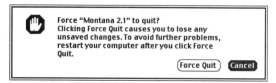

Figure 2.17   The Force Quit dialog box.

Connecting to a File Server at Startup by Using the Chooser

Remember when a 250MB hard drive seemed ridiculously large? That was in the old days when Microsoft Word was roughly 5MB in its entirety. Today, the Microsoft Web site says to allow 56MB for the easy installation of MS Word 98; Word 2001 will surely require even more disk space. Despite the fact that hard drives are larger than ever, more and more system administrators are deciding to run huge office applications from a central server. If you need to connect to the same server every time you start your computer, you may want to do so automatically by taking these steps:

1. Go to the Apple menu and select the Chooser.

2. Click on AppleShare and locate the server you wish to access automatically. Click on OK (refer to Figure 2.18).

3. Enter your username and password or select the guest button, if it is an option. Click on OK.

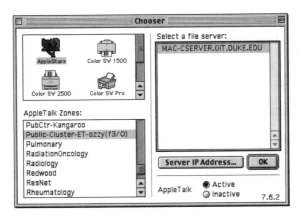

Figure 2.18   The Chooser.

4. In the third dialog box, if there are multiple volumes available on the server, select the one you need.

5. While still in this dialog box, click in the small box beside the selected volume to access this server whenever your computer is restarted. You can also save your name or save both your name and password. Most system administrators prefer that you not opt for the latter.

6. Click on OK and close the Chooser.

You will now automatically attach to this server each time you start your computer. If you encounter someone who has enabled this accidentally, you can advise them to cancel login at startup or delete the System Preferences to stop the automatic login. To learn more about how to work with non-AppleShare networks, see Chapter 10.

Related solutions:	*Found on page:*
Using DAVE	320
Configuring File Sharing and Program Linking	337

Connecting to a File Server by Using the Network Browser

The Network Browser is one of the most helpful applications included with Mac OS 9.1. It breaks the limitations of the Chooser and allows you to browse your network in the same way that you browse your computer. Figure 2.19 shows a network viewed through Network Browser. The Network Browser will be covered in depth in Chapter 11.

Figure 2.19   The Network Browser.

One of the most promising aspects of the Network Browser is the capability to keep a record of commonly accessed servers. This record is called a Favorites list. If you've used Microsoft's Internet Explorer, you are familiar with its use of Favorites as a method of remembering commonly accessed web sites. To add a server to your favorites list:

1. Open the Network Browser.

2. Locate the server you want to add to the Favorites list.

3. Click on the button with the Book icon (refer to Figure 2.19) and choose Add To Favorites.

You can now access this server, as well as any other server on this list, quickly.

Choosing a Reboot Option

If you press the power key on the keyboard while the system is active, the special Shut Down Options dialog box, shown earlier in Figure 2.8, appears. You have the following four options:

- Choose Restart to close open applications and perform a warm reboot on the system.

- Choose Sleep to put the system in a low-energy mode. Press the spacebar to wake the system.

- Choose Cancel to close the dialog box without making any changes to the system status.

- Choose Shut Down to close all open applications and shut down the system.

Choosing a Startup Disk

In this age of large hard drives, we find that power users often divide a large drive into multiple volumes either by choice or by necessity (older versions of the Mac OS had a size limit for drive volumes). Users can also easily add additional internal or external storage devices such as hard drives, which also mount separately on the Desktop. Mac OS 9.1 also changes the appearance of hard drive icons to indicate that a system is installed. Darker gray icons have a system installed; lighter gray ones do not.

You can install an operating system on any partition. This is an excellent solution if you are testing alpha or beta software applications and are concerned about the integrity of your system. To do so, take these steps:

1. Go to the Apple menu|Control Panels and choose Startup Disk.

2. Select the volume you want to use for starting the computer and close the window.

3. Restart the computer to use the chosen drive or volume.

Figure 2.20 shows the Startup Disk Control Panel.

The Startup Disk Control Panel has been revamped for Mac OS 9.1 You can now designate which System Folder you wish to use. This is useful if you have two or more System Folders on the same volume.

If your Mac has SCSI drives, you can choose an alternate SCSI drive as the startup disk by pressing Shift+Option+Command+Delete while starting the computer.

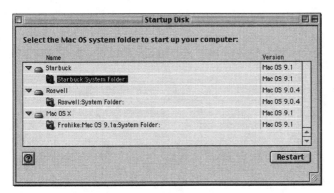

Figure 2.20   The Startup Disk Control Panel.

Booting from a CD-ROM

The most recent generations of Macintosh computers, beginning with the iMac, do not contain a floppy drive. Although this may seem frightening to the average user, most of us rarely use a floppy disk unless we are practicing "sneaker" networking. For newer Macs, it's more efficient to boot from a CD-ROM, which has a larger system because of the greater disk size. It may even be worthwhile to create a custom CD boot disc if you have access to a CD burner.

Follow these steps to boot from a CD-ROM:

1. Insert the CD-ROM in the drive.

2. Start or restart the computer.

3. Hold down the C key.

4. You should hear the CD-ROM drive spinning as the system launches from the CD-ROM.

5. If you have successfully booted from the disk, you should see the CD-ROM icon in the top-right corner of the screen, as shown in Figure 2.21.

You can also use the Startup Disk Control Panel to choose the CD drive as the starting volume (refer to the section "Choosing a Startup Disk," covered previously in this chapter, for instructions).

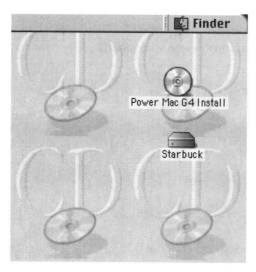

Figure 2.21   The CD-ROM as the primary boot volume.

Booting from Other Removable Media

You can boot from other media, including popular storage devices such as the Iomega Zip and Jaz drives and the SyQuest removable hard drive. Peripherals and drives, including FireWire hard drives and DVD disks, can hold much more data than CD-ROMs and are poised to be just as common . For most media, if an operating system is installed on the device, you can boot from it. Simply select it in the Startup Disk Control Panel.

Some exceptions exist in the USB world, however. Depending on your computer model, you may not be able to boot from a USB device as a startup disk because the drivers must be loaded before the device can be used. Check your computer manual for more information.

To boot from removable media:

1. Locate or create a medium with the appropriate version of the Mac OS installed.

2. Insert the medium while the computer is not up (either while it is off or in the dark screen phase during a warm reboot). Figure 2.22 shows a 100MB Zip disk with a minimalist version of Mac OS 9.1 installed.

3. Start the computer.

4. You should hear the medium being accessed, and the "Welcome to Mac OS" screen should appear.

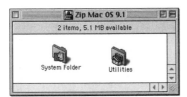

Figure 2.22   Boot from a removable medium such as a Zip disk to repair serious errors on your hard drive.

Chapter 3

The User Environment

In Depth

The most compelling aspect of the Mac OS is the user environment, and Mac OS 9.1 includes many new features for users to explore. This section highlights the essential aspects of the user environment, discusses its many configuration options, tells you where to find software and resources for enhancing the user environment, and offers tips to help you organize the contents of your computer.

Essential Configuration Options

Immediately after installing Mac OS 9.1, it's important to configure or check several elements of the user environment for accuracy. The sky won't fall if these matters aren't attended to promptly, but you may experience some degree of frustration if you delay. We consider the following items to be essential configuration options:

- *Hardware-related options*—Energy saving settings, auto wake-up and shutdown, monitor resolution, sound-in and sound-out, removable drive settings (such as Zip, Jaz, or Orb), virtual memory, local and networked printers, and mouse tracking and clicking speed

- *Software-related options*—Languages, color control, text and numbers, Internet preferences, and speakable alerts

These configuration options allow the computer to accurately store data on your hard drive (using the correct date, time, time zone, and daylight-saving time options, for example), as well as wake up or shut down on schedule (using Energy Saver or Auto Power On/Off, for example).

Additional Configuration Options

What sets the optional configuration options apart from the essential options is that once configured, the essential options are rarely modified. You can frequently change the following configuration options, however, to suit your (or your users') needs or whims:

- Appearance (themes, fonts, scroll bars, collapsible windows, Desktop pictures and patterns), sounds, and Desktop views

- Shortcuts (Apple menu, Applications menu, Control Strip, Launcher, and Favorites)

- Speech recognition

- Finder elements (View, Labels, and other preferences)

These options are most of what we consider alternative configuration options that are part of the Mac OS, but you may have other ideas about what's essential and what's optional.

Enhancing the User Environment

The Mac OS has never had a shortage of utilities and applications to enhance its usability, and many of these enhancements will run under Mac OS 9.1. Those that won't run either have been incorporated into the OS and may no longer be needed, or are being upgraded with new features. Over the years, Apple has incorporated many of these utilities and features, such as Kaleidoscope themes, hierarchical menus, and pop-up windows, because it was easy to do. Simultaneously, Apple has helped developers create even more enhancements by providing Application Programming Interface (API) specifications. By using these specifications, developers can write applications to take advantage of OS features, such as the Sherlock 2 search engine and the navigational services (Open and Save dialog windows).

We cover a few of the more popular user-environment utilities in the next section, as well as in the "Immediate Solutions" section later in this chapter. Visit the Web sites of your favorite software developers to obtain more information on the status of Mac OS 9.1 compatibility for their applications and utilities. For general information about enhancing the user environment, see these URLs:

- **www.macdesktops.com**

- **www.tazl-inside.de**

- **www.kaleidoscope.net**

- **www.iconfactory.com**

- **www.clixsounds.com**

- **macworld.zdnet.com**

- **www.macweek.com**

- **www.zdnet.com/mac/download.html**

- **hyperarchive.lcs.mit.edu/HyperArchive/HyperArchive.html**

ACTION GoMac

There are many great third-party utilities that can significantly enhance the user interface experience, and one of our favorites is ACTION GoMac from Power On, LLC. This utility is part of a suite of utilities called ACTION Utilities that are designed to complement the Apple menu. ACTION GoMac provides all the functionality of the Apple menu and adds several features found in other popular operating systems, such as a list of active applications. It also has numerous shortcuts to frequently used configuration options and utilities, such as the Sherlock search engine. Figure 3.1 shows several of ACTION GoMac's features, including its hierarchical menus, active applications, minimized applications, clock, and calendar (when clicked).

ACTION GoMac, which comes with very good documentation, has too many features to cover here. You can download it and several other venerable utilities for the Mac OS, such as Now Up-to-Date and Now Contact, from the Proteron Web site at **www.poweronsoftware.com**.

Finally, ACTION GoMac also offers an alternative to Mac OS 9.1's keyboard Application Switcher feature (Command+Tab). For people who want this functionality without the added features and cost of ACTION GoMac, this feature can be purchased separately from Proteron (**www.proteron.com**) in a utility called LiteSwitch, which uses customizable key combinations to toggle between applications.

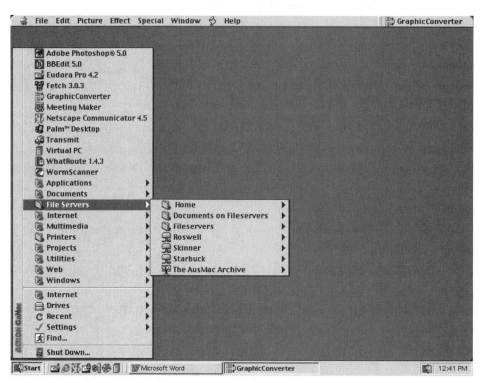

Figure 3.1   ACTION GoMac is a great alternative to many of the features of the Apple menu.

Organizing Content

You can organize and customize the user environment by organizing your files into folders using a plan that is logical to you. Our Macs usually hold between 30,000 and 50,000 files apiece, and Mac OS 9.1 installs some 2,000 files. So, it just makes good sense to organize the contents of storage devices in a consistent fashion.

Mac OS 9.1 utilizes a new folder structure that further streamlines the many files and folders installed by the Mac OS into four main folders (down from about nine folders in Mac OS 9.0). For example, Figure 3.2 shows the folder structure created with a default installation of Mac OS 9.1, which includes the following folders:

- *Applications (Mac OS 9)*—Apple Extras (additional applications, utilities, and OS components), Internet applications and utilities, multimedia applications such as QuickTime, the Utilities folder, SimpleText, and other applications

- *Assistants*—Internet Setup and Mac OS Setup assistants

- *Documents*—A catch-all folder that contains the Web Pages folder, consisting of HTML documents for use with the Web Sharing feature, and log files created by the Mac OS installer

- *System Folder*—The Mac OS and other system resources

These folders are a good start, but you'll want to add folders and subfolders as necessary for documents, images, projects, downloads, games, and other items. When you open a folder, the Mac OS has to read information from the Desktop database pertaining to that folder, including file names, sizes, modification dates, and the like. The more items that are in a folder, the longer it takes to open the folder. Therefore, we recommend that you consider creating subfolders if you have more than several dozen items in a folder. For example, we have one computer with about 4,500 files stored in the Utilities folder, so we created subfolders

Figure 3.2   The new folder structure created by Mac OS 9.1.

Figure 3.3   Use a collection of subfolders to organize large collections of related files.

that allow us to divide the utilities alphabetically among 26 subfolders within the Utilities folder, as shown in Figure 3.3. This makes it much easier to find a particular file without having to navigate huge scrolling lists of files and folders.

Of course, no "correct" way exists to organize the contents of your hard drives. Do what you feel is best for you and what makes it easiest to find your files.

The Setup Assistant

The Mac OS 9.1 installer places an alias to the Mac OS Setup Assistant in the Startup Items folder so that when the computer reboots after installation, the Mac OS Setup Assistant is launched automatically. A clean installation of Mac OS 9.1 will cause several of the default environments to lose their configurations; the Mac OS Setup Assistant helps users enter these configuration options, including:

• Keyboard layout

• Username and organization

• Time, date, and time zone

• Standard or Simple Finder

• File sharing username, password, and sharing folder

The Mac OS Setup Assistant alias will be deleted automatically from the Startup Items folder after the first time it is run, but you can always run it again from the Assistants folder if necessary. Figure 3.4 shows how the user interface appears in the Mac OS Setup Assistant.

Energy Saver

The Energy Saver Control Panel is installed on all new Macintosh computers (PowerBook, iBook, iMac, G4, and Cube) because they are all Energy Star compliant. First-generation PowerMacs that are not Energy Star compliant, however, can use the Auto On/Off Control Panel instead. Both Control Panels allow you to configure the Mac OS to automatically start up and shut down the computer on selected days of the week and at certain times. You can also configure computers that are Energy Star compliant to go into power-saving mode by:

- Putting the entire computer (CPU, hard drive, and monitor) to sleep

- Putting the monitor to sleep

- Putting the hard drive to sleep

For all these features to work, of course, each component—in addition to the CPU itself—must have its own power-saving features.

Navigational Services

Mac OS 9.1's dialog window for opening and saving files has far more functionality than previous versions of the Mac OS. However, only those applications and utilities that have been specifically programmed to take advantage of these features will be able to display the new dialog windows. For example, Figure 3.5

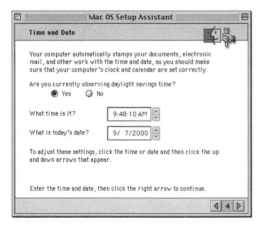

Figure 3.4   The Mac OS Setup Assistant.

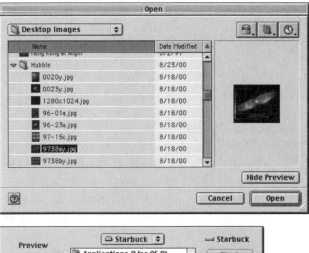

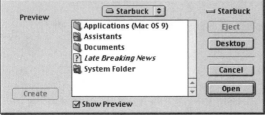

Figure 3.5   The new (top) and old (bottom) navigational services for the Mac OS.

shows the navigational services of the Appearance Control Panel (top) and the old-style open dialog window of SimpleText (bottom).

The advantages of the new open and save dialog window include:

- The entire dialog window is both vertically and horizontally resizable.
- The dialog box is no longer modal. This means that you can move to another application or view the Desktop while the open or save dialog window is still active.
- A more window-like interface displays your current location and the path to the folder, such as Option+clicking on a window's title bar.
- List items are sortable by name and date modified and are hierarchically expandable.
- You can easily jump to the Desktop, mounted volumes, and AppleTalk and AppleShare IP server and volumes by using the Shortcuts button.
- You can effortlessly access your Favorites folder by using the Favorites button.
- You can quickly locate recently used files and documents by utilizing the Recent button.
- You can easily access the Help viewer.

General Controls

The General Controls Control Panel, shown in Figure 3.6, has undergone a major design change in Mac OS 9.1, but it still allows you to configure most of the same features as before. To make any of the following changes, open the General Controls Control Panel, make your selections, and then close the Control Panel:

- *Show Desktop When In Background*—When unchecked, the Desktop and its contents are hidden from view, leaving only the windows of unhidden applications (see Figure 3.7).

- *Show Launcher At System Startup*—Opens the Launcher (described later in this chapter) at startup without placing an alias to the Launcher in the Startup Items folder.

- *Menu Blinking*—Controls whether an item in the Apple menu blinks when selected, and if so, how many times it should blink before opening the selected item. This is a cosmetic feature. Turn it off to enable the fastest response time when selecting an item in the Apple menu.

- *Insertion Point Blinking*—Chooses the blink rate of the insertion point (where you can enter text in a window or document) as slow, medium, or fast.

- *When Opening Or Saving A Document, Take Me To*—Selects the location where the OS will open automatically. If you select Documents Folder, a folder called Documents (if it does not already exist) will be created at the root level of the startup disk.

- *Check Disk If Computer Was Shut Down Improperly*—Checking this option ensures that you'll be warned, upon restarting in the wake of a crash or abnormal

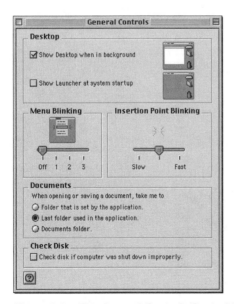

Figure 3.6   The General Controls Control Panel.

ending (*abend*), that the computer was shut down improperly. This option also ensures that the integrity of the startup disk will be verified when the computer is restarted. With OS 9.1, the dialog window that issues the warning dismisses itself after a few moments, whereas in previous versions of the OS it would stay on screen until dismissed by the user.

The following two options, found in previous versions of the General Controls Control Panel, do not appear in Mac OS 9.1; their functionality has been incorporated into the Multiple Users feature (discussed in Chapter 16):

- *Protect System Folder*—When checked, the OS locked down critical areas of the System Folder to prevent unwanted items from being installed into the folder and to keep critical items from being deleted.

- *Protect Applications Folder*—This option was similar to the Protect System Folder option, but was for the Applications folder instead.

Related solution:	*Found on page:*
Setting Up the Multiple User Environment	464

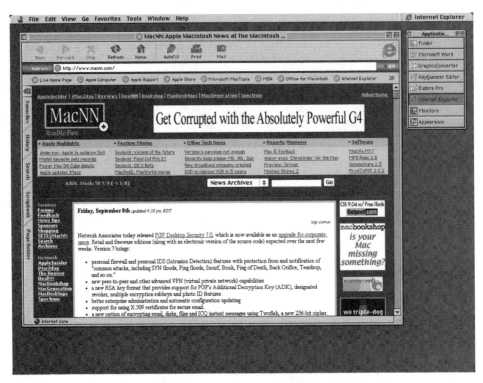

Figure 3.7   Hiding the Desktop when in the background can help clear up a messy environment.

Immediate Solutions

Configuring Energy Saver

To configure the Energy Saver to power down various Energy Star-compliant components of your computer:

1. Open the Energy Saver Control Panel.

2. Select the Sleep Setup tab, as well as the Show Details button (see Figure 3.8).

3. Configure the options you want.

4. Review the Schedule, Notification and Advanced Settings tabs. If your computer is acting as a file sharing or Internet server, be sure to check the Restart Automatically After A Power Failure option in the Advanced Settings tab to enable your computer to automatically restart itself after a power failure.

5. Close (or quit) the Control Panel.

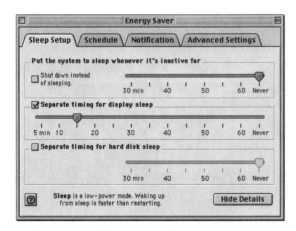

Figure 3.8   Configuring the Energy Saver Control Panel.

Configuring Startup and Shutdown

To configure your computer to automatically start up or shut down while unattended:

1. Open the Energy Saver Control Panel.
2. Select the Schedule tab (see Figure 3.9).
3. Configure the options you want, then close (or quit) the Control Panel.

For computers that are not Energy Star compliant:

1. Open the Auto Power On/Off Control Panel (see Figure 3.10).
2. Configure the desired options, then close the Control Panel.

Note that the Auto Power On/Off Control Panel has all its configurable options in the same window, unlike the Energy Saver, which has multiple configuration tabs and pull-down menu options.

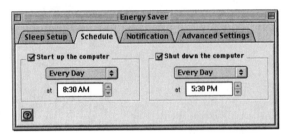

Figure 3.9   Configuring the Energy Saver Control Panel.

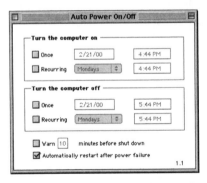

Figure 3.10   Configuring the Auto Power On/Off Control Panel.

Configuring Date & Time

Configuring the computer's date, time, and time zone settings allows you to track documents according to the date and time they were created or last modified. Therefore, a file with an incorrect date and time stamp may very well elude you in a search for a file created on a specific date. Also, some applications, such as databases, may not function properly if some of their files bear incorrect time stamps.

To configure the Date & Time Control Panel:

1. Open the Date & Time Control Panel (see Figure 3.11).

2. Enter the current date and time.

3. Click on the appropriate daylight-saving time checkbox and select a time zone.

4. To use a network time server to set the time on your computer automatically, select the checkbox and click on the Server Options button (see Figure 3.12).

5. Select a time server from the list, such as Apple's time server (**http://time.apple.com**), or choose Edit List from the menu and enter another selection, as in Figure 3.13. For example, the U.S. Naval Observatory maintains two atomic clocks (**http://tick.usno.navy.mil** or **http://tock.usno.navy.mil**) that are used to set the time for U.S. military operations worldwide, as well as for many astronomical observatories. Setting the time using a time server only takes a few seconds. You'll be connected to a time server only when Internet connectivity is available.

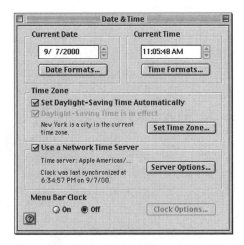

Figure 3.11   The Date & Time Control Panel in Mac OS 9.1.

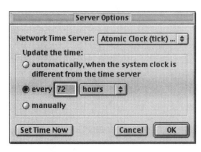

Figure 3.12   The time server option allows the computer's time to be set automatically by any time server on the Internet, including various atomic clocks.

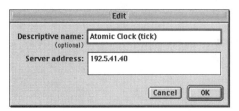

Figure 3.13   For the most accurate time possible, select a time server powered by an atomic clock, such as those of the U.S. Naval Observatory.

6. Finally, you may choose to display the time and date in the menu bar and select several clock display options by selecting the Clock Options button; then you can choose any appropriate configuration options.

Configuring Monitors

As we discuss in Chapter 9, the features that you configure in Mac OS 9.1's Monitors Control Panel have a big impact on how you interact with the OS. Most monitors built in the past few years are capable of displaying at multiple resolutions; the proper setting for your eyes can make life a lot easier.

To configure the basics of the Monitors Control Panel:

1. Open the Monitors Control Panel. Depending on what model of CPU and monitor you have, different options will be presented (an example is shown in Figure 3.14). PowerBook and iBook users will often have slightly different options, as will users who can adjust the physical geometry of their monitors with on-screen controls rather than knobs and dials.

2. Choose the Monitor button and select a color depth (commonly referred to as a bit depth).

3. Choose a resolution that suits your needs.

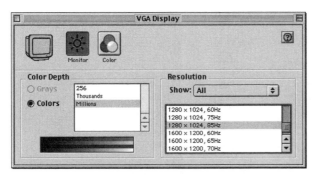

Figure 3.14   The Monitor section of the Monitors Control Panel for a computer with 6MB
              of video RAM (VRAM) and a 19" ViewSonic PS790 monitor.

The Color portion of the Monitors Control Panel will be discussed in Chapter 9 when we focus on the multimedia capabilities of the Mac OS.

The most important step in this process is selecting the proper resolution, refresh rate, and bit depth for your level of comfort. If the refresh rate is too low, causing the screen to flicker, the human eye can detect it. We suggest a resolution that supports a refresh rate of at least 75Hz, but a higher rate is always better. Select the maximum number of colors and purchase additional VRAM, if possible (as of this writing, VRAM is very inexpensive—only a few dollars per megabyte).

Related solutions:	*Found on page:*
Configuring ColorSync Workflow Files	268
Using DigitalColor Meter	271

Configuring Sound

Up through Mac OS 8.6, the sound settings were configured as part of the old Monitors & Sounds Control Panel. Since Mac OS 9, however, sound has its own separate Control Panel.

To configure the basic sound options on your computer:

1. Open the Sound Control Panel.

2. Use the Alerts tab to select or record your own system alert sound (see Figure 3.15). Sounds are stored in the System suitcase in the native sound format for the Mac OS.

3. Use the Input and Output tabs to choose appropriate sources for sound input and output (see Figure 3.16). Again, different computers display

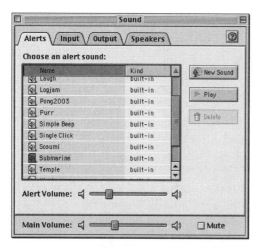

Figure 3.15   The Alerts tab of the Sound Control Panel.

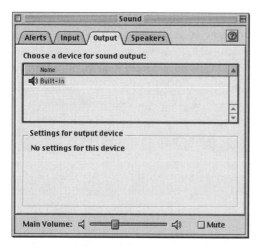

Figure 3.16   The Output tab of the Sound Control Panel.

different options depending on the speakers, monitor, and any additional
installed AV hardware.

4. Make any additional selections appropriate for your situation, and then
close the Control Panel.

Note that the Main Volume and Mute options appear in all the tabs of the Sound
Control Panel.

Configuring the Mouse

Most users have the standard Apple mouse and keyboard. If you've purchased a third-party keyboard or mouse, such as a Kensington mouse, you should refer to any additional software that may have been installed by that item.

The standard Apple mouse is configured via the same settings that are well known to most Macintosh users.

To configure a standard Apple mouse, take these steps:

1. Open the Mouse Control Panel (see Figure 3.17).
2. Select a speed for mouse tracking and double-clicking.
3. Close the Mouse Control Panel.

Changes made to the Mouse Control Panel immediately go into effect.

WARNING! Be sure to shut down your computer before unplugging an ADB device such as a mouse or keyboard. Newer Macs use Universal Serial Bus (USB) instead of ADB, so it's safe to plug and unplug devices while the computer is powered on.

Experienced Mac users should consider purchasing a multi-button mouse that allows you to create shortcuts using its programmable buttons. Figure 3.18, for example, shows the application that comes with a popular four-button Kensington mouse, which allows you to program the mouse behavior for specific applications such as the right-click option in Windows 98 running under Virtual PC.

Figure 3.17   The Mouse Control Panel.

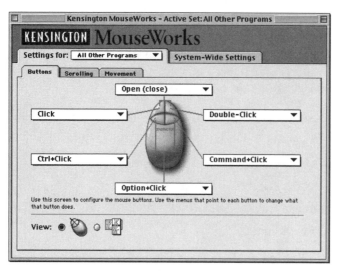

Figure 3.18   An example of configuration application for a third-party mouse
from Kensington.

Configuring the Keyboard

Because the keyboard layout options included in the Mac OS default to the U.S. layout, few American users will ever change their keyboard layout. Foreign-language users, however, will often find it necessary to change the layout to support a specific language, such as German or French. A keyboard layout assigns what we consider special characters, such as the German umlaut (¨) or an accented character (ò), to keys on the keyboard. The Mac OS supports multiple languages through WorldScript and keyboard layouts, which can be adjusted on the fly.

To configure the Keyboard Control Panel:

1. Open the Keyboard Control Panel (see Figure 3.19).

2. Select a script family (Roman is the default).

3. Select a keyboard layout. If you select multiple options, a new option will appear in the menu bar; this option allows you to select a keyboard layout from a pull-down menu. Click on the Options button at the bottom of the window to select a keyboard menu shortcut that will enable you to switch between keyboard layouts.

4. Configure the Key Repeat options.

5. Close the Keyboard Control Panel.

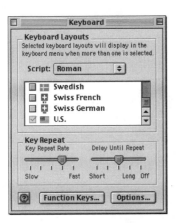

Figure 3.19   The Keyboard Control Panel.

Configuring Hot Function Keys

A more recent addition to the Mac OS is the Keyboard Control Panel's ability to map function keys to launch applications or open volumes, folders, files, and aliases. If you can double-click on an item in the Finder, then it's possible to map it to a function key.

To map a function key to open or launch an item in the Finder:

1. Open the Keyboard Control Panel.

2. Select the Function Keys button.

3. Select the Use F1 Through F15 As Hot Function Keys option, as in Figure 3.20.

4. Click on a function key button such as F1 and assign an item to that button, or drag an item from the Finder onto the field to the right of the button entitled "Nothing Assigned."

In this example, we've assigned a volume, folder, document, and two applications to function keys for very quick access.

However, many Mac OS users need more powerful shortcut and macro capabilities—we recommend two products for these needs:

- QuicKeys from CE Software (**www.cesoft.com**) is a visually oriented macro and automation tool that costs about $100. It is very powerful and easy to use.

- KeyQuencer from Binary Software (**www.binarysoft.com**) costs about $50 and uses natural-language scripts to perform shortcuts and automate tasks.

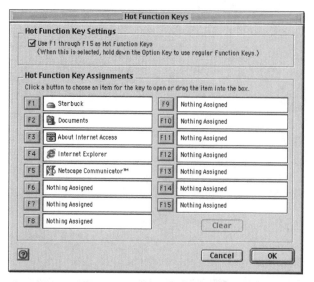

Figure 3.20   Use the Keyboard Control Panel to assign function keys as shortcuts.

Figure 3.21 shows one of many steps in a lengthy sequence that uses QuicKeys to complete a multitude of actions, including exporting data from one application, saving the data to file, switching to FileMaker Pro, and then executing a script that formats the data and imports it into a Web-enabled database.

With KeyQuencer, you can create very useful shortcuts that help automate everyday tasks. In the following example, the KeyQuencer macro remembers the current application, switches to SoundJam and pauses the music (if it is playing music), and then returns the user to the previous application:

```
SwitchApp remember "SoundJam" partial quiet
Menu "Controls" "Pause" partial quiet
SwitchApp restore
```

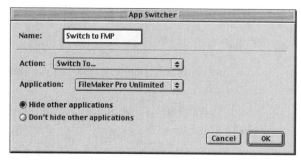

Figure 3.21   Part of a complex QuicKeys macro.

Both QuicKeys and KeyQuencer are extraordinary utilities that you should evaluate for your needs.

Configuring Numbers and Text

Like previous versions of the Mac OS, Mac OS 9.1 enables you to configure preferences for the display of numbers, currency, and text. For example, some people prefer to have a comma separate the hundreds from the thousands when viewing numbers (e.g., 1,234 versus 1234).

Number Configuration

To configure the Numbers Control Panel, take the following steps:

1. Open the Numbers Control Panel (see Figure 3.22).
2. Choose a predefined format, such as U.S., from the Number Format menu.
3. Alternatively, you can edit the Separator or Currency fields and use your customized preferences in place of the predefined formats.
4. Close the Control Panel; the changes will go into effect immediately.

To see how your choices will appear on screen, look at the Sample field after making your selections but before closing the Control Panel.

Text Configuration

Similarly, you can configure the Mac OS so that text items behave according to the rules of a particular language. Text Behaviors affect case conversions, sort order, and word definitions.

To configure the Text Control Panel, take these steps:

1. Open the Text Control Panel.
2. Choose a language from the Script menu.

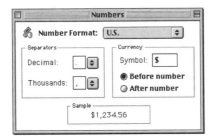

Figure 3.22   The Numbers Control Panel.

3. Choose a language from the Behavior menu (each script system may support multiple languages).

4. Close the Control Panel and the changes will go into effect immediately.

Configuring the Apple Menu

The Apple menu is probably the most recognized avenue for shortcuts and easy access to the contents of your hard drive. In some earlier versions of the OS, the Apple menu was not hierarchical and therefore displayed only the contents of the Apple Menu Items folder (located in the System Folder)—but not subfolders. In the early 1990s, Fabien Octave wrote a great shareware utility called BeHierarchic (**www.octave.net/BeHierarchic**) that provided hierarchical capabilities to the Apple menu. The most basic features of BeHierarchic were included in the Apple menu itself several years ago. Figure 3.23 shows the Apple menu and the Apple Menu Items folder, which holds the contents of the Apple menu.

The Apple menu in Mac OS 9.1 remains just as it has been in previous versions of the Mac OS dating back to version 8.0. To configure the Apple menu:

1. Open the Apple Menu Options Control Panel (see Figure 3.24).

2. Turn the Submenus option on or off.

3. Turn the Remember Recently Used Items option on or off and select how many items (0 through 99) are to be remembered for each category.

4. Close the Apple Menu Options Control Panel.

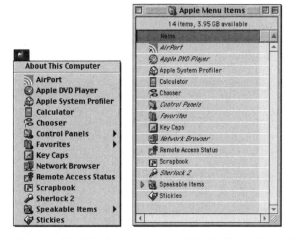

Figure 3.23   The Apple menu and Apple Menu Items folder.

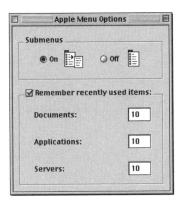

Figure 3.24   The Apple Menu Options Control Panel.

You can add items to the Apple menu by moving the original or an alias to the Apple Menu Items folder. Be aware, however, that because the OS must cache information about each item, including a large quantity of items in the Apple menu may slow its responsiveness.

Configuring ACTION GoMac

One of our favorite utilities, ACTION GoMac, consists of a Control Panel, an Extension, and two folders named Start Menu Items and Quick Launch Items that are housed in the System Folder. These folders contain the aliases of files, folders, and documents that are accessible through the Start menu created by GoMac. Items placed in the Start Menu Items folder appear in the uppermost portion of the Start menu in alphabetical order, with files at the top and folders at the bottom. The contents of the Quick Launch Items folder appear in the program bar area.

To configure ACTION GoMac, take these steps:

1. Open the ACTION Utilities Control Panel from the Start menu by choosing Start|Settings|ACTION GoMac.

2. In the Task Bar tab, select your configuration options, such as to show the clock and Start menu, as well as to automatically hide the program bar until activated by the mouse (see Figure 3.25).

3. Click on the Start Menu tab, shown in Figure 3.26, and make your configuration choices, such as adding a Drives menu to the Start menu and selecting an alternative find utility, such as Norton Fast Find, in place of Sherlock 2.

4. Close the ACTION Utilities Control Panel and the changes will take effect immediately.

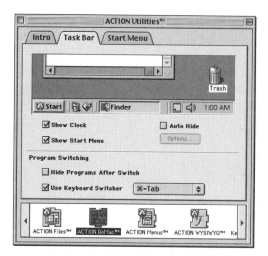

Figure 3.25   The Task Bar configuration tab of the ACTION GoMac Control Panel.

Figure 3.26   The Start Menu configuration tab of the ACTION GoMac Control Panel.

Configuring the Appearance

Mac OS 9.1's Appearance Control Panel will captivate users because its features allow you to customize the look and feel of the Finder, the Desktop, and the ways in which the Mac OS draws windows. Many of the features available in the wildly popular Kaleidoscope program (**www.kaleidoscope.net**) are now accessible through the Appearance Control Panel. The Appearance Manager consolidates several features from earlier versions of the Mac OS, such as the Desktop Pictures

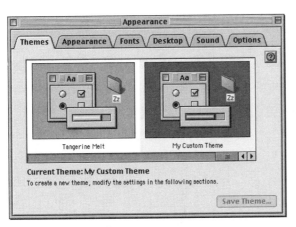

Figure 3.27   The Appearance Control Panel consolidates most of the features that affect the overall look and feel of the Mac OS.

and Appearance Control Panels, into the Appearance Control Panel, shown in Figure 3.27.

To change the appearance of windows, the Desktop, fonts, and sounds, open the Appearance Control Panel and select from among these options:

- *Themes*—A *theme* is a collection, or set, of appearance, font, Desktop pattern or picture, and sound options that can be saved and reloaded. To select a theme, scroll through the list of available themes and click on the one you want to activate. Mac OS 9.1 installs several default themes, including Bubbles, Convergence, Golden Poppy, Mono Blue, Rio Azul, Roswell, Sunny, and the ubiquitous Mac OS Default. To save your own theme, choose from the available appearances, fonts, Desktop patterns and pictures, and sounds, then return to the Themes tab, choose the Save Theme button, and assign it a name.

- *Appearance*—An appearance tells the Mac OS how to draw window elements such as the menu bar, window frames, scroll bars, buttons, and dialog windows. Currently, only the Apple Platinum appearance is available as part of Mac OS 9.1, but you can download others from various sites on the Web (see the list of Web sites in the earlier section entitled "Enhancing the User Environment"). See Figure 3.28 for an example of appearance selection.

- *Fonts*—Choose fonts (large and small) for system menus and for viewing window lists and the titles underneath icons. Mac OS 9.1 provides a font-smoothing option that allows fonts between 12 and 24 pt. in size to be anti-aliased for a smooth appearance (see Figure 3.29).

- *Desktop*—Choose a Desktop pattern or picture to replace the Mac OS Default pattern. To create your own pattern, drag a small picture to the Desktop preview area shown in Figure 3.30, then choose Edit|Pattern Name to edit the pattern name.

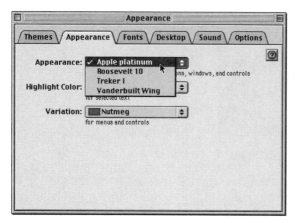

Figure 3.28   Choose an Appearance, which the Mac OS uses to draw Finder and
window elements.

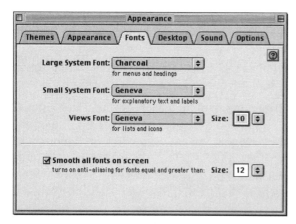

Figure 3.29   The Fonts configuration tab of the Appearance Control Panel.

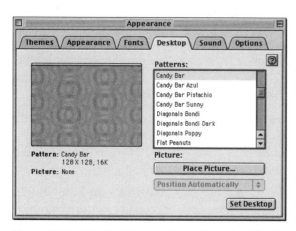

Figure 3.30   The Desktop configuration tab of the Appearance Control Panel.

To place a picture on the Desktop, repeat this step with an image that is larger than 128×128 pixels in size, or select the Place Picture button and locate a picture, such as those in the Desktop Pictures folder found in the Appearance folder within the System Folder.

Also, you may drag and drop pictures in several file formats—such as PICT, GIF, and TIFF—onto the System Folder and they will be automatically directed into the Desktop Pictures folder. To place a different picture on the Desktop every time your Mac is restarted, drag and drop a folder of images in JPEG format onto the Desktop preview area.

TIP: *Images dropped onto the Desktop preview area in the Appearance Control Panel that are smaller than 128×128 pixels will be converted into Desktop patterns by the Mac OS; larger images will be converted into Desktop pictures instead.*

- *Sound*—Choose a *sound track*, a collection of optional sound effects that play in conjunction with changes to the user environment, such as:
  - Opening and selecting menu items
  - Dragging and resizing windows
  - Clicking buttons, checkboxes, or scrollbars
  - Finder actions such as clicking, dragging, and dropping

  Mac OS 9.1 includes a sound track for the Apple Platinum appearance, but many others are available on the Web as well, such as those shown in Figure 3.31.

- *Options*—The Smart Scrolling feature has been around for some time, thanks to several third-party utilities, and was first incorporated into Mac OS version 8.5. This feature places vertical and horizontal scroll arrows at both the

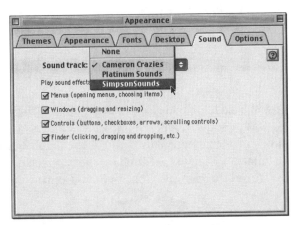

Figure 3.31   The Sound configuration tab of the Appearance Control Panel.

bottom and right corners of a window; it also uses *proportional thumbs* to indicate how much of a window's vertical and horizontal areas are visible. These features make navigating windows considerably easier.

For example, Figure 3.32 shows three views of the same window. The first shows Smart Scrolling off (top), whereas the second shows Smart Scrolling on (middle), where a large proportional thumb indicates that more of a window's contents is visible than not. A collapsed window is shown at the bottom of the figure.

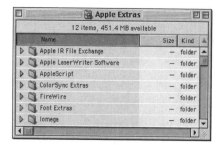

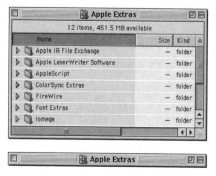

Figure 3.32   The Smart Scrolling and collapsible window features provide more scrolling options and visual clues as to the size of a window.

Using the Control Strip

The Control Strip was originally designed to provide PowerBook users with quick access to several of the more popular user environment options, such as changing the sound volume or selecting a printer. Eventually the Control Strip became part of the Mac OS standard installation. Mac OS 9.1 includes version 2.0 of the Control Strip, which can be configured through the Control Strip Control Panel, shown in Figure 3.33.

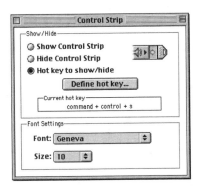

Figure 3.33   The Control Strip Control Panel.

Configuring the Control Strip

To configure the Control Strip, take the following steps:

1. Open the Control Strip Control Panel and indicate whether you want to show or hide the Control Strip; you can also activate the Control Strip by way of a user-defined hot key.

2. Select a font for viewing the contents of the Control Strip, and then close the Control Panel.

Many applications and utilities install a Control Strip module so that you can interact with that application via the Control Strip. To do so, such applications and utilities must install the module in the Control Strip Modules folder found in the System Folder. To disable a particular module, remove it from this folder and restart the computer. You might also want to try Vincent Jalby's Mac OS Items Manager 2 (**http:// hometown.aol.com/vjalby/MacOSIM/**), which works like the Extension Manager for several components of the System Folder, including Control Strip modules, Apple menu items, contextual menu items, and fonts, that are not managed by the Extension Manager. Figure 3.34 shows an example of this helpful utility.

Working with the Control Strip

To use the Control Strip, take these steps:

1. Activate the Control Strip and move it to a desired location on your screen by Option+dragging the Control Strip tab (the end of the strip closest to the center of your screen).

2. Resize the Control Strip horizontally by dragging the tab to show as much or as little of it as you wish. You can hide all but the tab by clicking on the square box closest to the screen border.

3. Access a Control Strip module by clicking on any of the items in the Control Strip. Figure 3.35 shows the choices contained in the Monitor BitDepth module.

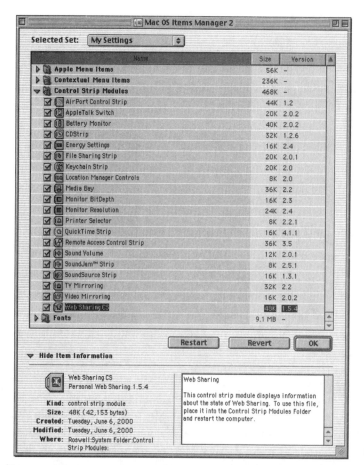

Figure 3.34   Use Mac OS Items Manager 2 to configure Control Strip modules.

Figure 3.35   The Monitor BitDepth Control Strip module.

Configuring the Launcher

The Launcher, which has been part of the Mac OS for some time, hasn't changed much over the years. It provides quick access to files, folders, and drives in a user-configurable palette. To activate the Launcher, double-click on the Launcher Control Panel or choose Show Launcher At System Startup in the General Controls Control Panel. The Launcher will appear as a Finder-like window, as in Figure 3.36.

Figure 3.36   The Launcher and its default contents.

To configure the contents of the Launcher:

1. Open the Launcher Items folder in the System Folder.

2. Add as many items as you like.

3. To create subcategories in the Launcher, create folders with a bullet (Option+8) as the first character and place them in the Launcher Items folder.

Any items in the root level of the Launcher Items folder (but not in a subfolder) will be accessible in the Applications section of the Launcher. Folders not preceded by a bullet will simply open on the Desktop when clicked in the Launcher. For example, Figure 3.37 shows the Launcher with two items at the root level (Script Editor and SimpleText) and three new subfolders (Apps, Docs, and Utilities).

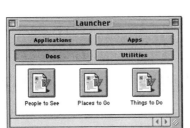
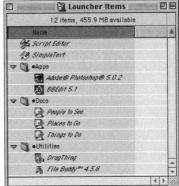

Figure 3.37   A customized Launcher with items at the root level and several customized subcategories.

Using the Simple Finder

The Simple Finder, which limits access to Finder menu items, is an ideal user-environment feature for schools and computer clusters where curious amateurs may want to explore all of the Mac OS menus and features. Figure 3.38 shows the File menu before (left) and after (right) the Simple Finder has been activated.

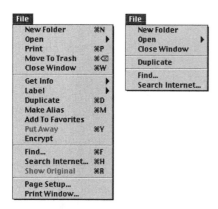

Figure 3.38   The Simple Finder, which deactivates several menu options in the Finder, is useful for young or inexperienced users.

To activate the Simple Finder, follow these steps:

1. Activate the Finder and select Edit|Preferences.

2. Click on the General preferences tab and then select the Simple Finder option.

3. Close the Preferences window.

Configuring the Application Switcher

The Application Switcher has been enhanced in several ways in Mac OS 9.1, as we've already seen in the "Switching among Applications" section of Chapter 1. You can select, hide, and show applications in the Application Switcher, as well as "tear off" the menu and place it elsewhere on the Desktop as a floating window, as shown in Figure 3.39.

Once it has been torn off, you can change the configuration of the Application Switcher and use AppleScript to change its appearance even more. Some of the actions to change the Application Switcher after tearing off the menu include the following:

- *View by small icon and name*—The default when you first tear off the Application Switcher

- *View by small icon*—Click on the Zoombox

- *View by large icon and name*—Option+click on the Zoombox

- *View by large icon*—Click on the Zoombox, then Option+click the Zoombox

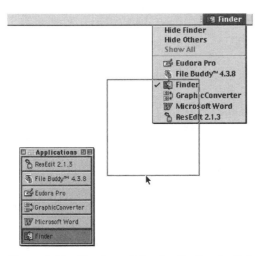

Figure 3.39   Tearing off the Application Switcher.

- *View horizontally by small icon and name*—Shift+Option+click on the Zoombox

- *View horizontally by small icon*—Shift+Option+click on the Zoombox, then click on the Zoombox

- *View horizontally by large icon and name*—Shift+Option+click on the Zoombox, then Option+click the Zoombox

- *View horizontally by large icon*—Shift+Option+click on the Zoombox, click on the Zoombox, then Option+click on the Zoombox

This may be a bit confusing, but remember that there are at least 24 unique ways to view the Application switcher, with the major categories being:

- Horizontal or vertical

- With or without the name of the application

- Short, medium, or long application names

- Small or large icons

- With or without the title

- In launch or reverse launch order

You can also hold down the Option key and resize the width (but not height) of the Applications menu. Figure 3.40 shows many of the various options for viewing the Application Switcher.

You can also use AppleScript to hide the title bar, display items in the order they were launched (rather than alphabetically), and position the Applications menu in

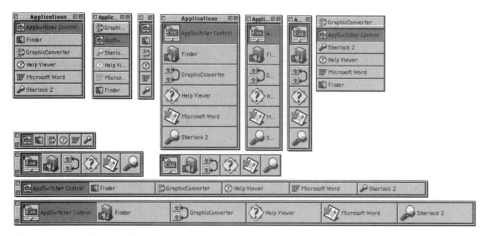

Figure 3.40   The possible ways to view the Application Switcher without using an AppleScript.

a specific location on the screen, such as the lower left. You can also Command+drag the Application Switcher anywhere on the screen.

To test some of these options, open the Help Viewer and search for the term "Application Switcher." Scroll to the bottom and select the options entitled Open The Application Switcher In A Horizontal Row For Me and Open The Application Switcher In Icon View For Me. Figure 3.41 shows how these two options appear when selected from within the Help Viewer. For more information on scripting the Application Switcher, follow the links provided.

The AppleScripts that control these actions are located on your hard drive as compiled scripts. To find them, search for the term "AppSwitcher" and open them using the Script Editor. See Chapter 14 for more details on using the Script Editor.

To use the Application Switcher:

1. Click on any of the buttons that appear in the Application Switcher to switch to that application.

2. Option+click on any of the buttons that appear in the Application Switcher to switch to that application and hide all the others (e.g., to unclutter the Desktop or speed up the foreground application). Option+selecting an

Figure 3.41   You can use AppleScript demos in the Help viewer to further enhance the Application Switcher.

item from the normal Applications menu also automatically hides all other applications.

3. Click on the close box to hide the Application Switcher from view.

Finally, if you want to try using an application to configure the Application Switcher instead of using cryptic keystrokes or AppleScripts, try AppSwitcher Control (**www.pascal.com/software**), shown in Figure 3.42.

Setting Up Talking Alerts

The Speech Manager, installed as part of Mac OS 9.1, allows the computer to speak alerts, called Talking Alerts, or read text in speech-aware applications. Speech recognition, which is not installed by default, has the capability to recognize human speech and execute commands in response. You can install it from the Mac OS 9.1 CD-ROM at any time by using the Add/Remove feature (choose English Speech recognition); if it's already installed, you can disable it by using the Extension Manager Control Panel.

Talking Alerts requires the basic speech software to be installed (Speech Manager Extension and the Speech Control Panel) and a few simple configuration options.

To configure Talking Alerts:

1. Open the Speech Control Panel (shown in Figure 3.43).

2. Select a voice and a rate at which alerts and readable text will be processed from the Voice options section.

Figure 3.42   Use AppSwitcher Control to configure the Application Switcher.

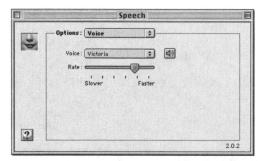

Figure 3.43   Selecting a voice in the Speech Control Panel.

3. Select the Talking Alerts option and indicate whether alerts should be announced, what phrase should be used to announce an alert, and whether the text of the alert window should be spoken (see Figure 3.44).

4. You can preview your settings and then close the Speech Control Panel.

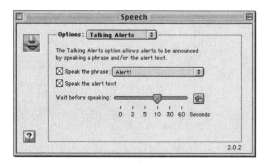

Figure 3.44   Configuring Talking Alerts to have the contents of warning dialog windows read to you.

Reading Text

Mac OS 9.1 allows speech-aware applications such as Eudora and SimpleText to use the Speech Manager to read documents in the voice selected in the Speech Control Panel.

To have SimpleText read the text of a document aloud:

1. Configure the Speech Control Panel by selecting a voice.

2. Highlight a section of text.

3. Select Speak Selection from the Sound menu.

Not all applications are capable of speaking, however.

Configuring Speech Recognition

Speech recognition requires custom installation via the Mac OS 9.1 CD-ROM, as well as a PlainTalk microphone or the built-in microphone found in most PowerBooks and iBooks. To configure speech recognition once it has been installed:

1. Open the Speech Control Panel.

2. Select a voice for the computer from the Voice section.

3. In the Listening section, Configure a hot key combination to enable/disable speech recognition, as well as to give the computer a name that is used when you want to issue a command. You may require the computer to listen for a command when the hot keys are pressed and to speak only after you first speak the computer's name. Because monosyllabic names are difficult for the Mac OS to recognize, you'll be prompted to rename the computer if you started off with something like Ralph. In this section of the Speech Control Panel, you may also select a microphone (see Figure 3.45).

4. In the Feedback section of the Speech Control Panel, select a character (or persona) to go along with the voice you've already selected; also, indicate how the computer should inform you that your command was recognized and will be executed. Figure 3.46 shows the Feedback section of the Speech Control Panel.

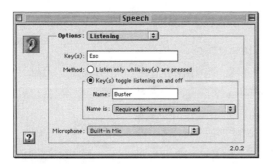

Figure 3.45 Speech recognition options for listening.

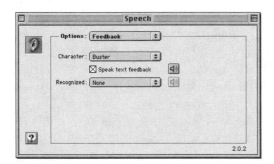

Figure 3.46 The Feedback section of the Speech Control Panel.

3. The User Environment

Figure 3.47   The Speakable Items folder contains commands that the Speech Manager can execute.

5. Finally, configure the Speakable Items section to allow you to issue commands located in the Speakable Items folder (see Figure 3.47), which is located in the Apple Menu Items folder. Close the Control Panel when you are finished.

Using Voice Commands

To issue a voice command, follow these steps:

1. Place the microphone in a desirable location, such as above the speech character floating window, where you can easily see whether your commands are being received.

2. Speak clearly and in a normal tone and ask the computer "What time is it?"

3. Sound waves will appear beside the character's ears to indicate the microphone is working; if the command is understood, it will be displayed in the window and then executed, as shown in Figure 3.48.

4. To add an item to the list of executable commands, place an alias to the command in the Speakable Items folder and rename it "Open *<application, document, or folder>*." This should result in the execution of the command in response to your saying "Open *<application, document, or folder>*". Or, to create an easy command, open the Script Editor and type "say "Howdy, partner!"" and save it as an application named "Hello." When you say "Hello" to the computer, it will respond with "Howdy, partner!"

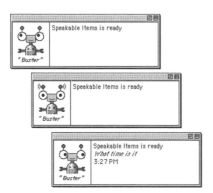

Figure 3.48　The speech character window displays your computer's persona and gives visual clues to its ability to listen for and execute voice commands.

For more robust speech recognition software that can process dictation, try IBM's ViaVoice (**www.ibm.com/software/speech/**). This is a piece of commercial software that has been very well received in the Macintosh community. It comes with a hands-free microphone customized for human speech recognition.

Changing Finder Window Views

The Mac OS makes it easy to change the way you view Finder windows. Depending on the options selected in the View menu, you can view a folder or disk as a regular or pop-up window, and you can view the contents of each window as icons, buttons, or a list.

To change the viewing options for a window, take these steps:

1. Open a folder or disk in the Finder.

2. Activate the View menu by selecting it from the Menu Bar or by pressing Command+J (a new feature in Mac OS 9.1). Then select one of the following:

   - As Icons

   - As Buttons

   - As List

3. Next, select one of the following options:

   - As Window

   - As Pop-up Window

If you drag a window to the bottom of the screen, it will automatically become a pop-up window—provided that no other pop-up window tabs were already in that location.

Setting Finder Window Preferences and Views

The Mac OS allows you to set your preferences for icon, button, or list views of Finder windows. Prior to Mac OS 8, it was possible to set a global view for Finder windows, but this ability was missing in 8.0 and 8.1. It reappeared in Mac OS 8.5 and continues in Mac OS 9.1.

Configuring Finder Window Preferences

Setting global Finder window preferences is a way of instructing the OS to consistently present each type of view (icons, buttons, or lists) in a particular way—except, of course, in the instances when you tell the OS to override your instructions. For example, you may specify that all button views should use large buttons while still allowing any individual window to override your preference and use small buttons instead.

To set Finder window view preferences, follow these steps:

1. In the Finder, choose Edit|Preferences.

2. Select the Views tab, as shown in Figure 3.49.

3. Indicate your view preferences, and then close the Preferences window.

Overriding Window View Preferences

To override the established preferences for a window view, follow these steps:

1. Select a window in the Finder.

2. Select the View menu and Arrange (with icons or buttons) or Sort List (with lists) the contents of the folder accordingly, as shown in Figure 3.50.

3. Next, select View|View Options (or press Command+J), as shown in Figure 3.51, and fine-tune your icon, button, or list window.

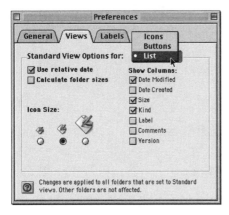

Figure 3.49   Setting default view preferences for windows viewed as a list.

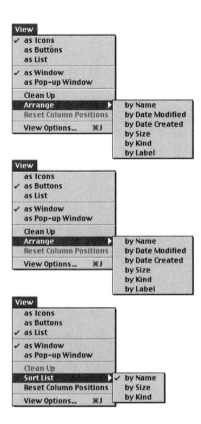

Figure 3.50   Arranging and sorting the contents of a window when viewed as icons (top), buttons (middle), and as a list.

Reverting to the Default Window View Preferences

To revert to the preferences for a specific type of view (icon, button, or list), take the following steps:

1. Select a window.

2. Choose View|View Options (or Command+J).

3. Select the Set To Standard Views button. Note that this button will be inactive if the current window is already viewed using the preferences defined in the Views tab of the Edit|Preferences menu.

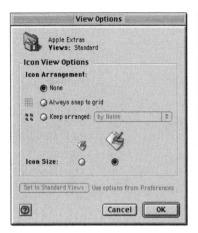
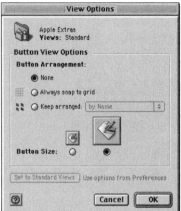

Figure 3.51   The specific options for viewing icon, button, and list windows.

Rearranging and Resizing Window Columns

Prior to Mac OS 8.5, users who wanted to seriously organize their list view windows had to turn to third-party utilities such as CoolViews in order to go beyond sorting by clicking on the column heading (Name, Date Modified, Size, and so on). Newer versions of the Mac OS made it possible to reorder columns by dragging and dropping them, as well as to resize column widths by clicking and dragging their margins. Mac OS 9.1 also includes this very cool—and very helpful—feature for rearranging and resizing columns.

Resizing Column Width

You can also resize the width of a column. Bear in mind that your changes to the columns' widths and order will remain until you select the Set To Standard Views button.

To resize the width of a column:

1. Open a folder or disk window and view it as a list.
2. Drag the right margin indicator in a column heading to the desired width, and then release it.

For example, Figure 3.52 shows a before (top) and after (bottom) view of a window whose columns have been resized. Note that the date formats change in proportion to the width of the Date Modified column.

Reordering Columns

To reorder columns in a list window, take the following steps:

1. Open a folder or disk window and view it as a list.
2. Drag a column heading such as the Date Modified or Kind and drop it onto any other heading except the Name heading, which will always appear first (on the left) in a list window.

For example, Figure 3.53 shows the Kind heading before, during, and after it has been reordered to appear second in the list instead of fourth.

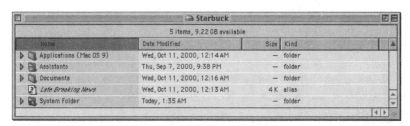

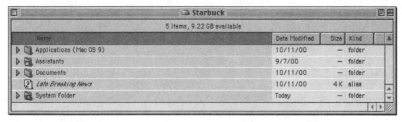

Figure 3.52   Resizing columns in a Finder window.

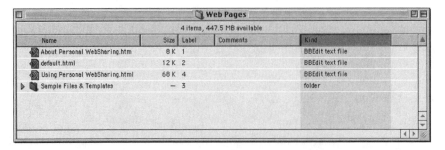

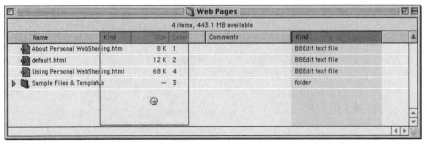

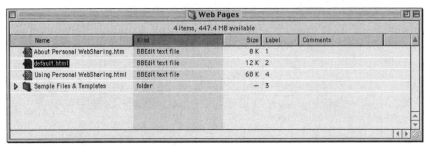

Figure 3.53   Rearranging columns in a list view.

Using Window Shortcuts

In Chapter 1, we discussed how to view folders under Mac OS 9.1. Nevertheless, here are a few additional shortcuts and features to help you get the most out of the Mac OS 9.1 user environment.

Collapsing Windows

You can collapse one or all open windows (the old Windowshade feature) to save room on your Desktop for viewing other elements, such as the Desktop itself, or simply to minimize the clutter on your screen. This feature works with all Finder and most application windows.

To collapse a window, follow these steps:

1. Select a window.

2. Double-click on the title bar (if enabled in the Options tab of the Appearance Control Panel).

3. Optionally, single-click on the collapse box (see Figure 3.54).

To collapse multiple windows, take the following steps:

1. Select any open window.

2. Option+double-click on the title bar (if enabled in the Options tab of the Appearance Control Panel). Alternatively, Option+click on the collapse box.

To undo this action, just repeat it.

Navigating Backward within a Folder

Another shortcut that has been available for some time but isn't well known to many users is the capability to navigate backward through a folder hierarchy.

To navigate backward from within a folder, take these steps:

1. Command+click on the window title until a pop-up menu appears, as shown in Figure 3.55.

2. Select a folder, then release the mouse button.

3. Choose Option+Command+click to navigate and close the current folder when the mouse is released.

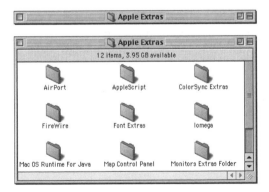

Figure 3.54   Collapsing and uncollapsing a window.

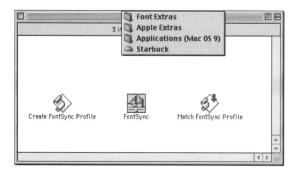

Figure 3.55   Command+click the window title to reveal the folder's path and to navigate backward through it.

Manipulating the Icon Proxy

Another great shortcut is the capability to move, copy, or alias a folder by dragging, Command+dragging, or Option+Command+dragging the icon proxy (the small icon in the title bar) to another location. Figure 3.56 shows the QuickTime icon proxy being moved to the Desktop.

To use an icon proxy, do the following:

1. Open a window.

2. Click and hold the mouse on the icon proxy.

3. While holding down the mouse, you can do one of the following:

   • Drag the icon proxy elsewhere to move the folder.

   • Drag the icon proxy to another volume to copy it to that volume.

   • Option+drag the icon proxy to copy the folder onto the same volume as the original.

   • Option+Command+drag the icon proxy to make an alias of the folder.

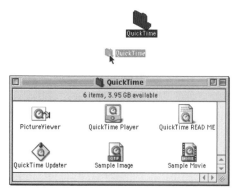

Figure 3.56   Using an icon proxy to move a folder to the Desktop.

Using the Command Key to Scroll

Mac OS 8.5 introduced a new way to scroll through windows without using the scroll bars on the right and bottom of all Finder windows. This scrolling method allows you to click in one spot and scroll left, right, up, and down, all without releasing the mouse; an example of this can be seen in Figure 3.57, where the hand-style cursor takes the place of the traditional pointer. This can be particularly useful if you have a multi-button mouse. You can configure a secondary mouse button to emulate the Command key, which makes it easier to target the entire window region for scrolling rather than the narrow scroll regions at the left and bottom of each window.

To scroll by using the Command key, take these steps:

1. Open any window to an icon, button, or list view.

2. Command+drag any portion of the active window region (except the title, scroll, or header areas).

3. Scroll along the vertical or horizontal axes, as well as on the diagonal or in circles, and the window will scroll as if you were moving the window itself instead of its contents. The scroll bars will move in the reverse direction, which is a little confusing at first.

Additional Sorting Options

You can also reverse the order in which a list is viewed by clicking on the small triangle (the Sort button) in the upper-right side of a Finder window. Figure 3.58 shows the default position (on the left) and the reverse position (on the right).

When the Sort button is selected:

• Lists viewed by Name will be alphabetized in reverse.

• Lists viewed by Date Modified will be sorted in reverse chronological order (oldest to newest).

Figure 3.57   Command+dragging a list view allows you to scroll in any direction.

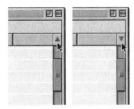

Figure 3.58   Reverse the sort order of any list by clicking on the Sort button.

- Lists viewed by Date Created will be sorted in reverse chronological order (oldest to newest).
- Lists viewed by Size will be sorted smallest to largest, with folders listed first.
- Lists viewed by Kind will be alphabetized in reverse by kind (utility, document, application).
- Lists viewed by Comments will be alphabetized in reverse according to the first character in the Comment field in the Get Info dialog window.
- Lists viewed by Version will be in reverse numerical order (3.3, 2.2, and 1.1, for example).

Using Default Folder and ACTION Files

Two great supplements to the Mac OS's open and save dialog windows are Default Folder from St. Clair Software (**www.stclairsoft.com**) and ACTION Files from Power On Software (**www.poweronsoftware.com**). Each provides unique features that enhance the user environment.

Default Folder, a Control Panel, adds numerous keyboard shortcuts and an extra button to every open and save dialog window. It also uses highly configurable shortcuts to your favorite folders. Webmasters and HTML developers will especially appreciate the ability to create multiple sets of favorite folders for different projects, for example. Figure 3.59 shows how the Default Folder shortcut button appears in an Open dialog window; the Default Folder button is the first of the four buttons above the preview area.

Figure 3.60 illustrates some of the Default Folder button's features. Default Folder is highly configurable, of course, and may look different depending on the features that are enabled or disabled.

ACTION Files also provides many more features than Mac OS 9.1's own navigational services, but the user interface alone is worth trying it out. Shown in Figure 3.61, ACTION Files uses a whole new way of displaying dialog windows by adding

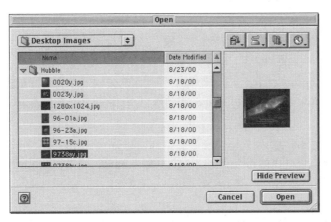

Figure 3.59   Default Folder's keyboard shortcuts and menu are added to every open and save dialog window.

Figure 3.60   The Default Folder menu.

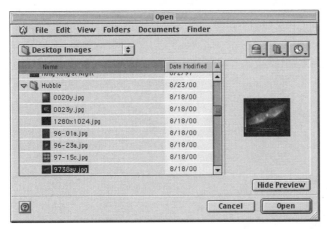

Figure 3.61   ACTION Files greatly enhances all open and save dialog boxes.

a much more Finder-like list view to represent the contents of a folder. It even comes with a Find utility that allows you to search for a file even while the open or save dialog window itself is open.

ACTION Files adds six menus to each open and save dialog window, including a handy File menu that mimics the File menu of the Mac OS itself. Figure 3.62 shows an example of this menu.

Both Default Folder and ACTION Files have far too many features to mention here. We urge you to try them out, along with ACTION GoMac, to sample ways in which you can further enhance the Mac OS user environment.

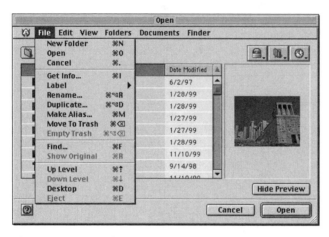

Figure 3.62   The File menu in ACTION Files.

Chapter 4

Installation and Basic Configuration

In Depth

As operating systems become larger and more complicated, it's more important than ever that each component resides in the proper place within the structure of the operating system. If a component is misplaced, the system itself or programs installed on the computer may malfunction. Gone are the days when you could upgrade the operating system by dragging a couple of folders onto your hard drive. Now you're required to launch an installer that has been scripted to correctly place the parts of the system and install the operating system appropriate for your computer. Of course, some users still try to cheat by copying a System Folder to the hard drive—only to see problems ranging from constant system errors to a computer that will not boot.

Despite the complexity of the system, Apple has made it very easy to install Mac OS 9.1. Although the installer has automated the process, you'll still be called upon to prepare for the upgrade and make certain decisions during the installation process.

Before You Install

Most Mac OS installations run smoothly even if the user does not take the time to prepare the computer. In some cases, however, lack of preparation can lead to serious problems or conflicts during installation. You can improve the odds that the new installation will be successful by getting your computer in the best possible shape.

Repair Your Disk

Free your hard drive from as many system problems as possible. If you've been experiencing problems with your system, run Disk First Aid or a similar disk repair and recovery utility to repair these problems. Although Disk First Aid can solve many problems, some are beyond its abilities. You may need a commercial utility such as Norton Utilities or TechTool Pro. Disk errors can carry over to the new system and continue to cause problems.

Even if your system has been operating well, it's a good idea to run a disk repair utility to check system integrity. Your hard drive may contain errors too small for you to notice.

Clean Your System Folder

Go through the System Folder and remove files that you no longer need. First check the folders containing disabled Extensions or Control Panels. These folders contain files that are not in use either because you disabled the file or, more importantly, because the program disabled itself (which means the program can't run at all). Remove these files and contact the software company for an upgrade.

Also check the Preferences folder within the System Folder. Remember that almost any program that you run on your computer generates a preference file, even if you delete the application immediately after running it. The items in this folder can be extensive, especially if you have used the computer for a while or are running lots of little programs and utilities. Your best approach is to remove preferences for programs that you know you've already deleted. However, don't remove a preferences folder just because you don't recognize the file name. Many applications require that you enter a serial or registration number before the program will run. This information is often stored in the program's preference file, which may have been given an unfamiliar name when the program was installed. If you don't have this number handy, you may not be able to run your application again.

Be cautious when you check the Extensions and Control Panels folders. Don't delete a file unless you know what it does. Some file names, especially the names of Extensions, can be rather cryptic. If you want to delete a program, try running its installer again. Many installers give you the opportunity to remove the application. This option is usually located within the custom options for the program installer. You may also find it helpful to employ a utility that's capable of intelligently searching the hard drive for all the files that accompany an application. Chaos Master (formerly Yank Pro) from Radiologic (**www.radiologic.com**) can move an application and all associated files to the Trash. Chaos Master also finds outdated or orphaned preferences and moves them to the Trash.

TIP: *When you're preparing to upgrade the operating system, don't forget about your software applications. People often assume that buying a software program is a one-time purchase, but in many cases software must be updated along with the operating system. Pay special attention to software programs that utilize system components such as libraries, Control Panels, and Extensions.*

Check Your Hardware

Take the time now to evaluate your hardware. Does it meet the system requirements for Mac OS 9.1? Apple has stated that, at the minimum, Mac OS 9.1 requires a computer that was manufactured as a Power Macintosh. Mac OS 9.1 is not supported for 68K systems that have been upgraded to a Power Macintosh. Watch out for problems if you've installed an accelerator card in an older Power Mac such as the 6100, 7100, 8100, or 9150—the main installer may not run. If so, Apple recommends that you run a specific installer for each part of the system. These installers are available in the Software Installers folder. If you have a Performa model in the 5200, 5300, 6200, or 6300 series, you must run a program called 5xxx/6xxx Tester (included with Mac OS 9.1), which will determine whether your computer needs a hardware repair. It isn't necessary to run this test on the Performa 5260, 6320, or 6360 models.

Check your available disk space. The Mac OS 9.1 basic installation requires approximately 195MB of disk space, or more if you install additional software utilities. The amount of free disk space determines what kind of Mac OS installation you should perform. Also, make sure that you have adequate memory installed on your computer. Macintoshes sold today include at least 32MB of memory, and most models have 64MB. If you have less than 32MB, you can purchase additional memory at somewhat competitive prices. Be aware that the system requirements for Mac OS 9.1 call for 40MB of memory (32MB RAM and 8MB virtual memory).

Back Up Your Hard Drive

In most cases, upgrades are relatively painless. Nevertheless, you should prepare for problems by backing up your System Folder, if nothing else. Because it isn't always possible to predict which third-party software will conflict with the new system, ensure that you can restore the computer to its original state in the event that you must run the conflicting software. You can also plan to perform a clean installation of Mac OS 9.1. If you encounter problems after the upgrade, you can easily remove the new system and return to the older operating system. Clean installation instructions are included in the Immediate Solutions section "Performing a Clean Installation."

Review Your Documentation

The Mac OS 9.1 installation program includes a document entitled "Before You Install," which contains special instructions. It's worth a few minutes of your time to read and review this document. It may provide important information that was not included in the printed manual (usually due to publishing deadlines). These documents may contain information regarding possible conflicts between Mac OS 9.1 and other applications, as well as suggestions for troubleshooting installation problems.

Installation Media

Mac OS 9.1 is usually installed from a CD-ROM. This medium is ideal for installing the OS because the CD-ROM includes its own System Folder, which allows you to boot from the CD-ROM drive. You can also run the installation from other removable media such as Zip, Jaz, or Superdisk volumes. Bear in mind that the Mac OS install program accesses individual installers for each component of the system.

If you use a Zip cartridge, you need to bypass the main installer program and run individual installers.

Alternatively, you can install Mac OS 9.1 from a network server. The software may be stored on the server itself, or the Mac OS 9.1 installation CD-ROM may be accessible from the network. In either case, running the Mac OS 9.1 installation from a network server is almost the same as installing it from the local CD drive.

Mac OS 9.0 was a major system release. Since then, Apple has released a slight update to the Mac OS, bringing the version number to 9.1. Updates such as this one usually fix program bugs and provide system enhancements. If you're running Mac OS 9, you can download the 9.1 update from the Apple software archive. An installer similar to the one used with a major system release is included. The Mac OS will undergo major revisions over the next year, and updates may include major system changes as the Mac OS moves toward release 10 (Mac OS X).

Mac OS X Beta

For the first time in years, Apple has released a beta version of an operating system for public testing. Mac OS X represents a major rethinking and revamping of the Macintosh operating system, and Apple has high hopes for its success. If you would like to participate in the beta testing, visit **www.apple.com/macosx/**.

Booting for OS Installations

Booting from a medium or partition other than the disk of the system you want to upgrade gives you the best chance of successfully overwriting all the components. You can boot from another hard drive partition if it has a valid system folder or from a system stored on a floppy, CD-ROM, or other removable media. However, if you must boot from the system you intend to upgrade, make sure that the following factors are in place:

- Boot with all non-Apple Extensions off. This reduces the risk that a third-party program will interfere or conflict with the installation process.

- Disable all security software such as Network Administrator or FolderBolt Pro. They will interfere with the installation process.

- Disable all virus protection software. If you're paranoid, run a virus check on the medium that contains the Mac OS installation software as well as on your own system, and then reboot with the virus protection disabled.

- If you're upgrading the system on a PowerBook, make sure that you have the power adapter plugged into the computer. The installation process can be rather long, and you don't want the battery to die in the middle of it.

- Don't attempt to install Mac OS 9.1 on a PowerBook operating in SCSI mode. During the installation process, the installer retrieves information about the computer and tailors the operating system to the type of computer. The Installer will treat the PowerBook the same way as the computer to which the PowerBook is connected.

Updating the hard disk driver is another potentially precarious step in the installation process. In the past, most hard drives were formatted at the factory by Apple. Today, many users purchase larger hard drives without upgrading the system and probably use a non-Apple hard disk driver. During installation, the installer will attempt to upgrade the hard disk driver. If the Installer cannot upgrade the driver, contact the company that manufactured your hard drive for a driver update.

Installation Options

Now that you're ready to upgrade the system, you want to take steps to ensure that the upgrade is accomplished as simply and as quickly as possible. Two kinds of installation methods—reinstallation and clean installation—are possible, and each method has merits.

Reinstallation

The simplest and fastest of the upgrade methods is installing the upgrade on top of your existing system and then allowing it to overwrite and update files. When you restart your computer, the OS will be upgraded and your additional software will still be functional.

By default, the installer reinstalls the software. When you launch the Mac OS installation program, you are greeted with a Welcome window that generally explains the steps for upgrading your software. Figure 4.1 shows the installation Welcome window.

Figure 4.1   The Welcome window for installing Mac OS 9.1.

The Select Destination window asks you to identify a destination disk. You can indicate another partition or medium. After you've made your selection, specific information about the destination disk will appear in the window. Don't despair if this screen indicates that you don't have enough disk space; you can still perform a minimum system installation. Instructions are included later in the Immediate Solutions section.

If you're reinstalling Mac OS 9.1 on top of an existing Mac OS 9.1 system, you'll encounter the dialog box shown in Figure 4.2. You can choose to cancel the installation, reinstall Mac OS 9.1, or add or remove components of Mac OS 9.1.

After you've selected an installation disk, you'll have an opportunity to read some additional information about installing Mac OS 9.1. Be sure to take a look at this document. It contains late-breaking information about changes in the OS or possible conflicts with older software. Read this document carefully to confirm that you can install Mac OS 9.1.

As you continue the installation process, you will be presented with the software license. You must agree to this license before you can install Mac OS 9.1. Much of the license is written in "legalese," but you should review it nonetheless. For example, if you purchased Mac OS 9.1, the license states that you can install it on only one computer. For the sake of all Mac OS users, please abide by this license.

After you accept the terms of the license, you can begin installing the software. However, now is the time to set a few additional parameters. When you perform the installation of a new operating system over an existing one, you may not know which files have been changed or upgraded. You can track this in the following two ways:

- Before you run the installation, change the labels on your system files, especially Extensions and Control Panels, to something other than *none*. After the installation, files that were changed will no longer have the label you designated.

- Set the option in the Mac OS installation program to create an Installation Report, which will list all changes that were made to your files during the installation. This option is enabled by default. To confirm it, simply click on the Options button in the Installation Software window. You should see a checkmark in the Create Installation Report box (see Figure 4.3).

Figure 4.2   The dialog box for overwriting the same operating system.

Figure 4.3   The option to create an installation report has been enabled.

This window also gives you the option of updating the hard disk driver. If your hard drive was formatted with a non-Apple utility, you should disable this option—otherwise, you'll receive an error message that the hard disk driver could not be updated (but you can still continue with the installation). If you know the formatting utility used on your hard drive, contact the developer of the utility for information on updated hard disk drivers. Then proceed with manually updating your disk driver. On the other hand, if you formatted your hard disk with an Apple utility, you should leave this option enabled. Updating the driver improves the interaction between the hard disk and the OS. In some cases, serious problems with the new OS may occur as a result of skipping the hard disk driver update.

By default, most of the following system components are installed by a basic Mac OS 9.1 installation:

- *Mac OS 9.1*—Includes the basic operating system.
- *Internet Access*—Used for accessing the Internet, such as Web browsers and email software.
- *Airport*—Allows late-model PowerMacs, iMacs, PowerBooks, and iBooks to utilize wireless network access (when used with Airport hardware).
- *Apple DVD Software*—Drivers and application software for viewing or supporting DVD discs.
- *Apple Remote Access*—Used for establishing PPP connections using a modem.
- *Personal Web Sharing*—Permits you to easily enable Web services on your Mac.
- *Text-to-Speech*—Allows your computer to read alert messages and other documents to you.
- *Mac OS Runtime for Java*—Enables your Mac to run Java applications.
- *ColorSync*—Helps you produce accurate color images both on screen and in print.
- *English Speech Recognition*—Enables your computer to respond to vocal commands.

At this point, you can begin the Mac OS 9.1 installation. Instructions for customizing the installation are included later in this chapter in the "Customizing the Installation" section. As the installation begins, the installer gathers information about your system and installs the appropriate OS. When installation is complete, your OS will have been upgraded.

The next step is to restart the computer. Upon restarting, the Desktop File may be automatically rebuilt and the Mac OS Setup assistant may run. This program gives you a chance to configure your Mac with your network parameters, or exit the program and perform the tasks manually. After the Mac OS Setup assistant has finished, you can use Mac OS 9.1. Your previous Extensions and Control Panels should be enabled. If not, use the Extensions Manager Control Panel to enable them, and then restart the computer. If these system files are compatible with Mac OS 9.1, you should see little or no difference in their function.

Be aware that reinstallation may lead to unexpected results. Control Panels and Extensions may fail to run. Occasionally, programs such as Virex (from Network Associates) and RAM Doubler (from Connectix) require an upgrade in order for the software to run successfully following a major system upgrade. If you encounter conflicts with your software, contact the manufacturer for upgrade information.

Clean Installation

Are you concerned about possible conflicts between your software and Mac OS 9.1? Or maybe you'd like to start off the era of Mac OS 9.1 with a clean slate? In either case, you may want to consider performing a *clean installation*. A clean installation differs from a reinstallation in that your old system software components are neither overwritten nor carried over to the new Mac OS. The Mac OS Installation program will disable your current System Folder and rename it Previous System Folder. All of your existing system software, now inactive, will be located in this folder. With Mac OS 9.1, you can reactivate an inactive System Folder via the Startup Disk Control Panel. This makes it easier to put the computer back "the way it was."

Differing schools of thought exist on the subject of clean installation. Some feel it is necessary only if you encounter problems following a reinstallation. Others recommend a clean installation with every major upgrade. This disagreement arises from the fact that whereas performing a clean installation is very easy, reconfiguring your System Folder afterwards is not. In fact, it's quite labor-intensive and definitely not something that new users should attempt without clear instructions. We recommend that you consider a clean installation if you are performing a major upgrade (for example, from System 8.x to Mac OS 9.1), or if you have not thoroughly cleaned out your system in the last 12 months. Of course, you can also employ it as a troubleshooting method for an unsuccessful installation of Mac OS 9.1 on a previous operating system.

The clean installation option occurs early in the installation process, but it's easy to overlook. You will find it if you click on the Options button in the Disk Selection window. Figure 4.4 shows the window where you can choose to perform a clean installation. By default, this option is not enabled. You must manually select it to create a completely new System Folder.

After you enable the Perform Clean Installation option, the rest of the installation process is the same as a reinstallation. However, after you restart your computer, begin placing the items from within the Previous System Folder into the new System Folder.

WARNING! Be aware that the safest route in this process is to reinstall your software rather than move it. If this is not possible, you should be able to move files safely. Just exercise caution with files you do not recognize.

Before you begin moving items, label all the files in your clean System Folder to differentiate them visually from the files you will be adding. This process takes time, and if you aren't careful, you may forget to move an item from one folder to the other. Compare each System Folder, and move files that are found in the Previous System Folder—but not in the new System Folder—to the newer folder. Do not overwrite files in the new System Folder. Preferences files are the exception, however. For example, you can replace the new TCP/IP preferences with the TCP/IP preferences file from your Previous System Folder, thereby eliminating the need to reconfigure TCP/IP. After placing the items in the new System Folder, restart the computer and watch for problems. You may be asked to reenter the serial numbers for some of your applications (some developers attempt to prevent software piracy by making it impossible to move a preferences file to another System Folder). Because some software applications will not function if they are moved from one System Folder to another, you should also try reinstalling the program that's causing your problems. If you encounter severe system Extension conflicts, contact the software manufacturer for an upgrade.

Finally, proceed with caution when overwriting Mac OS system components or adding "missing" components to the new System Folder. Control Panels and Extensions are renamed, combined, and separated in system releases. For example, starting with Mac OS 9, the Monitors and Sounds Control Panel was separated

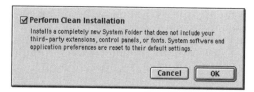

Figure 4.4   The option to perform a clean installation.

into two different control panels—the Monitors Control Panel and the Sound Control Panel. Some Extension libraries are incorporated into the System file and are no longer needed. Restoring these files may cause third-party software to malfunction. Your best bet is to work with third-party system components first. Restore Mac OS components only as a last resort.

Minimum Installation

Even after removing every piece of extraneous fluff from your hard drive, you may still not have enough available disk space to do a basic Mac OS 9.1 installation. Or, perhaps you want to create a bootable Zip disk. Zip disks have only 100MB of total space—not enough to contain a basic Mac OS 9.1 installation. When faced with these limitations, you can perform a minimum installation instead. You won't have many of the bells and whistles of Mac OS 9.1, but you can at least boot a computer with the disk.

Although the Mac OS installation program will tell you if you do not have enough space for a basic installation, it will nevertheless allow you to proceed with the installation. When you eventually reach the Install Software window, click on the Customize button, rather than the Start button, to perform a minimum installation. A window will list all of the system components that are being installed. Beside each component a pop-up menu offers three options: Recommended Installation, Customized Installation, and Customized Removal. To perform a minimum installation of Mac OS 9.1, click on the pop-up menu beside Mac OS 9.1 and choose Customized Installation. The window shown in Figure 4.5 will appear. Select Core System Software, which takes up a little more than 27MB of disk space. If you're installing Mac OS 9.1 on a removable medium such as a CD-ROM, Imation, or Zip disk, you probably have enough space to do a Universal system installation. You can then boot almost any computer supported by Mac OS 9.1. Please note that the option to install a Universal System has been moved in the

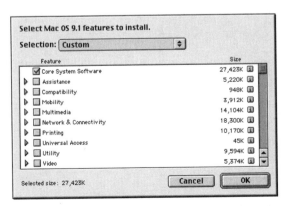

Figure 4.5   The Customized Installation options for Mac OS 9.1 system software.

Mac OS 9.1 installer. See the Immediate Solutions section "Performing a Universal or Minimum System Installation" later in this chapter for more details.

Customizing the Installation

Previously in this chapter, we showed you the list of components that the Mac OS installation program includes by default. You may not need some of the listed components. Perhaps you're satisfied with your email and browser programs and would prefer to disable the installation of new versions of those features. To tailor the installation to your needs, you'll also be required to manually enable other components that are not enabled by default. Each of the software components has its own installer and installation options that allow you to configure the settings you desire. Simply click on the Customize button in the Install Software window, and the listing shown in Figure 4.6 will appear.

To obtain general information about each component, click on the small "i" button. An explanation of what is being installed and how much space is necessary for the installation appears in a small window. To enable or disable a component, simply add or remove the checkmark beside it. You can further customize all of these options by way of the Installation Mode pop-up menu beside each option. Click on the menu and select Customized Installation to see exactly what will be included with or can be added to the individual component installation. For example, the default Web browser installed with Mac OS 9.1 is Microsoft Internet Explorer. However, by customizing the Internet Access installer options, you can select Netscape Communicator instead, as shown in Figure 4.7.

You can remove software with the Mac OS Install program by choosing Customized Removal from the pop-up menu beside the software component. For instance, if you're installing OS 9.1 on your home computer, you probably don't need

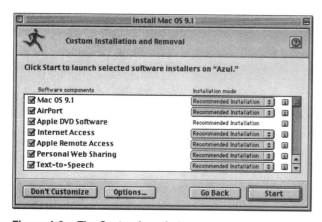

Figure 4.6   The Customize window.

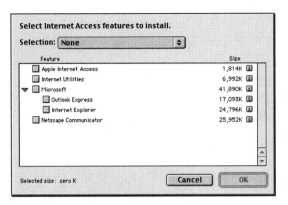

Figure 4.7   The custom installation options for Internet access.

Personal Web Sharing because this is a networking function that relies on a static Web address and constant access to the Internet. Go to the Customized Removal options and select each portion you want to remove, as shown in Figure 4.8. To remove the entire software component, select All from the pop-up menu at the top of the Customized Removal window.

Basic Configuration Issues

If you've just completed a clean installation of Mac OS 9.1, or if you're sitting in front of a brand new Macintosh computer, some basic system configuration may be necessary.

When the installation is completed, your hard drive window may look something like the one shown in Figure 4.9. Users who are familiar with previous versions of the Mac OS will notice that the number of initial folders has been reduced, presumably to make navigating the hard drive easier. The Desktop will display icons

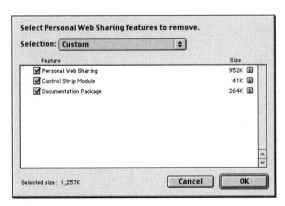

Figure 4.8   Removing Personal Web Sharing system components.

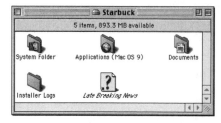

Figure 4.9   Desktop icons following a basic Mac OS 9.1 hard drive installation.

for browsing the Internet, utilizing QuickTime, and checking your email, as well as Assistants for configuring your computer and Internet settings. If you're supporting other Mac users, you may want to advise them to configure the system by running these Assistants.

Immediate Solutions

How to Determine Your Hardware Configuration

You have that Mac OS 9.1 CD-ROM in your hot little hands, but before you run the installation program, ask yourself a few questions about your hardware configuration. Do you have enough disk space? Is your computer capable of running Mac OS 9.1? How much memory do you have? To find the answers to these and other hardware questions, follow these steps:

1. Go to the Apple menu and launch Apple System Profiler. The window shown in Figure 4.10 will appear.

2. Look in the Processor Info field on the System Profiler tab to confirm that the computer is a Power Macintosh. Non-Power Macintosh machines cannot run Mac OS 9.1.

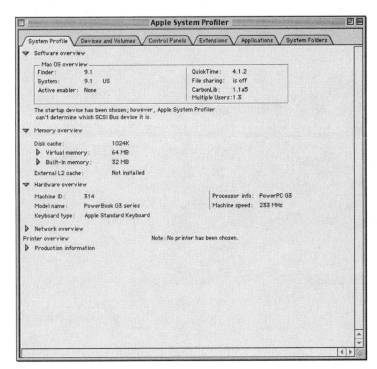

Figure 4.10   The Apple System Profiler.

3. Verify that you have enough memory to run Mac OS 9.1. Most new Macintosh computers come with at least 32MB of memory; Mac OS 9.1 requires 40MB of memory, although 8MB of that can be virtual memory.

4. Go to the Devices And Volumes tab and select the drive for your Mac OS 9.1 installation. For a basic installation, verify that you have approximately 195MB of free disk space.

5. If you do not have the Apple System Profiler, go to **www.micromat.com** and download TechTool. You can use it to retrieve the hardware and processor information. Launch the program and then click on the Hardware button. The window shown in Figure 4.11 will appear.

6. Confirm that your CPU type is Power PC chip (PPC), then exit TechTool.

7. From within the Finder, go to the Apple menu and select About This Computer or About This Macintosh to determine the amount of memory you have (see Figure 4.12).

8. Check free disk space by clicking on the drive icon and selecting File|Get Info (Command+i).

Related solutions:	Found on page:
Getting Information About Files and Folders	145
Using TechTool Pro	534

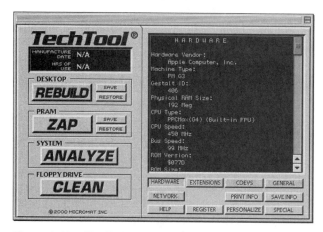

Figure 4.11   The TechTool hardware information window.

Figure 4.12   The About This Computer memory information.

Picking the Best OS Version

Now that you've analyzed your hardware, determine what version of the OS would be best for your computer (or the computer you are supporting). Not all Macintosh computers can run Mac OS 9.1, but that doesn't mean you can't upgrade the system at all. Many computers that are running older operating systems could benefit from an upgrade. Table 4.1 indicates what version of the Mac OS is best suited for various Macintosh models.

If you're still not sure which system is best for your computer, a search of Apple's Technical Information Library at **http://til.info.apple.com** will help you identify the right one.

The computer must have been manufactured as a Power Macintosh computer in order to run Mac OS 9.1. Support is not available for 68K machines that were upgraded to Power Macintosh.

Table 4.1   The best operating system for older Macintosh computers.

Processor	Example Models	Operating System
68000	Mac Plus, Classic, PowerBook 100	System 7.5.5
68020	Mac II, LC II	System 7.6.1
68030	Mac SE/30, IIx, IIcx, IIci, PowerBook Duo 210	Mac OS 7.6.1
68040	Quadra 610 and Centris 650	Mac OS 8.1
PPC	All Power Macintosh models	Mac OS 9.1

Preparing for Installation

Now that you've verified that Mac OS 9.1 can run on your machine, you're ready to prepare for the installation. Although the following tasks are not mandatory, performing them will increase your chances of a successful installation. Moreover, some of these tasks should be done on a routine basis anyway.

Follow these steps to prepare your computer for installation of Mac OS 9.1:

1. Run Disk First Aid on the disk on which you intend to install Mac OS 9.1. Disk First Aid will report any errors and indicate whether it can correct them. If you encounter errors that cannot be repaired, run Disk First Aid repeatedly—it may be fixing the problem bit by bit.

2. If Disk First Aid can't repair the drive, run a commercial utility such as Norton Utilities Disk Doctor or TechTool Pro. Repair the disk before you upgrade to avoid future problems with it. At this stage, defragmenting the hard drive is also a good idea.

3. Read the documentation that accompanies Mac OS 9.1. Specifically, make it a priority to read the files included with the installer. They contain important compatibility issues and installation guidelines. Reading these files now will help you reduce compatibility issues later.

4. Back up the contents of your hard drive. If this isn't possible, at least back up your System Folder in the event that the Mac OS 9.1 installation fails and you need to restore the original configuration. A backup also ensures that if you do a clean system installation you can easily restore your original system environment.

5. If you're going to install Mac OS 9.1 over your current system, label all the files within the current System Folder (for example, assign the color red to all files within the folders). After the installation, you'll be able to easily identify—by their lack of labels—the items that were replaced. This process is also helpful if you're having difficulties booting with Mac OS 9.1 and need to troubleshoot an Extension conflict. The program Installer Observer, developed by Zachary Schneirov (**www.macdownload.com**), is an alternate way to detect changes to the System Folder.

Related solutions:	*Found on page:*
Labeling Files and Folders	154
Using Disk First Aid	532

Booting Correctly for the System Upgrade

Of course, it's possible to boot your computer normally, run the Mac OS Install program, and install Mac OS 9.1. However, taking the easy way out could lead to problems with compatibility, Energy Saver, and system protection software. These problems could, in turn, severely interfere with your upgrade process.

Follow these steps to correctly boot your computer prior to a Mac OS upgrade:

1. Boot from the Mac OS 9.1 installation CD-ROM. You should be able to do this by holding down the C key during startup. If this doesn't work, choose the CD-ROM as the primary disk from the Startup Disk control panel.

2. If you must boot from the system that you intend to upgrade, boot with non-Apple Extensions off by going to Control Panels|Extensions Manager and choosing the Mac OS 9.1 Base set, as shown in Figure 4.13.

3. Disable all virus protection and security software; they will interfere with the installation.

4. Make sure that your screen saver and the Energy Saver Control Panels are disabled. The installation process can be quite lengthy; if you've configured these options to power up after short periods of inactivity, your installation time may be increased inadvertently.

5. On PowerBooks, make sure that the power adapter is plugged in. This eliminates the risk of the battery dying during installation.

Remember that you'll achieve the best results if the system you want to upgrade is not active. If possible, boot from a disk other than the one you're planning to upgrade.

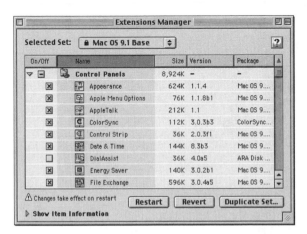

Figure 4.13   The Extensions Manager Control Panel with Mac OS 9.1 Base Extensions enabled.

Performing a Basic Installation

It's time to install Mac OS 9.1. You will most likely be running the Mac OS Install program from the CD-ROM. Some businesses or institutions may allow you to access the software from a server. For either source, the process is the same.

Follow these steps to install Mac OS 9.1:

1. Launch the Mac OS Install program. This is a "master" installer that interacts with the individual installers for each of the system components. You can customize each of these installations from within the Mac OS Install application.

2. The first screen that requires your input is the Welcome window, as shown in Figure 4.1. This window provides a brief overview of what you'll be doing during installation. Click on the Continue button to proceed.

3. The Select Destination window shown in Figure 4.14 allows you to choose the destination disk for your new software. It indicates what system software, if any, is currently installed and whether you have enough space to perform a basic installation. Select the disk and click on Select, but be aware of the following:

   • If you've chosen a disk on which Mac OS 9.1 is already installed, you'll be prompted to reinstall Mac OS 9.1 or add or remove system components.

Figure 4.14   The Select Destination window.

• You can continue with the installation even if you are warned that you do not have enough disk space. Consult the In Depth section "Performing a Custom Installation" earlier in the chapter if you receive this warning.

4. The Important Information window displays. This text file contains important information about installing Mac OS 9.1, including news about compatibility issues. Review this file and click on Continue.

5. The Software License Agreement is listed next. If you prefer to read this in a language other than English, select that language from the pop-up menu in the top right area of the window. After clicking on Continue, you are asked if you agree to accept the terms of the license. You must click on Agree to proceed.

6. The Install Software window appears (see Figure 4.15). By default, the program will attempt to update your hard disk driver and create a report of changes to your system folder. These settings are accessed by clicking on the Options button. If you know that a non-Apple utility was used to format your driver, disable the Update Apple Hard Disk Drivers setting and contact the manufacturer of the formatting utility.

7. Click on the Start button to begin installation. A progress bar indicates how much time remains in the process. When the installation is finished, restart your computer to use the new operating system.

Figure 4.15   The Install Software window.

Performing a Clean Installation

Perhaps you're concerned about the integrity of your System Folder, or maybe you ran into problems when restarting the computer after installing Mac OS 9.1. In these and other situations, a clean installation of Mac OS 9.1 may be advisable.

The instructions for a clean installation are almost identical to those for a basic installation:

1. Launch the Mac OS Install program.

2. You'll be greeted with a Welcome window that describes the steps you will be taking to install Mac OS 9.1. Click on the Continue button.

3. The Select Destination window indicates what disk is selected, the operating system currently on the selected disk, and whether enough space exists to perform a basic installation. Click on the Options button.

4. A dialog box similar to the one shown in Figure 4.4 will appear. Click in the box beside the Perform Clean Installation option and click OK.

5. Finish the installation by following the instructions starting at Step 3 in the previous section, "Performing a Basic Installation."

6. After completing the installation and restarting the computer, you'll notice that your customized settings are gone. All system preferences are set to their defaults, and your third-party software is inactive. Label the files in your new System Folder with the File|Label option to differentiate them from the files that you will be adding, then locate and open the Previous System Folder.

7. Compare all folders within each System Folder and move items from the Previous System Folder to the new System Folder (for example, compare the Apple Menu Items folders, then the Control Panels, and so on). Do not overwrite any files in the new System Folder if you are prompted.

8. After you move the items from the old to the new System Folder, restart the computer. If you experience any conflicts, see the "What to Do If Something Goes Wrong" section later in this chapter.

TIP: *As the Mac OS is upgraded, some Control Panels and Extensions are modified and may exist in Mac OS 9.1 in different form. For example, the Monitors and Sound Control Panel has been divided so that there is a Monitors Control Panel and a Sound Control Panel. The opposite may also happen in future system releases in that Extensions or Control Panels may be combined for efficiency. For this reason, you probably shouldn't move Control Panels or Extensions that were installed with the previous Mac OS version.*

Performing a Custom Installation

Perhaps you only want to upgrade the system itself, or you don't want all the other components that are installed along with Mac OS 9.1, or you'd like the English Speech software installed so that you can control your computer by voice. Whatever the situation, you can customize all parts of the Mac OS 9.1 installation to suit your needs. When you launch the main installation program, it interacts with the installer programs for each system component. In previous versions of the Mac OS installation program, these individual installers sometimes interrupted the process by asking you to interact with them. The Mac OS 9.1 main installer program bypasses all this by allowing you to set your options for each of these individual installers from the main installation program.

Follow these steps to customize the Mac OS 9.1 installation:

1. Launch the Mac OS Install program.

2. Select a destination disk. Click on Options to perform a clean installation; otherwise, click on Select.

3. Read the installation documentation window and click on Continue.

4. Click on Continue on the License Agreement window and, when prompted, agree to the terms of the license.

5. You should now be at the Software Install window. To control what is and isn't installed, click on the Customize button, rather than the Start button. The window shown earlier in Figure 4.7 will appear.

6. To disable entire system component installations, remove the checkmark beside the system component. To add system components to the installation, add a checkmark to the option.

7. Beside each component is a pop-up menu that allows you to choose Recommended Installation, Customized Installation, or Customized Removal. Choose Customized Installation beside the system component you want to customize. A few programs, such as Airport or Mac OS Runtime for Java, cannot be customized.

8. Decide what parts of a system component to add. Options with a triangle beside them can be expanded to include additional choices. By default, none of the items are selected. Use the pop-up menu at the top of the window to choose All, None, or Custom selections, or manually select the options you wish to install; click on OK.

9. Now click on Start to begin your software installation. The new OS will not be active until you restart your computer.

Performing a Universal or Minimum System Installation

Because each type of Macintosh requires a unique OS geared to the hardware specifications of that computer, dragging a System folder from one type of Macintosh computer to another is definitely not a good idea. Instead, you can

4. Installation and Basic Configuration

create a boot disk that should start almost any type of Power Macintosh computer. This is called creating a Universal System Folder.

If you don't have enough free disk space to accommodate the entire Mac OS 9.1 installation, you can perform a Minimum or Core System installation. Both of these options involve the same steps:

1. Launch the Mac OS Install program and click Continue at the Welcome window.

2. Select a destination disk and click on Continue.

3. Read the installation documentation window and click on Continue.

4. Click on Continue on the License Agreement window and, when prompted, agree to the terms of the license.

5. You should now be at the Software Install window. Click on the Customize button.

6. Disable all the other software component installations so that only Mac OS 9.1 is selected.

7. Click on the pop-up menu beside Mac OS 9.1 and choose Customized Installation.

8. Use the pop-up menu at the top of the window to select a Universal Installation or Recommended Installation (see Figure 4.16). Choose All, None, or Customize to determine what items are selected. If you want a minimum system installation, make sure Recommended Installation is chosen from the pop-up menu at the top of the window; under Features, activate Core System Software. If you want to create a disk that can boot almost any computer (in this case, a removable medium such as a Zip disk), choose Universal Installation and click on OK.

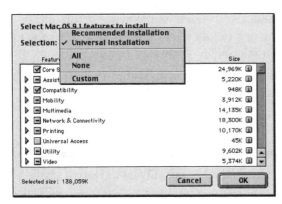

Figure 4.16   The customized installation options for the Mac OS 9.1 installer.

TIP: *Be aware that a Universal System installation requires more disk space than a system tailored to run on a particular machine. Make sure you have enough disk space available. If necessary, you can trim the size of the System Folder by deactivating some of the items that are selected by default. For example, you may not need all the items listed under Printing.*

---

9. Click on the Start button to begin the software installation. When the installation has finished, you will have upgraded your system or created a Universal System Folder.

What to Do If Something Goes Wrong

If everything goes right with your installation, you'll be able to reboot your computer and use Mac OS 9.1 and your existing applications. Sometimes problems arise, however. The following sections provide some suggestions for handling problems with your new software installation.

Computer Hanging Upon Restart

If your computer hangs after restarting, reboot with Extensions off (hold down the Shift key). If this fails, try booting from another system disk. If the computer boots, run Disk First Aid to look for problems in the hard drive. If you cannot boot with another system disk, you may have hardware problems. Try zapping the PRAM (boot and hold down Option+Cmd+P+R until the computer restarts). If you still cannot boot, your computer may need to be evaluated by an authorized repair shop.

Extension Conflict

If the computer can boot with Extensions off, launch the Extensions Manager Control Panel and select the Mac OS 9.1 Base Extension set from the pop-up menu at the top of the window. Restart your computer. If you can boot successfully, try booting from the Mac OS 9.1 All Extension set. If you're able to boot this time, you have an Extension conflict with a third-party program. Return to the Extensions Manager and enable a few Extensions or Control Panels and restart the computer. When you've identified the conflicting software, contact the manufacturer for an updated version that is compatible with Mac OS 9.1.

Cannot Boot with Extensions Enabled

If you cannot isolate an Extension conflict but are still having problems with your system, try performing a clean installation (refer to the "Performing a Clean Installation" section earlier in the Immediate Solutions section). Try booting with this new System Folder. If you succeed, gradually add items from the Previous

System Folder to the new System Folder and restart the computer until you isolate the problem or can successfully boot with the third-party programs enabled.

System Will Not Load

If you cannot boot after a clean installation, try performing a minimum installation. Customize your installation options and install only Mac OS 9.1, then try to boot. If you succeed, go back and run the installers for each system component you wish to add, noting whether any of them cause conflicts upon restart. If you discover a conflict, customize your installation again, choosing Customized Removal, and remove the offending component.

Upgrade Needs to Be Removed

If you still cannot boot your computer with only Mac OS 9.1 installed, it may be impossible to run Mac OS 9.1 on your hard drive in its current condition. It may be necessary to restore the System Folder from the backup you performed before upgrading. If you did create a backup, run the Mac OS Install program and customize your installation. On each component that was installed, select Customized Removal to remove the component. Then reinstall your previous OS (for example, reinstall Mac OS 8.1).

If you performed a clean installation of Mac OS 9.1, you can disable the current System Folder and select the Previous System Folder as your system of choice. Reboot to see if the old Mac OS will load. If not, reinstall the previous Mac OS that ran successfully on your computer.

Related solution:	Found on page:
Resolving Startup Conflicts	527

Chapter 5

Disk and File Systems

In Depth

Anything you create or produce on the computer is undertaken within the memory portion of the computing environment. When it's time to preserve your efforts, however, you'll need to access a permanent storage device. And if you ever want to see that file again, you should save it with some method of file organization in mind. In this chapter, we discuss different kinds of storage media and file formats, file organization methods, and remote storage options.

Storage Options

Numerous media exist on which you can store data. From the old reliable floppy disk to hard drives to DVD-ROMs, each one has its own plusses and minuses.

Floppy Disks

The floppy disk has gone through many transformations. It was once the size of an LP album. An unintentionally funny scene in the motion picture *War Games* involves the main character inserting an 8-inch floppy disk into the drive. As technology improved, the disks became capable of holding more data in smaller sizes. The last of the truly "floppy" disks was the 5.25-inch size. Although a protective envelope kept the Mylar disk from being damaged, data was still at risk because the disk medium was exposed.

The next step in the floppy disk evolution was the 3.5-inch disk. Not only could this disk hold more data, it was also protected by a hard plastic shell with a metal shield that retracted only after you inserted the disk into the drive. This format has endured—but not without some resistance from Apple. The absence of a floppy disk drive was one of the polarizing issues about the release of the original iMac. Many Mac users still want to have the option of storing data on objects they can hold. In fact, external storage devices such as the Zip or Imation Superdisk drive are some of the most commonly purchased iMac accessories.

The most popular floppy disks are, of course, in PC format. The original double-density disks, which can hold 640KB of data, are rarely seen today. High-density disks can hold 1.4MB of data, and double-density disks in a Macintosh format can hold 800KB of data.

Historically, the floppy disk was the most reliable way to boot an otherwise unbootable computer. In the modern era, however, the size of applications and operating systems has made it necessary to replace floppy disks with CD-ROMs.

Furthermore, floppy disks are unstable for long-term storage. Most users are familiar with the frustration that arises from discovering that a disk has become corrupted and no backup storage exists.

The floppy disk does have some benefits, however:

- It boots up older computers that are unable to boot from the existing system or are suffering from hard drive problems. In the latter case, the disk can verify and repair hard disk problems.

- It is the primary component of the "sneaker" network. Data is stored on the disk and exchanged with coworkers; this method of file sharing is often employed by users who are unaware of the extent of their storage options.

- It is an inexpensive storage medium.

CD-ROMs

CD-ROMs have replaced bootable floppy disks on newer Macintosh computers. CD-ROMs can hold over 650MB of data, including Mac OS software, disk utilities, and extra software. In fact, Macintosh systems have been supplying CD-ROMs for software installations, disk utilities, and troubleshooting since Mac OS 7.5. And as we've stated previously in this chapter, Apple no longer sells any computers that contain floppy drives.

CD-ROMs have become the standard format for software purchasing. A single CD-ROM can hold both PC and Macintosh data. One of the problems with the myth that no software is out there for the Mac is the fact that many titles do contain both system formats, but are grouped with other PC titles.

TIP: *When buying software, don't limit yourself to the Macintosh software section in your local Computers-R-Us retail store. Look at all the software. Many titles contain both Mac and PC formats but are grouped in the PC section to save space. More software is available for the Mac than most people realize.*

In most computers, the CD-ROM drive is read-only. However, CD-writing devices (also known as "burners") have become economically priced. In fact, the price of a burner is comparable to a second hard drive and the medium is very inexpensive, effectively giving you huge amounts of storage space for mere dollars. In our environment, we often use burners to write an image of a hard drive to a CD-ROM so we can configure multiple workstations at once. If you need to make copies of software to additional CDs, keep a central resource of departmental fonts or move installation programs from floppies to CD-ROMs, you may want to consider purchasing a CD read-write drive.

DVD-ROMs

Today's computer games and software have pushed the CD-ROM disk to its limit. DVD-ROM is the next generation of the digital storage format. DVD or *digital versatile discs* look exactly like CD-ROMs, but because the player angles the laser a little differently, a second layer of data on the disc can be read. DVDs can be double-sided, enabling them to hold much more data than CD-ROMs. However, this new industry has taken a while to agree upon a data format.

DVD drives have become popular options on iMacs and G4 systems as well as PowerBooks. Some G4 systems also include DVD-RAM drives, but there are still debates about the DVD-RAM standard.

While the software companies and advertising agencies are looking happily at the DVD format, the entertainment industry has been the real force behind this new standard. Thousands of motion pictures are available in DVD format. You can play these movies on a computer that has the proper equipment (a DVD drive and a specialized video card) installed.

Zip Disks

Although other removable storage devices were around before Iomega came out with its Zip drive, Iomega is responsible for making this device accessible to all users. Before the Zip disk, removable media was big, clunky, ugly, expensive, and occasionally unreliable. The Zip disk, only slightly larger and heavier than a 3.5-inch disk, has the advantages of being small, flat, economically priced, and stable. It holds up to 250MB of data, and you can format it for the Macintosh or the PC. You can install it internally or externally. (In fact, one of the external drive's greatest selling points is its portability.) Macintosh users favor the Zip drive so much that its driver has been included in the Mac OS since version 7.6.1. And with the advent of the iMac, which lacks a removable storage device, the Zip drive's popularity has been boosted by its easy connectability via USB.

SuperDisks

The SuperDisk drive from Imation goes a step beyond the Zip drive. Its greatest feature is its backward compatibility. The SuperDisk can hold 120MB of data, but it also can read and write to conventional 3.5-inch disks. The SuperDisk media looks and feels much like a conventional floppy disk.

The SuperDisk is a USB device. This has made it very popular with users who are converting to new Macintosh systems that lack floppy drives. The SuperDisk makes it possible to move data that has been stored on floppies to the new computer. In addition, it lives up to its name by providing an alternative, larger storage solution.

Jaz Drives

The Jaz drive from Iomega can hold even more data than the Zip and SuperDisk media disks. Jaz drives can hold up to 2GB of data. However, compared to the media we discussed earlier in this chapter, Jaz disks are somewhat large and clunky. They are also more fragile. Nevertheless, if you are faced with shrinking hard drive space and are debating whether to purchase another hard drive or go with a removable media device, the Jaz drive is very attractive in price and storage capacity.

SyQuest

At one time, SyQuest was a well-known name in the world of removable media. But the company has gone through some difficult times, including filing for bankruptcy. SyQuest was purchased by the Iomega Corporation and is now called SYQT. SyQuest/SYQT is worth mentioning because the company still continues to sell supplies and drives. Its drives come in a variety of sizes that range from 135MB to 1.5GB cartridges.

Magneto-Optical Disks

Magneto-optical disks are a cross between a floppy disk and a fixed hard drive. They can hold large amounts of data and write information to the disk many times. One tremendous advantage they have over other storage media is their stability around magnetic fields. Magneto-optical disks also have an extended storage life of 10 to 20 years.

When the first magneto-optical disks were released, some in the industry thought that they would replace floppy disks. However, the relatively slow data access rate of the magneto-optical drive has proven to be a drawback. For this reason, you may want to consider this system only if you have large data files or information that you don't need to access on a regular basis.

Hard Drives

The more well-known alternative to the floppy disk is the hard drive. Just a few years ago, the 1.4MB storage limit of one floppy disk made a hard drive with 40MB of storage seem huge. Inevitably, hard drives became larger. Today, many computers contain an internal hard drive with a minimum size of 6 gigabytes. Power users—especially graphic designers—insist on even greater storage capacity.

One of the most interesting issues with large-capacity hard drives has been the inability of operating systems to handle the larger partitions. On older Macintosh systems, this problem resulted in inaccurate statements of how much hard drive space was free. To resolve this issue, users would break or partition the hard drive into smaller chunks that the operating system could handle. Today, the Mac OS can handle drive partitions of two terabytes, a vast improvement for users with large hard drives.

An external hard drive is a hard drive housed in a case that sits outside the CPU. External hard drives serve a wide range of Macintosh users, from the novice who dreads the mere thought of opening the computer case to the professional who blithely stores his latest project on an external drive. And for those who make their living providing Macintosh support, these devices are a handy method of backing up users' hard drives.

WARNING! External hard drives are more expensive than internal drives and can cause problems for older Macs. For example, if the external drive spins faster than the internal one, system stalls may result.

External drives connect to the computer by several methods. The most well-known connection is SCSI, or Small Computer System Interface; however, Apple has moved away from SCSI connectivity and instead provides USB and FireWire ports on most of its computers. USB and FireWire connections are easier to support. They allow you to attach and detach devices while the system is on. In fact, you can detach a FireWire drive while a movie is playing, then reattach the drive, and the movie will resume at the same spot. See "USB and FireWire" later in this chapter.

Tape Backup Drives

If you are the manager of a network of Mac users or if you just want to protect your existing data, then you may want to consider purchasing a tape backup system. It is still the backup medium of choice for most companies. Tape cartridges can hold huge amounts of data and, with the right software, can perform data protection and recovery functions without interfering with your daily routine. Although tape backup systems are more expensive than other media that we have discussed, they are indispensable when you're faced with a corrupted database or a sobbing user who just overwrote an important file.

SCSI Issues

Apple may be pushing USB and FireWire, but many external devices are still attached to the computer via the SCSI port. SCSI is a processor-independent standard for communication between the computer and SCSI devices such as printers, scanners, hard drives, and CD-ROM drives. A SCSI chain consists of as many as seven devices, and each device is assigned a number in the chain. The number 7 is reserved for the Macintosh, and the number 0 is reserved for the internal hard drive. All other devices may use the remaining numbers.

Some Macintosh computers have more than one SCSI bus and therefore can contain up to 14 devices. If you have added a device to the SCSI chain and are experiencing difficulties accessing the device, or if your system fails to boot, then you may have a SCSI conflict. Mac OS 9.1's Apple System Profiler is invaluable for diagnosing these conflicts. Figure 5.1 shows the Apple System Profiler's report of the devices on a SCSI chain. After searching the bus, the Apple System Profiler identifies the devices associated with each number. In many cases, just changing the number of the device may resolve the conflict. Given this potential conflict, you can see why USB and FireWire are so attractive.

USB and FireWire

USB (Universal Serial Bus) is an industry standard for attaching external devices to computers. By including USB as a standard feature of the iMac, Apple has played a big part in popularizing it. USB has several advantages over SCSI, including the following:

- USB devices do not have to be manually numbered in the peripheral chain.

- You can have up to 127 devices in the USB chain.

- USB devices can be attached and removed while the devices are powered on. This capacity is also known as *hot plug* and *hot unplug* or *hot swappable*.

USB does have a big drawback—speed. SCSI connections are faster. In some peripherals, such as scanners, speed isn't a big deal. In external hard drives, however, you will notice the difference.

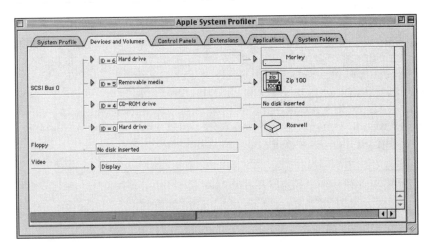

Figure 5.1   Apple System Profiler, showing the SCSI configuration.

FireWire, on the other hand, does not have a speed problem. It can transfer data at rates up to 300Mbps. FireWire was developed at Apple, but is an industry standard. You can have up to 63 devices in the FireWire chain, and the USB benefits such as hot plug and unplug are features of FireWire as well.

Understanding File Formats

The Macintosh file structure is unique. Each file in the operating system consists of two parts. The *data fork* contains what a user would normally see in a file. The *resource fork* contains information about the file such as its creator, icon bitmap, and program segments. The resource fork differentiates Macintosh files from Windows files. Files created on other platforms such as Windows contain only the data fork.

Information about the files on the Macintosh is stored in a hidden file named the *Desktop Database*. This database is a "roadmap" of the storage system, whether it is the hard drive, CD-ROM, or floppy disk. When you double-click on a file, the Desktop Database launches the appropriate software for reading the document. Occasionally, this database becomes confused. Symptoms include scrambled icons, poor performance, inability to connect to the network (if all cabling and network parameters have been correctly set), and an obvious failure of association (for example, you double-click on a plain text document and receive an error that the document's software creator cannot be found). To rebuild this database file and resolve some of these problems, refer to "Rebuilding the Desktop File" in the Immediate Solutions section of Chapter 18.

The resource fork includes information about the file creator. A broad category of creators exists; a good example is the **ttxt** category, which includes all plain-text documents. More specific creator information is available but is not as obvious. That's because every Macintosh software program assigns a unique four-character annotation to any document it creates. For example, Microsoft Word uses the creator identification of MSWD. You can find out this information by using specialized utilities such as ResEdit, File Buddy, or Cool Views. You can also search for documents by creator with the Sherlock 2 utility; this is very useful if you have trouble remembering information about a file, such as its name or where you saved it. You can use this information when creating AppleScripts or when transferring files, especially in some email programs.

TIP: Are you trying to identify a file's creator type, but don't have ResEdit or File Buddy? Sherlock 2 can help. Simply launch Sherlock 2, click the Edit button, and drag the file in question over the window. You will get all kinds of useful information such as creator and file type and the version and size of the file.

Standard vs. Extended Formats

The Macintosh standard format was revolutionary when it was first released in 1986. Until that point, the Macintosh file system could not even support the use of folders. By using allocation bits on a volume, the Macintosh standard format could support partitions up to 2GB in size (remember, at this time, large hard drives were 20MB). However, a standard number of allocation bits per volume was assigned. For example, for smaller volumes such as 256MB, the allocation bit for a file could be 4KB. However, for a 2GB volume, this allocation is 64KB. Therefore, the same file on both volumes would take up vastly different amounts of space, in spite of the fact that the files were identical. This was troublesome for very small files, especially text-only documents.

With the release of Mac OS 8.1, the Macintosh extended format was made available to Macintosh users. This new file storage format increased the number of allocation bits from 65,536 to over 4 billion, thus enabling disks to accurately represent and store files by their true size. Figure 5.2 shows a file listing on a standard format volume and Figure 5.3 shows the same files on the extended format volume.

The Macintosh extended format may not be for everyone. On current Macintosh systems, it's the standard drive type. For older systems, however, you may question whether you need to move to the Macintosh extended format at all. If the volume in question primarily stores large documents such as graphics files, then the extended format won't make much of a difference. On the other hand, if you maintain a file system (such as a Web server) that contains many small or plain-text files, you may want to consider the Macintosh extended format. You can

5. Disk and File Systems

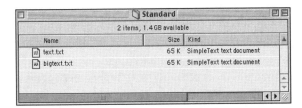

Figure 5.2   Files in the standard format volume.

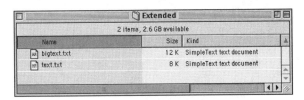

Figure 5.3   The same files in the extended format volume.

recover several megabytes of additional storage by using the newer format. Bear in mind that computers must be running Mac OS 8.1 or greater to see extended-format disks on the local system. Extended format volumes accessed over a network can be mounted on pre-Mac OS 8.1 systems.

Finally, if you support several computers that a user could modify, you need to know how to determine the format in which a disk has been formatted. Instructions are available later in this chapter, in the Immediate Solutions section entitled "Determining Mac OS Standard or Extended Format."

Server Storage

Several years ago, most computing environments featured a series of networked computers that shared data with a central file server. Today, servers are still very popular. The benefits of storing data remotely include data protection provided by the backup process featured in most servers. Furthermore, servers appeal to cost-conscious system administrators, who know from experience that purchasing 5 copies of a software program and using a server to meter them is more economical than buying and installing 100 copies of the program on each hard drive.

Problems can develop, however, depending upon the type of server and the server software. In an ideal world, the server would be an AppleShare device, and therefore easily accessed from the Chooser or Network Browser. In the real world, most servers run Novell NetWare or Windows NT/2000. Fortunately, these platforms allow Macintosh access by running certain processes on the server. Figure 5.4 shows files stored on a remote Novell server.

However, you may be working in an environment that is not Mac-friendly. Don't despair; programs are available that allow you to access the server without running special processes on the server itself. For Windows NT servers, you can use DAVE, a software utility from Thursby Software. DAVE allows you to access NT servers as well as other Windows systems up to Windows 2000. Moreover, DAVE enables you to access other Macintosh servers using TCP/IP rather than AppleTalk. We will be discussing utilities such as DAVE in more detail in Chapter 10, which covers Microsoft Windows compatibility issues.

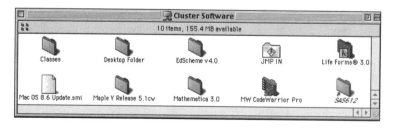

Figure 5.4   Files stored on a remote server volume.

Several companies offer remote data storage, usually in the form of Web space. In fact, most Internet service providers include data storage in their monthly fees. A search of the Internet for free Web space will turn up many sites that provide this service. Apple even provides data and Web storage in the form of iDisk, a component of their iTools suite. Go to **http://itools.mac.com/itoolsmain.html** for more information.

Using the Multithreaded Finder

In Mac OS 8, the Finder was improved to include multithreading capabilities. You'll see the most dramatic evidence of this improvement when you're manipulating files. For example, you can copy files from one volume to another and, while this operation is in progress, perform other functions in the Finder—including copying additional files to other folders or volumes. Figure 5.5 shows multiple copies in progress. Mac OS 9.1's contribution to the multithreaded Finder includes multiple searching sessions by using the Find or Sherlock utility.

Disk Fragmentation

Disk fragmentation occurs when gaps exist between files stored on the hard drive, as well as when files are broken up and stored over multiple areas of the disk. When a hard drive has barely been used, each new file is stored one after the other in neat alignment. However, as you make changes to files, delete them, save them under new names, and append data to them, data storage becomes messy. As you delete files, new files—rarely the same size as the old—are saved in their places and spread out over the disk. Eventually, you end up with gaps throughout your hard drive; each gap is too small for new data storage and therefore the space in the gap is wasted. To make matters worse, the tables that track the location of the parts of a file may become corrupt, rendering those files effectively lost. Defragmentation utilities remove these gaps while manually rewriting the data back to the volume. In the process, disk space for data storage is restored. Defragmenting your disk also improves hard drive performance.

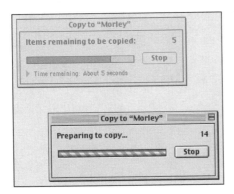

Figure 5.5   Multiple copies simultaneously in progress.

Several software makers offer disk defragmentation utilities. The most popular is Norton Utilities Speed Disk. In addition to defragmenting the hard drive, it can also organize files by type so that documents are immediately recognizable. The Norton Utilities package also includes Speed Disk; Disk Doctor, which is capable of repairing volumes that Apple's Disk First Aid cannot; a program to recover deleted files; and crash-protection software. If you are a system administrator, you should have some kind of disk or volume utility software. These programs can at least warn you that a drive is about to fail. At some point, every data storage volume needs maintenance. It's not a matter of *if*, but *when*.

Immediate Solutions

Mounting and Dismounting Floppy Disks

An administrator of multiple platforms who is new to the Mac may not be aware of the method of ejecting floppy disks, which are still commonly used in the workplace. Here are some simple guidelines for working with this medium:

1. Insert the disk in the drive.

2. The Mac OS will mount the disk on the Desktop.

3. You can store files on the disk or run programs from it.

4. When you are finished, dismount or eject the disk by any of these methods:

   - Drag the disk's icon to the trashcan.

   - Click once on the disk's icon, then go to the File menu and select Put Away.

   - Click once on the disk's icon, then go to the Special menu and select Eject Disk.

Using Removable Media

As a Macintosh user, you have access to many different removable media, including Zip and Jaz disks and removable hard drives. Installing, mounting, accessing, and dismounting any one of these media is very much the same:

1. If you are attaching a SCSI device, turn off the computer and devices. USB and FireWire devices can be attached while the computer is on.

2. Attach the device to the appropriate port.

3. If necessary, turn on the computer and device.

4. Insert the device's software disk and install the driver for the device.

5. If required, restart the computer and insert the disk or cartridge in the drive.

6. The icon of the medium should appear on the Desktop; you can use the medium to store documents or run applications (see Figure 5.6 for an example of a mounted Zip disk).

7. Drag the icon of the medium to the trash or use File|Put Away to dismount the medium.

5. Disk and File Systems

Figure 5.6   A Zip disk mounted on the Desktop.

TIP: *Mac OS 9.1 includes the Iomega Zip disk driver. You can attach the device, insert the disk, start the computer, and the Zip disk will be mounted on the Desktop automatically.*

Accessing Remote Servers and Volumes

You've had to use some cost-cutting measures and now have software stored on a local server rather than on each hard drive. You can use the Network Browser to access a remote server:

1. Go to the Apple menu.

2. Select the Network Browser utility (use this once, and you may never use the Chooser for accessing servers again).

3. If applicable, locate and double-click on the zone where your server resides (see Figure 5.7). If you have enabled File Sharing over TCP/IP you can also choose the option to Connect To Server and enter the machine's IP number.

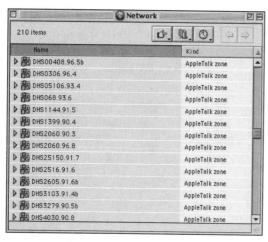

Figure 5.7   The Network Browser window listing zones.

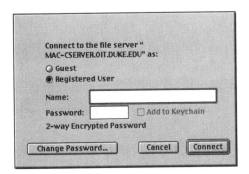

Figure 5.8   A password prompt.

4. To open your server, double-click on its icon within the browser (you'll probably be prompted for a password, as shown in Figure 5.8).

Getting Information About Files and Folders

You need to retrieve information about a particular file such as its status, path, creation and modification date, and version of the application. Much of this information is available in the Get Info window. Follow these directions to retrieve this information:

1. Click once on the file or folder to select it.

2. Go to the File menu and select Get Info|General Information or type Command+I. Figure 5.9 shows a standard Get Info window.

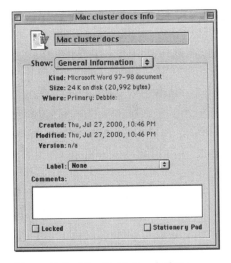

Figure 5.9   The Get Info window.

TIP: *You can also access this information by pressing the Command key as you click the object. This action brings up a contextual menu with the Get Info option.*

Making a File Read-Only

You have a particular file that you want to protect from changes. You can lock the file so that it is read-only. This protects the document from changes within an application and prohibits the user from saving a file of the same name to the locked file location. Follow these steps to make a file read-only:

1. Click once on the document you want to make read-only.

2. Go to the File menu and select Get Info|General Information.

3. Locate the small box in the bottom left of the Get Info window beside the word "Locked."

4. Click in the small box; a checkmark will appear in it. The file is now read-only.

By following these steps in reverse you can easily disable the locked setting.

TIP: *While the file is locked, it keeps this setting, even if you drag the file to the Trash. If you attempt to empty the Trash that contains the locked file, the dialog box in Figure 5.10 will appear. You can easily bypass this warning and delete the file by holding down the Option key and selecting Empty Trash.*

You can also save a file as stationery, rather than read-only. The file, still containing the information you added, will open in an untitled window. This option is great for creating templates.

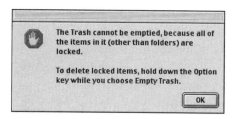

Figure 5.10   The warning for a locked file in the Trash.

Determining Mac OS Standard or Extended Format

You are unsure as to whether a particular volume has been formatted with the Mac OS Standard or Extended System. Follow these steps to determine the format of the volume:

1. Click once on the icon of the volume in question.

2. Go to the File Menu and select Get Info.

3. Look in the section entitled Format.

The term *Mac OS Standard,* shown in Figure 5.11, refers to the typical Macintosh file storage format. The alternate term, *Mac OS Extended,* refers to the new file allocation format.

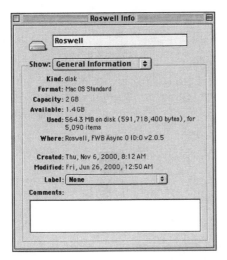

Figure 5.11   A standard format volume.

Finding Files and Folders by Name

In spite of your extraordinary organizational skills, you will often need help locating a particular file or document. Your best friend is the Sherlock 2 utility. This utility performs many search functions including searching local drives, the contents of documents, and the Internet. The default settings for Sherlock 2 make it easy to perform a search. Follow these steps:

1. Select either File|Find or Apple|Sherlock 2.

2. Check the volumes to be searched (see Figure 5.12).

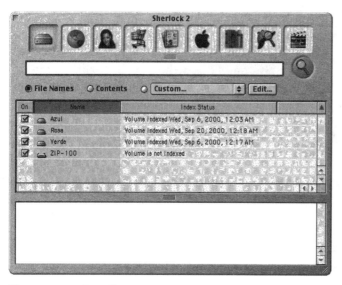

Figure 5.12   Selecting the volumes to be searched.

3. Enter the name of what you're searching for, then press Return or click on the magnifying glass button.

4. The results are shown in a separate window that has a split pane. If the bottom pane is not visible, click the grab handle on the bottom of the window to separate the panes. You can now click on a file in the upper window and the path will be displayed in the lower window (see Figure 5.13).

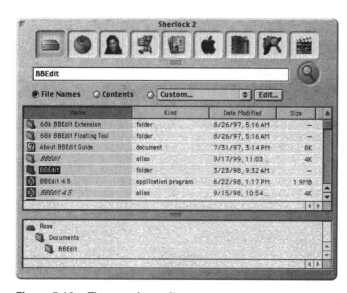

Figure 5.13   The search results.

You can perform many of the same functions in the Items Found window that you're accustomed to doing in the Finder. You can launch applications, drag files to the Trash, and Get Info.

Finding Files and Folders by Custom Search

Sherlock 2 is capable of searching within parameters more complex than just by name. You can also save these searches and use them again in seconds. Follow these steps to do a complicated search and save the results:

1. Select either File|Find or Apple|Sherlock 2.

2. Check the volumes to be searched (refer to Figure 5.12).

3. Click the Edit button. The More Search Options window, as shown in Figure 5.14, will appear. You can search by many methods, including name, size, kind, label, date created, date modified, version, comments, lock attribute, folder attribute, file type, and creator.

4. Enter your options and click OK—unless you think you'll want to search by this criteria again. If so, click Save to keep this custom search as an option. A dialog box will appear. Name the search and then click OK.

5. If you saved your search, you will see it selected in the main Sherlock 2 window. (Other personalized searches are listed in the Custom pull-down menu.) To begin your search, press Return or click on the magnifying glass.

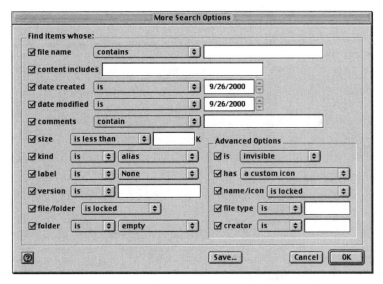

Figure 5.14 Sherlock 2 offers a wide variety of search options.

6. The results are shown in a separate, split-pane window. If the window is not split, click the grab handle near the bottom of the window and drag upward. You can now click on a file in the upper window and the path will be displayed in the lower window (see Figure 5.13 earlier in the chapter).

You can use these results to perform many of the functions that you're accustomed to doing in the Finder, including launching applications, dragging files to the Trash, and utilizing Get Info.

Indexing Content

Indexing content is the first and longest step in the process of searching volumes by file content. In fact, you cannot access the full power of this search style until you've created an index of the volumes that you want to search. You can program your Mac to index volumes routinely by taking these steps:

1. Select either Apple|Sherlock 2 or File|Find.

2. Select Find|Index Volumes. A window similar to the one shown in Figure 5.15 will appear.

3. Select the volume or volumes and click on the Create Index button. A warning dialog box will advise you that creating the index takes time. You'll be offered the options to proceed, schedule the index for later, or cancel the index.

4. Click the Create button to create your index.

A progress bar indicates how much of the volume has been indexed. If you can read quickly, you'll be able to spot the file names as they appear under the progress bar. When the indexing process is complete, you can search for files by their content, not just by their names.

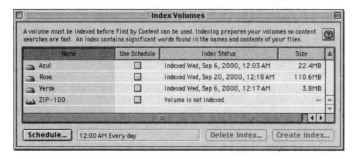

Figure 5.15   The Index Volumes window.

You can set special preferences for indexing by selecting Edit|Preferences. By labeling files and folders, you can indicate which ones should be indexed. You can also determine how you want your system to perform when Sherlock 2 is indexing a volume.

Finding Files by Content

It's no longer necessary to buy software that makes it possible for you to search the content of files in the way that a Unix user utilizes the **grep** command. The Mac OS contains the ability to search the contents of the file, not just the name of it. Follow these steps:

1. Launch Sherlock 2 from the Apple menu or select File|Find.

2. Enter your text or text string and click the Contents radio button, as shown in Figure 5.16.

3. Deselect any volumes you do not want searched.

4. Press Return or click on the magnifying glass. A window indicating your search results appears with the best matches listed first. Figure 5.17 shows a sample window.

TIP: You can search via Finder selection if you drag the selected files from Finder into the Sherlock 2 window before conducting the search.

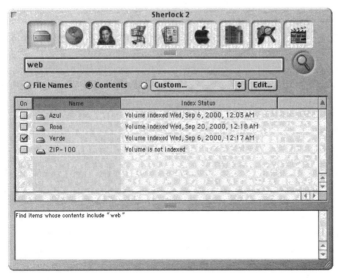

Figure 5.16   Setting the search parameters.

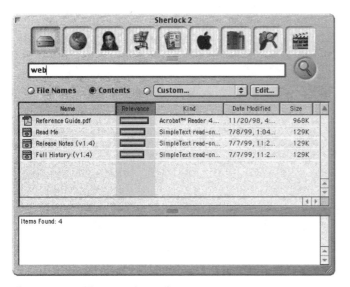

Figure 5.17   The search results.

Scheduling Content Indexing

Unless you want to create an index every time you want to do a file content search, it's a good idea to schedule indexing on a regular basis. Take the following steps to schedule indexing during the evening hours, so that you can work undisturbed:

1. Launch the Sherlock 2 utility.

2. Select File|Index Volumes.

3. Place a check in the box beside each volume you want indexed.

4. Click on the Schedule button.

5. Set the time of day and the day of the week for the automatic indexing (see Figure 5.18) and choose Okay. You can select more than one day.

6. Close all windows for the settings to take effect.

Automatic volume indexing will now occur. If you watch this process, you'll see the same progress bar that displays when you manually create an index. This feature will vastly improve your accuracy in searching by content.

Figure 5.18   Setting the schedule.

Searching the Internet

The Sherlock 2 utility also includes an interface that utilizes channels and plug-ins to search all the popular search engines on the Web. You can also search for diverse information on people and shopping or even create your own custom channels. Many Web sites provide Sherlock 2 plug-ins that you can use to add functionality to the utility. Follow these steps to search the Internet using Sherlock 2:

1. Launch the Sherlock 2 utility.

2. Select your channel for searching (see Figure 5.19). The most frequently used channel is the Internet, represented by a globe, but there are several others to choose from.

3. Enter the information you seek and, if necessary, modify the lists of sites you will be searching.

4. To begin the search, press Return or click on the magnifying glass.

5. Your search results will be listed in place of the search sites and will be ranked in order of relevance to your search criteria. This window has three panes. The second pane may be hidden; click the drag handle located below the search results to expose the URL pane. When you click once on a result, the URL will appear in the lower window. You can click this link or double-click a result in the list to view the complete page in a Web browser.

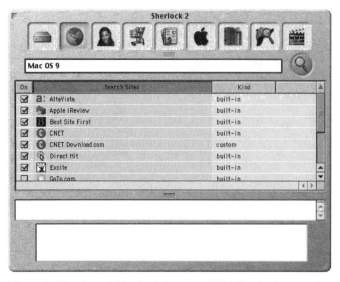

Figure 5.19   Searching the Internet within Sherlock 2.

Labeling Files and Folders

You can organize your files by type or by labels. Labels may be helpful when searching via Sherlock 2. It's also possible to use labels to group files in the list view. To label an item or items, follow these steps:

1. Select the item or items you want to label.

2. Choose File|Label.

3. Choose the most appropriate phrase or color.

4. The item now has a special property for organizational structure. Figure 5.20 shows a group of files organized by label.

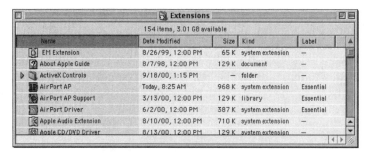

Figure 5.20   A list view of files labeled "Essential".

Creating and Using Custom Labels

OK, so now you can label icons. Your next question is, "How can I change the phrases to mean something?" After all, wouldn't it better if the label Project 2 could be changed to ACME or something more intuitive? You customize labels by following these steps:

1. Select Edit|Preferences.

2. Click on the Labels tab (see Figure 5.21).

3. Edit the phrases as necessary.

4. Edit the colors by clicking on the color by each phrase. This brings up the standard color selection window. Choose the color you want.

5. Save changes by closing the window.

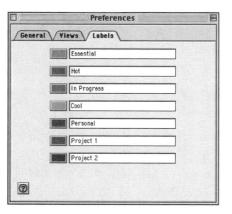

Figure 5.21   The Labels Preferences window.

5. Disk and File Systems

Selecting Items in the Finder

Occasionally you need to manipulate, label, copy, or open a file or group of files (yes, the Mac OS is wonderful in that you can open multiple files and applications at once). Use the following methods for selecting files in the Finder:

- Click once on a single icon to select it.

- Hold down the Shift key and click on multiple icons within a Finder view such as a window or the Desktop.

- Click and drag the mouse just outside a group of files to form a lasso; then catch the group of files with the lasso (the icons darken as you select them).

- Hold down the Shift key and drag to select noncontiguous groups of icons.

Creating Comments

You can enter additional text in the resource fork of a file by adding custom comments. Some examples of useful comments might be the reason the document was created and its URL or other relevant Web sites. You can create comments by taking these steps:

1. Select a file.

2. Choose File|Get Info or type Command+I.

3. In the Comments text box, enter whatever text you deem relevant to the file (see Figure 5.22).

4. Close the window.

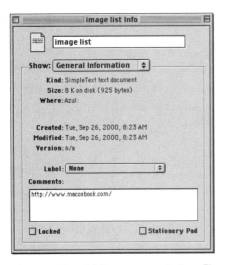

Figure 5.22   Adding comments to a file.

Creating and Using Aliases

Aliases are already heavily used in the Mac OS. If you see files with italicized text, you're looking at an alias of an original file or folder. The Apple menu often employs aliases. In fact, when you select the Control Panels option, you are actually selecting an alias that points to the original, which is located in the System Folder. Aliases are very easy to create:

1. Select the file that needs an alias.

2. Choose File|Make Alias or type Command+M.

3. Move the newly created alias file to the location of your choice. You can also press the Command key as you click on the object; this will bring up the contextual menu with an option to make an alias.

Figure 5.23 shows the difference between an alias and the original file.

In earlier versions of the Mac OS, you could put an alias almost anywhere you chose. If you moved the original file, however, the alias no longer functioned. Mac OS 9.1 includes a feature that fixes broken aliases. You can move the original file and the alias will still function.

TIP: *Make an alias in one swift motion by clicking the item, pressing the Command+Option keys, and dragging the file to the folder where the alias will reside. The file will not be moved; instead, an alias will be placed in the selected folder.*

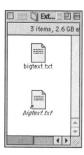

Figure 5.23   An original (top) and an alias (bottom).

Increasing Disk Performance

A volume that doesn't undergo routine maintenance is an accident waiting to happen. You can take several steps not only to prevent accidents, but also to improve disk performance:

- Defragment your hard drive. Several commercial products, including Norton Utilities and Disk Express Pro, do an excellent job.

- Run Disk First Aid at the first sign of trouble. Disk First Aid can now repair active volumes.

- Use a commercial utility to repair damaged volumes. Norton Utilities has an excellent program named Disk Doctor that can repair volumes beyond the capabilities of Disk First Aid. Make sure that you're using the latest version of the disk repair utility. This specialized software usually needs to be upgraded whenever the Mac OS is upgraded.

- Use some sort of virus protection. Symantec and McAfee offer excellent virus protection packages.

Configuring Disk Cache

You can improve system performance by setting your disk cache to a suitable level. The cache contains a history of commonly used commands. The smaller this file is, the more often the application must consult the hard drive for instructions on how to perform a function. A larger cache stores more of these common instructions. Mac OS 9.1 will set the default cache size to a size suitable to your machine, but you can modify these settings. To set your cache, take the following steps:

1. Go to the Apple menu and choose Control Panels\Memory.

2. Locate the cache section at the top of the window (see Figure 5.24).

3. Set the cache using this formula: Multiply 32KB by the amount of RAM installed (for example, someone with 16MB of memory would set the cache to 512KB).

4. Close the Memory Control Panel.

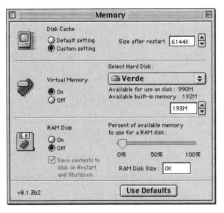

Figure 5.24   Setting the disk cache.

Accessing Damaged Disks

If you are experiencing strange system errors or your machine seems to be crashing frequently, you may have a damaged disk. Another obvious symptom of a damaged disk is that your computer doesn't seem to recognize the drive and wants to initialize it. You can utilize Disk First Aid as a first attempt at fixing the program. To do so, take the following steps:

1. Launch Disk First Aid, which is located in the Applications (Mac OS 9) subfolder of the Utilities folder (see Figure 5.25).

2. Select the volume that may be damaged (if you are using a floppy or Zip disk, insert it now).

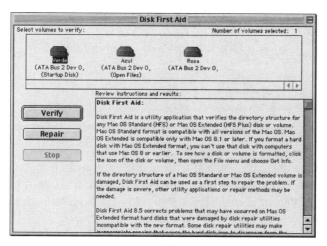

Figure 5.25   Disk First Aid.

3. Choose Repair to attempt to repair the volume (Verify will only tell you what is wrong).

4. When the process is finished, you will receive a report in the Disk First Aid window.

If Disk First Aid does not work, try running it several times. The program may need more than one run to fix the problem. However, if Disk First Aid cannot fix the disk, you may need to invest in a commercial disk-utility package, such as Norton Utilities.

Creating a Disk Tools Disk

Although the floppy drive is almost an antique, it has tremendous troubleshooting value when you're working on an older computer. Apple included a disk image with each system release up to Mac OS 7.6.1. Before you can create a disk tools disk, you need two things: a disk tools image and a program called Disk Copy. Disk Copy is available on the Apple Web site at **www.apple.com**. To create a disk tools disk, take the following steps:

1. Launch Disk Copy.

2. Choose Utilities|Make A Floppy.

3. Locate the disk image that you downloaded from Apple (you can also find disk tool disk images on your system CD-ROM).

4. After the image has loaded into Disk Copy, you will be prompted to insert a floppy disk. Be aware that all the data on the floppy disk will be erased.

5. Disk Copy will copy the disk image onto the floppy disk.

When this process is finished, you will have a disk suitable for booting your computer.

Creating Disk Images

In the past, disk images were used to copy installation programs onto floppy disks. Today, disk images are used to simplify distribution of installer programs. You can create your own disk images using the Disk Copy utility available from Apple by following these steps:

1. Launch Disk Copy.

2. Go to the Image menu and select Create Image From Folder or Create Image From Disk.

3. Locate the folder or disk and click on the Choose button.

4. A Save dialog box will appear. Choose a name for the image, and set the appropriate options such as image status (read-only) and image location.

5. Click on Save. The program will create and mount the image. See Figure 5.26 for the results.

This format is also an appropriate method for distributing files.

TIP: *Do you want to increase game performance? Create a disk image of a game CD-ROM, and mount the image rather than the CD. The game will play more smoothly and the movies and multimedia will load faster because a hard drive is much faster than a CD.*

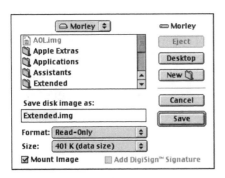

Figure 5.26   Creating a disk image.

Chapter 6

Memory Management

In Depth

This chapter explains how the Mac OS uses Random Access Memory (RAM) for the OS itself as well as for applications that run on top of the Mac OS. It also discusses Read Only Memory (ROM) and Video Random Access Memory (VRAM). Although memory management varies greatly among other operating systems, Mac OS 9.1—like most versions before it—remains true to the Mac OS model. You will notice, however, a few improvements, including faster memory usage (especially in the case of virtual memory) and more stability than ever.

How the Mac OS Uses Memory

The Mac OS uses one contiguous RAM pool for both system resources and applications. (Windows 95, 98, and NT use a similar approach to memory allocation, but earlier versions of Windows and MS-DOS used a very different method that caused many headaches for system administrators.) When the Mac OS boots, it loads most system resources into two areas in the memory pool: the System Heap and the High Memory area. The System Heap contains all elements of the System suitcase, such as fonts, sounds, and keyboard mappings, as well as icons and Desktop database resources. The High Memory area of the memory pool is home to the disk cache data and other system resources. The area between the System Heap and the High Memory area is available for use by applications, desk accessories, Control Panels, and Extensions.

The About This Computer feature offers basic information on how your computer has allocated memory, as shown in Figure 6.1. The level of information here only scratches the surface, however.

TIP: *For an overview of the most popular applications and RAM-related utilities, see the Immediate Solutions section later in this chapter.*

Understanding how the Mac OS uses memory can help you run more applications concurrently, avoid problems with memory fragmentation, recover unused and fragmented memory, and handle errors and crashes that occur as a result of memory-related issues.

Figure 6.1   You can obtain basic information on memory allocation from the About This Computer feature.

Physical Memory

RAM chips come in various sizes and speeds, and memory intended for one type of computer cannot necessarily be used in another computer. Because Macintosh computers enjoy a higher level of hardware interoperability than most other computers, RAM chips can usually be interchanged among families of Macintoshes, such as the first-generation PowerMacs with NuBus (6100, 7100, 8100), second-generation PowerMacs with a PCI bus (7200, 8500, and 9500), as well as third-generation (G3) and fourth-generation (G4) servers, desktops, PowerBooks, iBooks, and Cubes.

Today, Power Macintosh computers use several types of RAM chips, including the following:

- 30- and 72-pin SIMMs (Single Inline Memory Modules)
- 168-pin DIMMs (Dual Inline Memory Modules)
- 168-pin EDO (Extended Data Out) DIMMs
- 168-pin SDRAM (Synchronous Dynamic Random Access Memory)

PowerBooks and iBooks use similar types of RAM chips, but come in fewer configurations because most PowerBooks have very limited expansion slots (usually just a single slot) and all the memory must be put onto a single chip.

Moreover, different RAM chips are capable of transmitting data through the chip at different speeds, usually measured in nanoseconds, although some manufacturers and retailers list speed in megahertz:

- SIMMs: 80-120ns

- DIMMs: 60-70ns

- SDRAM: 10ns

RAM speed is important because chips of different speeds may not be completely compatible, and it's easy to accidentally mix chips with different speeds. This can generally slow the computer or cause it to be unable to recognize one or more of the chips. When possible, use chips with the exact same speed specifications.

G3 and G4 Macs have one or two banks of RAM expansion slots. When two banks are present, memory is best installed in like pairs to take advantage of memory interleaving. *Interleaving* enables chips of the same speed placed in the same spot on the two different memory banks to have a faster throughput than if the chips were placed in different slots. For example, if you place chips in slots A1 and B1, they are interleaved. If the chips are placed in slots A1 and B3, they are not interleaved. Although interleaved memory isn't required, it can yield a significant performance boost (some say up to 7 percent). Even Apple recommends that memory be interleaved when possible.

Similarly, be sure to use RAM chips of the same speed to obtain the highest level of performance.

TIP: *See the Apple Spec Database (**www.info.apple.com/applespec/applespec.taf**) for information about how much memory ships with which Macintosh, the maximum amount of RAM it will accommodate, and how many expansion slots are available. When ordering memory, it's important that your vendor understand Mac memory and whether matched pairs are required. If the vendor's unsure, at least verify that you can return or exchange the memory if it isn't acceptable for your computer.*

You use memory not only to store applications while they're in use, but also to assist the processor by temporarily storing processing instructions. All PowerPC processors include an on-chip memory storage area known as a *cache*, and most computers utilize additional cache chips on the processor daughter card or the motherboard, including the following:

- Level 2 (L2) cache

- Level 3 (L3) cache

- Backside cache

- Inline cache

- Look-aside cache

A typical on-chip cache is very small, usually 16KB or 32KB, and very, very fast when compared to the type of memory used for application data and the OS. L2 and L3 cache chips are also faster, and they range in size from 256KB to 1MB. Backside, inline, and look-aside caches are sometimes referred to as types of L2 caches. They're actually more similar to an L1.5 cache because they sit on or very near the processor card (or near the processor on the motherboard), but before the L2 cache. The G3 and G4 processors use these types of caches, which are so fast that they eclipse any other L2 or L3 cache. Cache chips can significantly increase the overall speed of just about any computer. Refer to the Apple Spec Database for information about your model's cache capacity.

Physical vs. Virtual Memory

Long before the first Mac came on the scene, mainframe, mini, and Unix computers were using hard drive space to mimic RAM to provide a very cheap substitute for it. Even in an era of cheaper-than-ever RAM prices, virtual memory—often abbreviated as VM—is a well-known concept to Mac users. Virtual memory takes inactive RAM, writes it to the hard drive in a protected and hidden file, and then transforms it from inactive data into active memory. Over the years, the Mac OS has become very efficient in its use of virtual memory. Many third-party developers have created alternatives to Apple's virtual memory routines, including RAM Doubler from Connectix and RAM Charger from the Jump Development Group. Figure 6.2 shows the Memory Control Panel, which is where you can configure Apple's built-in virtual memory capabilities, before (left) and after (right) virtual memory has been enabled.

Debates about using virtual memory persist. It is our opinion that if you need or want to use it, then do so, but if your computer has enough physical RAM installed

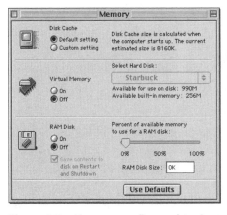
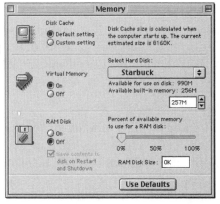

Figure 6.2   You can configure virtual memory through the Memory Control Panel.

to meet all your computing needs, then don't use it because it degrades system performance. The two most important reasons for using virtual memory are:

- It enables you to launch more applications.
- Applications launch faster and require less memory to load.

Drawbacks to using virtual memory include:

- The degrading effect virtual memory has on the overall speed of the Mac OS
- System instability (some say it has increased, others say it has decreased)

System degradation resulting from the use of virtual memory varies widely, depending on your computer's speed, hard drive speed and throughput, system bus speed, and SCSI or IDE adapter.

Every user's situation is different, of course, and virtual memory is more useful in some situations than in others. In some applications (such as Adobe PhotoShop), a built-in virtual memory routine makes it possible to open very large files and to write temp files to disk rather than holding them in memory. So, even if you're not intentionally utilizing virtual memory, some of your applications may use it anyway.

TIP: *Virtual memory relies on writing data to and reading data from your hard disk. A fast SCSI or ATA hard drive (7200 RPM or faster) will help speed things up when virtual memory is in use.*

Two of the most popular virtual memory utilities, RAM Doubler and RAM Charger, are discussed in the following section and in the Immediate Solutions section.

Allocating Virtual Memory

Mac OS 9.1 improves the speed and stability of virtual memory. Until the Mac OS is revised to allow for protected memory space, however, virtual memory will not be optimally efficient. Many experienced Mac users shy away from utilizing virtual memory because it slows some aspects of the Mac OS and introduces issues of system stability. The majority of us, however, use virtual memory because we have limited amounts of physical RAM and we run so many applications. Fortunately, several virtual memory solutions are available for use with Mac OS 9.1.

Mac OS Virtual Memory

The virtual memory options of the Mac OS have changed very little over the years. You can still opt to turn virtual memory on or off, select a hard disk to use, and determine the amount of disk space to use for virtual memory. The Memory Control Panel shown in Figure 6.2 is configured to use 1MB of additional virtual memory on the drive named Starbuck, providing 257MB of total system memory and consuming an equal amount of disk space.

How much virtual memory do you need? It's a matter of personal choice, depending on how much memory you need, how much speed you're willing to sacrifice by using virtual memory, and how much disk space is available for use with virtual memory. Any performance decrease may be offset by a decrease in the memory requirements of most applications when virtual memory is active and file mapping is therefore enabled.

RAM Doubler

For several reasons, RAM Doubler from Connectix Corporation (**www.connectix. com**) is a great improvement over Apple's virtual memory capabilities in Mac OS 9.1. First, RAM Doubler is reported to be faster and more stable than Apple's virtual memory, especially when it comes to launching applications. Also, it allows you to use virtual memory for file mapping only. File mapping makes it possible to open applications using less allocated memory than if virtual memory were turned off. RAM Doubler has few configuration options; Figure 6.3 shows its main configuration options.

With RAM Doubler, you can perform the following tasks:

- Enable file mapping only, which saves the time of having to page data to and from disk.

- Double or triple your computer's RAM using virtual memory, or adjust the amount of virtual memory to a maximum of 240MB.

- Default to doubling the amount of RAM by selecting the Use Default button.

TIP: *Remember, the more disk space you use as virtual memory, the more time your system will spend paging data to and from disk. Use the setting that best meets your needs.*

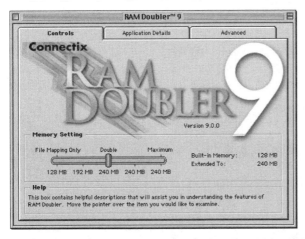

Figure 6.3   RAM Doubler is an appealing alternative to Apple's virtual memory routine in Mac OS 9.1.

Another nice feature of RAM Doubler is the way it displays information about how your memory has been allocated to a running application and to the operating system. For example, Figure 6.4 shows some of the same applications as in previous examples, as seen through the RAM Doubler Control Panel configuration window.

Unlike More About This Macintosh (MATM), discussed in the Immediate Solutions section, you can only view the memory allocation for each item; you cannot send a Quit Apple Event to quit an application and unload it from memory. However, it's helpful to see exactly how much RAM is being used by the various elements of your operating system. Finally, RAM Doubler also provides several useful memory management features in the Advanced configuration tab, shown in Figure 6.5.

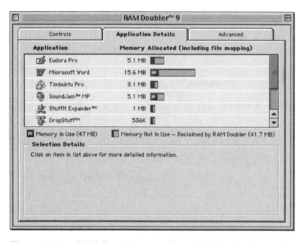

Figure 6.4   RAM Doubler provides detailed information on your operating system and applications' memory usage.

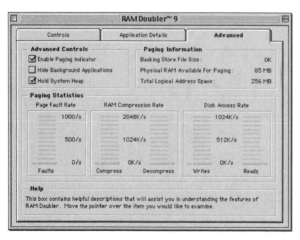

Figure 6.5   RAM Doubler's Advanced configuration tab.

The features you can configure in this section include a visual indicator that tells you when pages of memory are being written to and from virtual memory (referred to as the Paging Indicator), the ability to automatically hide background applications (which increases the performance of the foreground application), and to hold the contents of the System Heap in physical memory (which also speeds up system performance).

Other Types of Memory

In addition to RAM, the Mac OS may use at least four other types of memory:

- Read Only Memory (ROM)
- Parameter RAM (PRAM)
- Video RAM (VRAM)
- Synchronous Graphic RAM (SGRAM)

All Macintosh computers rely on what is referred to as an *Apple ROM*, a chip that is several megabytes in size and contains essential data for the operation of the Mac OS. Because it's a read-only chip, Apple ROM cannot be altered and doesn't lose its contents when the power is shut off. Apple ROMs are hardware-specific; each model of computer uses a ROM designed for that particular model. If the ROM is removed from the motherboard, the computer will not boot.

Parameter RAM is a very small chip, about 8KB in size, that stores information about several of your computer's settings, including the time and date, as well as the designated startup disk. When it is powered on, the computer needs to access this data. It is stored in PRAM by the computer's internal battery when it is off, or when the computer lacks a power source such as a battery (for PowerBooks) or an external power source. PRAM (referred to as *non-volatile memory*) will retain this information when the computer is turned off, as long as the battery on the motherboard is charged.

VRAM and SGRAM are two types of RAM that enable your computer's monitor to display at a higher bit depth (more colors) and faster refresh rate. These features are easier on the eyes, and are said to reduce stress. Most new G4 PowerMacs come with 16MB of VRAM. Third-party graphics cards, which often come with 32MB or more, enable monitors to display more colors at higher resolutions, and to show information on the screen more quickly. See your computer's "Technical Information" pamphlet for a breakdown of how much VRAM or SGRAM is required to display various resolutions and colors.

Determining Memory Requirements

Although it's possible to run Mac OS 9.1 with as little as 32MB or 64MB of RAM, it certainly isn't recommended. A good rule of thumb is to have at least 128MB of physical RAM for any PowerMac. (RAM is so cheap these days that you're really doing yourself or your users a disservice by having anything less.)

How much RAM do you really need? It boils down to your answers to the following questions:

- How many applications do you need to run at one time?

- How much RAM does each application require?

- How will you configure your Memory Control Panel to use virtual memory and the disk cache?

Unlike most other operating systems, the Mac OS allows you to allocate a predetermined amount of RAM for exclusive use by a particular application. To determine how much RAM you need, add up the minimum amount of RAM required for each application that must be run simultaneously and then add about 64MB for the Mac OS. Determine the minimum RAM for each application by selecting the application in the Finder and choosing the Memory section of the Get Info command (accessed from the File or contextual menu). For example, Figure 6.6 shows the Memory section of the Get Info command for the application BBEdit.

For the best possible estimate of an application's RAM requirements, turn off virtual memory, launch your applications, and see how much memory they actually use versus how much has been allocated to them. Remember that PowerPC-native applications take into account the presence of virtual memory when recommending memory requirements.

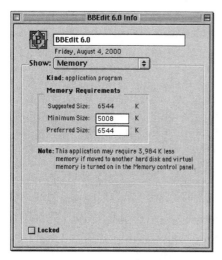

Figure 6.6   The Get Info command allows you to set memory requirements for applications.

Typical Memory Issues

As you explore Mac OS 9.1, you'll encounter a few memory-related issues. Some of them are manageable, some are mere limitations of the Mac OS itself, and some are the fault of computer programmers who created the applications we love so dearly (grin).

Not Enough Memory

The error message you're most likely to encounter is the "not enough memory" error. This error usually occurs when you're using an application or trying to launch an application. Two versions of the "not enough memory" error are shown in Figure 6.7.

The solution for this type of error is simple: Quit one or more applications to free up memory for another application (we'll cover this in detail later in this chapter in the Immediate Solutions section).

Memory Fragmentation

Many Mac users are unaware of the memory fragmentation issue. Memory can be fragmented in a manner similar to the fragmentation of files on a hard disk. This results in the failure of programs to launch or function properly once they are loaded into memory. Fragmented memory takes up memory that would otherwise be available for other programs. Because all programs need to be loaded into contiguous memory, the Mac OS will report that less memory is available than if fragmentation were not present. Figure 6.8 shows an application called Memory Mapper (**http://hyperarchive.lcs.mit.edu/HyperArchive**), which lists all the items currently in memory, including 12 fragments of free memory. Several of these fragments are large enough to prevent the launching of additional applications.

Identifying memory fragmentation is one thing, but how do you prevent it? Future versions of the Mac OS will probably eliminate most problems of this type, but for now here are a few tricks to keep in mind:

6. Memory Management

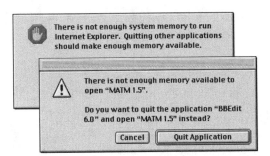

Figure 6.7   A good sign that your computer needs more RAM.

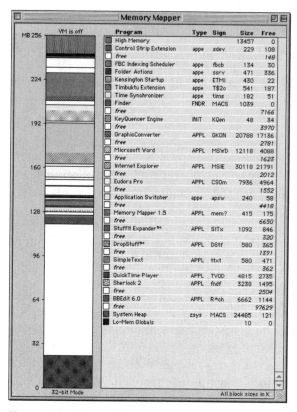

Figure 6.8   Fragmented memory can prevent applications from being launched.

- Don't quit applications unless necessary.

- Applications that you're less likely to quit prior to the next reboot of your computer should be loaded first.

- Quit applications in reverse of the order in which they were launched.

- Install Apple's MacsBug (**http://developer.apple.com/tools/debuggers/ MacsBug**) to identify problematic applications.

- Applications (such as Web browsers) that are more likely to crash or need to be restarted should be placed last in the load order of applications in the Startup Items folder.

- Use as little virtual memory as possible—preferably none at all.

Memory-Related Errors

While using the Mac OS, you may have encountered other types of memory-related errors, some of which you may not have known were actually memory errors. These "disguised" memory errors usually result in the crash of an application followed by the display of a Mac OS error message such as "The application

SuperApp has unexpectedly quit because of a Type 25 error." Sometimes a description of the error will accompany an error code number; at other times, only an error code, such as "Type -1" or "Type 3" will be displayed.

Memory errors occur when an application tries to read to, or write from, an address space. Most applications are programmed to avoid this type of problem or to tolerate other applications that infringe upon their own address space. Some offending applications are capable of crashing not only the current application, but other applications or the entire Mac OS as well.

Another common error involves the System Heap's habit of creeping upward in the memory pool. When an application occupying the space immediately above the System Heap has no more growing room, the Mac OS returns a "not enough memory" error whenever you try to launch it. You respond by quitting all other applications and relaunching the one you need—the one that has the bad luck of living next door to the System Heap. Sometimes this approach works, but occasionally you'll be faced once again with the memory error. Here's why: If the address space directly above the System Heap is fragmented, then the space cannot grow. The error will persist until you reboot the system. Similarly, if an application attempts to write to an address space already occupied by the Mac OS, the entire computer will probably crash. On the other hand, if the address space is occupied by another application, it's likely that only one or both applications—and not the entire computer—will crash.

TIP: *Quitting applications in reverse of the order in which they were launched can help prevent memory fragmentation.*

Finally, if the System Heap itself becomes fragmented, the Memory Manager will no longer be able to do its job and the Mac OS will crash. This type of error is usually the result of flawed programming, and the only solution is to try a utility such as Mac OS Purge (described in the Immediate Solutions section) that purges your computer's memory of unused blocks. This frees up more memory for use by the System Heap.

Immediate Solutions

Identifying Physical Memory

It's a hard fact of life that few of us actually have enough RAM in our computers, which leaves us wondering how the memory we do have is being used, and if it's being used efficiently. Knowing how much memory your computer has is the first step toward optimizing your system for peak performance.

To determine how much memory your computer has, and in exactly what configuration:

1. Launch the Apple System Profiler.
2. Look in the Memory Overview section.

Information about your computer's disk cache, virtual memory, physical memory, video memory, and backside L2 cache will be displayed. If your computer has more than one memory slot, only the slots that are occupied by memory chips will be displayed. Information about empty slots will not be shown. Therefore, you won't be able to determine the total number of available slots by using this command. Figure 6.9 shows an example of this method.

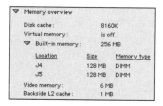

Figure 6.9   Using the Apple System Profiler to identify the various types of physical memory.

Using the About This Computer Command

Mac OS 9.1 offers limited information about the allocation of your system's physical and virtual memory. The About This Computer command (see Figure 6.10) gives a broad overview of allocated memory, but that's about it. In earlier versions of the Mac OS, this command was known as About This Macintosh.

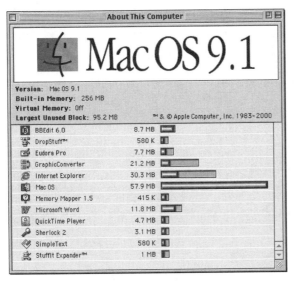

Figure 6.10 The About This Computer command offers only an overview of your system's memory allocation.

To issue the About This Computer command, follow the same steps you used when the command was called About This Macintosh (prior to Mac OS 8):

1. Select the Finder from the Applications menu.
2. Choose About This Computer from the Apple Menu.

Information about your system's memory will appear in the upper half of the window. Running applications, as well as memory usage of the Mac OS itself, will be listed (in alphabetical order) in the lower half of the window.

TIP: *The amount of memory used by the Mac OS, as reported by About This Computer, is equal to the memory occupied by the Finder, System Heap, High Memory area, and miscellaneous memory partitions used by the Mac OS.*

The upper half of the window displays the following information about your computer's memory usage:

- *Version*—The version of the Mac OS.
- *Built-in Memory*—The amount of physical RAM installed on your computer's logic board.
- *Virtual Memory*—The amount of hard drive space used when virtual memory is enabled. It also reflects the total amount of memory available to applications.
- *Largest Unused Block*—The largest contiguous allocation of RAM (physical or virtual) available for use by an application.

The actual amount of memory used by the Mac OS and applications will vary, depending on whether you're using virtual memory and if you've reconfigured the amount of memory each application is allowed to use. For example, Figure 6.11 shows the same set of applications as Figure 6.10, but with virtual memory turned on (and set to its default settings).

However, there are several utilities and applications that provide much more information about how your computer is using memory.

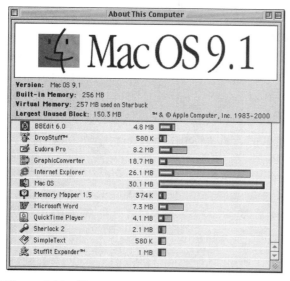

Figure 6.11   The About This Computer command with virtual memory turned on.

Using More About This Macintosh

Kevin Tieskoetter's application, More About This Macintosh (MATM), provides exactly what it says—more information about your computer (remember, the application used to be called About This Macintosh). You can download the latest version from Kevin's Web site at **http://pobox.com/~albtrssp/** (the standard version is bundled with RAM Charger—which we'll discuss later in this section—and a demo of MATM Pro).

MATM provides more detailed information about your computer's memory allocation, including free blocks of RAM. To launch MATM after you've installed it, double-click on the MATM application icon. A window like the one shown in Figure 6.12 will appear.

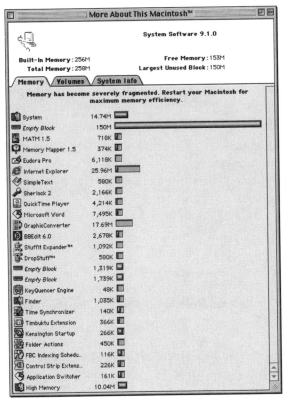

Figure 6.12 Kevin Tieskoetter's More About This Macintosh application provides more details on your computer's allocation of available memory.

MATM's interface provides information about four main features of your computer: the OS, memory usage, disk usage, and general facts about your hardware. The upper portion of the window shows some of the same information found in About This Computer, as does the Memory tab, at first glance.

As you can see in Figure 6.13, MATM shows much more about how your computer is using different types of memory:

• Memory used by applications

• Memory used by major Extensions, such as File Sharing

• Free blocks of memory

• Percentage of memory used by each entry

Double-clicking on an application's entry while holding down the Option key will cause that application to quit and automatically update the MATM Memory tab to show newly freed blocks of RAM. For example, Figure 6.13 shows the separate

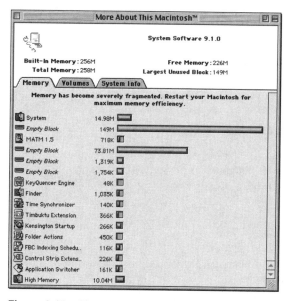

Figure 6.13   You can quit applications from within MATM to update information about empty blocks of memory.

"Empty Blocks" that are freed up after quitting each of the applications shown in Figure 6.12. Note the warning that indicates the presence of memory fragmentation.

The demo of MATM Pro that ships with RAM Charger allows you to customize the way information about your memory appears in the interface. For example, you can reorder the list of items that have memory allocated to them in several ways. Figure 6.14 shows the same information as in the previous examples, but here it is ordered so that the items requiring the most RAM are listed first.

View	
by: Name	⌘N
✓ Starting Size	⌘S
Starting Time	⌘T
Location In Memory	⌘L
with: No Bars	⌘1
✓ Standard Bars	⌘2
Enhanced Bars	⌘3
✓ Header w/ General Info	⌘4
Large Icons (& CPU Bars)	⌘5
"Never Listed" Apps	⌘6
✓ Allow Width Change	⌘-
✓ Auto-Adjust Height	⌘=
Zoom Window	⌘Z
Position as Switcher	⌘P

Figure 6.14   The Pro version of MATM that comes bundled with RAM Charger offers different views and is customizable.

Using Memory Mapper

Bob Fronabarger's Memory Mapper is another great solution for exploring how your system is using memory. Memory Mapper, a freeware utility, not only gives you more information than About This Computer, it draws a map of your computer's memory, which is a real bonus in understanding how the Mac OS allocates memory.

For example, Figure 6.15 shows the same active applications that are included in the previous examples as they appear in Memory Mapper. It does a great job showing how portions of the Mac OS are loaded into the High Memory area at the top of the map and the System Heap at the bottom, and is especially useful for detecting fragmented free memory blocks, five of which are shown in this example.

Double-clicking on an entry reveals detailed information about a process, as in Figure 6.16, including the type of process and how much CPU time has lapsed since it was launched. As with MATM, you can quit an application from within Memory Mapper by choosing File|Send Quit Event.

Another very useful feature of Memory Mapper becomes visible when virtual memory is enabled, either through Apple's built-in virtual memory scheme or by using an application like RAM Doubler. Memory Mapper uses a black vertical line

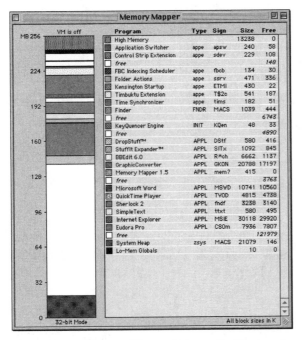

Figure 6.15   Memory Mapper lists applications and processes, and maps them out in an easy-to-read diagram of allocated memory.

Figure 6.16 Memory Mapper provides detailed information about each process.

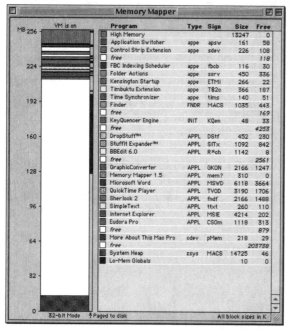

Figure 6.17 Memory Mapper also tracks memory blocks that have been paged to disk through virtual memory.

on the right side of the memory map, shown in Figure 6.17, to display memory blocks that have been paged to disk by virtual memory.

Allocating Default and Custom Disk Cache

Mac OS 9.1 allows you to set aside a portion of your RAM as a hard disk cache. This speeds up many applications that need to access your hard drive for information on a frequent basis. A large disk cache can really boost applications that are disk intensive. Keep in mind, however, that any memory you set aside for use by the disk cache will be unavailable for use by the OS or by applications. The Memory Control Panel in Mac OS 9.1 gives you two choices for allocating the disk cache.

Default Disk Cache Settings

The Default setting for the disk cache takes the guesswork out of allocating memory. Debates still rage over how much RAM is enough, but the engineers at Apple have consistently suggested using about 32KB of RAM for every megabyte of physical RAM installed on your computer. Therefore, for a computer with 128MB of RAM, a default disk cache setting would be 4096KB, or 1/32 of your installed physical RAM.

To allow the Mac OS to make this calculation for you, choose the Default setting in the Memory Control Panel, as shown earlier in Figure 6.2.

Customizing Disk Cache Settings

At times, of course, you may need to increase or decrease the size of the disk cache to gain a performance advantage. The minimum cache size is 128KB; the maximum is 64MB. Increasing the cache size will speed things up; decreasing it will optimize other aspects of your computer.

To customize your disk cache, follow these steps:

1. Open the Memory Control Panel.
2. Select the Custom Settings button.
3. Select Custom when the warning dialog appears, reminding you that changing the settings may cause poor system performance.
4. Increase or decrease the size of the cache using the Up or Down buttons, as shown in Figure 6.18.
5. Restart the computer to force the changes to take effect.

Having a large disk cache isn't always ideal, however. For example, if your computer crashes while a word-processing document is active, the changes to your document may not be written to disk fast enough. Consequently, you may lose some of your work. To help in these situations, St. Clair Software makes a fine utility, CacheSaver, that allows you to flush the cache to disk—at predetermined intervals or manually—when the computer has been idle for an extended period (see Figure 6.19 for an example).

Figure 6.18 Customize your disk cache settings as needed, or allow the Mac OS to calculate the standard setting size for you automatically.

Figure 6.19   CacheSaver writes the contents of your disk cache to disk to prevent data loss in case of a system failure.

You can download the latest version of CacheSaver from the St. Clair Software Web site at **www.stclairsw.com**.

Allocating Memory for RAM Disks

RAM disks are really the opposite of virtual memory because they use physical RAM to emulate a hard disk. RAM disks are typically used to store frequently accessed files and folders, such as databases or Web server documents. The speed at which a RAM disk can be accessed (measured in nanoseconds) is many times greater than that of a disk drive mechanism (measured in milliseconds). Although RAM disks are used much less frequently than virtual memory, several solutions are available for those who need RAM disks. Mac OS 9.1 has a built-in capability to allocate a portion of your computer's RAM to serve as a RAM disk, and you have other options as well.

RAM Disk

The RAM disk portion of the Memory Control Panel, shown in Figure 6.20, allows you to allocate a portion of your system's RAM for use as a RAM disk. As with virtual memory, any RAM utilized for a RAM disk is unavailable for use by the operating system and applications.

To create a RAM disk, take these steps:

1. Open the Memory Control Panel.

2. Turn the RAM disk on and select a size for the disk.

3. Restart the computer.

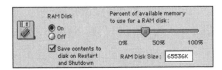

Figure 6.20   Open the Memory Control Panel to create and adjust RAM disk settings.

RAM disks work just like other disks on the Mac OS. You can share them and save files and folders on them. When you restart the computer, the contents of the RAM disk are saved and will reappear for continued use. However, remember that you cannot change the settings in the Memory Control Panel when the RAM disk is being shared. Also bear in mind that the memory used to create the RAM disk will be unavailable for use by other applications. Figure 6.21 shows a 64MB RAM disk with a few items that will be restored after the computer is rebooted.

Other RAM Disks

In addition to the Mac OS's RAM disk, there are a few other RAM disks that are excellent alternatives. Figure 6.22 shows some of the configuration options available with the following RAM disk alternatives:

- *AppDisk*—An easy-to-use RAM disk by Mark Adams that automatically saves the contents of the disk at predefined intervals and allows you to mount and unmount multiple RAM disks without restarting. You can find AppDisk at **http://members.aol.com/mavsftwre**.

- *ramBunctious*—An AppleScriptable RAM disk by Elden Wood and Bob Clark that offers more features than most other RAM disk utilities. It even supports

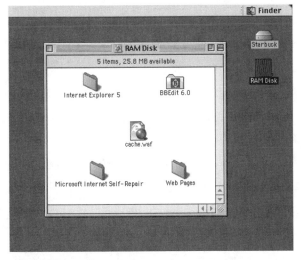

Figure 6.21   A RAM disk functions like any other disk, but much faster.

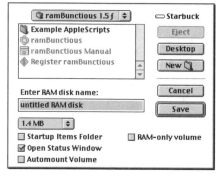

Figure 6.22   Three alternatives to the Mac OS's RAM disk feature.

write-through to disk—just in case the computer crashes. You can find ramBunctious at **www.clarkwoodsoftware.com/rambunctious/**.

- *RamDisk+*—A system INIT from Roger D. Bates that supports booting from the RAM disk, RamDisk+ can automatically copy files and folders from a hard disk onto the RAM disk on startup. You can find it at **www.teleport.com/~rbates/**.

Allocating Application Memory

The Mac OS is rather unique among mainstream operating systems because it allows you to decide how much memory an application may use. This feature was included in previous versions of the Mac OS, so you're probably accustomed to it. Little has changed in the Memory section of the Get Info command for Mac OS 9.1, an example of which is shown in Figure 6.23.

The Memory section of the Get Info command is configurable only for applications (foreground and background) that are not currently running; it is not available

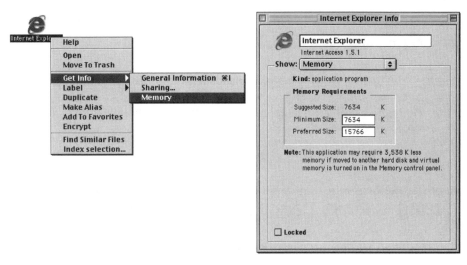

Figure 6.23   The Memory section of the Get Info command.

for documents and folders. The Memory Requirements section provides the following information and allocation options:

- *Suggested Size*—The amount of memory that should be allocated for normal use, as suggested by the program's author.

- *Minimal Size*—The smallest allocation that is necessary to sustain functionality.

- *Preferred Size*—The amount of memory you want to allocate to an application, if this amount of memory is available for use.

The Note section estimates the effect of virtual memory on RAM usage. Applications that are not PowerPC-native or FAT binary (for both PowerPC and 68K computers) will not have a Note section.

A good rule of thumb is to increase the Preferred Size setting only if an error message indicates the application is running low on memory, or system-level errors such as Type 1 or 10 errors frequently recur. Try doubling the amount of suggested memory, and then scale back if necessary. Also, keep in mind that some applications do not return portions of allocated memory to the Finder after they have been quit. This is a leading cause of memory fragmentation that will persist until the computer is restarted.

To increase the amount of memory allocated to an application, take these steps:

1. Quit the application.

2. Select the application and choose File|Get Info (or Command+I), then select Show|Memory. Or, select File|Get Info|Memory from the contextual menu when selecting the application.

3. Increase the Preferred Size to a figure higher than the Suggested Size.

4. Close the Info window and relaunch the application.

TIP: *Applications are capable of reporting various type of errors to the user in the event of a crash or malfunction in the program, including memory-related errors. However, programmers must accurately enable error reporting so that users will be properly informed of a memory-related error. See Appendix D for detailed information on the most common types of errors and their meanings.*

Reducing Memory Requirements with Get Info

The memory requirements of applications in Mac OS 9.1 can be reduced by several methods. You can manually reduce the amount of RAM in the Get Info command. Alternatively, you can employ shareware and commercial applications that do the job automatically.

If your computer is low on physical memory, take advantage of the Memory section of the Get Info command to reduce the amount of memory allocated to an application. Because reducing memory allocations may cause problems, it should be done only when necessary.

To reduce the memory requirements for an application:

1. Quit the application.

2. Select the application and choose File|Get Info (or Command+I), then select Show|Memory. Or, select File|Get Info|Memory from the contextual menu while selecting the application.

3. Change the Preferred Size to a figure higher than the Minimum Size but smaller than the Suggested Size.

4. Close the Info window and relaunch the application.

You can change the Minimum Size to an amount smaller than the default, but a warning dialog box will inform you that this could cause the application to crash. Do this only if absolutely necessary (see Figure 6.24).

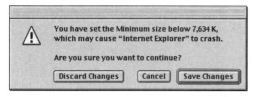

Figure 6.24   Mac OS 9.1 will let you know if your memory changes could cause problems.

Reducing Memory Requirements with RAM Charger

RAM Charger, a commercial application from the Jump Development Group, is a comprehensive solution for reducing and optimizing memory requirements for applications on the Mac OS. Don't confuse this application with virtual memory applications such as RAM Doubler—RAM Charger is an optimization tool, not a virtual memory tool. You can use RAM Charger in conjunction with RAM Doubler, the Mac OS's virtual memory scheme, or with no virtual memory at all. To get the latest version of RAM Charger, including a fully functional demo, visit the Jump Development Group Web site at **www.jumpdev.com**. At the time of this writing, RAM Charger was not completely compatible with Mac OS 9.1 because of a few cosmetic changes in the Memory Control Panel, but it is still a useful and informative tool. Check with the Jump Development Group for the latest information on compatibility.

RAM Charger evaluates an application's memory requirements and, when necessary, dynamically allocates additional memory by intercepting certain Apple Events between the application and the Mac OS. This prevents the application from running out of memory. RAM Charger also adds many configuration options to the Get Info command and allows you to preconfigure your applications for optimal memory usage.

RAM Charger has too many features to describe in detail here. The following example of how to "charge" an application should give you an idea of how it can help you with your needs:

1. Install the latest version of RAM Charger, reboot, and open the RAM Charger General Settings Control Panel, as shown in Figure 6.25.

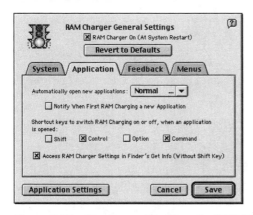

Figure 6.25   The General Settings for RAM Charger, which you can open from the Control Panels menu or from the newly installed RAM Charger menu next to the Applications menu.

2. Make sure that the Access RAM Charger Settings in the Finder's Get Info is selected. Then select the Memory section of the Get Info window for an application and refer to the new RAM Charger Memory Requirements section. Figure 6.26 shows before and after versions of this section.

3. Click on the More button to access the RAM Charger Application Settings menu, shown in Figure 6.27, and then configure the application for use with RAM Charger.

4. Confirm the current settings, or select the Wizard button and follow the instructions to have RAM Charger evaluate your usage of the application in comparison to its actual memory usage. This option is very helpful; in fact, Jump Development has already assessed many applications and their peculiar memory requirements.

RAM Charger does an excellent job of evaluating memory allocation usage and requirements for most applications. However, you may have to try a thing or three to optimize RAM Charger to work with your applications. For example, Figure 6.28 shows the result of our use of the RAM Charger Wizard with Disk First Aid.

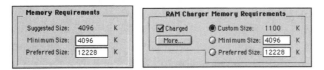

Figure 6.26   RAM Charger replaces the Memory Requirements section of the Get Info command with several new options.

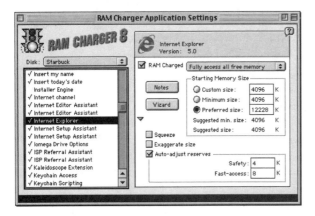

Figure 6.27   You can configure applications to work with RAM Charger one at a time, or select RAM Charger Application Settings from the RAM Charger drop-down menu and configure them *en masse*.

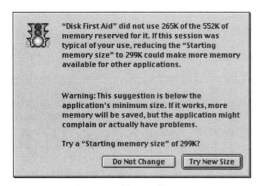

"Disk First Aid" did not use 265K of the 552K of memory reserved for it. If this session was typical of your use, reducing the "Starting memory size" to 299K could make more memory available for other applications.

Warning: This suggestion is below the application's minimum size. If it works, more memory will be saved, but the application might complain or actually have problems.

Try a "Starting memory size" of 299K?

Do Not Change   Try New Size

Figure 6.28   The RAM Charger Wizard evaluates how applications use memory and recommends a different approach for allocating memory if it deems necessary.

Purging the System Heap with Mac OS Purge

As we mentioned earlier, the System Heap grows and shrinks dynamically. When an application residing in the lower region of the memory pool blocks the System Heap's upward growth, trouble sometimes ensues. One way to temporarily fix this problem is to run Mac OS Purge, Kenji Takeuchi's freeware application, before launching—and after quitting—applications that rely upon System Extensions. By purging stale data from memory, it creates more room for the Mac OS.

To run Mac OS Purge, take these steps:

1. Copy Mac OS Purge to your hard drive. You can place it anywhere, but we suggest the Apple menu.
2. Launch Mac OS Purge.
3. Mac OS Purge will run, quit, and then display the About This Computer window.

The decrease in the amount of memory used by the Mac OS is proportional to the amount of stale data that was purged. For example, Figure 6.29 shows an excerpt from Memory Mapper after Mac OS Purge has been run (it offers detailed information on the System Heap). Notice that the System Heap now has twice as much free memory.

See the Info-Mac HyperArchive at **http://hyperarchive.lcs.mit.edu/HyperArchive/ HyperArchive.html** for updates to Mac OS Purge and many other programs.

6. Memory Management

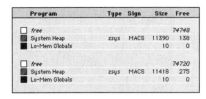

Figure 6.29   Mac OS Purge rids the System Heap of unused data, thereby reducing the occurrence of the "out of memory" error messages issued by the Finder.

Purging Application Memory with RAM Handler

Mac OS 9.1 doesn't allow users to purge unused memory from the System Heap—or from applications, for that matter. Mike Throckmorton's RAM Handler is a great utility that allows you to purge unused memory as well as view memory use. RAM Handler is similar to Memory Mapper in that it displays detailed memory allocation information; it is similar to Mac OS Purge because it allows you to purge unused memory. It goes one step further, however, by enabling you to purge unused application memory. RAM Handler is copyrighted by the Ziff-Davis Publishing Company, and you can download it from **www.macdownload.com**.

To use RAM Handler:

1. Copy RAM Handler to your hard drive. You can place it anywhere, but we suggest the Startup Items folder.

2. Launch RAM Handler.

3. RAM Handler will run, opening a floating palette like the ones shown in Figure 6.30.

To configure RAM Handler, go to the Options menu and choose the items you want displayed (see Figure 6.31). You can configure two views—a maximized view or a minimized view.

In the examples shown in Figures 6.30 and 6.31, RAM Handler is configured to display:

- The name of the application or process (left)

- The amount of memory in use (middle)

- The amount of free memory (right)

To purge and compact memory usage, just click on any of the buttons that list an application or a process, and RAM Handler will reclaim unused memory and update the palette to reflect the new values.

Figure 6.30   RAM Handler's floating palette gives you quick access to memory allocation information in two different views, a minimized view (top) and a maximized view (bottom).

Figure 6.31   Configure RAM Handler's floating palette to display as much information as you need.

TIP: RAM Handler's Process Manager lists only the amount of RAM that is free for use by other applications.

6. Memory Management

Chapter 7
Mobile Computing

In Depth

"Make it smaller without compromising on power" seems to be the mission statement of anyone who designs electronic devices. This motto pretty much sums up the history of Apple computer design in particular. The first computers filled entire rooms. Gradually the tubes gave way to circuits, which gave way to chips and microchips. Motorola's Reduced Instruction Set Computer (RISC) chip, which was among the smallest, coolest, and fastest of its kind, was one of the reasons Apple elected to move away from the 68K architecture. Meanwhile, the x86 architecture or the Complex Instruction Set Computer (CISC) chip was growing larger and running hotter. Intel, the dominant manufacturer of the x86 chips, occasionally aired commercials in which brightly colored technicians (also known as "bunnies") thrust the Intel Pentium chip toward the viewer. The chip was the size of a chalkboard eraser. Try fitting *that* into a notebook computer.

Portable vs. Desktop Computing

Mobility is one of the driving forces behind the development of portable computing. Whether traveling great distances or just commuting between home and work, people dislike leaving their computers—and the resources contained therein—back in the office. Fortunately the PowerBook, a standard-bearer in the world of portable computing, provides excellent portability options. In fact, PowerBooks are almost as good as desktop systems.

Expansion

In the expansion arena, desktop systems definitely have an advantage. Their size makes it easy to improve storage, memory, and performance. A PowerBook's system can be expanded by using expansion bays that hold different devices. The latest G3 models allow you to use two devices at once by removing the battery, but that requires plugging the computer into a power source. Other expansion options for the PowerBook include the PCMCIA card and additional storage and RAM, as well as Ethernet and modems. See the section on "PCMCIA Cards" later in this chapter for additional information on these devices.

Fragility

If you are debating the purchase of a laptop vs. a desktop system, you need to factor in the fragility of the laptop. Portable computers of the past were very hardy and computer salesmen would occasionally drop the computer during demonstrations, and then turn on the device to illustrate its durability. That is no longer true today. Portable computers are particularly vulnerable to harm. Desktop systems are equally fragile, but are at lower risk for damage because they are rarely in motion (except for the rare earthquake or other disaster).

Portability

If you need a computer that you can take just about anywhere, buy a PowerBook. Thanks to the PowerPC processor chip, PowerBooks can run at speeds comparable to Macintosh desktop machines.

PowerBook Limitations

A PowerBook can do just about anything a desktop computer can do. PowerBook users must recognize certain limitations, however.

When it's using its battery, a PowerBook is truly portable. Batteries have come a long way from the first PowerBooks—they're now capable of running for five hours (even longer, if you practice some of the energy-saving techniques covered later in this chapter). Many of the hardware components have been designed to use as little power as possible. Nevertheless, on a long airplane flight, invariably the battery begins to fade. The PowerBook G3 Series computers allow you to plug two batteries into the expansion bays—a helpful feature, but one that limits your options with other devices. Of course, if you plan to watch a DVD movie by using the DVD-ROM expansion device, make sure to fully charge the battery, since you won't have the luxury of two batteries.

Two G3 PowerBooks

Two PowerBook models have the G3 chip. The first PowerBook G3 computer was an older model; you can recognize it by the multi-colored Apple on the case. The more familiar PowerBook G3 computer that we see today has a sleek design with a large white Apple logo on the case. Apple has moved away from the multi-colored Apple in favor of the solid Apple logo, which is visible on desktop systems as well as PowerBooks and iBooks.

Energy Saving

Great strides have been made in the search for the combination of deadly chemicals that will provide the longest battery life. By utilizing batteries in both expansion bays of a PowerBook G3 Series computer, you can enjoy up to 10 hours of usage without recharging the battery. You can take certain steps to increase battery life. The computer also takes some steps on its own to preserve power.

7. Mobile Computing

Screen Dimming

By default, the computer dims the screen after a certain period of inactivity. The screen appears to darken slightly, although icons and the Desktop still display. Screen dimming is a vital energy conservation feature because the display itself consumes a significant percentage of battery power. The black-and-white or grayscale display uses roughly 20 percent; the color display uses a whopping 50 percent.

Previous versions of the Mac OS used a Control Panel called PowerBook Settings to configure many of the energy saving features. In Mac OS 9.1, these options reside within the Energy Saver Control Panel, as shown in Figure 7.1.

You can configure screen dimming to occur at different time intervals or not at all. The default settings are 3 minutes of inactivity during battery usage and 15 minutes while using the power adapter.

If you're really serious about saving battery power, choose to turn off the built-in display rather than dim the screen. Even when dimmed, the display uses more battery power than in the sleep state. In fact, passive-matrix grayscale displays found on older PowerBooks can be turned off altogether in direct sunlight.

Hard Disk

The hard drive must spin in order to access data stored on it. This spinning and data access require approximately 15 percent of the battery power. Most of your work is held in memory until you're ready to store it in a more permanent location (such as the hard drive)—especially if you're working in a word-processing package. All this hard drive activity may not be necessary, however. You can configure the Energy Saver settings to "spin down," or stop, the hard drive, as shown in Figure 7.2.

Each of the following measures will conserve energy that your hard drive uses:

• Reduce I/O usage by using memory-resident applications.

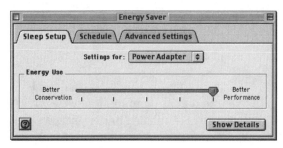

Figure 7.1   The Energy Saver Control Panel default view.

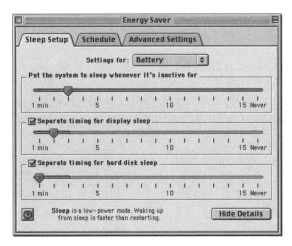

Figure 7.2   The Energy Saver Control Panel settings for hard drive spin down.

- Turn off virtual memory. It is enabled by default to improve memory performance, but you can live without it if you really need extended battery life.

- Install as much RAM as possible. It makes a difference in your computer's performance.

- Go to the Energy Saver Control Panel to configure the hard drive spin-down setting, which will stop the hard drive after a period of inactivity.

- If you have the Hard Drive Spin Down control strip module, use the Control Strip button to instantly stop the hard drive.

- Press Command+Shift+Control+0 to stop the hard drive.

- Create a RAM disk (see the instructions in the Immediate Solutions section entitled "Creating a RAM Disk").

How often should you spin down the hard drive? Keep in mind that the energy expended to bring the hard drive back up to speed equals the energy expended during 30 to 60 seconds of routine spinning. If you've loaded a long Web page that will take several minutes to read, energy saving may be a good idea. Otherwise, you may benefit by allowing the computer to engage this feature automatically via the Energy Saver settings.

Sleep

Computer *sleep* is a state in which very little energy is used. The sleep option was first developed for notebook computers as a way of conserving battery power. Owners of desktop systems also found it desirable, and so it became part of the Mac OS. However, the sleep state is not the same for all systems. Sleeping desktop systems conserve energy, even though the hard drive continues to spin. On the other hand, sleeping PowerBooks shut down everything but keep the contents of memory protected.

When a PowerBook is sleeping, the screen darkens completely and the hard drive ceases to spin. The computer looks as though it has been turned off, with the exception of a blinking light at the top of the monitor. However, pushing any key—with the exception of the Caps Lock and trackpad buttons—brings the system back to full power.

Each of the following methods will put a PowerBook to sleep:

- Configure the Energy Saver Control Panel settings so that sleep will occur after a specified period of inactivity.
- Select the Energy Saver Control Strip button to sleep immediately.
- Select Sleep from the Special menu.
- Press the power button to bring up Sleep as an option.
- Press Command+Shift+0.

Your computer will also go to sleep when the battery power is too depleted for the system to function. You will receive a series of warnings instructing you to plug in the adapter and charge the batteries immediately. If you ignore these warnings or cannot begin charging immediately, the system will eventually go into a sleep state and will not awaken until adequate power has been provided. Information stored within RAM may be held for a limited time only. Check the user's manual that came with your PowerBook for more information.

RAM Disk

You can designate part of your hard drive to function as additional memory; this function is called *virtual memory*. You can also allocate a section of memory to function as a high-speed storage disk called a *RAM disk*. PowerBooks utilize the RAM disk to increase speed and extend battery life by reducing the frequency of reading and writing to the hard drive. The drawback of a RAM disk is that the contents are lost when the computer is shut down. However, you can configure the system to save the contents of a RAM disk to the hard drive upon system shutdown. Figure 7.3 shows the RAM Disk options in the Memory Control Panel.

Network Access

Because the ability to access a network is essential these days, the latest PowerBook G3 and iBook computers come with built-in Ethernet. You can also use Airport wireless networking in iBooks and PowerBooks with the appropriate hardware. (See Chapter 12 for more information about Airport.) Internal modems are still commonly used in portable Macs. Even the earliest PowerBooks had

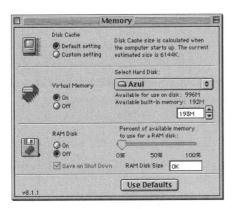

Figure 7.3   The RAM Disk options in the Memory Control Panel.

methods of accessing the network, and these devices still work today. The different ways to access a network include:

- *SCSI*—A SCSI solution made Ethernet access possible for users of first-generation PowerBooks. It's difficult to purchase the hardware today, but you may be able to find a SCSI network adapter on the Internet.

- *PCMCIA*—A more popular option is the PCMCIA card. Companies such as Farallon manufacture PCMCIA cards that provide Ethernet access to the PowerBook. These solutions are more portable than the SCSI network device. A wide variety of PCMCIA cards is available.

- *Infrared*—Some PowerBooks are equipped with an infrared port. Data can be exchanged between two computers in this fashion, provided the second computer also has an infrared port.

- *Modems*—Many laptops include a modem or a port to which you can add a modem. It is one of the most common methods of network access for mobile users.

When you have enabled network access, your portable computer can perform the same networking functions as a desktop system. Use the Chooser or the Network Browser to access network services and enjoy rapid file transfer between computers.

SCSI Ethernet

The SCSI Ethernet device, which plugs into the SCSI port in the back of the computer, is an alternate method for accessing the network. Asante used to manufacture SCSI devices, and still provides drivers for download. Although a SCSI device is larger than a PCMCIA card, products that use the computer's power supply (and thus allow you some mobility) are available. You can also find devices that provide network access and have their own power supply.

PCMCIA Cards

PCMCIA cards have greatly improved the expansion capabilities of PowerBooks. PowerBooks with this capability have up to two PCMCIA ports, usually located on the left side of the computer. PCMCIA cards, also known as *PC cards*, are the size of credit cards—though they're a little thicker—and come in three types:

- Type I cards are 3.3mm thick and can be placed in either the top or bottom slot.

- Type II cards are 5mm thick and can be placed in either the top or bottom slot.

- Type III cards are 10.5mm thick and can be placed in the bottom slot only (because of size limitations).

PC cards can perform a variety of functions, including acting as an Ethernet network card, a modem, a combination Ethernet network and modem card, and an option for additional disk storage. Because they're so small, you can carry several PC cards. Their small size, however, can also be a drawback. The connection cables for the cards are especially fragile and must be handled with care. If you damage the connection, you may have to purchase a replacement from the manufacturer.

Infrared

Today's network environment is full of cabling and connections. Each device is hardwired into the chain, tethered like a dog on a leash. Infrared attempts to change that. Infrared technology is already a part of everyday life. For example, millions of people use a device that sends signals to a receiver each time they watch television. Ambitious plans for wireless networks are in the works. PowerBooks have featured infrared ports for several years, and the first-generation iMac included infrared technology (subsequent models did not provide infrared). Some PDA devices such as the Palm Pilot also support infrared. You can exchange data between devices that contain these wireless connectivity ports.

The Apple IR File Exchange application allows you to exchange information between Macintosh devices that have infrared ports. Apple also provides two network protocols for data transfer. IRTalk is an AppleTalk-only protocol; IrDA supports both AppleTalk and TCP/IP. The devices must be no more than three feet apart, with their infrared (IR) windows facing each other. Enable infrared communication by selecting the Apple IrDA protocol within the AppleTalk Control Panel.

Modem

We are just beginning to enjoy fast Ethernet or broadband access in our homes. Asynchronous Digital Subscriber Line (ADSL) and cable modems are available in some areas of the country, and each of them provides speedy Internet access. But most home computer users rely on modems to access the Internet.

Modems use analog telephone lines to transmit digital information. Initially, modem connections were slow and primarily used to access text-based systems such as bulletin boards and terminal servers. As modem speeds increased, it became feasible to use network protocols that could function within a modem connection. Point-to-Point Protocol (PPP) and Serial Line Internet Protocol (SLIP) connections allow users to function remotely in almost the same way as they can with an Ethernet connection. Because PowerBook users will probably still rely on modems when traveling (even as some of the advanced technologies become more common), a discussion of modem options is in order.

PC card modems are excellent solutions for PowerBooks that are equipped with PC card ports. Installation is as simple as installing some software drivers and inserting the card in a free PCMCIA slot. Older PowerBooks have both internal and external modem options; external modems should work with all PowerBooks. More recent models have a printer and modem combination port, which means that printing becomes a challenge while you're trying to surf the Web. If you must use an external modem in this port, you may have to print offline.

USB and FireWire

The iBook and PowerBook G3 Series computers feature the latest in expansion ports. The USB port is much smaller than the SCSI port and provides access to hundreds of USB devices including hard drives, scanners, and cameras. FireWire provides even faster communication between the peripherals and the PowerBook computer. The iBook even includes iMovie so that you can create movies by plugging a digital camcorder into the FireWire port.

Automatically Remounting Servers

Suppose you're working on your PowerBook and accessing servers and file systems right and left, and a few remote server volumes are mounted on your Desktop. Your desperate need for caffeine forces you to leave your desk. By the time you return, your PowerBook has gone to sleep, those remote volumes are unmounted, and you're stuck with the task of locating and logging in to each one of them again. Or are you?

Earlier models of the PowerBook solved this problem by way of a special Control Panel called *AutoRemounter*; you could configure the system to automatically remount servers upon system wakeup.

In more recent PowerBooks, the AutoRemounter options have been incorporated into the Energy Saver Control Panel. Under the Advanced Settings tab, you can enable automatic remounting of servers and specify whether the password should be saved. For security reasons, it's not a good idea to save passwords if you're in an open environment.

The appearance of the Energy Saver Control Panel may vary according to the computer model. For example, in the PowerBook G3 Series computers, you cannot schedule automatic startup and shutdown of the machine—you can only schedule automatic sleep options. If any of your computer's Energy Saver options have not been discussed in this chapter, refer to your system's online Help or visit the Apple Technical Information Library at **http://til.info.apple.com**.

Processor Cycling

Processor activity is another routine PowerBook system activity that eats up your battery power. By default, an option is set in the Energy Saver Control Panel to enable processor cycling. This slows the processor activity down to an absolute crawl when little keyboard, mouse, or trackpad activity has occurred within a certain period of time. When system activity resumes, the processor immediately cycles back to normal speed. The user may not even notice that the processor has cycled.

Because processor cycling is quick and painless, Apple suggests that you leave it enabled. You can also manually reduce the processor speed by going to the Advanced Settings tab of the Energy Saver Control Panel, as shown in Figure 7.4.

Not all applications need full processor power; for example, a graphic-rendering program such as Adobe Photoshop uses more of the processor than a word processor such as Microsoft Word. However, if you prefer to run the processor constantly at top speed, you can disable processor cycling by unchecking the Allow Processor Cycling option.

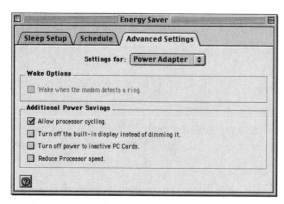

Figure 7.4   Processor cycling in the Energy Saver Control Panel.

File Synchronization

Here's a scenario that most PowerBook users will recognize. You create a file on the desktop computer in your office, then transfer it to your PowerBook so you can continue working on it at home. When you return to your desktop machine the next day, the original file is out of synch with the file on your PowerBook, and now you have to spend valuable time manually synchronizing the files on the different systems.

The File Synchronization Control Panel takes the pain out of this process. It allows you to synchronize files on different systems as well as files residing in different folders on the same system.

You can choose among several options for synchronizing files. If the arrow that connects the out-of-synch files or folders points in one direction only, a master copy will determine how the other file is updated. A two-way link means that the older copy will be updated to the newer copy. Table 7.1 shows what happens in the synchronization process between files.

File Synchronization occurs whenever you open the Control Panel, which is shown in Figure 7.5. You can synchronize files manually, as well. The files you select for updating must have the same name. Folders can have different names, however. You can add files to the right or left folder by dragging the files to the window or by manually selecting the file. You can see the path of the folders by clicking on the arrow by the volume name.

The File Synchronization Control Panel's Preferences window allows you to configure the application. For example, you can decide when and if error messages should be generated, as well as how the synchronization process should function when errors are encountered. More of the File Synchronization preferences are shown in Figure 7.6.

7. Mobile Computing

Table 7.1   File synchronization patterns.

File on Left	File on Right	Synchronization Results
Changed	Unchanged	The file on the right is updated.
Unchanged	Changed	For a left-to-right arrow, the right file is updated to match the left file. For a right-to-left and two-way arrow, the left file is updated.
Unchanged	Deleted	For a left-to-right arrow, the right file is replaced. For a right-to-left and two-way update, you are asked if you want to delete the left file.
Deleted	Unchanged	For a left-to-right and two-way arrow, you are asked if you want to delete the right file. For a right-to-left arrow, the left file is replaced.

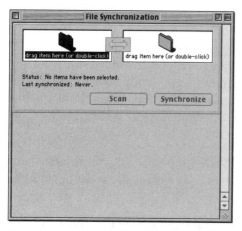

Figure 7.5   The File Synchronization Control Panel.

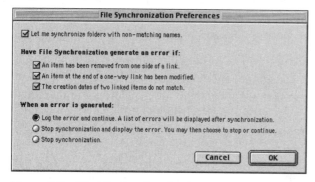

Figure 7.6   The File Synchronization Preferences window.

If you use more than one computer, one of which is a PowerBook, and you want to keep information accurate, then you should familiarize yourself with the File Synchronization functions. Life isn't always this easy.

Control Strip

The Control Strip, like Sleep, is one of those options that was originally developed for the PowerBook and proved to be so popular that it became part of the standard Mac OS installation for all systems. The Control Strip, a band of icons that represent shortcuts to standard system functions, was originally designed to help PowerBook users conserve battery power. For example, rather than going to the Monitors Control Panel to switch your system colors from thousands to 256 colors, you can just click on a Control Strip button and choose the new color palette.

Figure 7.7 shows a sample Control Strip for a PowerBook using Mac OS 9.1. Your configuration may differ, depending on the following factors:

Figure 7.7   A sample Control Strip.

- A clean installation versus an upgrade

- Your PowerBook model

- Additional programs you may have installed—some of them add buttons to the Control Strip

Each Control Strip button performs a particular task that can also be executed from another location in the operating system. The following list defines what some of the buttons do:

- *AppleTalk Switch*—Turns AppleTalk on and off

- *Battery Monitor*—Shows the battery charge level (if you're using a battery for your power source, you may also see a button indicating current battery activity)

- *CDStrip*—Controls your audio CD play program and ejects CD-ROMs

- *Energy Settings*—Chooses your system performance levels and puts your system to sleep or spins down the hard drive

- *File Sharing Strip*—Turns File Sharing on and off and lets you see who is connected to your computer

- *Keychain Access Strip*—Manages and opens keychains

- *Location Manager Controls*—Switches to a different location document

- *Expansion Bay Strip*—Indicates the status of the expansion bays in G3 Series PowerBooks

- *Monitor BitDepth*—Chooses the color depth of the system

- *Monitor Resolution*—Chooses the screen resolution (this setting may be limited on your PowerBook, depending on the model)

- *Printer Selector*—Changes printers

- *QuickTime Access*—Provides access to the QuickTime components as well as several QuickTime channels

- *Remote Access Control Strip*—Opens a remote access connection

- *Sound Volume*—Sets the system volume

- *Sound Source*—Selects the sound source for recording or listening

- *Web Sharing CS*—Enables or disables Web sharing

Don't worry if the strip crosses the whole screen. Arrows at either end permit you to access buttons that are no longer visible. You can move the Control Strip by

7. Mobile Computing

holding down the Option key and moving the mouse to the strip until the cursor changes to a hand, and then dragging the strip to the preferred location. You can also customize the Control Strip. Many software applications add icons to the Control Strip, and Web sites provide a host of buttons that you can add.

Location Manager

Before the advent of the Location Manager, PowerBook users manually changed their settings to suit their location. For example, at work you might have an Ethernet connection and use certain Extensions and protocols to support it, and you've configured your settings accordingly. While traveling, on the other hand, you might utilize a modem for Internet access, and also disable File Sharing to conserve system memory. In order for your PowerBook to meet your needs under these conditions, you have to reconfigure your options appropriately. Of course, the worst part is remembering all the variations.

The Location Manager, shown in Figure 7.8, allows you to tell the system how to perform certain tasks depending on your location. The Location Manager can handle a variety of settings, including those for network protocols or particular applications, in a location document. Setting a location document can take some time, but once each setting is completed, you can change locations easily from the Control Strip button or the Control Panel.

Additional Devices

The PowerBook G3 Series computers have expansion bays that can accept multiple devices, including CD, Zip, and DVD drives. You can use two devices at once, although you must give up battery power.

The devices that go in the expansion bays are hot-swappable—they can be removed or installed while the computer is running. (In older PowerBooks, which

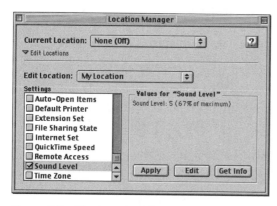

Figure 7.8   The Location Manager.

are sleep-swappable, the computer must be in sleep mode before the device can be switched).

More devices are being manufactured every day. Between the expansion bays, the PC card ports, and the built-in USB, FireWire, serial, and SCSI ports, your PowerBook has access to as many devices as you can afford.

Video Displays

Multimedia and animated slide presentations are some of the more common uses for a PowerBook computer. No longer are you limited to an overhead projector and transparencies. Your creative side can be unleashed in colorful presentations that can include special effects, as well as sound and movies, to drive home your point. Many PowerBooks have an external video port; if your computer lacks one, you may be able to purchase an expansion card to give you this capability. With video out, you can project the PowerBook display to another video device such as a projection device or another monitor (in some cases special cables may be needed to connect the PowerBook to the other video device).

When you connect another monitor to the PowerBook, you have one and possibly two display options (check your manual to confirm what options you have). You can use *video mirroring*, which allows you to see the same image on both displays. This is helpful when you're using a projection device to display a presentation—you don't have to contort yourself to see the screen image and still talk to the audience. What you see on your display will be the same as what is projected on the screen. You can use the PowerBook Display Control Panel (if available) shown in Figure 7.9 or the Monitors Control Panel to enable video mirroring. You may also have an *extended Desktop* that allows you to continue your Desktop to the next monitor, giving you twice as much screen area.

Security Issues

As we have mentioned, portability is one of the strengths of the PowerBook. It is also one of its greatest weaknesses. Portable computers are more expensive than comparable desktop systems and are very attractive to thieves. And because PowerBooks are small enough to conceal, one left unattended is very likely to be

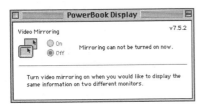

Figure 7.9   The PowerBook Display Control Panel.

stolen. Don't handcuff your PowerBook to your body like some secret agent—by using some common sense and a few security tools, you can protect your investment.

Password

The password, a hallmark of computing, secures a wide variety of systems, including network access, email accounts, and ATM machines. Older PowerBooks, including the (non-FireWire) G3, are protected by a password. Activate the password feature by accessing the Password Security Control Panel, as shown in Figure 7.10. After a password has been activated on the computer, it will no longer boot without the password. In fact, without it the computer's hard drive is no longer functional. In older PowerBooks, you had to reformat the hard drive to bypass this security, but newer PowerBooks go a step further: The drive cannot be reformatted without this password, because the password is assigned at the disk's driver level.

This is an excellent feature—unless you happen to forget your password. If you absolutely cannot remember it, go to an Apple Certified repair technician who has been entrusted with a password that will bypass the security and boot the computer.

Be aware that the previous paragraphs apply to older PowerBooks. The new G3 PowerBooks and iBooks do not have this Control Panel. If it is missing from your computer, do not add it. You could risk losing your data. Instead, utilize the multi-user login process included in Mac OS 9.1, or consider a third-party provider. Consult Chapter 16 for more information on system security options for your PowerBook.

Not only does the password security system protect your data, it also protects your hard drive. You can also use Apple's encryption options included with Mac OS 9.1 to provide file encryption (see Chapter 16 for more information on system security).

Figure 7.10   The Password Security Control Panel.

Using Good Passwords

Regarding passwords, make sure that you keep the rules of good passwords in mind:

- Do no use any word in the dictionary.
- Do not use telephone numbers, license plates, or other phrases that can be easily seen and guessed.
- Do not use names.
- If the system is case-sensitive, make some of the letters uppercase.
- Mix numbers and letters, as well as other non-alphabetical characters.
- The more secure the system must be, the longer the password should be.

Security Packages

When you are not mobile, you can lock your PowerBook down by using security cables. A security slot is located in the back of the PowerBook; you can attach cables and lock the PowerBook to a fixed object. Depending upon your environment, you can even equip the PowerBook in an alarm system. By utilizing both password and cabling options, you can protect your system against both data and physical theft.

Airport Issues

Walk through any airport during a weekday and you'll see thousands of business travelers carrying some sort of portable computer. Some users misunderstand airport security systems and the impact they could have on portable devices. Apple has stated that it is safe to allow PowerBooks to pass through properly tuned X-ray machines. However, some conveyor belts utilize magnetic components. For this reason, you should place your PowerBook close to the entrance or "tunnel" of the device and remove it immediately after it passes through the other end. Metal detectors do not damage PowerBooks, but if these devices make you nervous anyway, you can have the airport security personnel inspect your PowerBook by hand. Be aware that some airports personally inspect portable computers and request that you turn the computer on. Make sure that you have a fully charged battery ready to power the computer. You may even want to arrive at the airport with your computer in sleep mode rather than shut down.

Most airlines do not allow portable computers to run while the airplane is taking off or landing. This rule is in response to concern that these devices may interfere with certain airplane instruments, especially guidance systems. Although this has not been proven conclusively, respect this request and do not run your computer during flight until the captain gives permission to do so.

7. Mobile Computing

Immediate Solutions

Increasing Battery Performance (Simple Details)

Consult your user documentation for an estimation of your battery life. Then try some of the following methods to make it last a little longer, especially when you are in situations where you cannot recharge the battery.

To configure your energy conservation settings, take these steps:

1. Go to Apple menu|Control Panels and select Energy Saver, or click the Energy Saver button on the Control Strip and select Open Energy Saver Control Panel.

2. If it is not selected, click on the Sleep Setup tab.

3. In the Settings For pop-up menu, choose Battery.

4. To allow the system to determine the appropriate battery conservation methods, slide the tab to Better Conservation (choose Better Performance if battery usage doesn't matter). Figure 7.11 shows the Energy Saver Control Panel with these simple settings.

TIP: You can use your PowerBook without running batteries. However, when transporting batteries, make sure that the metal contacts are covered. Avoid touching the metal contacts. This will preserve and prolong the life of the battery.

Related solution:	Found on page:
Configuring Energy Saver	65

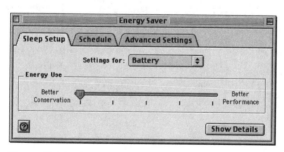

Figure 7.11   The Energy Saver Control Panel, hiding details.

Increasing Battery Performance (Customization)

You can let the system decide when the system sleeps, dims, and spins down, or you can take charge of your PowerBook and show it who's boss. In the previous section, we showed you how to access and set the Energy Saver Control Panel. However, you can control each function that saves battery power by going a little deeper:

1. Go to Apple menu|Control Panels and select Energy Saver.

2. If it is not selected, click on the Sleep Settings tab.

3. In the Settings For pop-up menu, choose Battery.

4. Click on the Show Details button. You will see the Control Panel shown in Figure 7.12.

5. On the sleep time slide bar on the top of the Control Panel, slide the tab to a preferred sleep time (one minute minimum). This will take effect when the system is idle for the designated amount of time.

6. If you prefer a different screen dimming time, click on the Separate Timing For Display Sleep checkbox and slide the tab. Notice that the maximum time allowed is the setting you chose for the sleep time.

7. If you prefer a different hard disk spindown time, click the Separate Timing For Hard Disk Sleep checkbox and slide the tab. Again, the maximum time allowed is the setting you chose for the sleep time.

You can follow these same steps for the Power Adapter settings, which are accessed via the Settings For pop-up menu. You'll notice that the settings for the Power Adapter are somewhat longer (see Figure 7.13) because energy saving is not as critical.

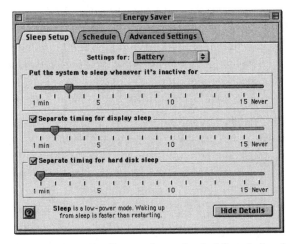

Figure 7.12   The Energy Saver Control Panel showing details.

7. Mobile Computing

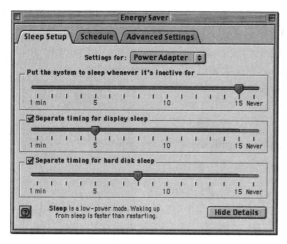

Figure 7.13   The Power Adapter settings.

Related solution:	Found on page:
Configuring Energy Saver	65

Using CD-ROMs

PowerBooks supported by Mac OS 9.1 have CD and, in some models, even DVD drives. iBooks also have CD drive bays. The PowerBook G3 Series computers allow you to use the CD and another data device simultaneously, although you must give up battery power.

CD-ROMs are inserted and mounted on a PowerBook the same way they are mounted on a desktop. However, if the CD-ROM does not mount and you do not hear the drive spinning, you may have improperly inserted the CD-ROM drive into the expansion bay. To correct this, take these steps:

1. If necessary, put the system to sleep (newer PowerBook models may not need this step—check your computer manual).

2. Use a straightened paper clip to eject the CD-ROM manually (carefully insert a straightened paper clip into the small hole located at the front of the drive and push gently until the CD-ROM bay glides out).

3. Remove the entire CD-ROM drive and insert it into the expansion bay again (push carefully but firmly).

4. Wake up the system and attempt to mount the CD-ROM disk again.

Ejecting Problem Floppy Disks

If Apple has its way, the floppy disk drive will go the way of all floppy disks—into big storage boxes or on museum shelves. Nevertheless, some older PowerBooks have floppy drives. Mounting and ejecting floppies in a PowerBook is very similar to the way you mount and eject them on a desktop system.

If the disk icon does not appear and you do not hear the drive spinning, you may have improperly inserted the floppy drive into the expansion bay. To correct this, take the following steps:

1. If necessary, put the system to sleep (newer PowerBook models may not need this step—check your computer manual).

2. Use a straightened paper clip to eject the floppy manually (carefully insert a straightened paper clip into the small hole located at the front of the drive and push gently until the disk comes out).

3. Remove the entire floppy drive and insert it into the expansion bay again (push carefully but firmly).

4. Wake up the system and attempt to mount the disk again.

Apple recommends that you push firmly on the floppy drive to insert it in the expansion bay. Remember the "firmly" part. For some reason, the floppy drive is more difficult to insert than other expansion devices (perhaps due to the location of the contact pins). You should hear a reassuring "click" when the drive is properly seated.

Related solution:	Found on page:
Mounting and Dismounting Floppy Disks	143

Swapping Removable Devices

You have been busily playing *Monopoly* when a colleague gives you a file on a disk that you are expected to open immediately. Follow these steps to do this quickly and properly:

1. Eject any media in the expansion bay drive.

2. If necessary, put the system to sleep (this step may not be required for later PowerBooks—check your PowerBook manual).

3. Remove the existing expansion bay device.

4. Insert the new expansion bay device. Make sure that you use a gentle but firm touch. The device should click into position.

5. Wake up the system.

You can now use other media.

TIP: *You can use the DVD-ROM expansion device to play DVD movies, but you may also need to insert a PC card that acts as a translator to view the movies playing on the DVD drive. Newer PowerBooks do not need this card.*

Configuring Energy Saver Scheduled Options

You can configure the PowerBook to sleep and wake up on a regular schedule. This feature can prevent you from accidentally leaving the system up all night. Business travelers may find this function especially useful.

To configure your PowerBook to start up and shut down on a regular schedule, take the following steps:

1. Go to Apple menu|Control Panels and select Energy Saver.

2. Click on the Schedule tab.

3. Place a check in the box beside Wake Up The Computer.

4. Choose the daily schedule (for example, you could choose to make the system wake up on Monday mornings and sleep on Friday afternoons).

5. Set the hour and minute you prefer for system wakeup.

6. Place a check in the box beside Put The Computer To Sleep.

7. Choose the daily schedule and set the hour and minute you prefer for putting the system to sleep.

8. Close the Control Panel to save changes.

The PowerBook will now sleep and wake up at the times and days you selected. Figure 7.14 shows a sample configuration.

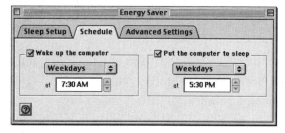

Figure 7.14   The sleep and wakeup schedule.

Related solution:	Found on page:
Configuring Energy Saver	65

Controlling Processor Cycling

We don't always run at top speed from one task to another, so why should we expect this from a computer? For example, when you're reading a Web page, you may need less horsepower. You can configure the system to slow down the processor when it has been idle for a certain length of time:

1. Go to Apple menu|Control Panels and select Energy Saver.

2. Click on the Advanced Settings tab.

3. Locate the section for Additional Power Savings.

4. Put a check in the box Allow Processor Cycling (see Figure 7.4 earlier in the chapter).

Although you can also manually reduce processor functions, it's best to let the system determine this energy saving option.

Automatically Remounting Shared Disks

Suppose you're talking on the telephone and decide it's time for a nap. You tell the party on the other line, "I'm going to sleep now." Normally the other party would say good-bye and hang up. You wouldn't expect him to stay on the line while you snooze, would you? PowerBooks behave the same way. When they go to sleep, connections to servers are broken. However, depending on your model PowerBook, you can tell it to automatically reconnect to these servers upon system wakeup:

1. Go to Apple menu|Control Panels and select Energy Saver.

2. Click on the Advanced Settings tab.

3. Locate the Network Connections section.

4. Place a check in the box beside Reconnect Servers On Wakeup.

5. If you work in a very secure environment or security is not a concern, place a check in the box Remember My Passwords. Otherwise you will be prompted to enter your password for each shared disk you're mounting.

6. Your system should now automatically remount these volumes.

If you do not have these options, your PowerBook may not support remounting shared disks.

7. Mobile Computing

Using PowerBook SCSI Disk Mode

Using your PowerBook as an external hard drive to another computer allows you to install, copy, and move software rapidly between the drives. Be aware that if you don't use the proper equipment you will not be able to treat the PowerBook as another device on the SCSI chain. Take the following steps to use your PowerBook as an external hard drive to another computer:

1. Purchase an Apple HDI-30 SCSI Disk Adapter cable. This is not a standard SCSI cable; it is designed specifically for this function. Additionally, try third-party cables that can switch between SCSI disk mode and a standard SCSI adapter cable.

2. If you have enabled password security on your PowerBook, disable it. You cannot mount a hard drive that has password protection.

3. Go to Apple menu|Control Panels and select PowerBook SCSI Disk Mode (see Figure 7.15).

4. By default, the ID is "2". If you know that a device on the desktop system will conflict with this number, select another number, then close the Control Panel.

TIP: *Remember that a SCSI chain can only have six additional devices. Each device on the chain must have a unique ID. If two devices have the same number, many strange problems can occur.*

---

5. Shut down the PowerBook.

6. Attach the HDI-30 SCSI Disk Adapter cable to the PowerBook; then attach a SCSI system cable from the adapter to the other computer. Connect these two cables.

7. Turn the PowerBook on. You should see the icon in Figure 7.16 on your PowerBook display (the number may be different if you chose a different SCSI ID number).

If your PowerBook begins booting normally or generates an error while booting, shut down the PowerBook, remove it from the SCSI chain, and repeat Steps 5 through 7. Make sure that you have the correct cables. Also verify that password

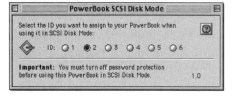

Figure 7.15   The Control Panel for SCSI Disk Mode.

Figure 7.16   The SCSI Mode icon on the PowerBook display.

protection has been turned off. This action isn't necessary for all PowerBooks, but may be required on your particular model.

TIP: Make sure that you plug in the power adapter when you are using the PowerBook in SCSI mode. This mode puts more intensive demands on the batteries. Also, you will not get a warning when battery power is almost gone; instead, the computer will simply shut down.

Creating a RAM Disk

If you're really serious about conserving battery power and you have memory to spare, then create a RAM disk. It behaves like a hard disk. You can save files to it, reducing the spinning of the hard drive and ultimately saving some battery juice. Just make sure that you save any documents stored in the RAM disk to a permanent storage location to minimize your risk of data loss. To create a RAM disk, take the following steps:

1. Go to Apple menu|Control Panels and select Memory.

2. Locate the RAM disk section at the bottom of the window.

3. Click on the On radio button.

4. Use the slide bar to indicate what percentage of RAM you want allocated to the RAM disk. Notice that the minimum RAM disk size increases as you move the slide tab. Figure 7.17 shows the Memory Control Panel with the RAM disk enabled.

5. The Save Contents To Disk On Restart And Shut Down option is checked by default. If you disable this, you will have to manually move the contents of the RAM disk to a permanent storage device. If you shut down the computer with files stored in the RAM disk, you will see the error message shown in Figure 7.18.

6. Close the Memory Control Panel and restart the computer.

7. A RAM disk icon like the one in Figure 7.19 should appear on the Desktop. You can now use this disk to save documents within computing sessions.

7. Mobile Computing

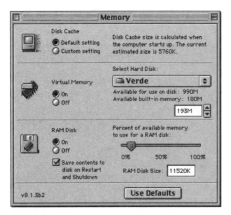

Figure 7.17   The Memory Control Panel with RAM Disk enabled.

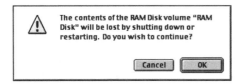

Figure 7.18   The warning for files in the RAM disk.

Figure 7.19   A RAM Disk icon.

Related solution:	Found on page:
Allocating Memory for RAM Disks	182

Removing a RAM Disk

A RAM disk is wonderful for extending battery life, but you may find that you need to remove it. This may especially be true if you need every scrap of available memory. Also, some systems behave better if the RAM disk is removed.

To remove a RAM disk:

1. Go to Apple menu|Control Panels and select Memory.

2. Locate the RAM Disk section.

3. Click on the Off radio button. The RAM disk should disappear from your Desktop immediately. In fact, if you really didn't intend to click on the Off

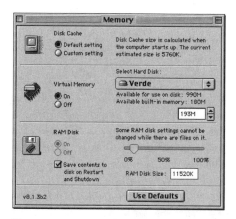

Figure 7.20   The RAM disk cannot be turned off.

button, you will find that you'll have to restart your computer to enable the RAM disk again.

TIP: *If you go into the Memory Control Panel and the On and Off buttons are grayed out, you will notice a message indicating that the RAM disk has files in it and cannot be modified (see Figure 7.20). This includes files that have been placed in the Trash. You must remove these files from the RAM disk and empty the Trash before you can remove the RAM disk.*

Related solution:	*Found on page:*
Allocating Memory for RAM Disks	182

Enabling Password Protection

One of the simplest ways to protect your PowerBook against intruder access is to require users to enter a password. This password works at the driver level and cannot be bypassed—not even by formatting the hard drive. In fact, you can't format the hard drive without entering the password. To set up a password:

1. Go to Apple menu|Control Panels and select Password Security.

2. If you have not set up password protection, click on the Setup button to view the dialog box for configuring your password information.

3. Follow the on-screen directions by entering a password in the first field, then retyping the password in the second field.

4. For extra convenience, Mac OS 9.1 provides a field to enter a hint that will help you remember your password (optional).

5. If you want password prompting both at system startup and upon wakeup, place a check in the Also Ask When Waking From Sleep box.

6. Click on the OK button to continue setting up your security and ownership information, or click on the Cancel button to stop the process.

7. At the main window, click on the On radio button to enable password protection.

If you want to delete password settings, go into the Setup section of the Password Security Control Panel and click on Reset.

WARNING! *The FireWire G3 Series PowerBook and the iBook cannot use this method of password protection. It should not appear as a Control Panel and you should not manually add it. If you do and enable password security, you could lose data. You may even have to take the hard drive out and put it in a PowerBook that does support password protection in order to disable the password.*

Related solutions:	Found on page:
Changing Passwords	346
Setting Up the Multiple User Environment	464
Adding Accounts to Multiple Users	466

Configuring the Control Strip

The Control Strip is a handy group of icons placed on a long tab that enables you to perform system functions with the push of a button. You can rearrange the order of the Control Strip icons, as well as add and remove them. The Control Strip behaves like the Application Switcher window: It remains in the front and cannot be placed in the background.

To access Control Strip settings, follow these steps:

1. Go to Apple menu|Control Panels and select Control Strip.

2. You have three options:

   • Show the Control Strip.

   • Hide the Control Strip.

   • Use a hot key to toggle between show and hide within the Finder.

   Select your preferred option and if necessary define a hot key combination for the show/hide function.

3. Select the font for the Control Strip menu options. Figure 7.21 shows the Control Strip Control Panel window.

Figure 7.21   The Control Strip Control Panel.

Customizing the Control Strip

You can add many more icons to the Control Strip. In fact, many applications add a button to the Control Strip during installation. You can also remove buttons that you don't use. And if you don't like the location of the Strip, you can move it or compress it easily.

To rearrange the order of the icons on the Control Strip:

1. Hold down the Option key.
2. Move the mouse over the icon you wish to move. The cursor will assume the shape of a hand.
3. Click and drag the icon to the preferred location (the hand will appear to grab the icon).
4. Release the icon. You have now customized the strip.

To add new icons or remove existing ones:

1. Drag the Control Strip module or file over the System Folder.
2. The Finder will tell you this is a Control Strip module and ask if you want the file put into the Control Strip Modules folder.
3. You can also manually install new modules by opening the Control Strip Modules folder located in the System Folder. Control Strip modules placed in the folder will be added to the Control Strip and items that are removed from the folder will be removed from the Control Strip.
4. Changes will take effect only after you restart the computer.

To move the Control Strip within the Finder:

1. Hold down the Option key.

2. Move the mouse over the tab at the end of the strip. The cursor will assume the shape of a hand.

3. Drag the strip to the preferred location. You can even move it to the right side of the screen.

TIP: *Occasionally, when you switch screen resolutions (especially lower to higher resolution), the Control Strip will end up stationed where the bottom of the screen used to be. Use the previous instructions to relocate the strip.*

Related solution:	Found on page:
Using the Control Strip	82

Configuring the Trackpad

The Trackpad Control Panel now allows you to tap the trackpad for mouse control. (Previously, you had to drag with the pad and click with the trackpad button.) Now, you can tap the trackpad to initiate a click, relieving the stress on your thumb joint.

To configure the trackpad:

1. Go to Apple menu|Control Panels and select Trackpad. See Figure 7.22.

2. Set the tracking speed in the first section. Use slower trackpad speeds for drawing applications and faster speeds to effectively use the trackpad space. For example, in some situations you run out of trackpad before you reach your destination. Faster tracking helps reduce this predicament.

3. Set the double-click speed. This determines the time lapse between clicks. If you are new to the trackpad device, you may want to increase this gap until you get accustomed to the art of double-clicking.

Figure 7.22   The Trackpad Control Panel.

4. Determine the trackpad uses. You can use the trackpad for clicking (tap the pad), dragging, and drag lock. If you choose nothing else, use the trackpad for clicking. Your thumb will thank you.

Configuring the Location Manager

Portability is a PowerBook's *raison d'être*. You bought it to take it to multiple locations—even if this means only between work and home, a lot of hard work is involved in switching between network and remote access. In Mac OS 9.1, you can use the Location Manager to expedite this process by using different Extension sets for different locations or applications.

To configure the Location Manager:

1. Go to Apple menu|Control Panels and select Location Manager, or click the Location Manager button on the Control Strip and select Open Location Manager. If this is the first time the Location Manager is being launched, you will encounter the window shown in Figure 7.23. Open the window to its full view by clicking on the triangle next to Edit Locations.

2. Go to the File menu and select New Location.

3. Give a name to your new location and click on Save. For our example, we'll use *Home*.

4. In the pop-up menu next to Current Location, select a location. See Figure 7.24 for an example.

5. Set your options such as Sound Level, Default Printer, and Extension Set. As you set the values for each option, the right side of the dialog box will display each setting.

TIP: *Setting up the locations involves more work than what Figure 7.24 may lead you to believe. For example, in the AppleTalk & TCP/IP option, you need to go into each of these Control Panels and create configuration sets with names other than Default. To use the Extension Sets option, you must first go into the Extension Manager and save sets with names other than My Settings. Several of the options listed in the Location Manager require pre-configuration, but the Mac OS will tell you what you need to do to use each option. Simply select the option and click on the Get Info button.*

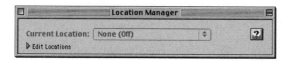

Figure 7.23   The Location Manager unconfigured.

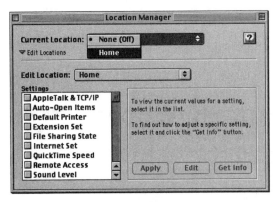

Figure 7.24   Selecting a location.

6. When you have set the options for the location, go to the File menu and choose Save Location (if you forget this step, you'll be prompted to save when you close this Control Panel).

7. To make a location active, select it from the pop-up menu beside Current Location (a restart may be necessary if you've specified custom Extension sets).

Related solution:	*Found on page:*
Creating Configuration Sets in the Internet Control Panel	366

Using PCMCIA Ethernet Cards

The latest PowerBooks come with a built-in Ethernet port. However, many PowerBook users do not have this luxury and must use one of the other methods for network access, including the installation of a network expansion card, an external SCSI Ethernet device, or a PCMCIA (PC) card. Of the three options, the PC card is the most economical and expandable.

To set up a PC card:

1. Purchase an Ethernet PC card (make sure that Macintosh drivers are available).

2. Install the drivers for the card and restart the computer.

3. Insert the PC card into a PCMCIA slot and attach the Ethernet cable (some cards use a small cable with the 10BaseT jack on the end; others include the Ethernet cable that attaches directly to the PC card). The icon of the PC card will appear on the Desktop (see Figure 7.25).

Farallon EN Card

Figure 7.25   The Ethernet PC card icon on the Desktop.

   4. Go to Control Panels|AppleTalk and choose Alternate Ethernet as your
      network option (if AppleTalk is disabled, you will be asked to enable it).

   5. Close the AppleTalk Control Panel and save changes. You should now be
      able to access your network.

If you fail to access the network, try disabling AppleTalk, then re-enabling it.

Using PCMCIA Modem Cards

Not every computer owner has access to a fast network. In fact, most of us rely
on modem connections to access the Internet. Many PowerBooks include a modem; all iBooks contain an internal modem. Older PowerBooks may need an alternative, however. Internal modems can be installed, but lack easy expandability,
and external modems lack portability. The PC card modem is an excellent and
economical alternative.

To install and set up a PCMCIA modem card:

   1. Install the PC card modem software (most importantly, make sure that you
      install any modem scripts).

   2. Restart the computer.

   3. Insert the PC card modem into a PCMCIA slot. An icon of the PC card
      should appear on the Desktop.

   4. Go to Apple menu|Control Panels and select the Modem Control Panel.

   5. In the Connect Via section choose Upper or Lower PC Card Slot (the upper
      or lower slot will vary depending on whether you chose the upper or lower
      slot for your card). Figure 7.26 shows the Lower PC Card Slot.

   6. Choose the correct modem script for your PC card.

   7. Close the Control Panel and save the settings.

You can continue setting the remote access options as detailed in Chapter 11.

7. Mobile Computing

TIP: *You can eject a PC card while the system is active (unless the card is in use) by dragging the PC card icon to the
Trash. The card will automatically pop out. If the computer is off, push the small button beside the PCMCIA slot to eject
the card. However, if the system is in sleep mode you must wake it to eject the card—pushing the button on the card
slot will not work.*

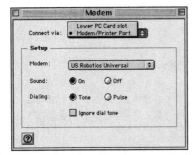

Figure 7.26   Choosing a modem port.

Related solutions:	*Found on page:*
Configuring the Remote Access Control Panel	362
Configuring the TCP/IP Control Panel	369

Chapter 8

Printing

In Depth

Everyone who has worked in computing technology has heard the phrase "paperless work environment." It seems to be the Utopian state of computing. Printers would become obsolete, and we would instead read and manage everything using an electronic display *à la* Captain Kirk. You've probably even wished that this dream would instantly come true when, for example, a frantic administrative assistant called because a report due in five minutes would not print. But the painful fact is that the paperless workflow has generated a greater need to print.

Many users take printing for granted, and may use the same printer for several years. They may even purchase an entirely new computer system, but keep an old printer. At the other end of the spectrum, graphic designers use expensive, specialized printers for high-quality output. And thanks to the iMac, USB connectivity for printing has emerged as a popular and easy method of printing connectivity. In this chapter, we hope to provide information about the printers, printing technology, and drivers that offer the best printing results. And because printing and text types are intertwined, we'll also cover font technology. As soon as a method for printing text clearly was developed, font usage exploded.

PostScript

Before PostScript, printers used a simple method of output. A series of tiny blocks would compose (or build a bitmap of) images or text using fonts that are often called *fixed size*. The results of this method were images and text with jagged edges. The technology of the time seemed to concentrate on making these blocks as small as possible, thus minimizing the jagged edges. The most commonly used printing device was a dot-matrix printer; Apple's version was called the ImageWriter. Because these printers used small dots generated by a print head to reproduce the data from the computer, the output was less than desirable, especially for business documents. The information on the screen frequently differed from the output because of the printer's inability to reproduce the displayed image. Then came the laser printer, which used toner and heat rollers instead of print heads and ribbons to print, and a font revolution was soon in the making.

In the pre-PostScript era, fonts were installed with a range of standard sizes. A set might include 9-, 10-, 11-, 14-, 18-, and 24-point sizes. In the earlier versions of the Mac OS, these fixed-size fonts were often represented by city names (Chicago, Geneva, and New York). If you wanted to use a size other than those included in the set, the output was not as attractive, especially the larger point sizes. The computer attempted to redraw the font, but instead, it produced huge, jagged text. When printed on a laser printer, the results were still unsatisfactory.

Then, Adobe developed PostScript, an entirely new method of printing. Rather than relying on a series of squares, PostScript used a printing language that used mathematical equations to create smooth outlines of the curves and lines of the font or image. This new method not only improved the quality of text, but also allowed graphic images to print with smooth, continuous lines and shading. Instead of generating output by a series of ribbon punches, PostScript took advantage of the printer's ability to smoothly spread the toner over the page. Using PostScript fonts, which were written for the printer so that it handled the output faster, better, and more easily, ensured even better results. It makes sense if you think about it. Using bitmap technology to print to a laser printer would be like trying to dry your hair in a clothes dryer: You may get the job done, but the results won't be pretty.

However, PostScript had problems within the operating system, which resulted in a big mess of font files. Read the "Fonts" section later in this chapter to learn more. Later, we will also discuss printing to a file, a feature that utilizes PostScript technology.

TrueType

When laser printers with PostScript technology were first released, they were a great success. At last the business community could print in-house, thanks to the tremendous improvement in quality. In the absence of competition, however, Adobe was able to charge a hefty licensing fee to include PostScript technology in printers—and laser printers were already expensive. To give Adobe a run for its money, Apple began to explore developing its own font technology to fix the problems inherent to PostScript fonts and, of course, to grab a share of the market. TrueType was the result of Apple's effort.

TrueType produced high-quality text output comparable to that of PostScript, and it was free. It eliminated the jagged edges by using a similar method of outlining the font with curves and lines. TrueType was also embraced by Microsoft (who says two companies can't get along?). Unlike PostScript fonts, TrueType housed all of the font information (both the display and the printing information) in a single suitcase file.

However, TrueType didn't cause the death of PostScript. First, many users had invested money in PostScript fonts and were not inclined to spend additional money on TrueType fonts. (The technology was free—the fonts were not.) Second, Adobe became very generous in light of the competition and gave the

PostScript technology away for almost nothing. Third, the two technologies actually coexisted quite nicely. They are very different, however, in one important aspect: TrueType is font-based and PostScript is graphics-based. You still need PostScript for printing clipart and images.

QuickDraw GX

We are mentioning QuickDraw GX briefly because you may see vestiges of it through system upgrades on Macs. QuickDraw GX is no longer included with the Mac OS, but it had great potential as a printing technology. However, during the period when Apple developed a hybrid of Mac OS and Rhapsody (now known as Mac OS X Server), QuickDraw GX became a casualty of standardization.

QuickDraw GX used such components as Desktop printer icons, simplified page-setup windows, printer sharing, and portable digital documents or PDDs (one of its best features). Specialized drivers and Extensions provided much of this functionality. Other aspects were built into QuickDraw GX itself.

QuickDraw GX Features

Before QuickDraw GX, you had to change printers by using the Chooser. This was rather annoying if you frequently used more than one printer. QuickDraw GX used the Chooser to install printer icons on the Desktop. You switched printers via the Finder. When you selected a printer icon, a new menu called *Printing* would appear; you could set the default printer from this menu. This functionality is included in Mac OS 9.1.

One specialized Extension was *portable digital documents (PDD)*, which allowed you to print a PDD document by dragging its icon over the printer icon. Regardless of the fonts used in the document or the application that created it, you could print the document.

However, now you can have the same PDD functionality by using the *portable document format (PDF)* from Adobe. The catch, of course, is that you must purchase Adobe Acrobat to create these files. However, you'll find that this file format preserves your fonts, images, and formatting so that the printed output will be what you intended.

As we discuss aspects of printing, you'll see that much of the functionality of QuickDraw GX has been included with Mac OS 9.1.

Printer Drivers

When personal computing was still new, printing was often a nightmare. You usually had to have a printer driver installed with each application. No centralized place existed to which all applications could send their data. Thank goodness for the Macintosh. Each application went its merry way and created documents; when it was time to print, the application simply sent the data to a driver within the system. The driver spooled the information, sent it to the printer, downloaded fonts if the printer did not have them installed, and stored large files in parts until the printer was ready to handle the next piece.

Today, many types of printers are available. You'll still find legacy dot-matrix printers around, but the more common types are laser and ink-cartridge printers. Consumers purchase the ink-cartridge printers because of cost. Ink-cartridge printers can produce excellent printed output and most have color capability. Supplies for ink cartridge printers are reasonably priced, and the quality of the more expensive ink cartridge printers is comparable to that of laser printers.

The business world is the domain of the laser printer. Although it's possible to share ink cartridge printers (easily, thanks to USB Printer Sharing), the laser printer has been developed for a networked environment. Many laser printers include PostScript technology, which results in superior print quality. Color laser printers produce excellent printouts. Although their prices are much lower today than when they were first introduced, laser printers are not cheap. Toner cartridges also contribute to the ongoing costs of owning a laser printer.

One of the best things Apple does for its customers is to provide printer drivers that will run almost any Mac-compatible printer. In fact, the driver for the ImageWriter (an Apple-manufactured dot-matrix printer) is still included with Mac OS 9.1, despite the fact that this printer is no longer in production.

Ink Technology Drivers

Many different manufacturers make ink-technology printers. For many years, Apple manufactured the StyleWriter and Color StyleWriter printer family. Capable of producing black-and-white or color output, the StyleWriter was aimed toward the consumer. Apple no longer manufactures the StyleWriter printers, but many are still in use. Canon also has the Bubble Jet family of printers, which used the same form factor as the StyleWriters. Hewlett-Packard also manufactures a line of Macintosh-compatible printers called DeskWriter. And Epson develops USB- and Macintosh-compatible printers and drivers.

The ink technology printer drivers included with Mac OS 9.1 are Color SW 1500, Color SW 2500, Color SW Pro, and CSW 6000 series (see Figure 8.1). These drivers can communicate with most StyleWriter printers. You also have the option of using the driver that shipped with your printer. Use the Get Info option to check the version numbers of the drivers and use the one with the latest driver. This enables you to take advantage of new printing options for your printer and reduces the risk of system errors when printing.

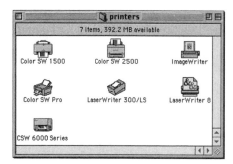

Figure 8.1   The printer drivers included with Mac OS 9.1.

Unlike laser printer drivers, ink cartridge printers require a specific driver that may not be included with Mac OS 9.1. If you do not see a compatible driver, install the one that came with the printer (printer drivers are placed in the Extensions folder) or download the latest driver from the manufacturer's Web site.

You should also check your printer's technical specifications to determine whether it has PostScript technology. If it does, you can use the PostScript drivers included with Mac OS 9.1 to achieve higher print quality. Be aware, however, that some programs using PostScript objects may not translate to the printer well. If you encounter this problem, a software program called StyleScript, available from Strydent, serves as a PostScript interpreter for ink-technology printers that don't have PostScript hardware interpreters.

Laser Printer Drivers

Each of the manufacturers previously named in this chapter—except Apple—produces laser printers. Laser printers provide speed, versatility, and durability to users. Most are designed to be shared in a work environment, although personal laser printers are also a desirable item. Personal laser printers are usually slower, and may not have PostScript technology installed (check your printer manual). Industrial laser printers frequently have several levels of PostScript installed (the count is currently at level 3).

Mac OS 9.1 includes drivers for many other printers, but usually two drivers are included for laser printers—one driver for a non-PostScript personal laser printer and one for a laser printer with PostScript capability. In most cases, you will use the latter driver (if you are in doubt, check your printer manual to verify if PostScript is a feature).

The driver included with Mac OS 9.1 that is used with PostScript printers is LaserWriter 8 (you can also use the Adobe PostScript driver). Although it is named for the brand of laser printers manufactured by Apple, the LaserWriter 8 driver can communicate with most PostScript printers. If AppleTalk protocol is enabled or if the printer can be reached via TCP/IP, then you should be able to print to it. However, to take full advantage of each printer's capabilities, you need a PostScript printer description (PPD) file, which allows you to use special features of the printers, such as bypass trays or custom paper sizes. PPD files usually come bundled with the driver installation software; they are located within the Extensions folder in the Printer Descriptions folder. Figure 8.2 shows some of the PPD files in this folder.

The latest LaserWriter 8 driver is version 8.7. Use the latest printer driver if possible. However, keep the older driver handy so that you can restore it if you develop system problems. The latest LaserWriter 8 drivers are available at **www.apple.com**. If you have a non-Apple printer, you may want to retrieve the latest driver from the manufacturer's Web site. Printer companies are usually very conscientious about distributing drivers for their printers.

Non-Macintosh Printers

If you have a PC-compatible printer, especially one that is a non-PostScript printer, software packages that will enable you to use the printer with a Macintosh are available. One of the more well-known of these packages is PowerPrint, a hardware and software solution. The package ships with an adapter cable and software that contains hundreds of printer drivers.

Connecting to Printers

Now that you have the appropriate driver, you can set up Mac OS 9.1 to print to the appropriate printer. Several files other than the driver and printer are involved in printing. Desktop PrintSpooler, Desktop Print Monitor, and Print Monitor work together to manage the printing process. These files are located in the Extensions folder.

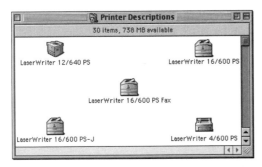

Figure 8.2   Printer description files in the Printer Descriptions folder.

Chooser

The Chooser has been a part of the printing process for years. This utility lists not only the drivers, but also AppleTalk zones and the printers within them (if the computer is connected to an AppleTalk or Ethernet network). Initially, the process is simple: Select the icon of the printer driver you will be using, the AppleTalk zone (if necessary), and the name of the printer or its port (printer or modem).

For non-PostScript printers that connect via serial port such as the ImageWriter or StyleWriter, you select a port (printer or modem). If you are not on a network, you also need to disable AppleTalk within the Chooser, as shown in Figure 8.3. In most cases, you plug the printer into the printer port, but if you must run AppleTalk, you can use the modem or Ethernet port to reduce conflicts (especially if the modem port is unused). Just make sure to select the modem port within the Chooser.

USB, or universal serial bus, is another very popular connectivity method. The original iMac provided only USB ports for connecting peripheral devices, including printers. You either purchased a new printer with your machine or purchased a serial-to-USB converter cable so you could attach your original printer to your new computer. Several printer models provide all three methods of connectivity: serial, parallel, and USB.

Mac OS 9.1 also has provided an easy method of sharing these USB printers. The USB Printer Sharing Control Panel allows you to specify printers that can be seen and used by other users on your network.

You don't choose a port for PostScript printers. Instead, the printer appears by name when you select the LaserWriter 8 icon. In some cases, especially if you're not on a network, it is the only name that appears. However, if you are part of a local area network, you may see many printers listed in many zones. Figure 8.4 shows an extensive listing of PostScript printers available in a particular networked environment.

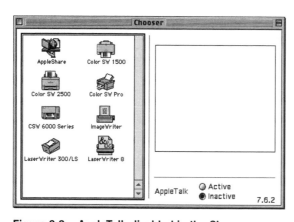

Figure 8.3   AppleTalk disabled in the Chooser.

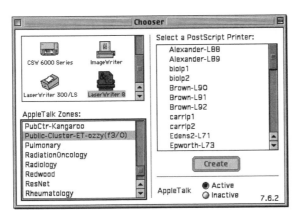

Figure 8.4   Networked PostScript printers in the Chooser.

After selecting a printer, regardless of whether it's a PostScript printer, you have the option of setting up the printer. Simply click on the Create button to initiate a connection to the printer. You can then choose from a variety of options, such as updating the printer information and customizing options.

Desktop Printing

In the previous section, we discussed selecting printers via the Chooser. But that's only half of the story. Before the advent of Desktop printing, you had to go to the Chooser every time you wanted to change printers. It was easy to forget to switch back to the original printer, and sooner or later you would be reporting lost printing jobs rather than checking the Printer dialog box to identify the selected printer. Desktop printing makes all this much easier. The first time you access a printer, you still need to select it in the Chooser. After you've done that, an icon for the printer appears on the Desktop, as shown in Figure 8.5.

The default printer's icon is differentiated by a heavy black border. When a printer icon is selected, a new menu called Printing appears within the Finder (see Figure 8.6). This menu replaces much of the function of the old Print Monitor.

NOTE: *Print Monitor was an application that launched when you sent something to print—you could also launch it manually. Print Monitor appeared in the Applications menu and allowed you to perform such tasks as deleting print jobs or halting the print queue. These tasks and more can be accessed from the Printing menu.*

Figure 8.5   A printer icon on the Desktop.

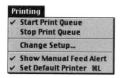

Figure 8.6   The Printing menu.

When documents are sent to print, the application prepares the document and sends it to the Print Spooler, which then prepares the document for the printer. When the Desktop Print Spooler is active, an image of a document will appear over the printer icon. Double-clicking on the icon reveals the Print Queue window, which provides information such as how much of the document has been processed and where it is located in the queue. You can rearrange and delete print jobs within this window. Figure 8.7 shows an active Print Queue window.

TIP: *You can print by dragging a document over a particular desktop printer icon. The Mac OS will launch the application that created the document, bring up the print dialog box, and close the application when printing is finished.*

You may find yourself using a locally attached laser printer that is plugged in to the printer port. If you are a home user, this is usually not a problem because AppleTalk is not normally required in a non-networked environment. However, if you must keep AppleTalk active yet still use the printer port for the printer, you may need a copy of LaserWriter Bridge (available at **www.apple.com**). This Control Panel enables you to use the printer and AppleTalk at the same time. A side benefit is that the printer can be seen and shared by multiple users with this software.

TIP: *If you are no longer using a particular printer, you can drag its icon to the trash. However, you must have at least one Desktop printer icon. If you attempt to drag the default printer to the trash, the icon will be re-created.*

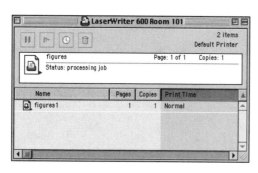

Figure 8.7   The Print Queue.

Fonts

Fonts and printing seem to go hand-in-hand. Fonts are used to communicate information in a legible and eye-catching manner. Fonts are used by the system as well as for printing; the default system fonts in Mac OS 9.1 are Charcoal and Geneva. There are basically three types of fonts:

- *Fixed-size*—Fixed-size fonts (not to be confused with monospaced fonts such as Courier) are created by a series of pixels and are installed in sets. As long as you print using one of the sizes in the set, output is acceptable. Results are more mixed when you use a size not in the set; your output will be very jagged.

- *PostScript*—PostScript fonts are created by outlining the font and filling in the white area, resulting in text that is smooth and professional. This technology also applies to image printing as well. Thousands of PostScript fonts are available, which creates a problem for the System Folder. One font may have files for bold, italics, and bold italics as well as separate files for the printer font.

- *TrueType*—TrueType uses a variable-size font technology which also produces excellent output. All of the font information relating to TrueType font files is stored in a suitcase file within the System Folder.

Thousands of PostScript and TrueType fonts are available for download or purchase. Both technologies result in excellent printed information. Several types of fixed-size fonts are also available.

Immediate Solutions

Configuring Local Printers

A *local printer* is a printer that is physically attached to your machine. Consult your manual for instructions on how to attach the printer to your computer. Be aware that some printers do not include the printer cable; you must purchase one separately.

To configure your printer, take these steps:

1. While all devices are turned off, connect the printer to the computer. If you don't need AppleTalk, use the printer port. If you do need AppleTalk, try using the modem or Ethernet port instead.

2. Turn on the computer and printer.

3. Install the software that came with the printer, unless it's a PostScript printer (which could overwrite the LaserWriter 8 driver included with the OS) or the driver for the printer is included in Mac OS 9.1. (You can still install the software; just be watchful for warnings that indicate your drivers are older than existing drivers.)

4. If you had to install new drivers, restart the computer. Otherwise, go to the Apple menu|Chooser option.

5. Select your printer icon.

6. Select the port (the same physical port that you chose in Step 1). Figure 8.8 shows the printer and port selected.

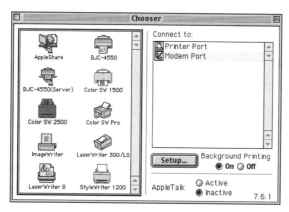

Figure 8.8   A locally attached printer selected in the Chooser.

7. Click on the Create button to set printer options and create a Desktop printer icon.

8. Close the Chooser.

Configuring Local USB Printers

USB printing has become very popular thanks to the iMac and the other newer Macintosh models. Setting up a USB printer is very easy. Consult your manual for instructions on how to attach the printer to the computer. Be aware that some printers do not include the printer cable; you must purchase one separately. USB printer cables are somewhat more delicate than serial cables, and crimps in the cable can lead to loss of connection with the printer.

To configure your printer, take these steps:

1. Connect the printer to one of the USB ports. It is not necessary to turn the devices off prior to this step.

2. Install the software that came with the printer.

3. You may need to restart the computer to use the drivers (you will be prompted by the system if this is necessary). Otherwise, go to the Apple menu|Chooser option.

4. Select your printer icon.

5. Select the port (only one option should be visible: USB Port).

6. Click on the Create button to set printer options and create a Desktop printer icon.

7. Close the Chooser.

TIP: *If you cannot see the USB Port option when you're setting up the printer, double-check those cables. Look very closely for any kind of crimping. Also, be aware that USB printers may not show up on the desktop when selected in Chooser.*

8. Printing

Configuring Networked Printers

Networked printers fall into two categories: those that have a built-in Ethernet port and those that are locally attached to a computer but visible over the network (some of the second-category printers can be converted to Ethernet with an adapter). The printers with built-in Ethernet ports have special software utilities that allow you to set options such as an IP address and printer name. Printer utility software also enables you to change printer options, such as the printer name, or disable the banner page of a locally attached laser printer. Newer laser printers utilize the Web for setting printer options. Some older or personal laser printers may require LaserWriter Bridge, a Control Panel that renders the printer visible on a network. LaserWriter Bridge is available from **www.apple.com**. You may also need LocalTalk cables if your printer does not have an Ethernet port.

Follow these steps to configure a networked printer.

1. Launch the printer utility (in this example, we will use the Apple Printer Utility).

2. Locate the zone where the printer resides (optional).

3. Select the printer you want to configure (the Apple Printer Utility has a series of dialog boxes indicating that the computer is communicating with the printer).

4. Set the printer options, such as the printer name or IP number. Figure 8.9 shows the Apple Printer Utility accessing a LaserWriter 16/600 and the options available.

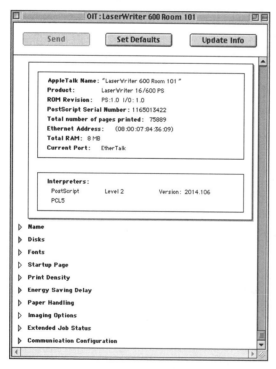

Figure 8.9   The Apple Printer Utility.

TIP: *By default, a banner page appears when a printer is turned on or restarted and is ready to print. The most useful information on this page is the page count. If you maintain many printers, you can use this information to determine how many pages each toner cartridge prints. The banner page can also warn you if the printer has lost its name or IP number. Users often disable the banner page option as a method of saving paper. Many printers allow you to print this page "on the fly," so you may want to enable it selectively.*

Selecting a Network Printer

Selecting a network printer is much easier than configuring one. And you can set up several printers at once while you're still in the Chooser.

To select a network printer:

1. Go to the Apple menu and open the Chooser.

2. Select the LaserWriter 8 driver.

3. Select the AppleTalk zone that houses the printer (optional).

4. Select the printer by name from the list that appears.

5. If this is the first time you have accessed this printer, click on the Create button.

6. You will see a series of dialog boxes as the computer communicates with the printer. You can also select the PPD file by clicking on the Select PPD button. If the PPD for your printer is not listed, you can install the files from disk or visit the printer manufacturer's Web site to see if the files are available via download.

7. When the printer and computer have finished communicating, you will be returned to the Chooser. Within the Chooser and on the Desktop, an icon will appear next to the printer. You can continue setting up printers; close the Chooser when you are finished.

Related solutions:	Found on page:
Managing a Network Using SNMP	335
Fixing Common Printing Problems	531

8. Printing

Configuring Printers Using the Desktop Printer Utility

Mac OS 9.1 includes the Desktop Printer Utility, a small utility that you can use to set up network and local printers as well as virtual printers. It is located in the Utilities folder in the Applications folder. The Desktop Printer Utility is also an easy program for setting up TCP/IP printing.

Follow these steps to create a desktop printer.

1. Locate and open the Desktop Printer Utility.

2. Select the driver that you want to use.

3. Select the type of Desktop printing you will be using. You have a wide variety of choices, including AppleTalk, LPR (the Unix command for printing; more commonly described as TCP/IP printing), and no printer connection. This list varies depending on your type of computer. For this example, the Printer (LPR) option has been chosen (see Figure 8.10).

4. If you do not want to use a generic printer description file, click the Change button to specify the PPD you want to use.

5. The other icon in this dialog box will vary depending on what type of desktop printing you will be doing. For Printer (LPR), the section for LPR printing has a Change button. Click this button.

6. Enter the IP address or domain name of the printer you want to access. You can also designate the queue name (most types of LPR printing suggest *raw* as an option). Click on the Verify button to communicate with the printer and determine whether it is accessible, but this step is not mandatory.

7. Click on the Create button and, if necessary, designate the printer name. Then choose Save.

Figure 8.10   The list of desktop printers available with the Desktop Printer Utility.

Changing Page Attributes

Most documents are printed in portrait orientation. Occasionally, landscape orientation is required (for example, when printing PowerPoint transparencies). Paper orientation is specific to the application and document; after you change it, the setting will not revert on its own. You may also need to indicate a different paper size or scale.

To change the orientation:

1. Go to File|Page Setup.

2. By default, the Page Attributes window should appear, as shown in Figure 8.11.

3. Select your orientation, printer format (from the list of your desktop printers), or scale.

4. Click on OK to close the window.

Remember that these settings will remain in effect until you manually change them in Page Setup.

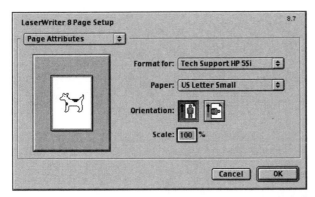

Figure 8.11   The Page Attributes window within Page Setup.

Setting PostScript Options

If you are printing to a PostScript printer, you can set specialized options, such as inverting the image. These options vary depending on the driver you are using. Consider that although some of these options can greatly increase printing time, they will produce better quality documents.

8. Printing

Follow these steps to set PostScript options.

1. Go to File|Page Setup.

2. Locate the Page Attributes button. Select PostScript Options via the pop-up menu located in the top-left corner of the window (see Figure 8.12).

3. Select or deselect the options you prefer. When you are finished, click on OK to initiate the options. For an explanation of the PostScript options, refer to Table 8.1.

Table 8.1   PostScript options.

Option	Purpose
Flip Horizontal	Produces a mirror image of the original document.
Flip Vertical	Produces an upside-down mirror image of the original document.
Invert Image	White areas are printed black and black areas are left white.
Substitute Fonts	Replaces certain fonts with better-printing fonts (for example, Monaco will be replaced by Courier). The end product can be disappointing, however, in that the text output may result in repagination of the document or overlapping text.
Smooth Text	Smoothes fixed-size or bitmap fonts.
Smooth Graphics	Smoothes graphic images.
Precision Bitmap Alignment	Reduces the image size to prevent image distortion.
Unlimited Downloadable Fonts	Downloads all the fonts needed for the document. This option will increase print time.

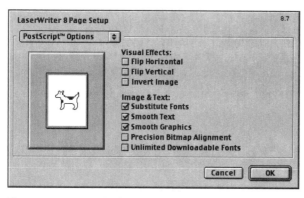

Figure 8.12   PostScript Options within Page Setup.

Using Desktop Printing

The nice thing about Desktop printing is that much of it is done automatically. Whenever you select a printer within the Chooser, a printer icon is placed on the desktop; the default printer is denoted by a bold border. Figure 8.13 shows the default printer beside an additional printer.

When you send a document to print, the icon changes to reflect that it is spooling the document to the printer (see Figure 8.14).

If you want to see the progress of your document, double-click on the printer icon to launch the window for the Desktop Print Monitor. This window lists all documents in the queue. You can rearrange jobs, cancel jobs, or halt the print queue.

You can also print by dragging a document over any printer icon. The Mac OS will launch the application for that document, open the Print command window, and quit the application after the document is printed.

Figure 8.13   Desktop printer icons.

Figure 8.14   A Desktop printer icon in action.

Setting the Default Printer

Although you can use the printer icons when you set the default printer, doing so will bring up the Printing menu. This menu only appears when a printer icon is selected.

TIP: *If you have chosen more than one printer, selections you make in the Printing menu will affect only the default printer.*

To set the default printer:

1. Click on the icon of the printer that you want to be your default printer. If the icon doesn't exist, go to Chooser and select the printer.

8. Printing

2. The Printing menu will appear. From it, select Set Default Printer.

3. A heavy black border should appear around the printer icon that you selected.

You can also perform this task by pressing the Control key as you click on the printer icon; a contextual menu with an option to Set Default Printer will appear. Figure 8.15 shows the contextual menu for Desktop printing.

Figure 8.15   The Desktop Printing contextual menu.

Foreground vs. Background Printing

When you send a document to print, you are using either foreground or background printing. By default, background printing is enabled. It allows you to continue working in an application while the document is printing in the background. As the application and the print queue use system resources to accomplish their tasks, the application's performance may be reduced. The size and type of document being printed will also affect system performance.

Foreground printing is faster than background printing. Foreground printing means that you allow the print driver to take over the computer, or dominate the foreground, while the document is printed. When the information has been sent to the printer and the queue is empty, you will be allowed to continue working in an application. Most users prefer background printing because, although it is slower, it allows you to continue using the application. If the speed of printing becomes a factor, you can easily disable background printing. To do so, take these steps:

1. Go to Apple|Chooser.

2. Select the printer driver and port or printer name.

3. Locate the Background section and click on the Off radio button.

Be aware that background printing may not be an option for some printers. If that is the case in your situation, you will not see the background settings in Chooser.

TIP: If you have not installed or enabled Desktop printing, then background printing is handled by the Print Monitor application. When you send information to print, the Print Monitor is automatically launched. It allows you to see the contents of the queue and remove print jobs if necessary.

Halting the Print Queue

Occasionally, you may need to disable printing from a particular computer. When you halt the print queue, print requests will remain on your computer until you're ready to begin printing again. Sometimes users who have halted the print queue accidentally will call the IT department because nothing they send to the printer will print. The print queue is one of the first places you should check.

Halting the Queue with Desktop Printing

To halt the print queue in Desktop printing, follow these steps:

1. Click once on the printer icon.
2. Go to Printing|Stop Print Queue.
3. To resume printing, select Start Print Queue.

You can also stop printing by holding the Control key and clicking on the printer icon. A contextual menu will appear with Stop Queue as a menu option. To start printing again, select Start Queue.

Halting the Queue with Print Monitor

To halt the print queue in Print Monitor, take the following steps:

1. Launch the Print Monitor application.
2. Go to File|Stop Printing.
3. To resume printing, select File|Resume Printing.

Printing to a File

When you are using a PostScript printer and the proper LaserWriter driver, you can print documents to a file rather than print them immediately on paper. Why would you do this? To save the files in a format that can be printed on another printer. Therefore, you could print a document to file and exchange it with a colleague who also has a PostScript printer. The output would be almost the same, depending on the options you chose. Printing to a file is also the first step in creating an Acrobat file. You can also create one-page PostScript files that can be placed in another document (such as Quark XPress or PageMaker).

To print to a file, take these steps:

1. Select File|Print.

2. Locate the unmarked pop-up menu under the General button. Select Save As File.

3. Select the Format pop-up menu and choose your option. Table 8.2 defines each option.

4. Determine your PostScript level. Level 1 will communicate with the most printers, but Levels 2 and 3 will provide better quality and handling.

5. Determine the Data Format. ASCII will print on most printers, but binary will provide greater speed on a compatible printer.

6. Determine the Font Inclusion option. The None option uses the least disk space, but may print incorrectly. The All option embeds every font used in the document, thus creating a larger file. The All But Standard 13 option indicates that fonts other than the 13 installed on all PostScript printers will be included. The All But Fonts In PPD File option includes fonts not listed in the printer description file.

7. In the top right of the window, change the Destination option to File. The Print button will change to a Save button (see Figure 8.16).

8. Click on the Save button. The Save dialog box will appear. Provide a name and location for the file and click on the Save button.

The computer will behave as if it is spooling a document, but instead of sending the output to a printer, a file will be created at the location you specified.

Table 8.2   Format options for printing to a file.

Option	Results
PostScript Job	Creates a normal PostScript file for later printing.
EPS Mac Standard Preview	Creates a black-and-white bitmapped preview image of the graphic.
EPS Mac Enhanced Preview	Creates a color PICT preview image of the graphic.
EPS No Preview	Creates the graphic with no preview image.
Acrobat PDF	Creates PDF files, working with Adobe Acrobat. (Adobe Acrobat Distiller must be installed.)

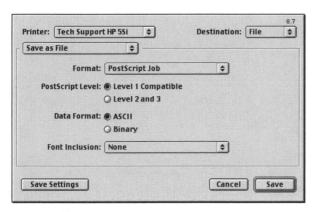

Figure 8.16   Printing to a PostScript file.

Sharing a Printer

Ethernet- or LocalTalk-enabled printers are not the only printers that can be shared over a network. You can also share printers such as StyleWriters. Software is included in the system software that allows for print sharing. However, the computer that is attached to the printer becomes a print server; any jobs sent to this printer will slow the host computer, especially if the document contains fonts that are missing from the host computer. This is a practical option if you use a dedicated computer as the printer server (no one is using the computer as a personal workstation), or if you are setting up a home network and want to share the printer. Your printer manual will tell you whether printer sharing is an option.

To share a printer, take these steps:

1. Go to Apple|Chooser.
2. Select the printer you want to share.
3. Click on the Setup button.
4. The window in Figure 8.17 will appear. Select the option to Share This Printer.
5. Set a distinctive name for the printer (this name will be visible over the network). You can also designate a password that must be entered before anyone can print to the printer.
6. If desired, select Keep Log Of Printer Usage. Click on OK.

The printer is now visible over the network. Other users can access it by selecting the printer driver within the Chooser. The printer and modem ports will appear, as will any other printers using the same driver that are being shared over the network.

8. Printing

Figure 8.17   Sharing a printer.

Configuring USB Printer Sharing

Mac OS 9.1 includes the option of sharing USB printers. This feature is handy in a networked home or office environment. The USB printer driver should be installed and selected before setting up USB printer sharing. Be aware that the network needs to be TCP/IP.

To share a USB printer:

1. Open the USB Printer Sharing Control Panel.

2. Turn on USB printer sharing by clicking the Start button. The Control Panel will then look like Figure 8.18.

3. Click the tab My Printers.

4. The USB printers will be listed. If you want to share the printer, place a check in the box beside the printer.

5. Click the Options button to enable logging of printer use and to specify the details to be included in the log.

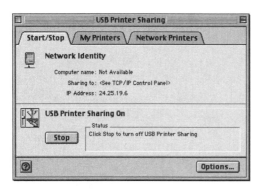

Figure 8.18   Enabling USB Printer Sharing.

6. Close the Control Panel.

The printer is now available for others to use.

TIP: Once a USB printer has been configured for sharing, other users in the network can access and print to it if the appropriate printer drivers are installed on their machines. Use Chooser to access the shared USB printer. You can also make things easy by dragging the name of the printer in the USB Printer Sharing Control Panel to the Desktop. Send the location clipping that appears to the other users. They can drag the location clipping to the Network Printers tab in the USB Printer Sharing Control Panel.

Related solution:	*Found on page:*
Configuring File Sharing and Program Linking	337

Getting Configuration Information

Mac OS 9.1 enables you to get printer information without obtaining special printer utility software. You can't make changes to the printer, but you can gain valuable information such as the IP number, amount of memory installed, PPD file in use, printer type, and printer name.

To retrieve status and configuration information, take the following steps:

1. Click the printer icon and go to the File|Get Info menu option. In the menu that branches to the right, select Status & Configuration.

2. The system will attempt to communicate with the printer to display the status in the upper window.

3. The lower window will contain printer information. Click on the Update button to retrieve configuration information from the printer. Figure 8.19 shows Status & Configuration information.

Related solution:	*Found on page:*
Getting Information About Files and Folders	145

8. Printing

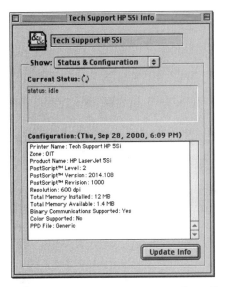

Figure 8.19   The status and configuration of a laser printer.

Getting Font Information

Most users believe that fonts are files installed within their system. Fonts, however, are also part of a printer's "operating system." In fact, you can install additional fonts in a printer.

When a font is installed on a printer, the printer recognizes and prints the document containing the font more quickly. However, when a requested font is not installed in the printer, it must be downloaded. This process increases printing time and the risk of poor output. Mac OS 9.1 includes an updated printer driver that allows you to see what fonts are installed on a PostScript printer.

To determine the fonts installed on a PostScript printer:

1. Select your printer and go to File|Get Info. In the menu that appears to the right, select Fonts.

2. The computer will communicate with the printer and produce a list of installed fonts. Figure 8.20 shows the fonts installed on a LaserWriter 16/600.

Figure 8.20   The font information window.

Chapter 9

Multimedia

In Depth

Some of you Macintosh old-timers may remember a saying that goes like this: "Macintosh *is* multimedia." This chapter covers everything in Mac OS 9.1 that makes this statement as true today as it was in 1984, including details on the latest versions of QuickTime (the Internet standard for multimedia) and ColorSync (Apple's color management architecture for the Mac OS).

Defining Multimedia

We define *multimedia* as the convergence of text, images, audio, and video in a single broadcast medium, in this case a computer. Not too long ago, we thought about multimedia only in terms of CD-ROM games. Now multimedia is more often associated with the Internet and the Web than with anything else. The Mac OS is supremely adapted for viewing multimedia over the Internet, thanks to QuickTime, a standard part of the Mac OS.

QuickTime is a series of Extensions and a Control Panel that enable you to view all the most popular multimedia file formats, including QuickTime, QuickTime VR, MP3, AVI, and MPEG. With the professional version of QuickTime, you can access additional file formats and even edit QuickTime movies. Numerous applications from third-party companies allow you to create complex movies and save them in QuickTime format for viewing over the Web or on CD-ROM. For the latest information about QuickTime, see the official Web site at **www.apple.com/quicktime/**.

Audio and Video Capabilities

All Power Macintosh computers have the ability to play basic audio and video, and some come with additional hardware components that provide more robust multimedia capabilities. The latest G4 computers sport 16MB of SD (Single Data Rate) RAM or 32MB of DDR (Double Data Rate) RAM and an AGP (Advanced Graphics Port) slot; additional multimedia capabilities found in most PowerMacs include:

- 16-bit sound
- 128-bit graphic acceleration
- 2D and 3D acceleration

9. Multimedia

- Microphone connector
- Speaker connector
- Telephony port
- NTSC, PAL, S-video, and composite support
- Dual-monitor support

Of course, you can always purchase alternative audio-visual (AV) hardware from any number of companies to provide these—and additional—capabilities. Except for a good set of speakers, which all but the Apple AV monitor lacks, the basic AV capabilities of all PowerMac computers are sufficient for viewing most of the Web's content.

TIP: *When downloading QuickTime files, Mac OS 9.1 retrieves the version (when available) that is optimal for the speed of your Internet connection.*

Most Macs also allow you to record sounds from a built-in or external microphone, CD player, or DVD player. Some older, non-PowerPC Macs don't include a sound-in port, but these models aren't capable of running Mac OS 9.1 anyway. Those that have a sound-in port accept only a monophonic microphone such as the Apple Microphone or the PlainTalk microphone. Some models have a microphone built into the computer or monitor, but these, too, are not capable of recording in stereo, for which you'll need to purchase third-party hardware and software.

QuickTime vs. QuickTime Pro

QuickTime is the heart of Mac OS 9.1's ability to play multimedia, and like most everything else these days, it comes in two versions, QuickTime and QuickTime Pro. QuickTime is free and comes with Mac OS 9.1; QuickTime Pro, on the other hand, will cost you about $30 and enable you to perform significantly more tasks. Our discussion here pertains to QuickTime Pro.

TIP: *QuickTime Pro doesn't require additional installation; a decryption key unlocks features installed as part of the standard version of QuickTime.*

We think the Pro version is worth the money. Besides, it stops that pesky advertisement—the one reminding you to purchase the Pro version—from popping up every time you launch QuickTime Player. Seriously, though, it does provide some cool features, including the capability to:

- Create and edit QuickTime movies and streaming movies
- Play and export more than 30 types of multimedia file formats

9. Multimedia

- Use filters to create special effects

- Create slide shows

The standard version is fine if you only view movies over the Web, but the Pro version opens several new doors to the world of multimedia.

QuickTime Essentials

QuickTime 4 has several components that provide just about all the multimedia capabilities you'll ever need, including the ability to open files to do the following:

- Play movies

- Navigate QuickTime VR panoramas

- View pictures

- Play audio, including MP3 files

- Explore 3D worlds using QuickDraw 3D

QuickTime's general preferences are configured through a Control Panel, as well as through a Web browser plug-in. These options enable you to use the applications discussed in the following sections to view multimedia content on your Mac.

TIP: QuickTime performance is dependent on the speed of your computer's processor, the type of video card, and the amount and type of video RAM.

QuickTime Player

The venerable MoviePlayer application has been renamed QuickTime Player because it supports so much more than just movies. When playing a movie or an audio track, as in Figure 9.1, it looks a lot different in comparison to previous versions. In fact, the Pro version allows you to selectively play the audio or video track of a movie, as well as export the movie in a wide variety of formats.

The radical changes in QuickTime Player's interface provide easy access to audio and video-enabled Web sites through the use of bookmarks for such sources as HBO and National Public Radio. QuickTime Player also allows you to add and delete bookmarks called Favorites.

PictureViewer

QuickTime 3 also includes the PictureViewer application, which uses the QuickTime component of Mac OS 9.1 to view, manipulate, and convert images into several popular file formats, including bitmap (BMP) (for Microsoft Windows) and Photoshop. Although PictureViewer is a no-frills application, it's essential for anyone

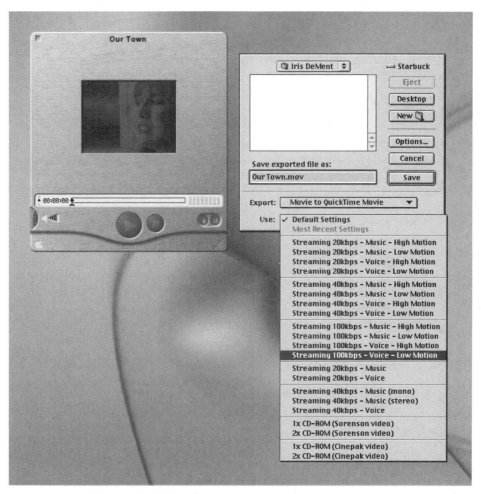

Figure 9.1   The QuickTime Player application, part of QuickTime 4.

who downloads images from the Web. Figure 9.2 shows a sample JPEG image as viewed through the PictureViewer application.

QuickTime Plug-In

The QuickTime Plug-in, also a standard part of Mac OS 9.1, enables some of the features found in the QuickTime Player application to be used in a Web browser, including Microsoft Internet Explorer and Netscape Navigator. This plug-in has its own set of controls that are configured independently of the Control Panel. Each browser may need a bit of assistance to work properly with the plug-in. Figure 9.3 shows some of the options associated with the QuickTime Plug-in.

Figure 9.2   The PictureViewer application is a handy utility and a good alternative to the popular (and no longer supported) JPEGView.

Figure 9.3   The QuickTime Web browser plug-in, as viewed through Internet Explorer.

QuickTime VR

QuickTime 4 incorporates the ability to view QuickTime VR (QTVR) movies in the QuickTime Player as well as Web browsers with the QuickTime Plug-in, a feature first introduced in version 3. For example, Figure 9.4 shows a sample QTVR file viewed in a Web browser (top) and the same file viewed in the QuickTime Player application (bottom).

QuickDraw 3D

QuickDraw 3D isn't as widely known as QuickTime. This situation will probably change in the near future, because the QuickDraw 3D metafile format (3DMF) has been chosen as the basis for the next generation of Virtual Reality Modeling Language (VRML). QuickDraw 3D, now part of QuickTime, is a cross-platform application programming interface (API) that allows Mac, Windows, and Unix users to view one version of a document on any of these platforms without modification. QuickDraw 3D images, such as the examples shown in Figure 9.5, can be exported to the QuickTime movie format or viewed using SimpleText.

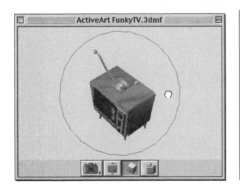

Figure 9.4   QuickTime VR files can be viewed in a Web browser window (top) or with the QuickTime Player application (bottom).

Figure 9.5   QuickDraw 3D's 3DMF format, now part of QuickTime, is also the basis for VRML 2.0 and Live3D.

QuickTime Streaming

An earlier version of QuickTime introduced the capability to stream movies over the Internet and allow recipients to start viewing the files before they completely downloaded (sometimes referred to as a "quickstart" feature). Because companies have found ways to use streaming multimedia to market products and services, this technology is becoming increasingly important. QuickTime has positioned itself very well as a standard file format to suit this purpose. QuickTime movies can be streamed using the Hypertext Transfer Protocol (HTTP) or Mac OS X Server's QuickTime Streaming Server, which uses the RTP/RTSP (Real-Time Transport/Real-Time Streaming) protocol to provide live streaming. QuickTime Pro enables you to save multiple versions of a multimedia file for streaming over the Web at different connection speeds.

---

*TIP: For more information about serving QuickTime movies live and on-demand using QuickTime Streaming Server, see **www.apple.com/quicktime/servers/qtssfaq.html**.*

QuickTime for Java

By porting QuickTime functions into Java class libraries, QuickTime for Java lets you view QuickTime documents with Java-enabled applications such as PlayMovie, shown in Figure 9.6. This capability is a tremendous boost for the Java programming community, as well as for Apple, because they both stand to gain increased interoperability and allow developers to focus on creating content for the widest possible audience.

See the QuickTime for Java Web site (**http://developer.apple.com/quicktime/qtjava/index.html**) for developer information and to download the latest version.

Figure 9.6   Any computer with a qualifying version of Java can view QuickTime movies.

Other File Formats

QuickTime is the Swiss Army knife of multimedia tools because it can open just about anything. Some of the more than 35 popular multimedia file formats that QuickTime can open and view include:

- AIFF
- AVI
- BMP
- Cinepak
- DV NTSC
- DV PAL
- DV Stream
- JPEG/JFIF
- MIDI
- mLaw
- MP3
- MPEG
- Photoshop
- PNG
- Targa
- TIFF
- WAV

Moreover, the QuickTime file format has been chosen as the basis for the MPEG-4 format by the International Organization of Standardization (ISO). Silicon Graphics, maker of the multimedia powerhouse SGI workstations, has also selected QuickTime as its preferred file format. It's a safe bet that if QuickTime doesn't support a certain file type now, it will in the future—or that specific file format isn't long for this world.

Color-Matching Issues

Color matching is a big concern in the world of multimedia (and desktop publishing). Whether you're viewing or creating multimedia, it's important for colors to be properly displayed on screen and in print. ColorSync 3, part of the default Mac OS 9.1 installation, provides more options than ever, including new monitor calibration features as well as the following:

9. Multimedia

- Photoshop plug-in support
- AppleScript support
- Multiprocessor support

A properly configured ColorSync profile will help ColorSync-savvy applications interpret colors and display or print them accordingly. The Monitor Calibration Assistant will guide you through calibrating your system and then generate a custom settings file (see Figure 9.7) that you can easily recall and use to switch among settings. This feature is useful in desktop publishing shops, where people share computers and work with dual-monitor workstations.

Enabling TV, Cable, Radio, and the Apple Video Player

Some models of Power Macintosh computers come with significantly more AV capabilities than others, and some are even cable-TV ready. Those that are cable ready will probably have the Apple Video Player—an excellent piece of software—

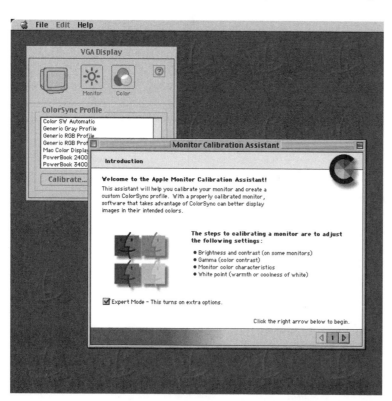

Figure 9.7   You can create and store ColorSync profiles to enhance color matching in Mac OS 9.1.

installed by default. It manages the AV hardware on your Mac and allows you to easily access cable TV, VCRs, regular TV and radio signals, camcorders, and other video- and audio-in sources. For example, Figure 9.8 shows a cable TV session, its controls, and an FM radio tuner.

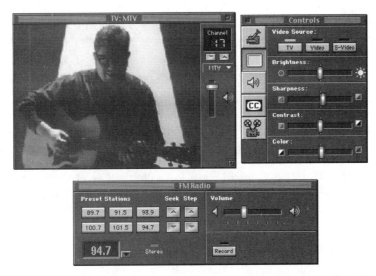

Figure 9.8   A few examples of AV hardware that you can easily add to your computer to provide additional multimedia capabilities.

Immediate Solutions

Configuring Monitors

Immediately after installing or upgrading to Mac OS 9.1, one of your first steps should be configuring the new Monitors Control Panel. (Starting with Mac OS 9, the old Monitors & Sound Control Panel was divided into two separate Control Panels, one for Monitors and one for Sound.) Figure 9.9 shows the Monitors Control Panel for a 15-inch Apple AV monitor (top) and a 19-inch ViewSonic monitor (bottom).

Several elements of the Monitors Control Panel have changed over the years. The options available to you will depend on the type of monitor that's attached to your computer (as illustrated in Figure 9.9). Note that the "Gamma" section is no

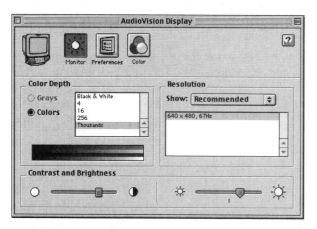

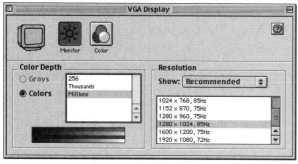

Figure 9.9   Two examples of the Monitors Control Panel, one of which has built-in AV
capability (top).

longer present, and that a button named Color appears in the upper section of the window used to configure ColorSync.

To configure the Monitors Control Panel, launch it from the Control Panels folder and follow these steps:

1. In the Monitor section (refer to Figure 9.9), choose a color depth and resolution. Additional options may be present—depending on the type of monitor you have attached—such as contrast, brightness, and additional hardware options.

2. Click the Color button to calibrate and create a display profile for a particular monitor. (If ColorSync is not installed, this button will not appear in the Monitors Control Panel.) Since monitors use different technologies to display images on screen, each monitor will have different display characteristics and will require calibration. See the section entitled "Configuring ColorSync Workflow Files" for more information on calibrating your monitor and ColorSync.

Configuring Sound

The Sound Control Panel options, formerly part of the Monitors & Sound Control Panel, will look substantially different to many users of the Mac OS (see Figure 9.10). The new Control Panel uses a tabbed interface to break out the following options:

- *Alerts*—Choose a sound as the default alert tone, record a new sound, and set the volume levels for alerts and the main system volume.

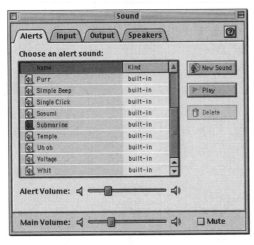

Figure 9.10   The Alerts section of the Sound Control Panel.

9. Multimedia

- *Input*—Select a source for sound input, such as CD-ROM, as well as play-through and signal level options.

- *Output*—Choose an output source such as the built-in speaker jack, AV connector, or a third-party multimedia card.

- *Speakers*—Configure your computer's internal or external speakers for balance or sound level.

To configure the various sound input and output options, open the Sound Control Panel, select the appropriate tab, and make your selections. The change will go into effect immediately. Again, depending on the make and model of your Mac and your speaker setup, your options may look a little different. For example, PowerBook and iBook users will have options for an internal microphone and speakers; Cube users will have no such options because it lacks these devices, and ships with a pair of USB-enabled external speakers. Also, AV monitors will often have software controls for bass and treble.

Configuring ColorSync Workflow Files

ColorSync allows users to create and store Workflow files, documents that describe how colors should be displayed on screen and in print. Although ColorSync isn't new to Mac OS 9.1, some of the calibration and Workflow file options are new. If you've never changed the old gamma settings in the Monitors & Sound Control Panel, you may find calibrating monitors to be a little complex. Fortunately, Apple provides well-documented configuration instructions.

Calibrating Monitors

To begin configuring ColorSync, open the Monitors Control Panel and calibrate your monitor as follows:

1. Click the Calibrate button and follow the seven or so steps required to configure your monitor's color characteristics, such as selecting the target gamma level (shown in Figure 9.11).

2. In the final step, review your settings and provide a name for your calibration.

3. Select your new profile and quit the Monitors Control Panel (see Figure 9.12).

Creating a Default ColorSync Profile

The ColorSync Control Panel uses default settings that you'll need to review and modify in order to create a usable Workflow file. To get started, launch ColorSync and follow these steps:

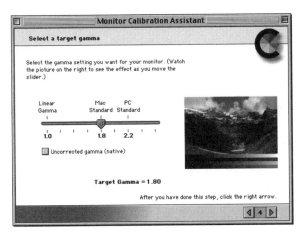

Figure 9.11   The first step in configuring ColorSync is to return to the Monitors Control Panel and calibrate your monitor.

Figure 9.12   Select a ColorSync profile in the Monitors Control Panel.

1. In the Profiles tab, configure ColorSync's Profiles For Standard Devices (shown in Figure 9.13), using the drop-down menus to select the appropriate options:

   - *Input*—Imaging device such as a digital camera or scanner
   - *Display*—Your computer's monitor, as defined in the Color section of the Monitors Control Panel
   - *Output*—Your primary printer
   - *Proofer*—Your primary printer used for proofing images

2. Next, select Default Profiles For Documents and configure the appropriate options for use with documents created using ColorSync-aware applications such as Adobe Photoshop. These options will be used only if a ColorSync profile is not attached to a document by the application with which it was created:

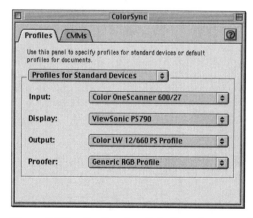

Figure 9.13   Configuring ColorSync for use with hardware input and output devices such as scanners and printers.

- *RGB Default*—Profile used for images stored using RGB (red, green, blue) values

- *CMYK Default*—Profile used for images stored using CMYK (cyan, magenta, yellow, and black) values

- *Gray Default*—Profile used for images stored using grayscale values

- *Lab Default*—Profile used for images stored using L*A*B values (a system created in the 1930s to define color values)

3. Click the CMMs tab in the ColorSync Control Panel and select a Preferred CMM (Color Matching Method). The CMMs installed in the Extensions folder will appear in the drop-down list.

4. Close the ColorSync Control Panel and save the changes when prompted.

Working with Workflow Files

ColorSync Workflow files can be edited, commented upon, and saved to file for reference with other computers. To work with a Workflow file:

1. Launch ColorSync and select File|ColorSync Workflows (or press Command+K).

2. Select an item in the ColorSync Workflows window.

3. Import, export, duplicate, delete, or activate the item by selecting the appropriate option. For example, Figure 9.14 shows a file being exported to a folder of other Workflow files.

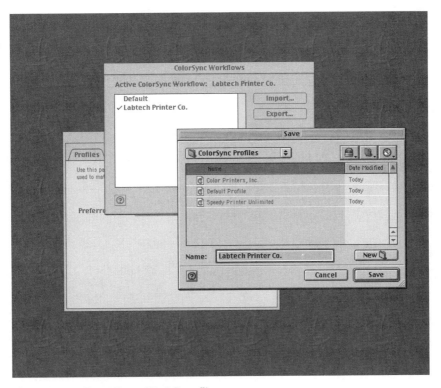

Figure 9.14   Exporting a Workflow file.

Using DigitalColor Meter

The DigitalColor Meter is a tool that allows you to sample on-screen images and translate the sampled area into industry-standard values as a means of color matching. ColorPicker Pro by Mike McNamara and Rootworks, LLC performs a similar task and is more friendly to HTML programmers. DigitalColor Meter, designed for advanced color matching in the publishing industry, matches an on-screen color to one of several industry standards, such as Pantone, CIE, and Tristimulus. Some matching features work in conjunction only with AppleVision and ColorSync monitors; RGB values, however, can be measured with any monitor.

To use the DigitalColor Meter to measure RGB color values of any element visible on your computer screen, follow these steps:

1. Launch the DigitalColor Meter application from the Monitors Extras folder, found in the Apple Extras folder.

2. Select the RGB (red, green, and blue) option.

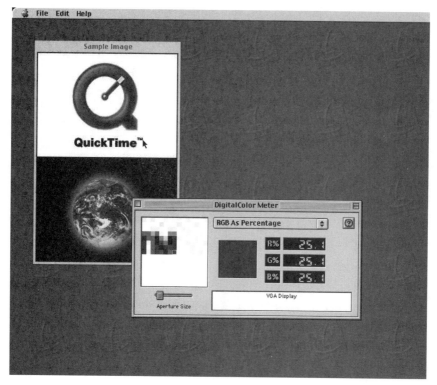

Figure 9.15   Using the DigitalColor Meter to measure a pixel's RGB color value.

3. Move the mouse pointer to any pixel on your display to display that pixel's RGB color value. For example, Figure 9.15 shows the DigitalColor Meter measuring the RGB value for the trademark symbol on the QuickTime Sample Image. An enlargement is shown in the detail window on the left side of the DigitalColor Meter window.

RGB values can be interpreted as percentages, actual values, or hexadecimal values, which are used in HTML documents to define colors in Web pages (for example, white equals #FFFFFF and black equals #000000). DigitalColor Meter allows you to view a pixel's color value by using any of these methods.

Configuring QuickTime

QuickTime is configured in two places: the QuickTime Control Panel and the QuickTime Plug-in. Some configuration information is shared between the two; perhaps someday, Apple will combine them into one configuration utility or Control Panel. The Control Panel is used to configure all QuickTime settings except for Web-browser-specific settings, which we will describe in the section entitled "Configuring QuickTime for Web Browsers" a bit further in this chapter.

To configure the QuickTime Control Panel, open the Control Panel and make the following selections:

1. In the AutoPlay section, enable or disable audio and CD-ROM AutoPlay, as in Figure 9.16. (Disabling AutoPlay is a good idea because of the AutoWorm virus, which spreads when the CD-ROM AutoPlay option is enabled.)

2. In the Browser plug-in section, you have three choices to make:
   * Should movie and sound files be played automatically or saved to disk?
   * Should the files be cached in the browser's disk cache?
   * Should kiosk be enabled (which hides control settings from within the QuickTime Plug-in when files are viewed inline)?

3. In the Connection Speed section, select an Internet connection speed to assist QuickTime in choosing from multiple files that have been optimized for streaming over the Internet (see Figure 9.17). Making the right decision here will allow you to view multimedia files more quickly.

4. In the Media Keys section, enter, edit, or delete any media keys that you have obtained to give you access to protected files (see Figure 9.18).

5. In the Music section, enter, edit, or delete music synthesizers installed on your computer. The QuickTime Music Synthesizer is installed by Mac OS 9.1 (see Figure 9.19).

6. In the QuickTime Exchange section, enable or disable the ability for QuickTime to automatically attempt to open multimedia files belonging to

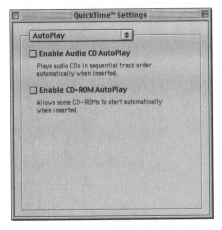

Figure 9.16   You should disable AutoPlay to prevent the AutoWorm virus from infecting your computer.

9. Multimedia

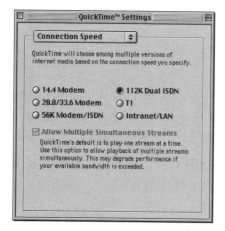

Figure 9.17   Choose the best connection speed for your computer.

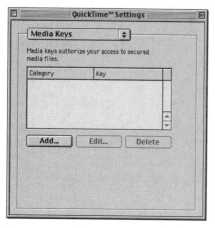

Figure 9.18   Media Keys configuration options.

other computer platforms, such as AVI files created by Windows users. Checking this option is a good idea because many non-QuickTime files are readable using QuickTime.

7. If your computer is behind a firewall that is configured to disallow the standard port assignments for QuickTime, select the appropriate options in the Streaming Proxy and Streaming Transport sections.

8. Finally, click on the About QuickTime section to see information about the version of QuickTime you're using and the technology companies Apple has partnered with to create QuickTime. Click on the Registration section to enter or reenter your QuickTime Pro registration information.

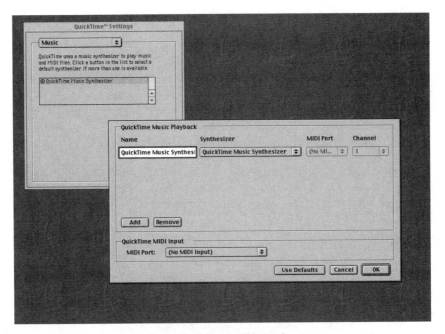

Figure 9.19   The default QuickTime Music Synthesizer.

Playing QuickTime Files with QuickTime Player

The best part about QuickTime is playing movies with the QuickTime Player. Unless you have the Pro version, playing movies is pretty much all you can do. QuickTime allows the Mac OS to recognize the most popular multimedia file types and assign the QuickTime Player creator code (TVOD) to them for easier viewing with QuickTime Player.

TIP: *The Mac OS uses creator codes to identify applications and their associated documents, such as QuickTime (TVOD), BBEdit (R*ch), and Netscape Communicator (MOSS). Each application is supposed to use a unique creator code so that when documents belonging to that application are double-clicked, they open in the appropriate application.*

To use QuickTime Player's basic functions, follow these steps:

1. Open a movie by double-clicking on its icon, or by launching QuickTime Player and choosing File|Open Movie In Player and selecting a file, as in Figure 9.20.

2. Use the controls shown in Figure 9.20 to control the basic options for a movie, including the following:

9. Multimedia

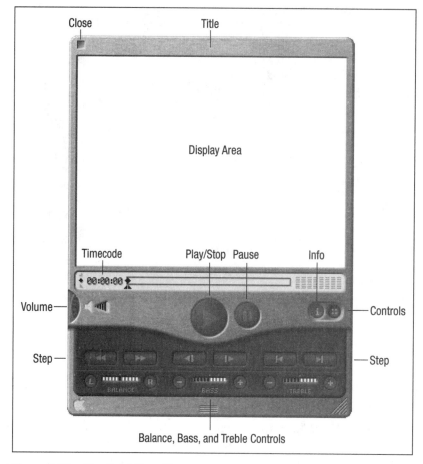

Figure 9.20   The QuickTime Player.

- *Volume control*—Increase, decrease, or mute the volume of a movie or sound track (not all movies have sound tracks, however).

- *Play/Stop button*—Start and stop a movie or sound track.

- *Timecode*—Drag the diamond to move forward or backward; Shift+drag the triangles to select a section.

- *Step controls*—Step forward or backward through a movie or sound track; click and hold to fast-forward or fast-reverse.

- *Display area* (movie files only)—Area to view movie data.

Saving and Exporting Movies with QuickTime

The standard version of QuickTime doesn't allow you to save or export movies. The Pro version, however, allows you to save files in many formats. Table 9.1 lists the import and export file types that QuickTime Pro is capable of handling for the Mac OS 9.1.

Table 9.1 QuickTime import/export file types.

Format	Import	Export
3DMF	Yes	No
AIFF	Yes	Yes
AU	Yes	Yes
Audio CD Data (Macintosh)	Yes	No
AVI	Yes	Yes
BMP	Yes	Yes
DV	Yes	No
DV Stream	No	Yes
FlashPix	Yes	No
FLC	No	Yes
GIF	Yes	No
Image Sequence movie exporters	No	Yes
JPEG/JFIF	Yes	Yes
Karaoke	Yes	No
M3U (MP3 playlist files)	Yes	No
MacPaint	Yes	Yes
Macromedia Flash	Yes	No
MIDI	Yes	Yes
MP3 (MPEG-1, Layer 3)	Yes	No
MPEG-1 (Macintosh)	Yes	No
Photoshop	Yes	Yes
PICS	Yes	No
PICT	Yes	Yes
PNG	Yes	Yes
QuickTime Image File	Yes	Yes
QuickTime Movie	Yes	Yes
SGI	Yes	Yes

(continued)

9. Multimedia

Table 9.1   QuickTime import/export file types *(continued)*.

Format	Import	Export
Sound	Yes	No
System 7 Sound	No	Yes
Targa	Yes	Yes
Text	Yes	Yes
TIFF	Yes	Yes
TIFF Fax	Yes	No
Virtual Reality (VR)	Yes	No
WAV	Yes	Yes

To save a QuickTime movie after it has been opened in QuickTime Player, follow these steps:

1. Choose File|Save As and indicate whether you want to save the movie *normally*, which creates a link to the actual data file, or as a self-contained QuickTime movie file.

2. Name the new file and select a location for it.

To export the movie into another file format, take these steps:

1. Choose File|Export, as shown in Figure 9.21.

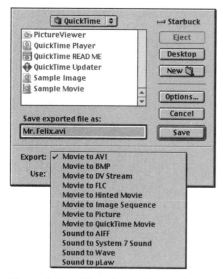

Figure 9.21   The primary Export Options settings window for exporting a QuickTime movie.

2. Choose from one of the export formats:

- Movie to AVI

- Movie to BMP

- Movie to DV Stream

- Movie to FLC

- Movie to Hinted Movie

- Sound to Image Sequence

- Sound to Picture

- Sound to QuickTime Movie

3. Next, click on the Options button in the Export dialog window, and prepare to select from a potentially long list of detailed configuration options, depending on the export format chosen. For example, some of the many export options include decisions that must be made for video tracks as well as sound tracks. Figure 9.22 shows the different options present for these two kinds of tracks.

For software and tools to help you manage QuickTime files, see the QuickTime home page at **www.apple.com/quicktime/** and the QuickTime Developer site at **http://developer.apple.com/quicktime/**.

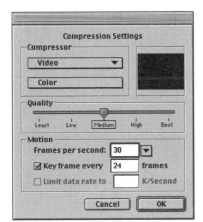

Figure 9.22   Some of the Export options for video and sound tracks in QuickTime format.

9. Multimedia

Configuring QuickTime for Web Browsers

Once configured, using the QuickTime Web browser plug-in isn't much different from using the QuickTime Player application, although the save and export features are limited in comparison. However, once a file has been saved as a QuickTime movie, you can always use QuickTime Player to perform any further conversions. Currently, the QuickTime Plug-in works with the following browsers on both Mac and Windows platforms: Netscape Navigator 3 and later; Internet Explorer 3 and later; America Online 3 and later. The plug-in allows users to view the same media types that can be viewed with the QuickTime Player.

To configure the QuickTime Plug-in, follow these steps:

1. Make sure that the QuickTime Plug-in is in your Web browser's plug-ins folder, which is usually located in the browser's application folder. Both Netscape Navigator and Microsoft Internet Explorer use Netscape plug-ins, so don't be alarmed if the plug-ins in your Internet Explorer folder have Navigator icons.

2. Open the QuickTime Control Panel, select the Browser plug-in section, and click the MIME settings button.

3. QuickTime will access the settings for your Web browser and allow you to selectively enable or disable the ability of the QuickTime Plug-in to handle each (see Figure 9.23).

4. Select OK, quit the QuickTime Control Panel, and open a sample QuickTime movie in your Web browser.

5. If you want to change the way in which your browser displays QuickTime files, you'll need to edit the Application settings (Netscape Navigator) or File Helper settings (Internet Explorer), examples of which are shown in

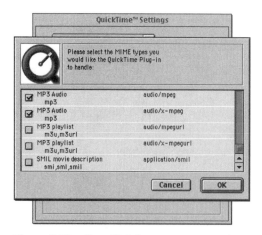

Figure 9.23   Your Web browser may need some assistance in recognizing QuickTime files, although the presence of the QuickTime Plug-in should be sufficient.

Figure 9.24. QuickTime content can be displayed using the plug-in or the application's built-in capabilities, which are limited when compared to the plug-in. Files may also be downloaded or post-processed with a user-specified application.

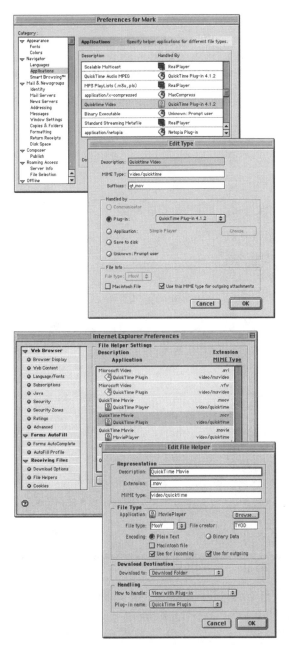

Figure 9.24   Accessing the QuickTime Plug-in's settings in Netscape Navigator (top) and Internet Explorer (bottom).

If the QuickTime Plug-in won't load, check your browser's preferences and make sure that the browser is configured to view QuickTime files via the QuickTime Plug-in, rather than trying to save the file to disk or viewing the movie with the Web browser. If the QuickTime Plug-in is properly recognized by the browser and configured to view content, the movie will begin playing. Figure 9.25 shows the controls for a movie viewed using the plug-in, as well as a shortcut to configure its settings (Figure 9.26). When you're ready to save a movie or sound file, just click on the triangle again and choose to save the files as a source (to preserve the original file format) or as a QuickTime file. The settings are only present when using the professional version of QuickTime.

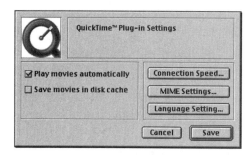

Figure 9.25   A streaming QuickTime movie view with the QuickTime Plug-in and Internet Explorer.

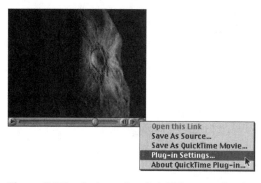

Figure 9.26   Configuring the QuickTime Plug-in settings via the plug-in's shortcut.

Viewing QuickTime VR Files

As we mentioned previously, QuickTime VR is now part-and-parcel of QuickTime, the QuickTime Plug-in, and the QuickTime Player application. Now you can view QTVR files with any QuickTime-savvy application or plug-in, just as you view a QuickTime movie. QuickTime VR movies come in three basic formats:

- *Panoramas*—These are created using a stationary camera with images taken in 360 degrees and then stitched together. For example, Figure 9.27 shows a QTVR panorama from the Martian probe Pathfinder using QuickTime Player (top) and Internet Explorer (bottom).

- *Walk-throughs*—Also called scenes, these are taken with a camera that is advanced in any direction with images stitched together as "hotspots" to navigate forward, backward, left, or right. Figure 9.28 shows a virtual tour of a street in Vancouver with a hotspot in the middle of the image.

- *Objects*—Object movies allow you to manipulate a 3D object by spinning it around, up, and down, depending on how the object movie is created. Figure 9.29 shows an object model of a famous brand of soup that would make Andy Warhol proud!

However, because QTVR files are panoramas that you can navigate through and around, the controls are a bit different from those for a regular QuickTime movie.

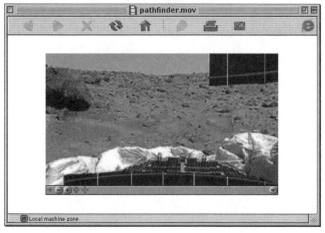

Figure 9.27   Two views of a QuickTime VR movie.

9. Multimedia

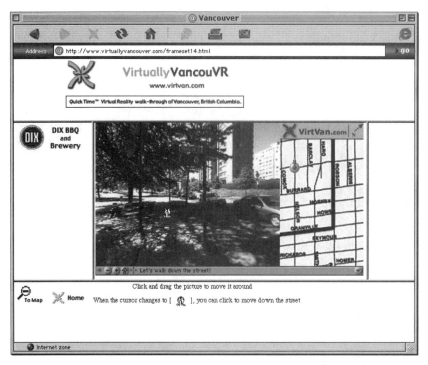

Figure 9.28   A QuickTime VR walk-through.

Figure 9.29   An object movie in QuickTime VR.

Rather than stopping and starting a QTVR movie, use the controls shown in Figure 9.30 to do the following:

- *Back*—Step backwards to the previous hot spot.
- *Zoom out*—Move further away from the image.
- *Zoom in*—Move closer to the image.
- *Reveal hotspots*—Reveal a file's hotspots.
- *Pan*—Move up, down, left, or right.

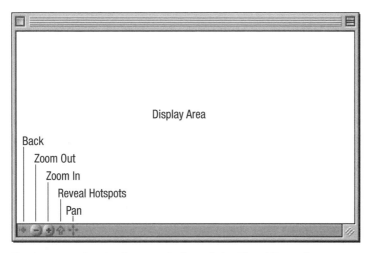

Figure 9.30   The basic controls for a QuickTime VR movie.

Viewing Images with PictureViewer

PictureViewer is a great addition to the QuickTime family because it serves as a no-frills helper application for general Internet use. You can do some basic image manipulation, such as change the size and rotate the image, as well as export images into the following formats:

- BMP
- JPEG
- MacPaint
- Photoshop
- PICT
- PNG
- QuickTime Image
- SGI Image
- TGA
- TIFF

To export an image using PictureViewer, take these steps:

1. Open an image in PictureViewer and make any changes, as in Figure 9.31, which shows an example of how you can reverse (or rotate) and image.

2. Choose File|Export, select a file format, name, and location, then select Save. All changes you make in size or perspective will be saved.

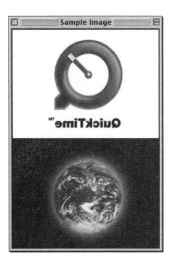

Figure 9.31   Using PictureViewer to make changes to an image.

Operating the AppleCD Audio Player

The AppleCD Audio Player has been around for a long time, and it hasn't changed a lick in Mac OS 9.1. Just as before, you can mount and play an audio CD as well as customize the playlist.

To configure a playlist with the AppleCD Audio Player, follow these steps:

1. Insert an audio CD into your computer's internal or external CD-ROM player.

2. Click on the Track List show/hide triangle to reveal the track list, as shown in Figure 9.32.

3. Enter a title for the CD, as well as a name for each track in the playlist area. You can use any name.

The user interface is about as easy as it gets, because it mimics many household CD players. The upper-left buttons of the AppleCD Audio Player are (from left to right):

- *Normal*—Plays the track in its original order, then stops.

- *Shuffle*—Reorders the tracks randomly, then stops.

- *Prog*—Allows you to program the order in which the tracks are played, as shown in Figure 9.33.

- *Repeat*—Repeats the CD over and over without stopping.

The upper-right buttons use conventional icons to start, stop, pause, jump to the previous or next track, scan forward and backward, and control volume. Also,

Figure 9.32   The AppleCD Audio Player's track list.

Figure 9.33   Use the Prog button to program your own playlist.

clicking on a track's pop-up menu allows you to skip to that track, as does double-clicking on a track number in the track list.

TIP: The playlists for your audio CDs, including programmed playlists, are stored in the Preferences folder in a file called CD Remote Programs. You should occasionally back up this file to preserve your playlists.

9. Multimedia

Manipulating QuickDraw 3D Objects

QuickDraw, QuickDraw 3D, and the QuickDraw 3D Meta File format, essential elements of Mac OS 9.1, are installed as part of Mac OS 9.1 and QuickTime. QuickDraw-savvy applications such as SimpleText and even the Scrapbook tap into the power of the 2D and 3D rendering capabilities of QuickDraw. For example, Figure 9.34 shows a SimpleText and a Scrapbook document embedded with QuickDraw 3D objects.

The QuickDraw controls, shown in Figure 9.35, are easy to use (much easier, in fact, than Netscape Navigator's LiveWorlds VRML controls):

- *Perspective*—See front, back, left, right, top, and bottom views
- *Zoom*—Zoom in or out
- *Rotate*—Move the object freely
- *Relocate*—Move the object to another region of the window

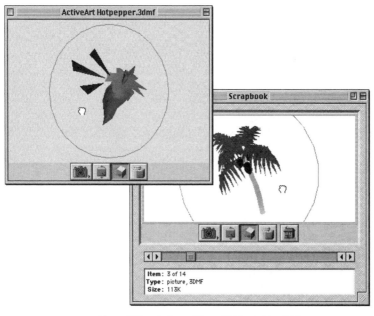

Figure 9.34   A couple of sample QuickDraw 3D objects.

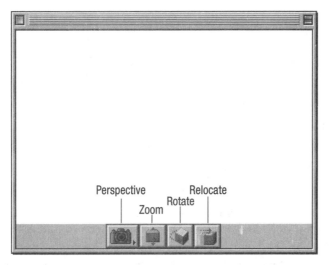

Figure 9.35   QuickDraw controls

Configuring the Apple DVD Player

All of the new G3- and G4-based computers come with a DVD-ROM player and the latest version of the Apple DVD Player; some come with a DVD-RAM player/recorder, and both will play industry-standard DVD discs. Of the many different types of DVD formats, the Apple DVD Player is capable of playing DVD Video, the industry standard, an example of which is shown in Figure 9.36. The many types of DVD formats include:

- *DVD-Video*—Full-screen, full-motion video via hardware or software compression

Figure 9.36   The Apple DVD Player.

9. Multimedia

- *DVD-ROM*—Read-only multimedia discs, capable of reading and playing CD-ROMs as well

- *DVD-RAM*—A 5.2GB storage drive that is readable and writable

- *DVD-ROM/RAM*—All the capabilities of DVD-ROM, as well as the capability of writing DVD-RAM discs (available as an option in some G4 models)

- *DVD+RW*—An erasable DVD format similar to CD-RW technology

- *DVD-R*—A DVD format that allows for one recording session up to 3.95GB

- *Divx*—A special DVD format that allows a disc to be used for a limited amount of time

The Apple DVD Player, which is very easy to use, has a few preferences that you should review. For example, Figure 9.37 shows two of the four configuration tabs for the Apple DVD Player: the Language tab, used to configure foreign language options, and the Parental Controls tab, used to provide password-protected settings that enable you to restrict the types of DVDs shown on your computer.

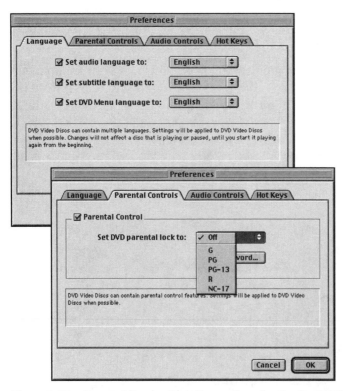

Figure 9.37   Some of the configuration options for the Apple DVD Player.

Check your computer's specifications to determine what AV hardware options are available as well as what expansion options it will accept, such as USB and FireWire ports for connecting external CD-ROM drives or digital cameras. Also look for internal PCI and expansion slots for adding decoder cards and DVD-RAM drives.

Playing Multimedia-Audio CD-ROMs

Finally, many new audio CD-ROMs come with a bonus multimedia track. It's no big surprise that the multimedia track is based on QuickTime with a front end created with Macromedia Director, one of the most popular CD-ROM gaming creation tools. Because these CD-ROMs are hybrid (audio and data) CDs, you can insert them into your Mac's CD-ROM drive and play the audio portion by using the AppleCD Audio Player, or you can follow the directions on the data portion.

For example, Figure 9.38 shows a QuickTime movie placed in the center of the screen with Macromedia controls in the lower half of the screen that allow you to advance through the CD or return to the main menu.

Because Mac OS 9.1 installs the latest version of QuickTime, you usually don't need to install anything else; you can just double-click on the application icon and start watching, listening, or interacting with the CD.

Figure 9.38   An example of an audio CD with a bonus multimedia track that features the band's videos and witticisms.

9. Multimedia

Chapter 10

Microsoft Windows Compatibility

In Depth

One of the best features of the Macintosh operating system is its ability to function in a Windows world. Apple and other developers have gone to great lengths to accommodate PC disks, files, networks, and even operating systems. As a Mac user, you have many options for working and playing well with others.

Windows Compatibility Issues

Why would you be interested in this chapter? More than 90 percent of computers run some version of Windows operating system. It's rare to find a predominantly Macintosh network, much less a network that contains only Macintosh computers. Most business environments are diverse; if you are a network administrator, you may be supporting both platforms and need to provide server access to all users. Also, we are increasingly sharing and exchanging files electronically, unaware of what operating system is on the other end. Perhaps the most important reason you are interested in this chapter is that you want access to all those great games without buying a new system.

File Problems

Sharing files between platforms can be a huge headache. If you can acknowledge this fact up front, you can learn to deal with problems such as Windows applications that use identical file extensions, unfamiliar document extensions, and the DOS-based 8.3 naming convention.

File Extensions

Some file extensions are exclusive to certain applications. For example, in the PC world, the .xls extension indicates that the document is in some way associated with Microsoft Excel. On the other hand, some extensions can be associated with more than one application. The .txt extension indicates a plain-text file, which can be opened by any number of programs, from SimpleText to Microsoft Word 98. The monkey wrench appears when you have proprietary applications assigning similar document extensions. The .doc extension indicates a word-processing document. Although it is most commonly associated with Microsoft Word, the extension is also used with Lotus Word Pro. However, the files cannot be opened cleanly between applications. Microsoft Word 98 doesn't even list Lotus Word Pro as a translation format.

Unknown Files

Occasionally, you will receive files with an unrecognizable extension. If possible, contact the person who gave you the file for more information. Otherwise, you can open the file within a text editor and browse the file to look for hints about the application that created the file. Some Windows applications identify themselves near the top or bottom of the file. Later in this chapter, we discuss how you can educate your Mac to deal with new or unfamiliar file formats.

WARNING! You should be aware that email attachments have become the preferred method for transporting computer viruses. In the summer of 2000, lots of people received a message saying "I Love You." The message included a file attachment containing Visual Basic script. When run, the attachment managed to delete files from the computer. The email was not dangerous to Macintosh users, but was a lesson on how to deal with unknown attachments: Don't open them. If you don't recognize it, contact the sender for more information before handling the attachment.

8.3 Naming Conventions

The number 8.3 refers to the DOS file-naming convention that limited you to eight characters in the file name, followed by a period and a three-character file extension. You weren't obligated to create a file name that was exactly eight characters long or to have an extension, but 8.3 was the maximum length of the file name. Windows 95 introduced long file names for the Windows community, but fat32—as it was known—was not understood by the Macintosh PC/DOS mounting software until Mac OS 8.1. You will find this restrictive naming convention on some CD-ROMs that use the ISO 9660 format. Level 1 of this standard used the 8.3 file name and was even more restrictive in its use of characters within the file name (the only characters allowed were the letters A through Z, the numbers 0 through 9, and the hyphen). Level 2 allowed long file names but still disallowed certain characters. To guarantee that the greatest number of users can view your documents, use the 8.3 naming convention. At the very least, use conventional file name extensions so Windows programs can properly translate the file.

File Format Issues

Mac and Windows users exchange files in a variety of methods: We send them through email, hand them over on disk, save them on local servers, and FTP them to remote servers. In some situations, we print them and exchange hard copies. Whatever the method, a variety of obstacles can arise in the exchange process. Table 10.1 shows some file formats that are considered "safe" because they have a good success rate of manipulation between platforms.

If you know the platform, operating system, or software application of the other user, you should do your best to accommodate him or her by saving the file in an easy-to-read format. In the Save As dialog box, you'll usually find a Save File As

Table 10.1   Safe file formats.

Application Type	File Format
Word processors	RTF, DOC
Bitmapped graphic	TIFF, GIF, and JPEG
Vector art	Generic EPS or export as safe bitmap
Spreadsheet	Excel 3 or 4, DIF, dBASE3, comma- or tab-delimited
Database	Comma- or tab-delimited, dBASE3

Type pop-up menu that lists other file formats. Figure 10.1 shows the list of file formats available for Microsoft Word 98.

If the application's developers have designed the product with both the Mac and Windows platforms in mind—and if the company releasing it makes a good-faith effort to keep both platforms synchronized—then saving files in the appropriate format is easy. In many cases, the program can open the file without any effort from you and save it in a special format. As the Windows platform has become dominant, however, the reality is that the Macintosh version of the software is often released well after the Windows version (case in point: Windows Office 2000 was released in 1999, but Office 2001 for the Mac was released in the latter half of 2000).

In most cases, you can save the file normally and easily exchange it with a Windows-using coworker. Problems arise when it's returned to you, however, because most programs are written to be backward compatible, not forward compatible. For example, Microsoft's Office 97, the updated software suite for Microsoft Office 4, was released for Windows 95 users only. Mac users were still running Word version 6 or even 5.1, which made exchanging files between the two operating systems precarious. Microsoft eventually wrote a translator that enabled Word 6 for Macintosh to open Word 97 for Windows files. However, Macintosh users couldn't save files in the Word 97 format. This created lapses in work productivity because

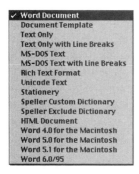

Figure 10.1   A listing of file formats in Microsoft Word 98.

files had to be constantly converted to the accessible formats. Finally, the scales were balanced in 1998 when Microsoft released Office 98 for the Macintosh.

It's a good idea to have an advance plan for dealing with gaps between Windows and Mac versions of software. Because no one can think of every eventuality, however, you may want to take advantage of software that can translate and convert files for your use even if the application in which they originated isn't on your computer. Mac OS 9.1 includes a file translator in the File Exchange Control Panel. This Control Panel, which is preconfigured with many standard file extensions, will launch the appropriate application for the document you want to open. You can also purchase a commercial utility, such as MacLinkPlus Deluxe from DataViz (**www.dataviz.com**), that can convert files in unknown formats into files that your computer can understand.

SuperDrive

The SuperDrive is actually the official name of your floppy drive. Once considered standard equipment on a Macintosh, floppy drives are no longer included in the iMac and G4 series. The SuperDrive is capable of reading data from, writing data to, and formatting several file formats, including the following:

- Macintosh
- ProDOS
- DOS

The SuperDrive can also read from and write to 1.6MB formatted disks for Windows 95. However, file naming has not always been reliable. Previous versions of PC Exchange, the utility used to mount non-Mac volumes, couldn't handle the long file-name format used by Windows 95 and Windows NT. It instead displayed the truncated 8.3 naming convention. However, in all versions of the Mac OS since 8.1, this shortcoming has been eliminated.

In this age of the floppyless Macintosh, the Imation SuperDisk has taken over the role previously played by the SuperDrive. The SuperDisk can handle and format Mac and PC disks. Imation also manufactures the Zip disk's major competitor, the SuperDisk diskette. The SuperDisk diskette looks very much like a floppy disk, but holds 120MB of data and can be formatted for the Mac or PC.

File Exchange Control Panel

When SuperDrives were first installed in Macs, you had to use a utility called Apple File Exchange to put information on PC-formatted disks. The PC disks would not mount on the Desktop, however. The PC Exchange utility, which enabled you to mount and manage a PC-formatted disk, was the answer. Figure 10.2 shows a PC-formatted disk on the Desktop. Note that the initials "PC" are the only difference between a Mac and non-Mac disk icon.

Figure 10.2   A DOS floppy disk on a Macintosh Desktop.

With PC Exchange, you could easily mount DOS disks and media on the Desktop, and any application could recognize and use them. This was also true for other removable media, including Zip and Jaz disks, CD-ROMs, and SyQuest removable hard drives. PC Exchange could also be configured to open a corresponding application whenever you double-clicked on a file bearing a particular three-character extension.

PC Exchange worked hand-in-hand with the Mac OS Easy Open Control Panel. This Extension employed translation databases, such as those created by DataViz, to search and locate the application that could open the file. If Mac OS Easy Open could not locate an exact match, it notified you and suggested other applications for launching the program.

TIP: *Actually, it isn't harmful to work exclusively with PC disks and media; in some settings, it's entirely appropriate (such as in a computer-lab environment, where you may need to use PCs, Macs, and even Sun computers). The one drawback is that it takes longer for the Mac OS to open PC disks than Mac disks.*

In Mac OS 9.1, PC Exchange and Mac Easy Open are combined in the File Exchange Control Panel. The file mappings within File Exchange are also displayed within the Internet Config Control Panel, and can be modified from either Control Panel. The PC Exchange portion, distinguished by the tab of the same name, now contains a huge library of file extension mappings. As new programs are developed and released, you can customize File Exchange to include appropriate file mappings. The File Translation tab contains many options that were originally found in Mac OS Easy Open. It allows you to set options for file translations as well as add mappings for new programs as they are released.

MacLinkPlus Deluxe

MacLinkPlus Deluxe from DataViz is a commercial package that enhances File Exchange. It converts many different file formats, including image and HTML files and email attachments (probably the most difficult files to handle). An extensive database of file extensions built into MacLinkPlus enables it to locate the appropriate software to open the document. DataViz continues to upgrade the product with a larger library of translators. Although previous versions of the Mac OS included MacLinkPlus, it is no longer bundled with the installation. You can purchase MacLinkPlus Deluxe at **www.dataviz.com**. The cost per copy is approximately $100, but if you work with Windows users extensively it will be a worthwhile purchase.

Graphic Converter

File Exchange is preconfigured to launch certain applications when you open a file with a particular extension. One of these applications, Graphic Converter, is a shareware utility that can import over 100 image file formats and save files in roughly 40 formats. It can also perform editing functions, such as creating a transparent GIF image (*transparent* means that a certain color in the image disappears; in a Web page, this can eliminate the white box around a graphic). It can open and save several Windows file formats including BMP, as well as cross-platform files such as GIF and JPEG. It can also do file conversions in batches, and even manage some movie and animation files. If you don't have the time or money to spend on a big graphics-editing program, Graphic Converter is certainly an excellent alternative. You can download Graphic Converter from most Macintosh software sites, including **www.macdownload.com**.

Zip Files

More and more of us are retrieving files from the Internet, and many of those files are compressed. Macintosh files are routinely compressed using StuffIt Deluxe from Aladdin Systems, Inc. You can recognize these archives by their file extension, which is usually .sit. In the PC world, most files are compressed with PKZIP or WinZip, both recognizable by the .zip extension. For some of us, it's difficult to think of Zip files as anything other than applications that, of course, do not run on your Mac. However, you can certainly use audio files from the Web's huge sound archives; many of these files may be zipped archives. You can also find sites that contain free clipart and images, which may also be compressed as a Zip file. As a Mac user, you've learned to live with the fact that although you can easily download a Zip file to your computer, you may have to move the file to a disk and then decompress it on a PC. Good news: This is no longer necessary, thanks to excellent shareware and freeware utilities, such as the following, that can unzip these files:

- *ZipIt*—A shareware utility that also can decompress and compress Zip files, as shown in Figure 10.3.

- *StuffIt Deluxe and Drop Stuff (with Expander Enhancer)*—These two utilities can open Zip files as well as tar and gzip files.

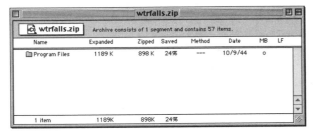

Figure 10.3   ZipIt in action.

Unix Files

In the Unix world, most files are compressed in the gzip or tar format. MacGZip is a freeware utility that can open archives and create new ones. It is available at most Macintosh software archives, including **http://download.cnet.com**. StuffIt Expander can also decompress these files.

Network Access

No man is an island—at least not in our networked environments. Sharing information as simply as possible with as many users as possible is the primary reason for setting up your own computer as a server or attaching to one on the network.

Setting up your computer so that other Mac users can access your files is simple. The difficulties arise when you need to access Windows or Novell servers, which run programs that allow you to access the file system. However, some environments may not be friendly to the AppleTalk or TCP/IP protocol. If you cannot convince your system administrator to run Macintosh-friendly programs on the server, you can install applications and Extensions such as DAVE and NetWare Client for MacOS that will help you access the servers you need.

DAVE

DAVE, a utility from Thursby Software Systems, Inc., uses the TCP/IP protocol to connect machines. TCP/IP has become the standard method of communication over the Internet. By focusing on this protocol, DAVE allows you to access Windows NT servers as well as Windows 95 and 98 machines; it also allows Windows users to access your files. You can even access other Macintosh computers via a TCP/IP connection. Using the Network Browser, you can attach to other Windows machines and utilize the Domain Logon feature to log on to an NT Server domain, thus gaining access to the resources and servers in that domain. DAVE also features a messaging service that allows you to send and receive short messages in pop-up windows. This service is very useful for broadcasting important messages regarding the server status. DAVE also supports AppleScripting for automating the mounting and dismounting of volumes. More information about DAVE can be found at **www.thursby.com**.

NetWare Client for Mac OS

Although Windows NT servers are gaining in popularity, Novell servers are very common and have been around for a long time. In many cases, the administrator may have activated the NetWare-loadable modules necessary to allow Macintosh computers to access, read, and write files to the server and run applications from it. In some cases, however, this application may not have been enabled (some network administrators are skittish about confidential servers appearing in

AppleTalk zones). By installing the NetWare client, you can access any server to which you have been granted rights. The client enables your computer to speak IPX, the language of Novell. You also increase your functionality by using this client rather than relying on AppleTalk access. The NetWare client is developed and maintained by Prosoft Engineering (**www.prosofteng.com/netware.asp**).

Running Windows on a Mac

In the average business environment, you're likely to encounter specialized software that has been customized to enable the company to perform unique work processes efficiently. This type of innovation requires skill, hard work, and money. Unfortunately, Macintosh users definitely find themselves at a disadvantage when it comes to these specialized programs. In cases where Macintosh clients are created, they are often buggy and unstable. This happens because the program may have been created and customized for a Windows client, then "ported" to the Mac OS platform. Because the application wasn't written specifically for the Mac OS, the software is often slow, unstable, and downright ugly. In fact, several software developers label themselves as "enterprise" companies, which means that their products are written to work on all popular platforms. Between the lines, however, you may detect the very scenario we describe here. In fact, a site-license purchaser often has to balance the economical questions of a do-it-all package versus the "best-of-breed" (but more expensive) approach. In today's "do-more-with-less" atmosphere, you can guess that the cheaper (but not-as-good packages) usually win.

To make matters worse, the Mac OS platform is often not supported at all. Mac users who are scrambling for a solution frequently end up running Windows in some fashion. You can do so in two ways:

- You can run Windows using a client that emulates Windows, such as SoftWindows 98 or Virtual PC.

- You can run Windows by installing a PC expansion card.

Emulation Clients

The cheaper—but slower—solution is to run Windows in emulation mode. If you occasionally need to run a particular Windows application, you may want to consider this option. An *emulator* is a software application that runs Windows within your Mac OS environment. One of the first emulation packages was SoftPC (no longer available) from Insignia Solutions. Insignia later created SoftWindows and SoftWindows 95/98. SoftWindows 95/98, which includes Windows software, certainly makes installation a little easier. However, the price of the software reflects this. SoftWindows products, including SoftWindows and RealPC, are now available through FWB software at **www.fwb.com**.

Virtual PC from Connectix approaches emulation a little differently. Because it emulates the entire PC, rather than just a particular operating system, you can run any operating system that will run on a PC. In fact, Virtual PC can run Windows NT and Windows 2000, the business user's operating system of choice. Connectix even has a version of VirtualPC that includes Red Hat Linux. Provided you have a large amount of RAM and disk space as well as a fast processor, you can successfully run Windows 95/98/NT while also performing tasks on your Mac. Figure 10.4 shows Virtual PC running Windows 95. You can find more information about Virtual PC at **www.connectix.com**.

You can also use emulation clients for fun. In fact, one of the biggest reasons people want a DOS or Windows solution is so that they can play all the games that are out there. Some very economical solutions are available to do so.

FWB, the distributors of SoftWindows, also sells a product called RealPC (available at **www.fwb.com**). Although Real PC is capable of running any DOS or Windows application (provided you have purchased a Windows license), it is targeted for the recreational user who occasionally wants to play a game or two. Real PC, economically priced, comes with several games.

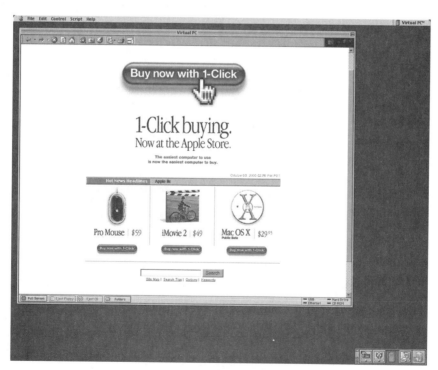

Figure 10.4   Virtual PC running Windows 95.

Virtual Game Station from Connectix is hands-down one of the most interesting gaming products to come along. It allows you to emulate the Sony Playstation on your Macintosh. You can play many games that in the past could only be played on the Playstation console. And it's economically priced at $49.95, much cheaper than the original Playstation.

You can also find free emulation packages. For example, if you are in the grip of nostalgia and want to play some of the old arcade games, you can run an emulation package called MacMAME, which attempts to reproduce the 1980s experience of playing arcade games. It allows you to run hundreds of arcade games and is frequently updated to add support for additional games. Figure 10.5 shows MacMAME running the old "why did the frog cross the road" diversion.

PC Cards

A few years ago, PC compatibility cards were popular with Macintosh users. They are not as popular today because you can purchase an entire computer for the cost of the card (approximately $600). However, if you find that Windows is fast becoming a part of your daily life but you just don't have the desk space for another computer, you may want to consider a hardware solution. The biggest benefit of installing a PC card is the fact that it runs almost separately from the Mac OS—yet information can still be shared between the two environments. The PC

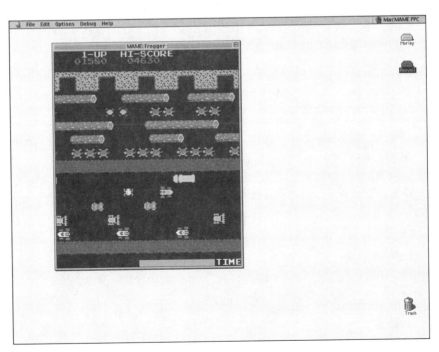

Figure 10.5 MacMAME running an arcade game.

card has its own memory and uses a portion of hard drive space allocated to it. It allows you to begin a process within the Windows environment and then switch to the Mac OS and continue performing other tasks. PC cards also support separate monitors and even separate keyboards, as well as other peripheral devices such as joysticks.

Orange Micro was the major distributor of PC compatibility cards. Unfortunately, Orange Micro has discontinued its line of PC cards. However, their cards are still available at many Macintosh online retailers. Go to **www.orangemicro.com** to determine whether a PC card can meet your needs.

Apple also manufactured DOS compatibility cards, but no longer supports them. Fraser Valley Distributed Computing Systems updated the original software, renamed it pcSetup, and continues to update the appropriate drivers and files for both the Mac and Windows components. You can purchase pcSetup software from **www.pcsetup2x.com**.

Client/Server Issues

Businesses often use the client/server model for productivity. Consequently, some platforms do not receive the development needed to produce a decent application, or are not supported at all. When this happens, users are often forced to use an operating system that they neither know nor like. They are advised to purchase emulators or PC cards or are told to switch platforms. However, if the affected user base is large enough, alternative solutions are available.

Browsers

One of the trends in the client/server industry is to develop clients with a Web browser interface. As long as the developer adheres to Internet standards, the resulting application should be accessible by Mac and Windows users via Web browsers. In the recent past, developers created applications for one platform (usually Windows) and ported to the other platforms (usually Mac and Unix). The results were mixed. Web browser client interfaces don't have this problem. As a side benefit, your productivity isn't dependent on one computer. As long as you can launch a Web browser, you can send information to and retrieve information from the server.

Java Applications

Some software companies are writing applications that will work effectively in a Web browser capable of running Java. By doing so, an application could truly be universal and not necessarily rely on a particular platform. Of course, this solution does require extensive programming, and Java standards seem to change daily. Nonetheless, this approach looks promising, and Mac OS 9.1 continues to improve its Java support.

WinFrame and MetaFrame

Several large companies that release specialized software have stated up front that they will not release software for a particular platform or operating system. In many cases, the Macintosh platform is the first item on the black list (some of these same companies still provide OS/2 and Windows 3.1 software!). As these specialized applications become larger and larger, even Windows users are finding that they need a better way to accommodate these disk space and memory monsters. WinFrame by Citrix is an excellent solution to this category of user needs. WinFrame works in two parts. Part one of WinFrame is a thin client that is installed on your computer. Part two is a WinFrame server. WinFrame is actually a customized version of the Windows NT 3.51 server software. When launched, the client accesses a WinFrame server and then begins a session that appears to be running locally on the computer but is actually executing from the server. WinFrame supports multiple platforms, including Macintosh and Unix. The WinFrame client is so thin that it barely takes any bandwidth on the network. It can even run successfully over a modem connection.

MetaFrame is an update of WinFrame, but is based on Windows NT 4. It runs on Windows 2000, and is an improvement over WinFrame in that WinFrame resembles a Windows 3.x user environment.

Expense is the drawback to these solutions. WinFrame and MetaFrame require a dedicated server and—depending upon your user base—you may want to dedicate more than one server to this purpose. However, if you have a large group of users frustrated by emulation and PC cards, these solutions may be worthwhile.

Color Differences

The uniform color table is one of the biggest and most-undisputed advantages that Mac users can claim. Although differences will inevitably arise when viewing a particular color from Macintosh to Macintosh and even monitor to monitor, the Macintosh color palette has been standardized. This is great if you're preparing and exchanging images with other Mac users. However, the Windows color palette uses a different interpretation of color, so that the color red on your computer may look orange-red on a PC. For this reason, if you're creating images for Web documents that will be viewed on Windows computer systems, check your Web page on the Windows platform. Be prepared for a shock. You may not like the results.

Macintosh Advocacy

Apple is devoted to working with software developers and encouraging them to begin or continue developing applications for the Macintosh platform. Your business may have only a few users who are affected by the lack of Macintosh platform support, but remember: Thousands of users like you are eager for more Macintosh-friendly products. Your combined voices could be very persuasive. By contacting Apple, you may be adding fuel to the fire that could justify the development of software for the Macintosh platform. You can find out more information about programs made for the Mac and development information at **http://guide.apple. com/usindex.html**.

Immediate Solutions

Formatting DOS Disks

If you have a Mac with a disk drive (many newer Macs don't have them) and anticipate sharing information with anyone via disk, you need to know how to create a DOS-formatted floppy disk in Mac OS 9.1. Your files will be handled just fine, and you can continue using the disk on your computer (just make sure you back up the data—disks do not have a long life).

To create a DOS-formatted floppy disk in Mac OS 9.1:

1. Insert a disk in the drive.

WARNING! Make sure the disk you're using does not contain files that you need to keep.

2. Select the disk icon, and then go to the Special menu and choose Erase Disk. (This menu selection also works on other media, including hard drives.)

3. The Erase Disk dialog box will appear. Select DOS 1.4MB and click on the Erase button, as shown in Figure 10.6.

4. You will see a series of messages informing you of the status of the formatting process. After the disk has been reformatted as a PC disk, the icon will change, as shown in Figure 10.7. You can now store data on the disk.

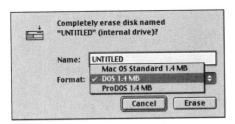

Figure 10.6   Choosing the correct format.

Figure 10.7   The Desktop disk icon, before (left) and after (right) formatting.

Zip disks are erased in the same manner. Keep in mind, however, that you may need to download the Tools software from Iomega (**www.iomega.com**) in order to change the format of the disk from Mac to PC.

Related solution:	*Found on page:*
Mounting and Dismounting Floppy Disks	143

Editing File Exchange Entries

The File Exchange Control Panel already contains an extensive library of file mappings. However, you may have a different application in mind for opening files bearing a particular three-character extension.

To edit the existing File Exchange entries to launch your preferred application, follow these steps:

1. Go to the Apple menu and select Control Panels|File Exchange (if necessary, select the PC Exchange tab).

2. Select the entry you wish to edit and then click on the Change button (see Figure 10.8).

3. After searching the hard drive for other appropriate applications, File Exchange will display the dialog box shown in Figure 10.9. Choose the application you want to use to open the file and click on the Select button.

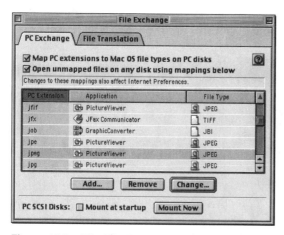

Figure 10.8   The File Exchange window.

Figure 10.9   The Change Mapping window.

4. A new dialog box will appear. Locate the application and click on the Select button.

5. Now add the application information. Click on the Change button to accept your changes.

Adding File Exchange Entries

As new applications are written, you will need to add file extension mappings to the database already included with File Exchange. To do so, follow these steps:

1. Go to the Apple menu and select Control Panels|File Exchange (if necessary, select the PC Exchange tab).

2. Click on the Add button.

3. Type the extension that you want to add (see Figure 10.10).

4. Click on the Select button and locate the application that you want to use to open the file.

5. After you have located the application and it is highlighted, click on the Select button.

6. Click on the Add button to accept your new entry. Figure 10.11 shows the new addition listed with the other file extension mappings.

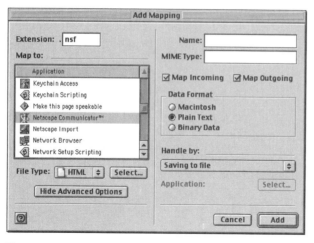

Figure 10.10 Entering the new extension.

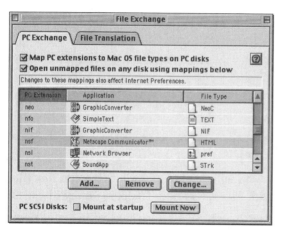

Figure 10.11 The new addition to the PC Exchange Panel.

Editing the File Translation in File Exchange

The File Translation part of File Exchange goes a step beyond file extension mapping. It also converts certain files to a particular file format, provided the file has a resource fork (this dictates that the file was created on another Mac). If the file is in the Windows format, File Exchange will attempt the translation based on the file extension. If it doesn't recognize the format, it will tell you that your only option is to open the file in the application that created it.

Use the following steps to modify File Exchange entries.

1. Go to the Apple menu and select Control Panels|File Exchange (if necessary, select the File Translation tab).

2. Click on the Add button. A dialog box prompts you to locate an example file. We've selected a GIF image, shown in Figure 10.12.

3. A window displays with the message shown in Figure 10.13. Locate the application you want to be linked to the example file and click on OK.

4. When the process has finished, you should see the new File Translation option listed (see Figure 10.14).

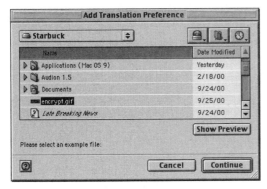

Figure 10.12   Selecting an example file.

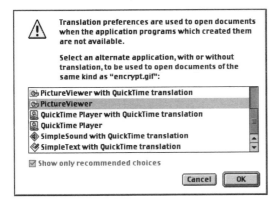

Figure 10.13   Selecting the appropriate application.

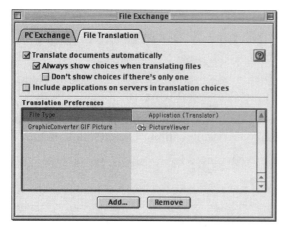

Figure 10.14   The new File Translation configuration.

Using MacLinkPlus Deluxe

If you really want to cover all the bases when it comes to file translation, you should definitely consider MacLinkPlus Deluxe. It's worth the expense for the additional extension translations, and is very easy to configure using the following steps:

1. Go to the Apple menu and select Control Panels|MacLinkPlus.

2. Look at the two options, but accept the defaults. Figure 10.15 shows the default configuration options (in case you play with the drop-down menus and then forget what the default was).

3. MacLinkPlus is now ready for action.

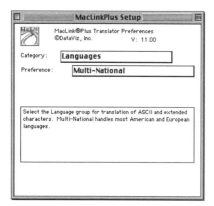

Figure 10.15   MacLinkPlus.

Using GraphicConverter

Do you want to do a little image editing but don't have the money for a copy of Photoshop? GraphicConverter, an excellent shareware application, not only includes some nifty image editing features, but also can import and export a huge number of image formats. It can open just about any image file, including Windows and Unix formats. If you locate a new format that the software can't handle, contact the author of GraphicConverter at **www.lemkesoft.com**. He really puts a lot of effort into keeping this utility up to date.

Just to get your feet wet, here is a simple file-import and -export session:

1. Launch GraphicConverter (you can also double-click on the image file in question).

2. Select File|Open. Locate your file, and open it with GraphicConverter.

3. The image will display in a window, similar to the window shown in Figure 10.16 (several other tool windows give you additional information about the image).

4. Edit the image if you like, or go ahead and switch it to another format by choosing File|Save As to view the Save window.

5. Click on the drop-down menu beside the word "Format" to choose from over 40 file types. For Figure 10.17, we chose the GIF format.

6. If necessary, click on the Options button to choose additional settings for the image. See Figure 10.18 for some GIF options. When you have finished, click on Save to create the new image.

TIP: *GraphicConverter automatically adds the appropriate extension to your file. However, you can change this to suit your needs. For example, you can make the file name extension three letters instead of four.*

Figure 10.16   An open image in GraphicConverter.

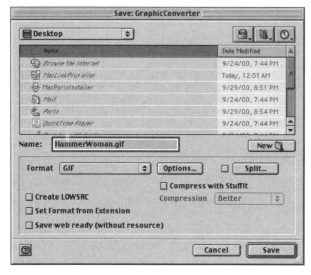

Figure 10.17   Choosing the GIF image format.

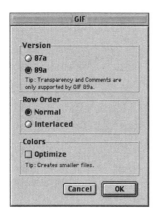

Figure 10.18   Additional GIF options.

Decompressing a ZIP File

The majority of PC files online or in network transfers are compressed. You can recognize them by the .zip extension. Because many of these files are universal, you can use them on your Macintosh.

Try using StuffIt Expander from Aladdin Software. You've probably been using it to open Macintosh files, but as the following steps will show, StuffIt Expander can also decompress files with the .zip extension:

1. Download your file.

2. Drag the downloaded file icon over the StuffIt Expander icon.

3. You will see a progress bar indicating files and folders that have been decompressed.

4. When the file has been decompressed, StuffIt Expander will quit on its own.

Creating a Zip File

Let's say that you need to create some archived or zipped files. You need a utility that can compress files. Consider using another great utility written for the Macintosh—the shareware program ZipIt. You can use ZipIt to decompress files (like StuffIt Expander, it features drag-and-drop expanding) and create new archives. It can even preserve the resource fork in your files. Moreover, if you need to distribute your archive via floppy disks, ZipIt can break the archive into manageable chunks.

To create a Zip file, take these steps:

1. Launch ZipIt. An empty archive will appear. Use this window to decompress zipped documents or add files to an archive.

2. Go to the Zip menu and select Add.

3. The window in Figure 10.19 will appear. Choose the files or folders you want to add (you can continue adding all files for the archive within this dialog box). When you are finished, click on Done.

4. Go to the File menu and select Save.

5. If necessary, change the file name and click on the Save button (note that ZipIt adds the .zip extension automatically). ZipIt also allows you to create self-extracting archives for Mac and PC users.

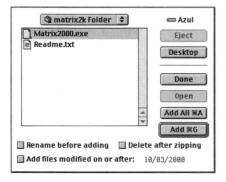

Figure 10.19   Adding items to the Zip archive.

You have now created an archive that can be opened from a PC. This is a useful tool for exchanging compressed files between Mac and PC users.

Installing a PC Coprocessor Card

So, you've decided that you need to run Windows. However, you don't have the money or the desk space for two computers. If you choose to purchase a PC coprocessor card, you will find that it runs at competitive speeds and can put Windows access, even Windows NT, within reach. Unfortunately, Orange Micro, the leading vendor of PC coprocessor cards, has discontinued its line of PC cards. Orange Micro still provides excellent drivers for its products so that you can really work between the two environments. Figure 10.20 shows the PC side of the computer, running in a window within Mac OS 9.1.

If you already have an Orange Micro PC coprocessor card, we recommend that you follow its enclosed instructions. However, what follows are some general instructions for installing the card:

Figure 10.20   The PC side of a Macintosh in which an Orange Micro card has been installed.

1. With the computer turned off, install the card in the expansion slot of your PowerMacintosh. You may need to connect additional wiring, such as video and sound cables, to take advantage of multimedia processes.

2. Turn the computer on and install the software necessary for the Mac to access the Orange PC card.

3. Launch the application OrangePC and configure the PC environment (Figure 10.21 shows an example of the configuration options).

4. Switch to the PC side of your Mac and install the operating system of choice, as well as any specialized drivers, for communicating with the Mac OS.

5. You should be able to run Windows and the Mac OS at the same time. To switch between the environments, you can use the menu provided in the OrangePC application or see the next section for keystroke combinations. Figure 10.22 shows the OrangePC Commands menu.

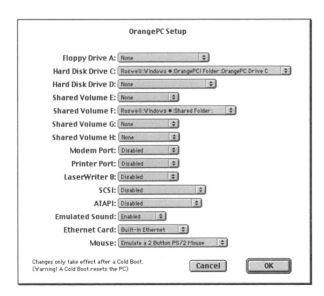

Figure 10.21   Setting up the OrangePC card.

Figure 10.22   The OrangePC Commands menu.

Key Combinations for PC Coprocessor Cards

Keystroke combinations are the preferred method of accessing the PC environment from the Mac OS and vice versa. Use Table 10.2 as a handy reference guide.

Table 10.2   Common keystroke combinations for PC cards.

Command	Function
Command+E	Eject a floppy disk (works on all PC cards)
Command+Y	Eject the CD (use with Apple-style DOS cards)
Command+Return	Switch between PC and Mac environment (use with Apple-style DOS cards)
Command+D	Switch between PC and Mac environment (use with the OrangePC)
Command+M	Switch to Macintosh menus
Command+F	Select a floppy image file (use with the OrangePC)
Command+U	Eject the CD (use with the OrangePC)
Command+R	Reboot the OrangePC

Installing a Windows Emulator

If running an emulator seems intimidating, you may want to remember that in reality, it's just one more software program running on your Mac. It just takes a little longer to set up, as the following steps will show. It is also the most common method of running Windows on a Mac:

1. Insert the software CD in the drive and run the installer program.

2. If necessary, reboot the computer and then launch the emulator application. It's that easy.

Emulators such as SoftWindows95 and Virtual PC come with an operating system that allows you to be productive immediately. You can install a different operating system, of course. Virtual PC can even run Windows 2000 or Red Hat Linux.

Deleting Resource Forks

Files on the Mac OS are made up of two parts: the data fork and the resource fork. The *data fork* contains the actual document information. The *resource fork* is the part of a file that contains Mac-specific information, such as the icon of the file, the file's creator, and the kind of file. Because this information is useful only within the Mac OS, you can remove it. Why would you want to do so? The answer is a simple one: If the resource fork information is merged into the data fork during the file compression or transmission process, it can hopelessly corrupt the file. Another reason to remove the resource fork is to decrease file size. For plain-text documents, this may not be as evident, but Photoshop places a large amount of extraneous information in the resource fork of a graphics file, making it appear much larger than it really is.

You can remove the resource fork from documents that you need to exchange with Windows users. You can also use it to strip the resource fork information from HTML files. There are several utility programs that can perform this process. File Buddy is a shareware program available at **www.macdownload.com** that allows you to remove the resource fork, as well as modify attributes of files such as creation date, creator, and kind. Here are some instructions for using File Buddy:

1. Launch File Buddy.

2. Select File|Get Info and locate your file. A window similar to the one in Figure 10.23 will appear.

3. Click the Additional Actions button and select Delete Resource fork. Figure 10.24 shows an active Additional Actions button.

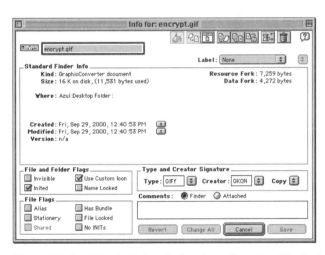

Figure 10.23   The Get Info window for a file using File Buddy.

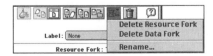

Figure 10.24   The Additional Actions button menu.

4. You will receive a warning indicating that deleting the resource fork will make some files unusable. Click Delete to remove the resource fork.

5. If you change your mind, you can click the Revert button to restore the resource fork. Otherwise, click the Save button to modify this file.

Using DAVE

DAVE is a utility that uses NetBIOS over the TCP/IP protocol to allow Macintosh computers to talk to other computers that also use NetBIOS over TCP/IP. Examples of these systems include Windows 95 computers and Windows NT servers. Normally, as a Mac user you would have to wait for the NT server administrator to enable the AppleTalk protocol enabling you to access the server. With DAVE, you can bypass this process and configure your computer to access Windows 95, NT, or 2000 computers, as well as Macintosh computers, without having to install additional software on the Windows computers. The best part is that the Windows machines won't even know you're a Macintosh. To them, you're just another Windows computer. You also can share printing devices and exchange pop-up messages.

DAVE is available from Thursby Software Systems, Inc. Contact them at **www.thursby.com** for more information about using DAVE.

To install and use DAVE, take these steps:

1. Use the standard installer to use the software (you will have to reboot).

2. Launch the NetBIOS Control Panel and enter the license key and user and machine information (see Figure 10.25).

3. Go to the Apple menu and choose DAVE. A window will appear listing servers in your particular Windows workgroup.

Figure 10.25   The DAVE NetBIOS Control Panel.

Figure 10.26   The DAVE toolbar.

4. Go to Access|Command Palette to view a handy toolbar. The icons in Figure 10.26 will appear. Click on the appropriate button to log on to other servers in the domain.

Related solutions:	Found on page:
Accessing Remote Servers and Volumes	144
Sharing Files and Folders	339

Connecting to a WinFrame or MetaFrame Server

For many Macintosh users in large or specialized organizations, it is difficult to obtain a decent client to access the application server. Even worse, some of these software developers will not even write a client for the Mac. In the past, your solutions were to use an emulator or purchase a PC coprocessor card.

However, a sufficiently large and vocal group of disenfranchised Macintosh users may be able to persuade their organization to purchase or set up WinFrame or MetaFrame Server. WinFrame from Citrix is a modified version of Windows NT 3.51. It is a thin client, which means that the local machine receives screen images of what is going on in the session on the WinFrame server. In most cases, servers are more powerful than local machines; because of this, some tasks actually run faster on the WinFrame server. WinFrame runs on a variety of platforms and can even perform in low-bandwidth situations, such as a modem connection. MetaFrame follows the same principles as WinFrame but is modeled on Windows NT 4.

To connect to a WinFrame server, take these steps:

1. Install the ICA client on your computer.

2. Launch the ICA Client Editor, as shown in Figure 10.27.

3. Enter the IP address of the WinFrame server, and (if necessary) your login and password.

4. Click on the Connect button. The Citrix ICA client will launch and create a window on your desktop. Figure 10.28 shows the client session.

5. You can perform the functions within the client window.

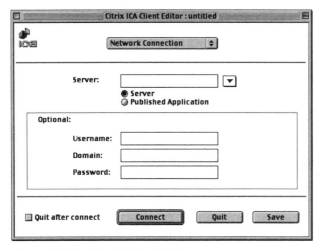

Figure 10.27   The ICA Client Editor.

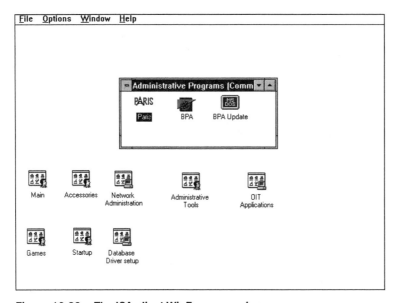

Figure 10.28   The ICA client WinFrame session.

In the client editor, you can also save settings for distribution to other users in the department. They will only need to launch the file to go into the server and can bypass entering IP and server information.

Chapter 11

Networking and File Sharing

In Depth

Creating a local area network (LAN) of Macs is almost as easy as changing a Desktop pattern. Mac OS 9.1 supports all the most popular networking protocols, including TCP/IP, SNMP, and AppleTalk, as well as network cabling such as 10Base2, 10BaseT, Ethernet, Fast Ethernet, Gigabit Ethernet, and LocalTalk. This chapter explores the many ways to network Macs to share files, services, and applications among themselves.

Supported Networking Protocols

If you're a networking junkie like we are, then you might agree with us when we say that one of the greatest things about the Mac OS is that it supports all the most popular networking protocols, and provides limited support for a few less popular protocols. Open Transport 1.0 was introduced with the first line of PCI-bus PowerMacs, and has been through several revisions since then. Mac OS 9.1 ships with Open Transport 2.7, which offers more robust networking support for several protocols, including:

- AppleTalk
- AppleTalk IP
- Transmission Control Protocol/Internet Protocol (TCP/IP)
- IRTalk
- Point-to-Point Protocol (PPP)
- Serial Line Interface Protocol (SLIP)
- Bootstrap Protocol (BootP)
- Dynamic Host Configuration Protocol (DHCP)
- Reverse Address Resolution Protocol (RARP)
- Apple Remote Access Protocol (ARAP)
- Open Transport Printer Access Protocol (OT PAP)

Mac OS 9.1 also adds support for Simple Network Management Protocol (SNMP), which is now bundled with the OS. The majority of you will use the AppleTalk and TCP/IP protocols, which are transmission protocols, in conjunction with non-transmission protocols such as BootP and DHCP, which are protocols that assist Open Transport in obtaining an IP address.

Modem users will most likely utilize PPP instead of SLIP. Both PPP and SLIP are used to connect remote computers to a LAN or the Internet using a plain old telephone service (POTS) or ISDN line. However, cable modems and various versions of Digital Subscriber Line (DSL), such as Asynchronous DSL (ADSL) and Synchronous DSL (SDSL), are growing in popularity. Therefore, more and more Mac users will be configuring their Internet connection using Ethernet and some form of cable or DSL modem. Considering how easy it is to configure IP settings for the Mac OS, this is decidedly a good thing.

Under Mac OS 9.1, you can still employ a tunneling protocol, such as AppleTalk IP, and the Apple LocalTalk Bridge to communicate using TCP/IP via AppleTalk. For example, AppleTalk IP hides (or tunnels) TCP/IP packets inside an AppleTalk network datastream and delivers them to a TCP/IP-based network by using a gateway that connects both networks or devices. This kind of multiprotocol network is alive and well today on networks, such as those in public school systems, that have many older Macs.

Supported Network Hardware

Most Mac users are connected these days via standard Ethernet running at 10Mbps or Fast Ethernet running at 100Mbps, whereas in the early days they were connected via LocalTalk running at about 230Kbps. However, with the newest G4 PowerMacs, the standard networking speed is now 100Mbps or even 1000Mbps (Gigabit Ethernet). Mac OS 9.1 and Open Transport support the following networking hardware options:

- 10Mbps Built-in Ethernet
- 100Mbps Built-in Ethernet
- 1000Mbps Built-in Ethernet
- LocalTalk
- Infrared
- Third-party PCI- and PCMCIA Ethernet adapters (additional drivers required)

Note that Apple will no longer develop or test products to support Token Ring networks, including Token Ring adapters and TokenTalk drivers. Consequently, connecting to a network will be a challenge for Macs that are used in IBM or mainframe computing environments.

Apple has centered its networking and Internet strategies on TCP/IP instead of AppleTalk and Fast Ethernet (100Mbps) rather than LocalTalk and standard Ethernet. This makes Apple the first computer company to use the most widely used networking protocol (TCP/IP) and the fastest common hardware protocol

(Fast Ethernet) in a home or business computer. We suspect Gigabit Ethernet will become the standard within the next two years; however, for this to happen, the price of network equipment such as hubs and switches will first need to come down.

Of course, other network hardware options that make creating Mac-based LANs a snap are available from third-party vendors such as Farallon (**www.farallon.com**). When purchasing additional networking equipment such as Network Interface Cards (NICs), hubs, and switches, make sure you select products that support 100Mbps connections. This is the standard for the computer industry as a whole, as well as Apple's established direction for the development of new products.

File Sharing

File Sharing, along with support for multiple hardware and software protocols, has been a standard part of the Mac OS for quite some time. Mac OS 9.1 supports File Sharing via AppleTalk as well as using TCP/IP, thanks to technology acquired from Open Door Networks (**www.opendoor.com**). Users can also access AppleShare IP and Mac OS X Server via AppleTalk and TCP/IP, as in the past. In addition, Mac OS 9.1 supports a lightweight Web server called Web Sharing. Each of these methods of sharing data has its advantages and disadvantages.

Built-In File Sharing

File Sharing under Mac OS 9.1 has a new interface that combines the old File Sharing, Sharing Setup, and Users & Groups sections of the File Sharing Control Panel into a single Control Panel called File Sharing. It still uses the AppleTalk protocol and has the same limitations (10 shared folders, 10 concurrent users, and 5 concurrent requests) that it had in previous versions of the Mac OS, but it now allows access via TCP/IP in addition to AppleTalk. Small networks can employ File Sharing with little or no noticeable impact on the overall speed of the network or computers; now, however, enabling TCP/IP dramatically increases the speed of file transfers. Figure 11.1 shows the new File Sharing Control Panel.

In terms of security, File Sharing has not changed under Mac OS 9.1. Passwords, which are case-sensitive, are encrypted on both ends of transmission over AppleTalk and TCP/IP. For more information on passwords and security, refer to Chapter 16.

AppleShare IP and Mac OS X Server

Large networks will probably need the support of dedicated file servers that run AppleShare IP or Mac OS X Server. Each of these server operating systems from Apple uses a much more robust file sharing protocol and has fewer restrictions on the number of users that it can support and the number of volumes, folders,

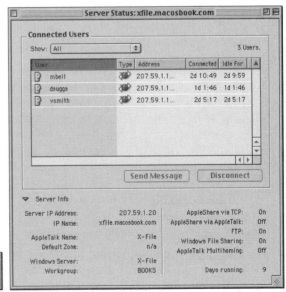

Figure 11.1   The File Sharing Control Panel.

and files it can serve. Both include Web, print, and email servers in addition to the file sharing capabilities, making them ideal solutions for medium or large LANs. Very large LANs or wide area networks (WANs) will most likely require the support of several file servers. Figure 11.2 shows the Server Status window for an AppleShare IP 6.3 server running on top of Mac OS 9.1.

Figure 11.2   You can remotely manage users and groups on an AppleShare IP server with the Mac OS Server Admin application.

The future of AppleShare IP and Mac OS X Server is limited, however, because they are sure to be surpassed in features and speed with the release of Mac OS X in early 2001.

Web Sharing

Finally, Mac OS 9.1 allows you to share files using the Personal Web Sharing feature, which is installed by default but disabled until activated through the Web Sharing Control Panel. Sharing files over the Web isn't as flexible as traditional File Sharing, of course, but it may help meet the needs of some networking environments, such as those that do not support the AppleTalk protocol. See Chapter 13 for more information on providing Web services. Figure 11.3 shows an example of a folder that is shared via the Web.

File Sharing Concerns

You should be aware of a few peculiarities concerning file sharing under the Mac OS. In terms of access restrictions, file sharing isn't nearly as flexible under the Mac OS compared to other operating systems (most notably, Unix or Windows NT). For example, Mac file sharing is geared toward folder-based access rather than per-individual access. This means that you must configure access for each folder first, then maintain users and groups and assign access restrictions accordingly. A better system would allow you to create accounts for individual users on your Mac and then assign access privileges to sections of your hard drive as needed.

Here are a few tips to keep in mind when using file sharing:

- You cannot assign guests a level of access that is higher than that of users, groups, or the owner. If you do, the Mac OS will automatically grant the same level of access to everyone.

- You cannot share an individual file; instead, you must share the parent folder containing that file.

- You cannot grant different levels of access to more than three entities: the owner, a particular user or group, and guests. For example, if the owner has full access, user A has read-only access, and Everyone has no access, you cannot also grant write access to user B.

File Servers

Small networks may not need a dedicated file server, but if you have more than a few computers and need to provide services such as backup, email, or Web access, having a dedicated file server is probably a good idea. Using individual Macs to share files with each other is often called a *distributed* file-sharing network, whereas a network with a dedicated file server is referred to as a *centralized* network. Of course, having a dedicated Mac as a file server means that one less workstation is available for use by someone on your LAN; however, if it can provide several essential services, then it's a good investment.

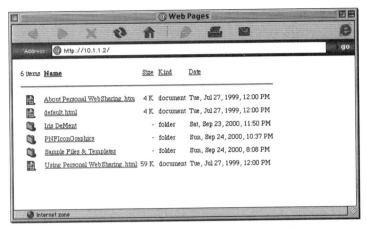

Figure 11.3   Personal Web Sharing can meet the needs of some users to share files over a LAN or the Internet.

Although you can use just about any PowerMacintosh as an AppleShare IP or Mac OS X Server, or for traditional file serving, it's best to use at least an entry-level G4 Macintosh as a server. G4s have several advantages over ordinary PowerMacs, including:

• A faster system bus

• A much faster processor (over one billion calculations per second)

• A faster hard drive (Ultra ATA/66, for up to 66MB per second (MBps) of throughput on most computers; the G4 server line includes even faster hard drives, up to 160 MBps with Ultra 160 SCSI)

You'll need a Network Operating System (NOS) for the server that is tuned for serving files. The current NOS options are AppleShare IP, Mac OS X Server, or MkLinux or LinuxPPC, which are freeware Unix derivatives created by Linus Torvalds and ported to the PowerPC by various groups. The pros and cons of these NOSs are as follows:

AppleShare IP

• *Pros*—Easy to use, provides many services in addition to file sharing, large install base, supports Windows users and shows up in the Network Neighborhood, Web-based administration, many resources for support.

• *Cons*—Expensive, file system is a bottleneck, no protected memory or preemptive multitasking.

Mac OS X Server

• *Pros*—Fairly easy to use, provides many services in addition to file sharing, uses protected memory and preemptive multitasking, very fast.

- *Cons*—Expensive, requires advanced skills to administer, cannot use as many storage and backup utilities as AppleShare IP.

MkLinux or LinuxPPC

- *Pros*—Free, very fast, dedicated user support group, supports AppleTalk and most TCP/IP services.

- *Cons*—Difficult to administer, must compile own software, requires Unix experience.

So, if you are a Unix geek and want to give it a go, we recommend LinuxPPC (**www.linuxppc.com**). For only $20, it's certainly worth a try. Otherwise, AppleShare IP is the way to go. It isn't cheap (currently $1,000 for a 50-user license), but when you consider that it provides Web, email, FTP, and print services in addition to robust file sharing, it may be the right product for your LAN.

Apple Remote Access

Another resource for connecting Macs is Apple Remote Access (ARA), a client/server application. Apple developed ARA several years ago so that Macs could connect to a LAN and to each other using modems, as well as share AppleTalk and TCP/IP resources. The current version of ARA (4.0) allows connections using AppleTalk and TCP/IP in addition to direct-dial using a modem. The components of ARA include:

- Apple Remote Access Personal Server (part of Mac OS 9.1)

- Apple Remote Access Client (part of Mac OS 9.1)

- Apple Remote Access MultiPort Server (a discontinued product from Apple)

Mac OS 9.1 includes the ARA client, which uses either the Apple Remote Access Protocol (ARAP) or Point-to-Point Protocol (PPP) to connect to an ARA Personal or MultiPort Server. The ARA Personal Server is a single-user server that is de-signed to allow you to remotely connect to a networked Mac and access that computer's files and folders, as well as network volumes and printers. The ARA MultiPort Server, designed to run on a dedicated file server, can support up to 16 simultaneous users who have access to the ARA server's local resources, as well as all resources or services that may be available on the LAN to which the server is connected. Using a modem to connect to an ARA Personal or MultiPort server enables the client to access the Internet as well as the LAN to which the server is attached, provided the server is on the Internet.

Timbuktu

Another method of networking Macs (as well as PCs) is Timbuktu from Netopia (**www.netopia.com**). Timbuktu is primarily used for screen sharing, but it provides many other services as well, including:

- File exchange
- Chat
- Intercom
- Direct dial-in access

Timbuktu provides several unique benefits. It allows you to remotely command another computer to do anything except start up. It also gives you the ability to control a Windows-based PC with the same level of capability as a Mac. For example, Figure 11.4 shows a Timbuktu session with a PC running Windows 98.

LAN Hardware

Since just about every Mac that is capable of running Mac OS 9.1 comes equipped with an Ethernet adapter, the hardware necessary to create a LAN falls into two categories:

Figure 11.4 Use Timbuktu on your LAN to control Macs as well as PCs.

11. Networking and File Sharing

- Cabling
- Switches/hubs

Cabling

Whereas LocalTalk networks require cables that are used in no other networks (as far as we know), Mac Ethernet networks use the same hardware as does any other Ethernet network. In general, these networks run at either 10Mbps or 100Mbps; we're now seeing 1000Mbps networks, which require special cables, hubs, and repeating devices. Ethernet cabling comes in two basic types:

- *10Base2 (also called ThinWire or Thin Coax)*—A coaxial cable similar to the type that is used to connect a VCR to a TV.

- *10BaseT (also called Twisted Pair)*—Looks like a telephone cable (known as RJ11), but is slightly bigger and has more pins.

Unless it's being used in conjunction with an existing network, no compelling reason for using 10Base2 cabling remains. 10BaseT has been the standard for several years now. Both 10Base2 and 10BaseT support 10Mbps throughput, but only 10BaseT supports 100Mbps or 1000Mbps, depending on the type of cable. 10BaseT cable comes in several levels, or categories, that measure throughput capacity; the following levels are the ones you're most likely to encounter:

- *Category 3*—10Mbps

- *Category 5*—100Mbps

- *Category 5e*—1000Mbps (the *e* stands for *enhanced*)

To identify which category (or *Cat*) of cable you are using, read the shielding and look for a description. If you don't find any description at all, throw it away and use confirmed Cat 5 or Cat 5e cable.

When purchasing 10BaseT cabling, don't confuse *straight-through* cables with *cross-over* cables. Straight-through cables are used to connect Ethernet ports or transceivers to ports on a hub. The pinouts (arrangement of pins) on both ends of a straight-through cable match when viewed side by side and face up, as shown in Figure 11.5.

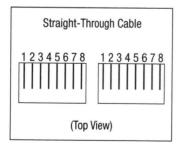

Figure 11.5   Diagram of a straight-through cable.

Cross-over cables connect networking devices such as switches, hubs, and routers to one another, and cannot be used to connect a Mac to a hub. However, a cross-over cable can be used to create a two-node, hubless network by connecting the built-in Ethernet ports of two Macs. The pinouts of a cross-over cable will mirror one another when viewed side by side and face up, as shown in Figure 11.6.

AppleTalk cable also comes in two flavors: One is manufactured by Apple and uses a coaxial-style cable, which is thick and brittle. The other uses standard indoor telephone cable (RJ11), which is cheap, easy to find, and much more flexible than Apple's cable. Each AppleTalk cable has a special adapter on either end called a *LocalTalk connector* that plugs into the serial port (modem or printer); both types of cable have the same 230Kbps throughput. An RJ11-based LocalTalk connector is usually cheaper than the traditional Apple-style connectors. The RJ11 wire is also cheaper and easier to work with—that's why it's our preference by a long shot.

Choosing Switches and Hubs

A standard 10BaseT (10Mbps) hub is sufficient for small LANs, unless your Macs have Fast Ethernet capabilities and you have Cat 5 cabling. 100Mbps hubs are more expensive than 10Mbps hubs, but prices are steadily dropping. For example, a typical 8-port 10Mbps hub sells for around $40, whereas a similar hub that supports 100Mbps might cost as much as $80. Also, in mixed environments (where you have both standard and Fast Ethernet), you'll have to purchase an auto-sensing 10/100Mbps hub to be able to accommodate both speeds, which is even more expensive.

Switches are better than hubs because they eliminate all unnecessary network traffic from flowing from one computer to all the others on your network. With a hub, network "chatter" is broadcast to all the computers on the network. With a switch, on the other hand, it is isolated to only those network devices that need to receive the signal. In laymen's terms, it prevents network saturation.

Furthermore, switches (theoretically) don't allow packets to collide when being routed from one node to another. Hubs, on the other hand, have no way to prevent

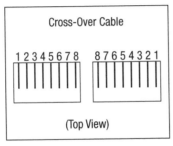

Figure 11.6   Diagram of a cross-over cable.

collisions, and networks can become seriously congested if too many collisions are present.

Bridging LocalTalk and Ethernet Networks

Some LANs have LocalTalk segments that need to be connected to Ethernet segments. In large networked environments, such as schools and publishing corporations, many workstations may be located on LocalTalk segments, but also need access to Ethernet segments and the Internet. Another common situation involves LocalTalk devices such as printers that are connected through LocalTalk ports on a Macintosh, but need to be accessible to other computers over an Ethernet network.

Several hardware and hardware/software options bridge the gaps between these two networks. An example of a hardware bridge that connects AppleTalk and Ethernet devices is the AsanteTalk 10BT LocalTalk Bridge from Asante (**www.asante.com**), a device that connects an Ethernet-based Mac to a LocalTalk device such as a printer.

Apple's LocalTalk and LaserWriter Bridge applications are software solutions for bridging LocalTalk and Ethernet networks. LocalTalk Bridge allows connections to and from LocalTalk and Ethernet networks, including printers and TCP/IP services. LaserWriter Bridge provides access to a printer on a LocalTalk segment from an Ethernet segment. A simple Control Panel, shown in Figure 11.7, is all it takes to allow Ethernet users to print to a LocalTalk printer as if it were located on the Ethernet segment as a networked printer. It also appears to the host computer on the LocalTalk segment as a networked printer. The host computer is therefore serving as a print server, and may take a performance hit if the printer is used heavily.

Other solutions, such as Stalker Software's PortShare software (see **www.stalker. com/PortShare/**), exist for bridging LocalTalk and Ethernet networks as well as sharing LocalTalk devices (printers and modems).

Figure 11.7   Apple's LaserWriter Bridge allows Ethernet users to access a LocalTalk-based laser printer as a networked printer.

Immediate Solutions

Managing a Network Using SNMP

The Simple Network Management Protocol (SNMP) is implemented in the SNMP Administrator, a tool included in Mac OS 9.1 that provides advanced AppleTalk and TCP/IP management capabilities. SNMP works by allowing administrators to create groups of computers that can be monitored using SNMP Administrator or another tool that uses SNMP, such as SNMP Watcher from Dartmouth College (**www.dartware.com/snmpwatcher/**).

SNMP Administrator is not installed as part of the Easy Installation of Mac OS 9.1. However, you can install it by choosing it from the Custom installation option in the Mac OS 9.1 CD-ROM, as shown in Figure 11.8.

Once installed, you can create customized groups of computers and monitor network activity for all computers that have the Open Transport SNMP Extension installed.

TIP: *In order to be managed via SNMP, each Mac on your network must have the Open Transport SNMP Extension installed.*

To create and monitor a group, follow these steps:

1. Launch SNMP Administrator and click on the New button to create a group, as in the new Community group shown in Figure 11.9.

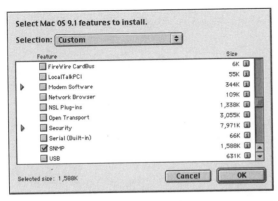

Figure 11.8   You can install SNMP Administrator from the Mac OS 9.1 CD-ROM.

Figure 11.9   Creating a new group by using SNMP Administrator.

2. Double-click on the new group to open and view the group's agent properties.

3. To view information about an agent, single-click the triangle beside an agent to expand it, or double-click an agent such as AppleTalk Agent, shown in Figure 11.10, to open it into a new window.

SNMP Administrator monitors just about every aspect of network activity for several protocols, including AppleTalk and TCP/IP. For example, you can monitor network activity by Ethernet hardware address, AppleTalk node or file sharing name, or IP address or domain name. You can find most of these capabilities in SNMP Watcher as well, as shown in Figure 11.11.

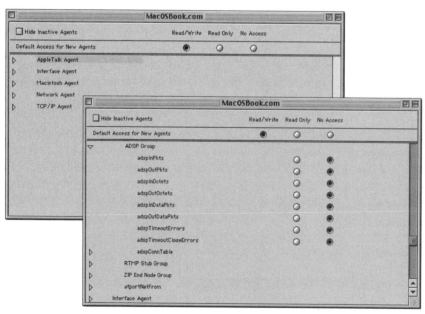

Figure 11.10   Selecting and monitoring an agent in SNMP Administrator.

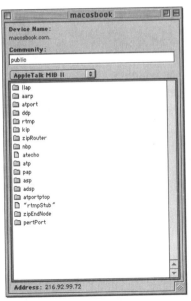

Figure 11.11 SNMP Watcher provides similar capabilities to Apple's SMTP Administrator.

Configuring File Sharing and Program Linking

File Sharing and Program Linking are Open Transport-native and capable of communicating via TCP/IP as well as AppleTalk (starting in Mac OS 9.0). To enable and disable File Sharing and Program Linking:

1. Open the AppleTalk Control Panel, click on the Options button, and make sure that AppleTalk is active. File Sharing cannot be enabled unless AppleTalk is active.

2. Open the File Sharing Control Panel and enter information for the Owner Name, Owner Password, and Computer Name in the Network Identity section of the Start/Stop tab, as shown in Figure 11.1 earlier in the chapter. You must enter a unique name in the Computer Name field for each computer on your LAN. If your LAN is divided into zones, you can use the same name in different zones.

3. Click on the Start button to enable file sharing and/or program linking, then close the File Sharing Control Panel. This enables file sharing for the owner, but no one else.

4. To enable services using TCP/IP in addition to AppleTalk, check the appropriate checkboxes in the File Sharing and/or Program Linking sections.

5. To disable File Sharing or Program Linking, open the File Sharing Control Panel and click on the Stop button for File Sharing and/or Program Linking, as shown in Figure 11.12. You can individually enable or disable file sharing and program linking.

When connecting to a Mac in which TCP/IP is enabled for File Sharing, you must enter the computer's IP address or host name in the Server IP Address section of the Chooser. Otherwise you'll connect to the server via AppleTalk, which is the default, rather than via TCP/IP. Figure 11.13 shows an example of this type of connection.

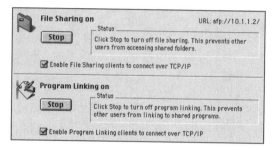

Figure 11.12   Stopping file sharing and program linking.

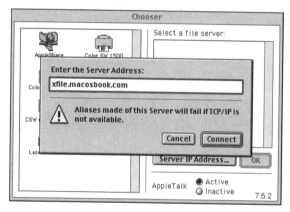

Figure 11.13   Specifying a host name when connecting to a Mac using File Sharing will ensure that the connection is made via TCP/IP instead of AppleTalk.

Monitoring File Sharing

The performance of your file server, whether it is on a personal computer or a dedicated file server, is an important resource to measure. If you are working away and all of a sudden your Mac grinds to a halt, it is very easy to find out if File Sharing is the culprit. Just follow these steps:

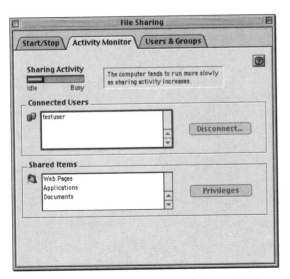

Figure 11.14   Monitoring the level of file-sharing activity.

1. Open the File Sharing Control Panel and select the Activity Monitor tab, as shown in Figure 11.14.

2. The Sharing Activity progress bar will display the level of activity, and the Connected Users and Shared Items will allow you to quickly access disconnected users and reconfigure shared folders.

Sharing Files and Folders

Mac OS 9.1 allows you to share 10 folders, host 10 concurrent users, or issue 5 concurrent requests to your computer using File Sharing. You can set the access privileges for each folder for the following kinds of users:

- Owner

- Individual network users or groups

- Guest users (anonymous)

When sharing an application, however, access is either enabled or disabled.

To share a folder and its contents, take these steps:

1. Open the Users & Groups section of the File Sharing Control Panel, shown in Figure 11.15, and click on the New User or New Group button.

2. Select a user account and give the account a name and password in the Identity section. Check the Allow User To Change Password option if you want a user to be able to change his or her password.

Figure 11.15   Creating user accounts.

3. Select the Sharing portion of the Show pop-up menu, and check the Allow User To Connect To This Computer box to enable access, as shown in Figure 11.16. Deselect this option to disable access without deleting the account.

4. Select the Remote Access section of the Show pop-up menu and indicate whether you want the user to be allowed to dial into your computer. Also enter the automatic call-back number (see Figure 11.17).

5. Next, identify a folder or volume in the Finder to be shared and choose File|Get Info|Sharing (Command+I, then select Sharing), as shown in Figure 11.18.

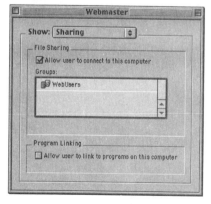

Figure 11.16   Enabling an account.

Figure 11.17 Allowing a user to dial into your computer using Apple Remote Access Personal Server.

6. Select from the following options to set the level of access for the folder:

- *Can't Move, Rename, Or Delete This Item (Locked)*—Prevents users from deleting the folder, but not the contents of the folder.

- *Share This Item And Its Contents*—Enables others to access the folder (the owner always has access, as long as file sharing is enabled).

- *Owner*—Enables you to grant ownership status to a user or group. Owners can then change access privileges for all others, but not add or delete users and groups themselves.

- *User/Group*—Sets the level of access privileges for a particular user or group.

- *Everyone*—Sets the level of access privileges for guests.

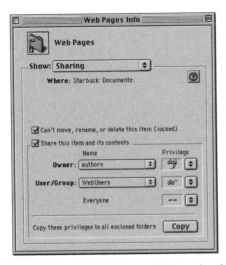

Figure 11.18 File sharing information for a folder.

7. Select a privilege level for the owner, user or group; for guest access, select from the following options:

- *Read & Write*—Allows you to read and modify existing files, add and edit new files and folders, delete files and folders, and view all the items in the folder and subfolder.

- *Read Only*—Allows you to read existing files and view the contents of the folder and subfolders, but not add, edit, or delete files or folders.

- *Write Only (Drop Box)*—Allows you to upload new files to a folder, but not view, edit, or delete files or folders.

- *None*—Denies a particular user or group the ability to mount or open the folder.

Browsing File Servers with Network Browser

The Network Browser, an interesting addition to the networking capabilities of Mac OS 9.1, has many helpful features, including navigation buttons for Web-browser style navigation of network resources (see Figure 11.19). In fact, the Network Browser may eventually replace the venerable Chooser for logging into AppleShare and AppleShare IP servers (but not for accessing printers).

To view the servers that are available on your network:

1. Launch the Network Browser; all available servers will appear in the Network window. If your network is divided into zones, the zones will appear in the browser window (see Figure 11.20).

2. Click on the triangle and enter the password to view the volumes that are available on a particular server, as in Figure 11.21.

Choose one of the following three methods to log in to an AppleShare server:

- Double-click on a server or volume in the Network window.

- Select a server or volume and choose File|Open In Place.

- Select a server or volume and choose File|Open in New Window.

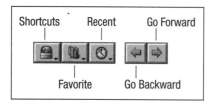

Figure 11.19   Use the Network Browser's navigational buttons to "browse" your network.

Figure 11.20   Multiple AppleTalk zones viewed in the Network Browser.

Figure 11.21   Use the Network Browser to view a list of volumes on an AppleShare server.

To access your iDisk or log in to an AppleShare IP server by IP address or host name, follow these steps:

1. Choose Connect to iDisk or Server from the Shortcuts button in the Network Browser (on the far left).

2. Enter the username and password for your iDisk, or the AppleShare IP server's IP address or host name (see Figure 11.22 for examples). The iDisk will appear on the Desktop and the AppleShare IP server will appear as a regular AppleShare server in the Network window.

3. Use the Network Browser's buttons to add a server to your list of favorite servers. When added to the list, a special type of alias is created in the Favorites folder, which is located in the System Folder.

Figure 11.22   Logging into an iDisk (top) and an AppleShare IP server (bottom) using the Network Browser.

To add or select a favorite file server by using the Network Browser, log in to a file server and choose Add To Favorites from the Favorites menu button; select a favorite from the same menu, as shown in Figure 11.23.

TIP: You can create an alias to a file server from within the Network Browser by selecting File|Make Alias and following the instructions.

To delete a favorite:

1. Choose Favorites|Remove From Favorites, and select an item from the Remove Favorites window, an example of which is shown in Figure 11.24.

2. Alternatively, you can quit the Network Browser, then manually delete the server's entry from the Favorites folder inside the System Folder.

Figure 11.23   Selecting a favorite file server from the Favorites menu.

Figure 11.24   Removing a favorite file server.

Saving Passwords in the Keychain

Finally, you and the users on your network will want to change passwords on a regular basis as a security precaution, as described in greater detail in Chapter 16. File Sharing passwords are encrypted when they travel across the network and when they are stored by the Mac OS on your hard drive.

Mac OS 9.1 enables users to create keychains—passwords (keys) stored on your computer in sets (keychains). This isn't a new concept for the Mac OS, but in Mac OS 9.1 its implementation is particularly well designed. We'll talk more about the keychain in Chapter 16 because all kinds of passwords, not just passwords to AppleShare and AppleShare IP servers, may be stored in keychains. But for now, let's review the basic steps for creating a keychain.

To create and test a keychain:

1. Open the Keychain Control Panel.

2. If you don't already have a keychain, follow the prompts and create one.

3. When the keychain is unlocked, you can add a password to it using the connection dialog window shown in Figure 11.25. This window appears when you're logging into a server via the Chooser or Network Browser.

4. Make an alias of an item on the remote volume such as a folder or the volume itself.

5. Log off of the server, then open the aliased folder or volume. You should be able to access the item without having to reenter your username or password.

To make the Keychain feature a bit easier to use, check out Chaotic Software's utility called KeyChain AutoUnlock (**http://chaotic.digitalchainsaw.com**). This utility is designed to automatically unlock your default keychain at startup and mount any servers whose alias resides in a folder called Startup Servers, which

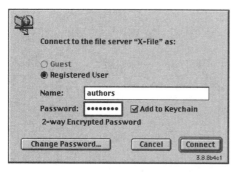

Figure 11.25   When logging into a file server, check the Add To Keychain option.

resides in the System Folder. Without this utility, you'll have to manually unlock the default keychain on the first attempt to access a password stored in the keychain.

Related solutions:	*Found on page:*
Creating and Adding Items to a Keychain	479
Setting Keychain Access Preferences	480

Changing Passwords

To change the password of a File Sharing user on your system:

1. Open the Users & Groups section of the File Sharing Control Panel.

2. Select the user, type the new password in the Password field, and then close the window.

The password will not appear in clear text as it did in previous versions of the Mac OS.

To change a password on a remote server:

1. Open the Chooser and select a server.

2. Instead of logging in to the server, click on the Change Password button.

3. In the password change window, enter the old password, the new password, and then click on the OK button.

4. Confirm the new password when prompted; any errors will result in your having to start over.

Related solution:	*Found on page:*
Choosing a Good Password	469

Chapter 12

Internet Connectivity

In Depth

Today's Internet is a place of business, commerce, hobbies, and entertainment. People of all ages have found something of benefit by getting "wired." But some fundamental components must be in place before network access can become a reality.

Internet Service Providers

The development of the World Wide Web has contributed to the desire for Internet access. Before the Web, Internet users retrieved information by employing software applications written for the particular kind of information they sought. For example, information contained in a database could only be accessed with Gopher software or a Telnet application. Obtaining information from a software archive required file transfer applications such as Fetch or Anarchie, and newsreaders like InterNews or NewsWatcher were necessary if you wanted to check out a newsgroup. Above all, searching for specific information required patience and luck.

The development of the Web, a system of documents connected with hyperlinks, streamlined the search for information. Browsers were designed to display Web documents; hyperlinks made it easy to access additional documents. In addition, these browsers handled existing (non-Web) information systems. Today, browsers perform a variety of tasks, including accessing databases, transferring software, and reading newsgroups. They've also branched into new methods of communication such as chat and teleconferencing. Web search engines and portals have made searching for information much easier. Overall, the Web and its browsers have made Internet access appealing to all users. In fact, the hardware and software necessary for connecting to the Internet are standard features of most computers sold today.

To take advantage of the built-in Internet access features, you may need an *Internet service provider* (ISP). Most ISPs are companies that allow you to dial a number and, with proper authentication, establish a network connection over a phone line. Some ISPs, such as America Online, provide proprietary services, including online magazine subscriptions and specialized discussion groups, in addition to Internet access. These companies usually provide special software for accessing their services.

On the other hand, some ISPs provide Internet access only. Although they may have a specialized dialer, you can often use the software included with Mac OS 9.1 to establish network services over a telephone line. These ISPs initially catered to the savvy computer user or small business owner but now target anyone who is looking for high-speed access and reliable connection times. Some ISPs specialize in helping you set up your own domain, which enables you to publicize a unique email address or Web site. Earthlink is one of the best examples of this type of ISP.

Most ISPs charge for access. Some companies provide free Internet access in exchange for subjecting you to a parade of advertisements whenever you access the Internet. Until recently, the downside of this arrangement—apart from the ads—was that most of these companies favored Windows users. However, these free ISPs are wising up to the strong Mac market and beginning to include options for Macintosh connectivity. Some free ISPs that provide Macintosh connectivity are **www.freeinternet.com** and **www.freelane.net**. You can find more information by searching in Sherlock 2 for "free isp."

Which ISP is the best? That's for you to decide. Although the nationally known ISPs are more familiar, a local company or free ISP may be a better match for you. Make a list of the services you want and then shop around for the ISP that can provide them at the best cost. Some questions to ask yourself include:

- How many hours per month will you be connecting to the ISP?

- Do you need unlimited access?

- Do advertisements bother you?

- Do you need multiple accounts?

- Does the ISP supply local access telephone numbers or toll-free access?

TIP: The Web site **www.ispfinder.com**, which specializes in listing ISPs by area code, may prove helpful.

Dial-up vs. Permanent Connections

Internet users fall into two groups (and depending on your financial position or job, you may fall into both of them): those who use a modem and those who have a wired Ethernet connection. Modems were originally used to establish a terminal emulation session with a remote bulletin board service or database. Back then, modems were slow because only text was exchanged. The speed of the connection and the corruption rate made transferring files difficult. Network protocols capable of running over a telephone line, including Serial Line Interface Protocol (SLIP) and Point-to-Point Protocol (PPP), an improved version of SLIP, were developed next. Apple's AppleTalk Remote Access (ARA) allows Macs to communicate with each other and see AppleTalk zones over a telephone connection. Modem speed has been increased to meet the demands of these network protocols. Modem access is still a very popular Internet access method, but no modem is fast enough to compete with the speed of a permanent Ethernet connection.

An Ethernet connection is 50 to 100 times faster than a dial-up connection. With this type of permanent connection, an Ethernet cable directly connects your computer to a larger network. The network cable is usually 10BaseT, although occasionally you may still come across thin coaxial cable (this looks like cable television wire). It is connected to a network interface card or a network port. (In newer systems, including the Power Macintosh and iMac computers, the network interface is wired to the motherboard.) Provided that the appropriate network software has been installed, the computer can send and receive data over the network wire. Permanent Internet connections are usually found in businesses and educational institutions. However, newer technologies such as ADSL and cable modem connectivity are becoming a reality for home and small business users in many areas of the country.

Hardware Requirements

In order to establish any kind of network connection, certain hardware elements must first be in place. Hardware requirements vary depending on the connection you plan to establish.

Modem

The average home user accesses the Internet with a modem. To establish a reliable connection, you need a fast modem. A productive PPP connection should be a minimum of 14.4Kbps (28.8Kbps is the most common speed, these days). Watch for the other extreme, however. Some ISPs don't support 56Kbps or the V.90 protocol. If you have a 56Kbps modem, you can easily determine whether your ISP supports these speeds by attempting to dial in to the service. If your modem connects but "squeals" much longer than usual and never establishes a network connection, you can assume that your ISP doesn't support 56Kbps or the V.90 standard. Adjust the modem script to force the modem to connect at slower speeds. Apple has just such a script for the iMac, available for download at **ftp.apple.com/ Apple_Support_Area/Apple_Software_Updates/US/Macintosh/iMac/**.

You also have the option of an internal or external modem. External modems are easier to configure, install, and upgrade. However, like most peripherals, an external modem requires a power supply. Internal modems don't add to the clutter on your desk. Both internal and external modems can serve as answering and fax machines. Most Macintosh computers sold today include an internal modem. In fact, the iMac and iBook come with both internal modems and a built-in Ethernet port.

Ethernet

Many businesses, schools, and other organizations maintain Ethernet networks for their employees. An Ethernet connection is much, much faster than a modem connection and provides fast access to information available on the Web. Plus, if your Ethernet network assigns static IP addresses, you can set up a computer as a Web server or email host.

For several years, Macintosh computers have included two varieties of built-in Ethernet ports. The Apple Attachment Unit Interface (AAUI) port is found on most models (including older machines such as the Centris 610 and 650). This unusual port must have an additional hardware device, a *transceiver*, in order to access the network. When Apple began adding Ethernet capability to its computers, the cabling was not universal; some environments used 10BaseT cable whereas others used thin coax wire (other wiring solutions existed as well). The AAUI port allows access to the network using a transceiver with the cable connection that matched the network environment. It isn't necessary to adjust jumpers on a card or to change driver configurations.

The second variety of Ethernet port is the 10BaseT port. Because 10BaseT, which resembles a telephone connection, is the more popular of the Ethernet wiring solutions, Apple included it on its newer model computers. The 10BaseT port allows you to connect an Ethernet wire directly to your computer, without needing a transceiver.

Some Macintosh computers, including several of the Performa computers, lack Ethernet capability. If your computer is missing an AAUI or 10BaseT port, see if it has a free expansion slot. If so, you can purchase a network interface card with the appropriate connector for your environment. PowerBooks also have an expansion slot that can be filled by an Ethernet card. PCMCIA Ethernet cards are also available.

Software Requirements

The Mac OS includes software that enables you to connect to a permanent Ethernet connection or dial into a modem pool. It's easy to set up either type of connection. However, if you purchased a PCMCIA card for your PowerBook, you will need to install the drivers for the card.

Protocol Software

Open Transport is the software suite of Extensions and Control Panels that enables the computer to connect to various types of networks. Open Transport comes bundled with Mac OS 9.1. You can also use the DialAssist, Internet, Modem, and

Remote Access Control Panels in conjunction with Open Transport to establish Internet connectivity.

Some of the Extensions used with Open Transport begin with *Open Transport* or *Open Tpt*. However, other Extensions may not be labeled as such. For example, modem scripts are located in the Extensions folder and work with Open Transport Remote Access.

TIP: *You may see vestiges of Classic Networking, especially within the Control Panels. Classic Networking is the term used to describe the network software that preceded Open Transport. Network and MacTCP Control Panels were used with Classic Networking; AppleTalk and TCP/IP are the Open Transport Control Panels that replaced them. If you have the newer Open Transport Control Panels, you can disable Network and MacTCP.*

These Control Panels and Extensions work together to establish a network connection. Other software packages are available for dial-up connectivity, however. FreePPP, a freeware connectivity package that can be found on older Macs, is a relic of the era prior to System 7.6, when the Mac OS did not have a built-in connectivity software package for a PPP connection. FreePPP allows you to have multiple dial-up configurations and to adjust options such as the modem speed and initialization string.

You can also have multiple configuration sets with the Open Transport Modem Control Panel. However, you cannot change the modem speed or initialization string; you must manually edit the scripts or obtain updated dialing scripts from the modem manufacturer. For the average user who has struggled to find the correct initialization string, this is a blessing. On the other hand, users who are accustomed to the many options of FreePPP may find this disconcerting.

ISP Software

We mentioned the different kinds of ISPs at the beginning of this chapter. If you have no ISP, Earthlink is accessible via the Remote Access software included with Mac OS 9.1; other ISPs offer a dialer created for their users. Still others provide a complete Internet access package with proprietary email and Web browser software. Analyze your needs. Be aware that the cheapest ISP many not be the best one for your needs.

IP Number

An *IP number*, a unique number assigned to your machine, identifies you to the rest of the Internet and allows you to access Web sites, send email, and transfer files. Your IP number can also be used to set up Internet services such as email, Web, and FTP functions. Permanent Ethernet users may have a number assigned to the computer that usually does not change. In some settings, such as computer lab environments, you may see numbers assigned by a server. In this case, you don't need to remember the IP number; a server will assign one to the computer. Depending on the network configuration, the computer may have a new IP number each time the machine starts up and connects to the network, or the number may last for several months. Dial-up connections usually receive a new number with each connection.

If your number is not unique, you will receive an error that the number is in use. This error message usually indicates the hardware address of the machine that is currently using the number. This type of error can occur in environments that manually assign IP numbers to machines. It rarely occurs during a dial-up connection. Figure 12.1 shows an example of this error. If your number is in use, you will not be able to access Internet services; you must change your IP numbers or locate and ask the offending computer user to change his or her numbers.

Keep Track of Your Information

Document the hardware address of your computer and your assigned IP number. If your computer is ever stolen, you may be able to use the IP number to track it down. In some networks, an administrator can determine the physical location of a computer on the network if the IP number is in use. You can also assign the IP number from your stolen computer to a different computer and see if a duplicate IP number error occurs; the error message may list the stolen computer's hardware address. You can then alert your network administrators and the proper authorities that the stolen computer is in use.

It's also a good idea to document your IP number so that you can easily reconfigure your computer if your hard drive crashes. You may be forced to configure your system from scratch.

New Technologies

Modems today are rather slow compared to permanent Ethernet connections. Emerging technologies that can change the way you access the Internet may already be available in your area. Other high-bandwidth technologies, including wireless and satellite networking, are on the horizon.

Airport

When Airport debuted with the release of the iBook, mobile computing suddenly really meant *mobile computing*. Airport is a wireless networking environment.

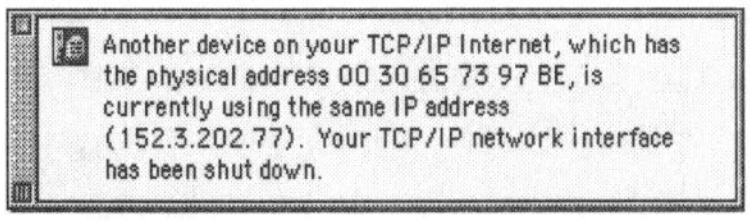

Figure 12.1   A duplicate IP number error.

With it, you can walk around your house or sit outside on the deck and still be able to browse the Web. Airport is also a blessing for users who are sick of wires. In fact, an entire classroom of computers could access the Internet without plugging in a single cable. Even if you're not particularly mobile, you could probably benefit from Airport.

Airport includes a base station that is actually the connection to the Internet. This connection can be via Ethernet cable or modem. From the base station, wireless signals are transmitted to and from the receiving devices in which the proper hardware has been installed. In most cases, this hardware is an Airport card, although some PowerBook G3 series computers use third-party cards. Airport base stations, which can accommodate up to 50 computers, can transfer signals as far as 150 feet. These signals can even penetrate walls.

Fast Ethernet

Fast Ethernet refers to improved network cards, wire, and hubs capable of exchanging data packets at 100Mbps or greater, such as Gigabit Ethernet. Compare this to the common 10BaseT standard that passes data at 10Mbps. Before you can use Fast Ethernet, your network hardware must be upgraded. You can purchase Macintosh computers with Fast Ethernet, but unless the hubs and wires used in the network are also upgraded, you will not enjoy a speed increase. Fast Ethernet doesn't involve special software configuration. If the hardware elements are in place, you can use Fast Ethernet immediately.

ISDN

When it came out, Integrated Services Digital Network (ISDN) promised to be the future of telephone communication. Not only can ISDN transmit voice, it can transmit voice and data simultaneously. However, although ISDN is rather popular in several European and Asian countries, its use is spotty in the United States because of competing telecommunication protocols. Also, the existing telephone lines may not support it. ISDN may require the installation of additional hardware, some of which can be expensive. Although ISDN can transmit data faster than standard modem communication (up to 164Kbps), other competing technologies are faster. In the United States, ADSL and cable modems are more popular choices for fast network access.

ADSL

Asynchronous Digital Subscriber Line (ADSL) is a technology that radically improves the existing telephone line communication, making it possible for you to talk on the telephone while accessing the Internet. With specialized hardware, you can achieve data exchange rates as a fast as 9Mbps downstream and 1.5Mbps upstream. The rationale behind this speed gap is that more users are pulling data down to their computers than putting data up on a remote server. Also note that these speeds usually apply to businesses. Consumer packages generally feature speeds of 1.5Mbps downstream and 90Kbps upstream. ADSL requires a hardware device that interfaces with your computer, and may also require an upgrade of your telephone lines. You can determine whether ADSL is available in your area by checking with your local phone company or a local ISP.

Cable Modems

ISDN and ADSL are services provided by your local telephone company. Cable modems are obtained through cable television providers. Using the existing cable television line in your home, your cable provider can install a hardware device that transmits data over the cable line. As with ADSL, a speed discrepancy exists between downstream and upstream data transmissions. Downstream transmissions can equal 10BaseT speed. Upstream is much slower, but is nonetheless faster than standard modem speeds.

What is the difference between ADSL and cable modems? The nature of each network is structured differently. ADSL connections are transmitted over telephone lines from your computer to the call center. The line is not shared, but is subject to speed loss due to poor equipment along the wire. Cable modems, on the other hand, are shared among the other subscribers in your area. If everyone in your area has a cable modem on the network, then you may see a speed loss, because the more people who use the service, the slower the connection will be. Cable modem lines can also lose speed due to aging equipment, although this difference has been minor thus far. Each provider likes to point out the weakness of the competition, but both are excellent solutions with practically identical results.

*TIP: If you use technologies such as ADSL or cable modems for your home or small-business network, you may find yourself locked into a single IP number. However, if you have multiple computers that need to access the Web simultaneously, Vicomsoft offers software solutions to this problem. SurfDoubler allows two Macs to access the Web using the same IP number, and Internet Gateway can connect small or large networks to the Internet. Find more information about these products at **www.vicomsoft.com**. Apple's Airport wireless network can also allow you to share one IP address among multiple machines on the Airport network in your home.*

Immediate Solutions

Running the Internet Setup Assistant (Part 1—All Configurations)

When you first run Mac OS 9.1, you are given an opportunity to configure your computer and Internet settings via two utilities, the *Mac OS Setup Assistant* and the *Internet Setup Assistant*. With the Mac OS Setup Assistant, you can establish the basic configuration of your computer, including time zone and computer name. After Mac OS Setup Assistant is finished, the program will allow you to go into the Internet Setup Assistant. This program asks a series of questions and uses your answers to configure Control Panels that regulate Internet access. If you close the Mac OS Setup Assistant when it first displays, you can launch it or the Internet Setup Assistant at a later time, or manually configure your computer. If you launch a program that depends on these settings, a dialog box will give you the opportunity to launch the Internet Setup Assistant.

If you prefer to use the Internet Setup Assistant to configure your system, take the following steps:

1. Launch the Internet Setup Assistant.

2. The first dialog box directly asks if you want to get on the Internet. If you answer Yes, the utility continues. Answering No shuts down the utility.

3. The second dialog box asks if you already have an account on the Internet. If you answer No, you will be given an opportunity to create an account with an ISP. If you answer Yes, the Internet Setup Assistant process will continue.

4. An introductory window appears next. Make sure that you know your DNS address, the type of connection you will be using, and your IP information, including the IP address, subnet router, and router address. In addition, if you're using a modem, you'll need the phone number of your ISP, your name, and your password. If you have the required information, click on the right arrow in the bottom-right corner of the window.

5. In the next window, you have an opportunity to name the configuration you are creating, as shown in Figure 12.2 (you can have multiple configurations). You also specify whether you're using a modem, network, or DSL connection.

Figure 12.2 Naming your Internet configuration.

At this point, Internet Setup Assistant continues on a particular path that is based on the type of connection you're configuring. If you're using a modem to create an Internet connection, select it and click on the right arrow. Continue to the next section, "Running the Internet Setup Assistant (Part 2—Modem)" for the next steps. If you're using a permanent Ethernet connection, select Network (Ethernet/LAN) and click on the right arrow. Proceed to the section, "Running the Internet Setup Assistant (Part 3—Network)" for further instructions.

Related solution:	*Found on page:*
Configuring File Sharing and Program Linking	337

Running the Internet Setup Assistant (Part 2—Modem)

Please make sure you've followed the steps in the previous section before you continue here. When you've completed the following steps, you should be able to connect to an ISP with Mac OS 9.1:

1. The Modem Settings window, shown in Figure 12.3, asks you for the type of modem you're using and the port to which the modem is connected. You can also indicate whether the telephone line is capable of tone dialing and whether the dial tone should be ignored (non-U.S. modems may require this setting in order to use the U.S. phone system and vice versa). After entering this information, click on the right arrow to continue.

2. In the next window, enter the telephone number and account information for your ISP, as shown in Figure 12.4. Then, click on the right arrow to continue.

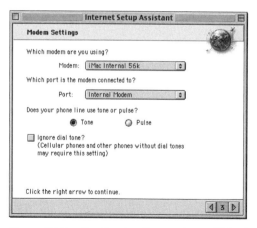

Figure 12.3   Configuring the modem within the Internet Setup Assistant.

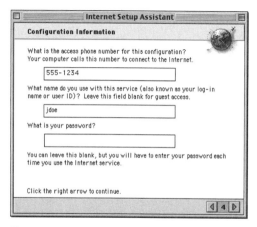

Figure 12.4   The ISP information.

3. Some ISPs require that you use a PPP connection script to access their services. If you have such a script, store it in the PPP Connect Scripts folder within the Extensions folder. The next window gives you the option of designating a PPP connection script. If you select No, you will be taken to the section for setting up the IP information (skip to Step 5). If you select Yes, continue to Step 4. Choose an option and click on the right arrow to continue.

4. Use the PPP Connect Scripts window (shown in Figure 12.5) to indicate a connection script. If a script is present in the PPP Connect Scripts folder, you should be able to select it from the pop-up menu. If it is located elsewhere on the computer, you can use a navigator window to locate it and have the Internet Setup Assistant copy it to the proper folder. Choose a script and click on the right arrow to continue.

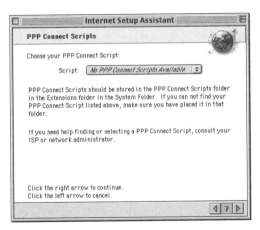

Figure 12.5   Choosing a connection script.

5. The Internet Setup Assistant will ask if you have been assigned an IP number. Many permanent Ethernet connections have an IP number; most dial-up connections do not. If you select No, go to Step 7. If you select Yes, you'll be prompted to enter your IP number.

6. If you selected Yes in Step 5, you are given an opportunity to enter the subnet mask and router address. Click the arrow to continue.

7. You are now prompted to enter the DNS information and domain or host name (see Figure 12.6). The domain or host name is optional. Click on the right arrow to continue.

8. Next, you are prompted for email information, including your published email address and password (optional). Enter the information and click on the right arrow to continue.

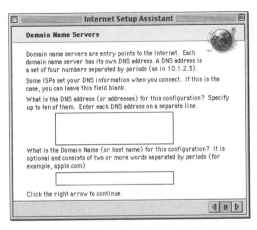

Figure 12.6   Entering DNS information.

9. Figure 12.7 shows the next window in which you are prompted to enter more detailed email account information. Enter the incoming mail server address and the outgoing mail host. Then click on the right arrow to continue.

10. Enter your news server host name (this step is optional). The news server provides Usenet groups to a software package that can display them (both Netscape Communicator and Outlook Express have this capability). Click on the right arrow to continue when done.

11. Your network may have security measures in place to prevent unauthorized access, and may require you to use proxy servers. This window asks if you must use proxy servers. If you answer Yes and click on the right arrow, you are prompted to enter the information shown in Figure 12.8. Enter the appropriate proxy server addresses and click on the right arrow. If you answer No, skip this screen and continue to Step 12. Click on the right arrow to continue.

12. At this last window, you can select Go Ahead to finish the process and make the changes. If you want to verify your settings, you can click on Show Details for a list. After you click on Go Ahead, the Internet Setup Assistant will make the changes to the appropriate Control Panels and automatically quit. You are now ready to access the Internet.

Figure 12.7   Email account information.

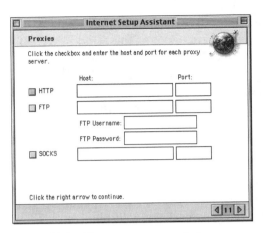

Figure 12.8   The proxy server window.

Running the Internet Setup Assistant (Part 3—Network)

Make sure that you've followed the steps within the section "Running the Internet Setup Assistant (Part 1—All Configurations)." If you have, you should be ready to configure your network and IP information:

1. The Internet Setup Assistant will ask if you have been assigned an IP number. Many permanent Ethernet connections have an IP number; most dial-up connections do not. If you select No, go to Step 3. If you select Yes, you'll be prompted to enter your IP number.

2. If you selected Yes in Step 1, you are given an opportunity to enter the subnet mask and router address. Click the arrow to continue.

3. You are now prompted to enter the DNS information and domain or host name (see Figure 12.6). The domain or host name is optional. Click on the right arrow to continue.

4. Next, you are prompted for email information, including your published email address and password (optional). Enter the information and click on the right arrow to continue.

5. Figure 12.7 shows the next window in which you are prompted to enter more detailed email account information. Enter the incoming mail server address and the outgoing mail host. Then click on the right arrow to continue.

6. Enter your news server host name (this step is optional). The news server provides Usenet groups to a software package that can display them (both Netscape Navigator and Outlook Express have this capability). Click on the right arrow to continue when done.

7. Your network may have security measures in place to prevent unauthorized access, and may require you to use proxy servers. This window asks if you must use proxy servers. If you answer Yes and click on the right arrow, you are prompted to enter the information shown in Figure 12.8. Enter the appropriate proxy server addresses and click on the right arrow. If you answer No, skip this screen and continue to Step 8. Click on the right arrow to continue.

8. At this last window, you can select Go Ahead to finish the process and make the changes. If you want to verify your settings, you can click on Show Details for a list. After you click on Go Ahead, the Internet Setup Assistant will make the changes to the appropriate Control Panels and automatically quit. You are now ready to access the Internet.

Configuring the Remote Access Control Panel

You can use the Internet Setup Assistant to set up Internet access, or you can manually configure the different Control Panels that allow you to access the Internet. The Remote Access Control Panel is used for modem connections. To configure the Remote Access Control Panel:

1. Open the Remote Access Control Panel (see Figure 12.9).

2. If applicable, enter your login name and password. To remove these fields, click on the Guest radio button.

3. Enter your ISP telephone number.

4. Click on the Options button to access additional settings.

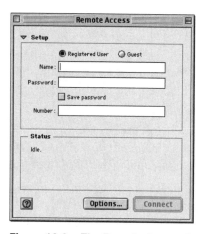

Figure 12.9   The Remote Access Control Panel.

5. Click on the Redialing tab. You can access the pop-up menu to determine if redialing is enabled, how many times the modem should redial, and if an alternate number should be used when redialing.

6. Click on the Connection tab (see Figure 12.10). You can turn on logging to troubleshoot connection problems. You can configure settings, such as a flashing icon or a message that appears every 10 minutes, to remind you that you are connected to the Internet. You can also automatically disconnect yourself if you are idle for 10 minutes; this option is useful if you are billed for the time you are online. Both time settings are adjustable.

7. Click on the Protocol tab. The default protocol used in modem connections is PPP. Previous versions of the Mac OS allowed you to use AppleTalk Remote Access; that protocol is no longer an option. You can set several options within the PPP tab, such as automatically connecting to an ISP when you launch TCP/IP applications (see Figure 12.11). You can also indicate compression options. If you connect to an ISP via a command-line prompt, you can set the PPP option from this panel. You can also indicate a particular script to use when dialing the ISP.

12. Internet Connectivity

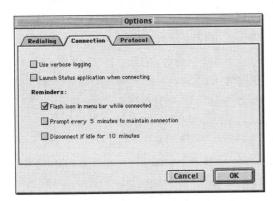

Figure 12.10   The Connection tab within the Remote Access Control Panel.

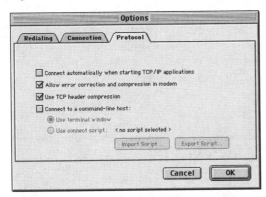

Figure 12.11   The PPP options in the Protocol tab.

When you have set your preferred options, click on OK to return to the main window. You still must configure the Modem and TCP/IP Control Panels in order to access an ISP. These Control Panels can be accessed from the Remote Access menu in the Remote Access Control Panel.

Creating a Remote Access Script

For some ISPs, you connect via a command-line interface in which you must respond to a series of prompts before you can establish a network connection. To save time and keystrokes, you can create a script that records this information automatically when you connect.

Take these steps to create a remote access script:

1. Launch the Remote Access Control Panel.
2. Click on the Connect button to begin the PPP connection process.
3. When you connect to your ISP, you should be prompted with a terminal window. Click on the Settings button.
4. Activate the option Prompt To Save Connect Script On Close and click on OK.
5. Enter your information as you normally would. When the PPP connection has been established, you are prompted to save the script. You don't have to save the script in a particular place—you just need to know where you saved it.
6. Click on the Options button (you should still be within the Protocol window).
7. Click on the radio button for Use Connect Script.
8. Click on the Import Script button, locate the script you created, and then click on OK.

The next time you connect to your ISP, you can test your script. You may have to repeat this process until the script is perfected. For example, some connections are noisy and insert additional characters at a command-line prompt. A quick workaround is to hit Enter to clear the characters. You should be given a clean prompt at which you can enter your information correctly.

Configuring the Internet Control Panel

The Internet Control Panel was developed from a software application called Internet Config. The Internet Control Panel, shown in Figure 12.12, contains information that can be referenced by TCP/IP applications such as email programs

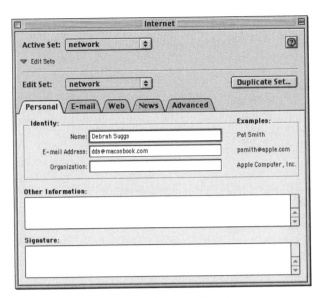

Figure 12.12   The Internet Control Panel.

and Web browsers. Much of this information is collected during the Mac OS 9.1 Internet Setup Assistant session. You can also set up multiple configuration sets with this Control Panel. See the following section entitled "Creating Configuration Sets in the Internet Control Panel" for instructions.

You can set the following options with the Internet Control Panel:

- *Personal*—These settings are not used for accessing servers; they are just personal settings such as your name, email address, and organization. You can also create a signature file that will be appended to the end of your email and newsgroup messages.

- *Email*—These settings are used to access email servers. You can enter your user account, incoming and outgoing mail server addresses, and password. You can also set your options for email notification. Mac OS 9.1 uses Outlook Express as the default email application. You have the option of changing this to another application.

- *Web*—These settings are used with Web browsers such as Microsoft Internet Explorer and Netscape Navigator. You can set your default home page and search engine, designate a folder to contain files that you download from the Internet, and set defaults for Web browser colors and links. Microsoft Internet Explorer is the default Web browser; you can select another browser if you wish.

- *News*—These options are used when reading Usenet newsgroups. You can set the news server address and your login options (if necessary), and select the preferred news reader (Microsoft Outlook Express is the default reader).

- *Advanced*—The Advanced settings, which were hidden in previous Mac OS versions, are easily accessible in Mac OS 9.1 You can set default FTP hosts, helper applications, fonts, file mapping, firewalls, messages, and hosts.

Creating Configuration Sets in the Internet Control Panel

The Internet Control Panel contains useful information about your Internet settings. But what if you share a workstation with another user? What if you have more than one email account? Situations like these call for more than one configuration set. You can use these sets as part of a shared workstation, or combine them with Location Manager to control different work environments.

Follow these steps to create configuration steps:

1. Launch the Internet Control Panel.

2. Go to File|New Set. If you need to make minor changes to an existing set, you can also click on the Duplicate Set button and select a new name for the set.

3. Fill in the appropriate fields or make changes to existing fields, then go to File|Save Settings.

4. If you would like to use the new set, click on the Active Set pop-up menu and choose the desired set. It will become active.

5. Close the Internet Control Panel and, if prompted, save your settings.

Configuring the Modem Control Panel

The Modem Control Panel tells the Remote Access Control Panel how to dial the ISP. If these settings are inaccurate, you will not be able to connect. Follow these steps to configure the Modem Control Panel:

1. Open the Modem Control Panel, as shown in Figure 12.13.

2. If necessary, indicate the port you will use to communicate with the modem. In newer computer models, such as the iMac, you cannot change the port.

3. Click on the Modem pop-up menu and locate your modem model. If it is not listed, try using a generic script. You can also try installing the scripts from the software that came with the modem (scripts are also available from the manufacturer).

Figure 12.13   The Modem Control Panel.

4. Use one of the Sound radio buttons to turn on or off the dialing sound.

5. Use one of the Dialing radio buttons to select tone or pulse dialing.

6. If necessary, select Ignore Dial Tone.

TIP: If you anticipate dialing your ISP from outside the U.S., you may need to enable the Ignore Dial Tone option. Modems are sensitive to the frequency of a telephone line, which may be different in a particular country. If you attempt to dial and can hear a dial tone, but receive an error message indicating that there is no dial tone, then you need to enable the Ignore Dial Tone option. The Modem Control Panel will force the modem to ignore the apparent lack of connectivity and dial the ISP number. Cell phone users may also benefit from this option.

Related solution:	Found on page:
Using PCMCIA Modem Cards	225

Configuring the AppleTalk Control Panel

The AppleTalk Control Panel is used with an Ethernet or LocalTalk network. Before you can configure the AppleTalk Control Panel, you must enable AppleTalk. If you launch this Control Panel while AppleTalk is inactive, you will be prompted to activate AppleTalk when you close the AppleTalk Control Panel. To configure the AppleTalk Control Panel for Ethernet:

1. Open the AppleTalk Control Panel (see Figure 12.14). If AppleTalk is inactive, you will be given an opportunity to make it active.

2. In the Connect Via pop-up menu, select Ethernet. If your network utilizes zones, the current zone should appear when you switch to Ethernet.

3. Close the Control Panel and save the settings.

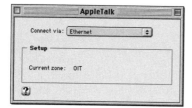

Figure 12.14   The AppleTalk Control Panel.

Configuring the DialAssist Control Panel

The DialAssist Control Panel works with the Modem Control Panel. DialAssist makes connecting easier and helps when you are dialing under unusual conditions, such as long distance or from within a telephone network requiring special settings. In the past, you had to type long numeric strings separated by commas to accomplish such tasks as dialing a particular long-distance provider or entering your calling card information. With DialAssist, you can enter this information and then use this Control Panel when you need to dial additional numbers in order to access your ISP or network. Not all settings must be completed to use DialAssist (you may only need to dial 9 for an outside line).

To configure DialAssist, take these steps:

1. Launch the DialAssist Control Panel, as shown in Figure 12.15.

NOTE: *All of the DialAssist settings reference the telephone number that is active within the Remote Access Control Panel.*

2. Optionally, indicate the area code of the number.

Figure 12.15   The DialAssist Control Panel.

3. Select the country from the Country pop-up menu. If the country isn't listed, you can click on the Country button to add a new country to the listing.

4. Indicate a special prefix such as 9 for dialing an outside line. If your prefix isn't listed, you can click on the Prefix button to add new ones.

5. Indicate your method of long-distance access (such as dialing 1+the area code) or a particular long-distance provider. If the provider isn't listed, click on the Long Distance button to add additional carriers.

6. Indicate your calling card or credit card number in the Suffix pop-up menu. (If you select this option, you need to click on the Suffix button and edit the settings to include your card numbers.)

TIP: If you choose to add the Suffix option within DialAssist, don't worry that someone can retrieve your credit or calling card information by opening the Suffix settings. The numbers entered are protected in the same way passwords are protected—they are encrypted.

Configuring the TCP/IP Control Panel

TCP/IP settings are vital for successfully connecting to the Internet. If the settings are configured incorrectly, problems ranging from the inability to connect to certain Web sites to the inability to connect to any site or server can occur. The settings vary depending on the type of Ethernet connection you will be using; it may be a permanent Ethernet connection or a remote access configuration. Follow these steps to configure the TCP/IP Control Panel for Internet access:

1. Launch the TCP/IP Control Panel, as shown in Figure 12.16.

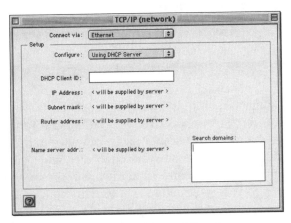

Figure 12.16 The TCP/IP Control Panel.

2. Select the connection protocol you will be using from the Connect Via pop-up menu. Each selection changes the options in the Setup portion of the TCP/IP Control Panel. You have several options that may include PPP, Ethernet, or AppleTalk (MacIP).

3. In the pop-up menu next to Configure, choose how you will configure TCP/IP. You can enter the information manually or use DHCP, BootP, PPP, or RARP servers. If you have an assigned IP number, manually configure the TCP/IP Control Panel. Figure 12.17 shows a TCP/IP manual configuration.

4. If you select any of the other options such as DHCP or PPP, you will only need to fill in select fields, such as the Search Domains or the DHCP client ID.

5. Close the Control Panel and click on Save Settings when prompted. You should be able to utilize TCP/IP applications. If you can't, try restarting your computer (especially if you had to edit an existing TCP/IP configuration).

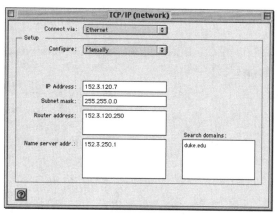

Figure 12.17   A manually configured TCP/IP Control Panel.

Configuring Airport

Airport, Apple's wireless networking solution, is used most often in newer systems such as the G4 Tower, G4 Cube, PowerBook, iBook, and iMac. It requires the purchase of a base station and an Airport card for each computer in the network. The signal from base station to computer is about 150 feet, and you can have up to 50 computers on the network. The Airport hardware comes with the appropriate software and instructions for setting up the network, but you can follow these general steps for using Airport:

1. In order to use Airport, you must configure the computer's network settings and install an Airport card before running the Airport Setup Assistant.

If the computer is not configured, the Airport Setup Assistant will give you an opportunity to launch the Internet Setup Assistant and configure the computer.

2. Run the Airport Setup Assistant to configure the Airport base station.

3. Install the Airport card and appropriate software in each client.

4. Configure the TCP/IP and, if necessary, AppleTalk clients to connect to the network via Airport.

5. Depending on how you configured the base station in Step 2, the clients may need to enter a password upon first-time contact with the Airport base station.

Find out more information about Airport at **www.apple.com/airport/**.

Creating and Saving Configuration Sets

The AppleTalk, Modem, Remote Access, and TCP/IP Control Panels all use the same method for creating different configurations. These configuration sets can be used with the Location Manager to control the network environment. For example, you may be using a PowerBook with an Ethernet connection at work and PPP connectivity at home. Follow these steps to create configuration sets:

1. Open the appropriate Control Panel.

2. Go to File|Configurations. The window shown in Figure 12.18 will appear.

3. Click on the Duplicate button and designate a new name for your configuration.

4. When you have created and named a set, click on the Make Active button so you can edit the configuration.

5. Return to the Control Panel and make the changes so that your configuration set is unique.

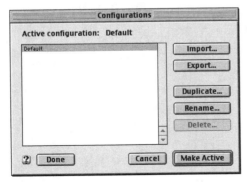

Figure 12.18   The Configurations window.

6. Close the Control Panel and choose Save Settings.

7. You can now go back into the Control Panel and select Configurations to make a different set active or create a new set.

TIP: *You can also use the Configurations dialog box to import and export information. To use these settings on multiple computers, simply export the settings to a file, go to a new computer, and use the Configurations dialog box to import the settings. This is handy when you must configure and administer several computers. You can also use the Configurations dialog box to delete old configuration sets.*

Related solution:	Found on page:
Configuring the Location Manager	223

Chapter 13

Providing Internet, Intranet, and Extranet Services

In Depth

This chapter shows how you can use a Macintosh running OS 9.1 to provide Internet, intranet, and extranet services. The Mac OS has been network-ready right out of the box since the first Macintosh was introduced in 1984. The first Macs communicated via AppleTalk as well as TCP/IP, and one of the first popular Web servers, MacHTTP, ran on the Mac OS. Mac OS 9.1 continues to be an inexpensive and incredibly easy way to provide all the most popular TCP/IP services over the Internet, as well as on intranets and extranets.

Internet, Intranet, and Extranet Services

Internet, intranet, and extranet services share some basic characteristics: They typically rely on the same transmission protocol, TCP/IP, and use the same wiring and routing technologies, such as frame relay, Ethernet, and ISDN. What makes them different, however, is the scope of their availability to users. Internet services are usually made available to the general public as part of a commercial venture or a public service; intranet services are usually part of a private local area network (LAN), and are restricted to a specific group of users. Intranets that provide limited access to outside users are referred to as *extranets*. That's all well and good, but what, you may ask, makes this discussion relevant in this book? The Mac OS, of course. If you're connected to the Internet or a corporate intranet or extranet on a full-time basis, you can provide services to users with your Macintosh.

Common TCP/IP Services

Many people assume that the Web is synonymous with Internet services—but that's not true at all. Internet services include the Web, for sure, but with the Mac OS you can provide many services beyond just Web access. It is possible—not to mention incredibly easy—to provide multiple Internet services such as the following:

- Web
- Email
- Mailing list servers
- FTP
- Proxy and gateway
- Usenet News

- Domain Name Servers (DNS)

- Gopher

- Chat

- Talk

- Finger

- Whois

- Ident

- Streaming audio and video

Until fairly recently, these Internet services were provided almost exclusively by Unix computers, which required a resident computer expert for installation and maintenance. Linux and Windows NT have also been used in this capacity. With a Macintosh, however, just about anyone can provide these Internet services. They all rely on TCP/IP, as do all Internet-based services, and Mac users have multiple options when it comes to choosing an application to provide these services.

NOTE: *To provide Internet services on most any computer, you will need one or more dedicated IP addresses instead of dynamically assigned IP addresses from DSL, cable, and dial-up services.*

Hardware Requirements

Computers that are configured to provide Internet, intranet, and extranet services are typically faster and more expensive than your typical workstation. However, you can take a workstation and convert it into an efficient server without too much difficulty or expense, depending on the intended task. Of course, faster computers are usually better, but you may be surprised to learn that in some cases, speed is almost irrelevant—even the slowest PowerMacintosh will be more than sufficient.

In general, look for the following hardware requirements or extras when selecting or building an Internet server:

- Fast G4 processor (400MHz or better)

- 7200 RPM (or faster) hard drive(s)

- RAID (redundant array of inexpensive disks)

- SCSI accelerator

- Fast Ethernet (100Mbps)

- Regular backup schedule

- UPS (uninterruptible power supply)

- Rebound or PowerKey (to restart the server automatically)

Of course, don't forget the human requirements. Make sure that the procedures for operating your servers are well documented and that someone is always available who can fill in for the primary caretaker. You never know when he or she may be hit by a name-brand beer truck (not just any beer truck!) on the way to work.

Connectivity and Disaster Recovery Issues

When planning your server setup, you should also consider the kind of connectivity you'll have to the Internet or your internal network, and what to do in the event that your connection isn't stable or goes down for a prolonged period. Several utilities, which we'll discuss in Chapter 17, can help you monitor your servers and alert you to problems; nevertheless, a backup plan for dealing with a lost connection or a catastrophic hardware failure is essential.

A redundant server co-located on another network is the most effective way to overcome prolonged downtime on a usable server. Maintaining two identical servers in different locations is a daunting task. In fact, it may be overkill if your ISP guarantees minimal downtime, which would make co-locating a second server unnecessary. In this case, having a redundant server on site is sufficient. Even maintaining two identical servers may be overkill; in some situations, a backup Web server that provides basic services may be sufficient.

On the other hand, it is likely that you can find a peer institution or organization with which you can create a reciprocal agreement for monitoring each others' servers or co-locating backup servers. Mac people tend to stick together, so don't dismiss the possibility of creating this type of arrangement.

Account Administration

Providing Internet, intranet, and extranet services involves the creation of user accounts, usage rules, and regular accounts maintenance. This is equally true for commercial services and personal or departmental intranet accounts; the more users you have, the more work you'll have to do in order to maintain the accounts. Tools and utilities are available to help you, and some of them, when compared to less reliable shareware and freeware applications, are worth paying for.

The creation and enforcement of rules for acceptable use constitute one area of account administration that is often overlooked. In our opinion, it's better to define—at the outset—exactly what users can and cannot do with your services. This beats bickering with disgruntled users whose accounts have been restricted for misuse. When creating an acceptable use policy for your servers, consider the following for each account:

- Maximum levels of file transfer traffic
- Tech support limits

- Disk quotas

- Offensive language and flame wars

- Passing spam, chain letters, and the like

- Reselling of account resources

- Copyright laws and legal restrictions

It's a good idea to post your policies where everyone can read them and remind your users of the policies on a regular basis, perhaps with a monthly "help file" distributed on a mailing list.

Commercial Web Services

Mac users have long had multiple software options for operating commercial or high-volume Web sites, but the field has really narrowed to only two commercial Web servers: WebSTAR from StarNine and WebTen from Tenon Intersystems. WebSTAR, the more familiar of the two, has been around in one form or another for about eight years. It has an easy-to-use interface and supports several million connections per day, depending on what kind of hardware is utilized. WebTen is a virtual Unix server that runs the Apache Web server, a public-domain server that is quickly becoming the most popular Web server on the Internet. WebTen is a bit trickier to administer, but its performance is unmatched on the Mac OS and most other platforms. Running on a fast G4 computer, WebTen is capable of supporting 60 to 80 million hits per day, which ranks it as a first-class Web server by any standard. Both WebSTAR and WebTen cost around $500.

The features of WebSTAR and WebTen are too numerous to cover in detail here. In case you're not using either one, or you're considering changing from one to another, we will summarize them to help you decide on the one that's most likely to suit your needs.

WebSTAR

WebSTAR 4 provides faster performance, more features, and easier administration than its predecessors. WebSTAR is also more than a Web server—it furnishes all the services you'll need to run multiple Web sites using a single server. WebSTAR Version 4 includes:

- Web server

- Proxy server

- FTP server

- Mail server

- SSL (Secure Sockets Layer)

- High-performance caching
- Virtual domain hosting
- Integrated search engine
- SSI (Server-Side Include) support
- Byte-server
- Keep-alive support

Version 4 is capable of running on a variety of Macs. However, to take advantage of all the plug-ins and services, you'll want a G4-powered computer because WebSTAR is enhanced to take advantage of the AltiVec floating point instruction set. Other requirements include:

- Mac OS 8.6 or higher
- 14MB of RAM (minimum)
- 20MB of disk space, not including space for user files
- A dedicated IP address

WebTen

WebTen uses a very different approach to providing commercial Web services on the Mac platform. To overcome certain limitations in the Mac OS's input/output and file systems, the makers of WebTen found a way to combine elements of MachTen, their virtual Unix operating system, and Apache, a freeware Web server, to produce a hyperfast Web server. By taking full advantage of the PowerPC processor, file caching, and an alternative to Open Transport, WebTen created a Web server that is several times faster than WebSTAR. The latest version of WebTen requires:

- Mac OS 8.6 or higher
- 16MB of RAM (minimum)
- 40MB of disk space, not including space for user files
- One or more dedicated IP addresses

The main features of WebTen include:

- Web server
- FTP server
- Proxy server
- DNS server
- NFS server
- Support for 1,000 hits per second
- High-performance caching

- Support for CGIs, Server-Side Includes (SSI), WebSTAR plug-ins, AppleScript, Apache plug-ins, and Perl scripts
- True virtual hosting
- Support for multiple Ethernet adapters

Email Services

The Internet service most heavily relied upon by users of all kinds is email. It may not take up bandwidth and generate excitement like the Web, but it has become a standard form of communication vital to many organizations. When choosing an email server, you need to consider several issues, including the email protocols your server should use and the ability of email clients to access your server. Several email server solutions, as well as many utilities and helper applications that enhance these servers, are currently available for the Mac OS.

POP vs. IMAP

The most popular email protocols are Post Office Protocol (POP) and Internet Message Access Protocol (IMAP). Both POP and IMAP use Simple Mail Transfer Protocol (SMTP) to exchange data and connection information. SMTP is a server-to-server protocol, meaning that it is used to transfer email from a sending email server to a receiving email server. Most Unix-based computers employ SMTP in conjunction with sendmail, part of many Unix operating systems since the late 1970s, and are themselves email servers. Version 3 of POP (POP3), the most popular Internet server protocol, is widely available on several platforms, including the Mac OS.

The POP protocol is structured as a "store and forward" or "store and download" email server, where email clients such as Qualcomm's Eudora log in to the server and then download the contents of a user's inbox to the hard drive. This makes the load on the email server minimal, compared to IMAP-based email servers, because POP-based email servers delegate email storage, processing, and other system-intensive tasks to the client. IMAP, on the other hand, keeps the user's email on the server and maintains a constant connection with its clients, which requires huge amounts of processor, RAM, and storage space. The greatest benefits of POP, therefore, are that it is much faster, isn't "chatty," and places less demand on the server. IMAP's greatest benefit is that a user's email is accessible from any IMAP email client from anywhere on the Internet because it isn't downloaded off the server to a local hard drive.

Eudora Internet Mail Server (EIMS)

The Eudora Internet Mail Server (EIMS), formerly the Apple Internet Mail Server (AIMS), is a feature-rich SMTP, IMAP, and POP3 email server for the Mac OS. EIMS, which Apple acquired from Glen Anderson in 1995, is a complete server application that has minimal hardware and OS requirements yet delivers everything needed to provide robust Internet email services to organizations of all sizes.

In fact, we run an EIMS server with over 1,000 users on a 200MHz PPC 601, and it does just fine! To run this email server, your Mac needs to meet only the following requirements:

- Any PowerMac
- Mac OS 8 or higher
- Open Transport 1.1.2 or higher
- 1MB of hard drive space (minimum)
- An Internet connection
- DNS services

Other Email Servers

Several options are available for Mac OS email servers, but most are part of moderately priced commercial packages. Their abilities and prices vary, and your best choices include:

- NetTen from Tenon is an IMAP, POP3, DNS, and BIND server that uses a Unix virtual machine, as does WebTen, to bring very high-performance mail services to Mac OS 9.1. See **www.tenon.com/products/netten/** for more information.

- Stalker Internet Mail Server from Stalker Software supports both POP3 and IMAP, and is reasonably priced at just a few hundred dollars. See **www.stalker.com/SIMS/** for more information.

- WebSTAR has built into its Server Suite an email server that provides SMTP, POP3, IMAP4, APOP, and MIME as well as WebMail. See **www.starnine.com** for more information.

Mailing List Services

A *mailing list server*, often called a *listserv*, is a program that manages and sends email to lists of subscribers and provides email on demand. For example, you could have one email address such as **staff@mycompany.com** and be able to send a message to dozens, hundreds, or thousands of people by entering this single address. Mailing lists can be public or private, and can be configured to allow people to subscribe and unsubscribe themselves, as well as to post messages to the list. These servers can also allow you to provide email-on-demand services, which allow people to send email to the server and have the server reply to their requests with information, documents, and attachments.

TIP: Mailing lists come in two general formats: distribution lists and discussion lists. Distribution lists are typically used to distribute messages to large groups of people and are not used to generate topics for discussion among their recipients. Discussion lists, on the other hand, are usually configured to allow their subscribers to send messages to one another, either freely or through the assistance of a moderator.

Although EIMS and other mail servers contain basic mailing list capabilities, they often are not robust enough to meet the needs of large or complex lists, nor do they offer email-on-demand and other services.

Macjordomo

Macjordomo is freeware, but don't let that fool you: Macjordomo meets the needs of almost all organizations requiring an Internet list server. A product of Leuca Software and the Office of Academic Computing at Cornell Medical College, Macjordomo is extremely easy to set up and requires a POP3/SMTP email server (such as EIMS) to handle the actual mail delivery. Macjordomo serves as an intelligent email client that responds to email sent to one or more of its accounts. Its requirements include:

- Any PowerPC processor
- 2MB of application memory
- 1MB of disk space, plus space for list messages and archives
- An Internet connection
- POP3 server (such as EIMS)

See **http://macjordomo.med.cornell.edu** for more information and software downloads.

LetterRip Pro

The most powerful commercial mailing list application for the Mac OS is LetterRip Pro from Fog City Software (**www.fogcity.com**). It is fairly expensive as far as Mac software goes ($395), but if you host multiple mailing lists, or a few lists with high volume, then LetterRip Pro is what you should use for your mailing lists. To run LetterRip Pro, you'll need a Mac with the following meager requirements:

- Any PowerPC processor (or even a 68030 or 68040 processor)
- 2MB of application memory
- 10MB of disk space, plus space for list messages and archives

It is both an SMTP and POP3 server, and can handle lists with thousands of subscribers. Accounts may be managed via email or an administrative application that runs on the server itself, or from any computer on the Internet.

FTP Services

File Transfer Protocol (FTP) is used to transfer files from one computer to another using TCP/IP. FTP was once the workhorse protocol on the Internet—before the Web became the top dog. Several good FTP server options have been available for the Mac OS for many years; let's look at three that are sure to meet just about everyone's needs.

Better Telnet (NCSA FTP)

The easiest—and cheapest—FTP server is part of Better Telnet, formerly known as NCSA Telnet. Sure, it's a little outdated, but Better Telnet is one of the few free FTP servers still available. Better Telnet is easy to configure and has a minuscule memory footprint, taking only about a 1MB of RAM. See **www.cstone.net/~rbraun/mac/telnet/** for the latest version.

Anonymous FTP

Anonymous FTP refers to an account on an FTP server that anyone can access. Anonymous FTP is very useful for distributing software and data files to the general public, but it has its risks. If access restrictions are improperly configured, it's possible to accidentally grant too many privileges to tens of millions of Internet users, many of whom would like to see—and possibly erase—the contents of your server.

It's proper netiquette to request that anonymous FTP users employ the user ID "anonymous" and use their actual email address as a password. Most FTP servers keep a log file of anonymous visitors, so if anything goes wrong with their server, they have a detailed account of who was on their server and when, where they looked for information, and for how long. Of course, it's easy to misrepresent yourself when doing anonymous FTP by entering a false email address during login. We wouldn't recommend this, however, because a log file can contain visitors' IP names and numbers—which goes a long way toward tracking them down.

NetPresenz FTP Server

If you require a more secure FTP server, try Peter Lewis's $70 shareware program NetPresenz, formerly FTPd. NetPresenz, an FTP/Web/Gopher server, requires System 7 or higher and uses the Mac OS's built-in file sharing capabilities to control user access and restrictions through two programs, a setup application and an FTP daemon. To get the latest version of NetPresenz, see **www.stairways.com**.

Rumpus

Rumpus, from Maxum Development, is the most powerful solution to providing FTP service on the Mac OS. Rumpus is unique among FTP servers for the Mac OS for several reasons:

- Rumpus is an Open Transport-native FTP server.
- It can use File Sharing's users and group accounts when File Sharing is not active.

- It has the capability to automatically encode files, using MacBinary and BinHex.

- It supports more than 32 simultaneous connections.

Rumpus is easy to set up and accommodates several different levels of FTP security. To begin using Rumpus, you'll need a computer that is running the Mac OS and meets the following criteria:

- System 7.5 or higher

- 3MB of free RAM

- 1MB of disk space for the application

- MacTCP or Open Transport

Providing Gopher Services

Gopher servers for the Mac aren't as plentiful as FTP and Web servers, and, once again as with many FTP servers, most of them come as part of a multi-server package. Over the past few years, Gopher usage has been decreasing because Web servers can deliver the same file-searching and -retrieving features with an interface that has more cross-platform features. Nonetheless, Gopher servers still have a place on the Internet, especially in university and library settings, where Gopher services are frequently used. If you're interested in hosting a Gopher server on your Mac, you have at least two good options to choose from: Peter Lewis's NetPresenz and the University of Minnesota's GopherSurfer.

NOTE: *For the latest information on Internet Gopher servers and clients, consult the University of Minnesota's Mother Gopher at **gopher://gopher.tc.umn.edu**.*

Immediate Solutions

Providing Personal Web Services

Personal Web servers have been part of the Mac OS for a couple of years; the two most popular servers come from Apple and Microsoft. Mac users who are connected to a LAN may be more interested in running a personal Web server than those who dial up to an ISP only on occasion.

Mac OS 9.1 includes a personal Web server capable of serving hundreds of thousands of "hits" per day. Most users will find this to be more than sufficient. The personal Web server is easy to set up and configure, and includes a Finder-like interface that helps visitors to your Web site feel more like Mac users than Web surfers.

To configure your Mac as a personal Web server, open the Web Sharing Control Panel, shown in Figure 13.1, and follow these steps:

1. Select a folder to serve as the root folder for your Web server. Mac OS 9.1 installs a folder named Web Pages on your hard drive; this folder is the default location for the Web server.

2. Select a default home page for your Web site. The default option is None, in which case the Web server uses Apple's Personal NetFinder to present the contents of your Web site to users. Figure 13.2 shows how the Personal NetFinder looks when viewed through Internet Explorer.

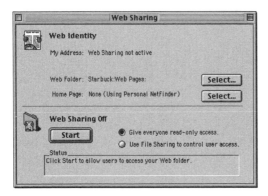

Figure 13.1   The Web Sharing Control Panel.

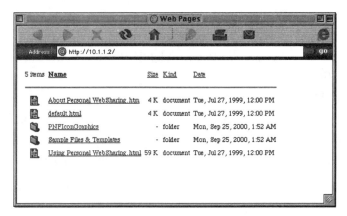

Figure 13.2   You can use the Personal NetFinder in place of a default HTML document for each folder in your Web server's folder hierarchy.

3. Open and edit the Preferences under the Edit menu, and make any necessary changes to the logging, port, access, memory, MIME, and actions settings (see Figure 13.3).

4. Return to the main window and click on the Start button to enable Web services; choose Stop to turn off the Web server.

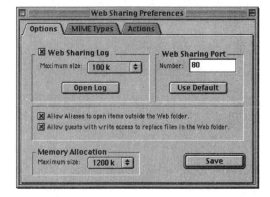

Figure 13.3   You can edit more settings through the Web Sharing Preferences window, which is accessible through the Edit menu.

Providing Commercial Web Services with WebSTAR

To install and configure WebSTAR, download the latest version of the software from **www.starnine.com** and follow these steps:

1. Run the WebSTAR Installer and launch WebSTAR.

2. Go to the Edit menu and enter a password for administrative access.

3. Launch the WebSTAR Admin application and connect to your Web server using the server's IP address, port number, and administrative password.

The WebSTAR application has very few configuration options; most of the real administration is accomplished through the WebSTAR Admin application. Figure 13.4 shows the WebSTAR Status window, which is automatically displayed on startup.

Version 4's very well thought-out administrative user interface makes it much easier to administer virtual domains, realms, and user accounts. The Web Settings section of the Edit|Server Settings is shown in Figure 13.5.

Some of the most important options in the Web Settings section include:

- *File Names*—Sets the default file names for index, error, and "no access" documents, pre- and post-processors, and the default MIME type.

- *Connections*—Sets the number of maximum connections to the Web server, as well as persistent connections (for Web browsers that support this type of connection).

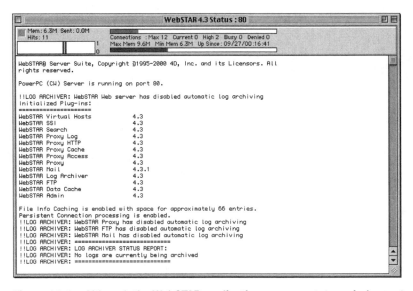

Figure 13.4   Although the WebSTAR application opens a status window automatically, virtually all the administration is performed via the WebSTAR Admin application or over the Web using a Web browser.

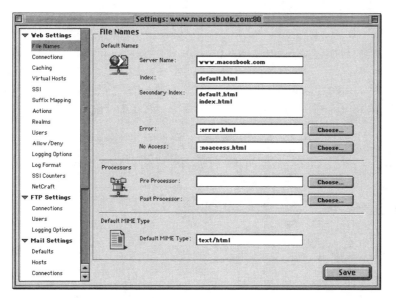

Figure 13.5   The Settings window of the new WebSTAR Admin application.

- *Caching*—Sets allocation size for caching of Web pages in memory; this allows them to be served much more quickly than if they were read from the hard drive.

- *Virtual Hosts*—Configures virtual hosts, which allow your server to host multiple domains (such as **www.debbie.com** and **www.mark.com**) using one or more IP addresses and/or domain names.

- *SSI (Server-Side Includes)*—A series of commands, executed by the Web server, that inserts items such as page counters, time and date, and last modified information into Web pages.

- *Suffix Mapping*—Configures the Web server to serve files based on their file suffix and MIME type, such as QuickTime movies (which have the extension .mov or .moov).

- *Actions*—Configures plug-in and CGI scripts.

- *Realms*—WebSTAR's main security feature, which allows you to password-protect files and folders based on their names and paths.

- *Users*—Add, modify, and delete users, and assign access rights based on realms.

- *Allow/Deny*—Sets global access restrictions based on visitors' IP and domain name information.

- *Logging Options*—Allows you to choose logging and log-archiving options.

- *Log Format*—Selects which elements, such as date, time, and host name of visitors, are to be logged.

The FTP Settings and Proxy Settings sections of the Settings window control the FTP and Proxy servers by using interface designs similar to the Web Settings. This version of WebSTAR contains excellent documentation, which is easily accessible via the Web server, and an easy-to-use search engine. For example, it took us only about five minutes to learn how to create a search session, index the documentation folder, and perform a search (see Figure 13.6).

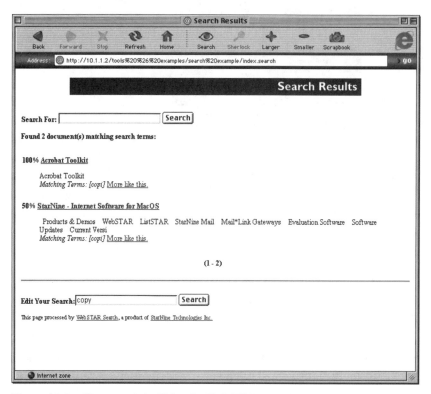

Figure 13.6   The search facilities for WebSTAR 4 are fast and easy to use.

Providing Commercial Web Services with WebTen

Be forewarned: WebTen is more complex to administer than WebSTAR, and is not for the faint of heart. To install and configure WebTen, visit **www.tenon.com** for the latest version, then follow these steps:

1. Launch the WebTen application and fill in the WebTen Preferences (shown in Figure 13.7), which can be found under the File menu.

2. Choose Admin|Set Admin Password and assign a username and password for access to the Administration Server.

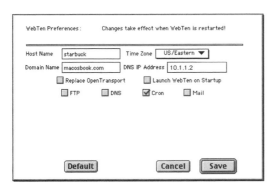

Figure 13.7 The first step in configuring WebTen is to set the application's preferences.

3. Open a Web browser to the server; on the default home page, look for a link entitled "WebTen's Administration Server." Click on this link to access the Admin Server, or enter **www.*yourservername*.com/webten_admin/**. Figure 13.8 shows the main configuration page after the username and password have been accepted.

The main configuration page is divided into two sections. The upper section is for systemwide configuration of the entire Web server, and the lower section is for the virtual domains that are hosted by the Web server. You can create multiple

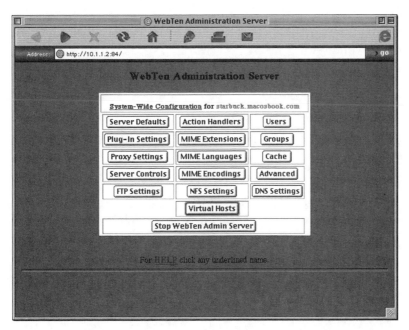

Figure 13.8 You configure WebTen, for the most part, by using a Web browser.

domains and configure each with its own preferences and settings, just as you can with WebSTAR.

The System-Wide Configuration section contains the following elements (reading top to bottom, left to right):

- *Server Defaults*—Set default file names and locations, logging, pre- and post-processors.

- *Plug-In Settings*—View the status and settings for any plug-ins, including WebSTAR and Apache plug-ins.

- *Proxy Settings*—Change the configuration options for proxy server.

- *Server Controls*—View server status and error messages, as well as flush the cache and restart the server.

- *FTP Settings*—Enable and disable FTP server, and configure logging.

- *Action Handlers*—Configure plug-in and CGI scripts.

- *MIME Extensions*—Edit user-definable MIME extensions and assign actions to specific MIME extensions.

- *MIME Languages*—Assign languages such as German or Italian to MIME extensions such as .de and .it.

- *MIME Encodings*—Assign MIME encodings to provide "meta information" about document types, such as compressed files or PDF documents.

- *NFS Settings*—Configure the Network File System (NFS) server to allow access to NFS volumes.

- *Users*—Manage user accounts.

- *Groups*—Manage groups of users.

- *Cache*—Configure various cache settings.

- *Advanced*—Configure various advanced settings that affect the performance of the Web server.

- *DNS Settings*—Configure DNS services.

- *Virtual Hosts*—Add, modify, and delete virtual domains. Figure 13.9 shows the settings for the default domain **starbuck.macosbook.com**.

Notice that many of the settings are inherited from the default host settings, so if you plan to add many virtual hosts in the future, make sure that you configure the System-Wide Configuration with this in mind.

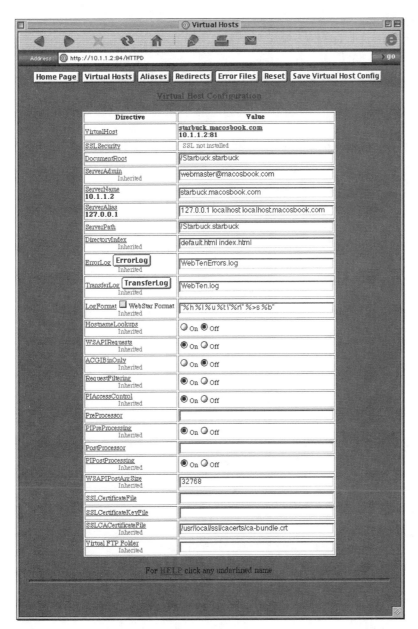

Figure 13.9   Virtual Host settings for the default domain.

Providing Email Services with EIMS

Installing EIMS couldn't be any easier. Just launch the installer, reboot, launch the application, launch the EIMS Admin application, and configure the preferences.

The main configuration options found in the Admin|Preferences menu are as follows:

- *General*—Default expansion name and logging options.

- *Connection Settings*—EIMS uses three types of server processes: POP, SMTP, and Password. Each of these utilizes one or more of the Mac OS network sockets. For small to medium offices, the default options will be adequate. Because POP uses a quick login-logout method of email retrieval, you don't need to increase the number of POP3 Server connections (unless your users have to wait more than a few seconds to check their inboxes for new messages). The same holds true for SMTP, Password, and Ph server options (see Figure 13.10).

- *Sending Setup*—Queue and timeout values for each domain, including expiration time for messages that cannot be transmitted.

- *Mail Routing*—Routing options for each domain.

- *Relay Restrictions*—Rules for routing mail, on a domain basis.

- *IP Range Restrictions*—IP-based restrictions for POP3, SMTP, password, Ph, and mail relay services.

Adding or deleting email accounts and groups is easy. Figure 13.11 shows the properties for a user whose ID is *itestuser*. The account is active; no limit exists on the forwarding of email or on the size of the user's inbox; and the user is a member of a group called Bookwriters.

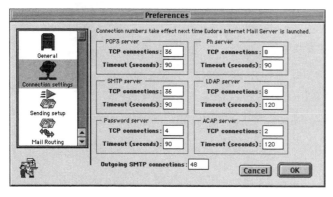

Figure 13.10   EIMS Connection Settings preferences.

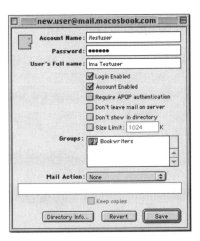

Figure 13.11   EIMS user account information.

By default, EIMS creates an account for the Postmaster, which is a requirement for email servers. The Postmaster account is used by the administrator of EIMS to receive email from users who need to contact the administrator without knowing the proper address to which to send a message. Someone should be designated to either check for email sent to this account or to receive email that can be forwarded from the Postmaster account to the user's Inbox.

Because EIMS maintains different configuration options for each domain it serves, it's very easy to maintain mail services for multiple domains. Figure 13.12 shows one of several domains that can be configured for each EIMS server, with several users and one group configured.

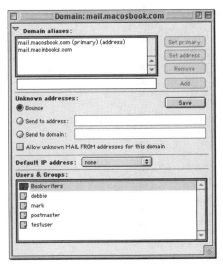

Figure 13.12   EIMS stores preferences and account information for each domain in its own window.

Providing Mailing List Services with Macjordomo

The configuration options for Macjordomo are powerful, yet easy to use. To get started, download Macjordomo from the Web (**http://macjordomo.med.cornell.edu**), install it, and follow these steps:

1. Choose Edit|Prefrerences and make some choices about message processing, character wrapping, and a few others matters (see Figure 13.13).

2. Choose Lists|New List to create a new mailing list, such as the one shown in Figure 13.14.

3. Edit the General settings, as well as any relevant advanced settings, for the new list.

4. Create an account, such as an EIMS account, on a mail server that will accept and distribute mail sent to and from the list.

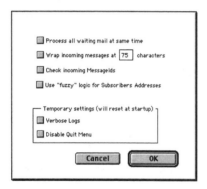

Figure 13.13   Because Macjordomo has few general preferences, it's a snap to get started.

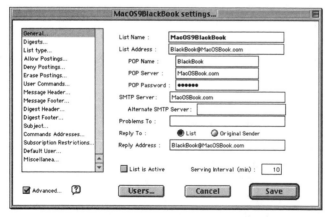

Figure 13.14   Creating lists is very easy with Macjordomo.

Macjordomo has a very easy-to-use interface for general listserv management as well as mailing lists configuration. Several default error messages are provided, as well as a message that is sent to new subscribers of a mailing list which you can customize to include information specific to your list. You may edit the text of the message, but you must not rename the LISTNAME variable because this response message is used with multiple subscriptions.

Providing Mailing List Services with LetterRip Pro

To get started with LetterRip Pro, download the demo version (**www.fogcity.com**), install it, and follow these steps:

1. Install the server and administrative applications.

2. Using the LetterRip Pro Administrator application, connect to the server from the same computer on which the server application is running. If the administrator and server applications are in the same folder, no password will be required.

3. Next, choose Server Settings from the Setup menu, then enter the basics of your server's domain information, the name of an account to which subscription requests may be sent, and an administrative username and password. Figure 13.15 illustrates these options.

4. Create a new list by choosing Mailing Lists from the setup menu, then clicking the Add button to start a new list.

5. Give the new list a name and choose an Address List (a.k.a. a list of subscribers) to associate with the new mailing list (see Figure 13.16).

6. Configure the remaining options for the list, including whether to offer a digest for subscribers who prefer to receive messages in bulk, say, once per

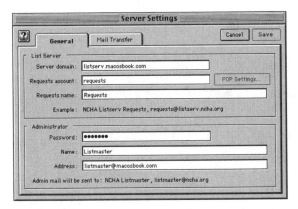

Figure 13.15   Configuring LetterRip Pro's server settings.

13. Providing Internet, Intranet, and Extranet Sevices

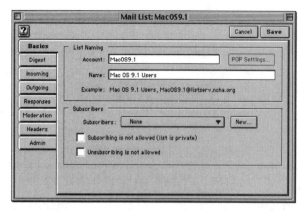

Figure 13.16   Creating a new mailing list in LetterRip Pro.

day; headers and footers on the list messages; customizing responses sent to the list (see Figure 13.17); choosing a moderator if you want someone to approve or reject individual postings to the list; headers for each message sent through the list; and assigning a secondary moderator for the list apart from the list's default administrator.

LetterRip Pro can be configured to serve distribution lists in addition to moderated or unmoderated discussion lists, and digest lists can be configured to be mailed once per day, week, or month, depending on the needs of your subscribers.

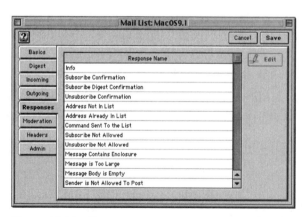

Figure 13.17   Response messages sent by the LetterRip Pro mailing list server.

Providing FTP Services with BetterTelnet

Go to **www.cstone.net/~rbraun/mac/telnet/** to download the latest version of BetterTelnet, then follow these steps to provide FTP services:

1. Launch BetterTelnet, then choose Edit|FTP Server, as shown in Figure 13.18, and configure the FTP server. The BetterTelnet FTP server has very basic control options and three levels of functionality:

   - Off

   - On, No Passwords Needed

   - On, Username & Passwords Required

   It allows you to select the default text and binary transfer file creator type, as well as to use MacBinary II, which is helpful when communicating with older Macs.

2. Add users via Edit|FTP Users. Each user is assigned a unique username, encrypted password, and a default directory. Unlike more sophisticated FTP servers, however, you cannot restrict users to certain areas of the server's hard drive.

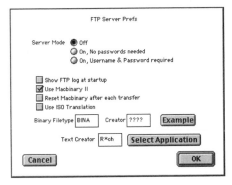

Figure 13.18   NCSA FTP server preferences.

Providing FTP Services with NetPresenz

To get the latest version of NetPresenz, go to **www.stairways.com**, then follow these steps:

1. Because NetPresenz relies on Apple's built-in file sharing capability for configuration and security, you must first go into the File Sharing Control Panel and enable file sharing, then configure the Users & Groups portion of the File Sharing Control Panel.

2. Next, launch NetPresenz and go to the FTP Setup window, where general access privileges and miscellaneous FTP-server settings are made, as shown in Figure 13.19. Note that, as in file sharing, users are categorized into three groups—Owner, Users, and Guests—and no place is available to edit usernames and passwords.

3. Go to the FTP Users configuration window, where you can customize login directories and commands on a user-by-user basis.

4. Finally, review the Security options (Figure 13.20), where you have control over read, write, delete, and copy access to directories (defined through Apple file sharing), files, and logging. One interesting feature is the capability to speak messages or play sounds during FTP sessions to inform the administrator about FTP activity!

5. Launch the NetPresenz application.

NOTE: *NetPresenz uses AppleShare's "Guest" account restrictions to control anonymous FTP access.*

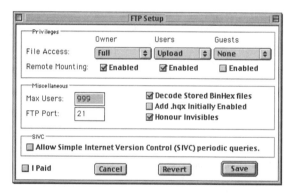

Figure 13.19   NetPresenz FTP Setup options.

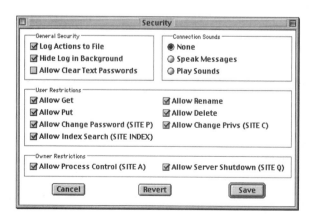

Figure 13.20   NetPresenz security settings.

Bear in mind that the Guest account is the equivalent of an anonymous FTP user in NetPresenz, and you must check the Remote Mounting checkbox to allow anonymous FTP. In the example shown in Figure 13.19, this option is not enabled.

Related solutions:	*See page:*
Configuring File Sharing and Program Linking	337
Sharing Files and Folders	339
Configuring the TCP/IP Control Panel	369
Locking Files	470
Using the File Sharing Activity Monitor	496

Providing FTP Services with Rumpus

To start using Rumpus, just follow these steps:

1. Launch Rumpus and configure it in the Basic Configuration tab, shown in Figure 13.21. This is where you'll set all the most important configuration options except the security options, which we'll discuss next. In the Basic tab, you'll decide the following:

   - The location of the root FTP directory, which can be anywhere on your system.

   - The port that will be used by Rumpus (the default is 21).

   - The maximum number of simultaneous connections that Rumpus will accept before denying access to incoming connection requests. The standard version of Rumpus allows up to 32 connections; Rumpus Pro supports 256 concurrent connections.

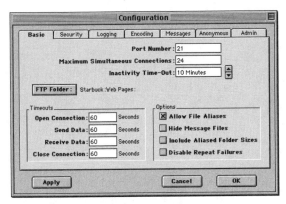

Figure 13.21 The Basic Configuration tab for Rumpus.

- The amount of time a connection may remain inactive before Rumpus disconnects the user.

- Other miscellaneous options, including timeout settings, whether Rumpus will follow aliases outside the root FTP folder, and so on.

2. Open the Security tab, shown in Figure 13.22. Pay special attention here, because Rumpus provides a new paradigm for FTP server security. Rumpus resembles a Web server more than an FTP server because it serves files and aliases to folders from a common folder, which may be different for administrators who are used to sharing folders scattered across a computer's file system. The Security tab allows you to select:

   - *Anonymous Login Only*—Tells Rumpus to use the base FTP folder (configured in the Basic Configuration tab).

   - *Users & Groups Security*—Allows you to use the File Sharing database for authentication without activating File Sharing.

   - *Built-in Security*—Uses Rumpus's own security features.

3. Configure the Logging, Encoding, Messages, Anonymous, and Admin configuration tabs.

4. If you use Built-in Security, choose the Define Users option from the File menu (or Command+U), shown in Figure 13.23, and create accounts for each user.

Rumpus is easy to learn and provides far greater flexibility than other FTP servers for the Mac OS.

Figure 13.22   The Security Configuration tab for Rumpus.

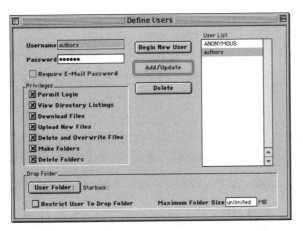

Figure 13.23   The Rumpus user account manager.

Providing Gopher Services with NetPresenz Gopher Server

Configuring NetPresenz for Gopher access entails only one more step in addition to the steps previously described for FTP access setup:

1. Launch the NetPresenz Setup application and select the Gopher Setup tab. Figure 13.24 shows the Gopher Setup options, which are all optional because these settings are read from the file-sharing setup.

2. Launch the NetPresenz application.

Note that, as with anonymous FTP, the Guest user account must be enabled in the Users & Groups portion of the File Sharing Control Panel.

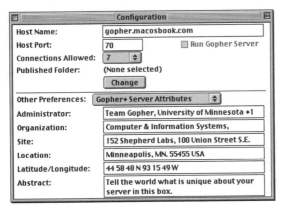

Figure 13.24   NetPresenz Gopher server setup.

Providing Gopher Services with GopherSurfer

GopherSurfer is a freeware Gopher server for the Mac OS from the University of Minnesota, home of the Golden Gophers. See **www.macorchard.com/server.html** for the latest version.

GopherSurfer requires about 1MB of RAM and has several more configuration options than does NetPresenz.

To configure GopherSurfer, take these steps:

1. Launch GopherSurfer and select Gopher|Configure.

2. Configure the elements in the upper half of the window. Then, select the Other Preferences pop-up menu and configure any additional options that are relevant to your needs. Figure 13.25 shows the main configuration options for GopherSurfer.

GopherSurfer allows from 1 to 50 simultaneous connections. Along with the host name and path to the base directory (Published Folder), these are the only settings you'll need to change in order to start running a Gopher server on your Mac.

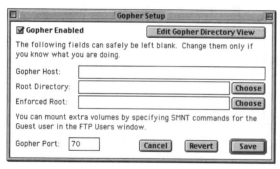

Figure 13.25   GopherSurfer Configuration options.

Chapter 14

AppleScript

In Depth

Many people don't rely on AppleScript on a daily basis, but those of us who do simply can't live without it. If you're one of these people, you can share the good news about AppleScript in Mac OS 9.1. Not only is it PowerPC-native, which makes it faster than previous versions, but it also contains improvements that enable users to automate more tasks than ever before. This chapter explores all the fundamentals of AppleScript, as well as everything that's new in the latest version.

The Usefulness of Scripting

Scripting has been around for a long time. In fact, just about every major operating system has some type of scripting facility. Scripting under Mac OS 9.1 makes it possible for you to automate repetitive tasks; programmers use scripting to create intricate solutions and even build entire applications. Scripting also makes it easy for you to access application features such as printing, as well as to manage Finder elements such as files, folders, and windows.

For example, suppose that you have a Web site that contains a few thousand documents and you need to edit them to replace the name of your company's main product, SuperGizmo, with its new name, SuperUltraGizmo, Deluxe Edition. No problem—AppleScript can do the job. But what if you want to change the name of the product only in documents that also contain the name of your competitor's product, Very Fast Special Gizmo, Standard Edition? AppleScript can handle that too, with the assistance of an Open Scripting Architecture Extension (OSAX), which is a special scripting addition. An extremely scriptable application, such as BBEdit, would also be an effective collaborator for AppleScript.

AppleScript is employed daily in the publishing industry, where complex AppleScripts are teamed with applications such as QuarkXPress to automate time-consuming production tasks. For example, AppleScripts can crop, filter, and apply special effects to batches of images, then send them to a printer. These tasks would otherwise require hours of work by a graphic artist; an AppleScript, however, can perform them automatically and free the artist to do other tasks.

Network managers can use AppleScripts to automate any number of repetitive tasks, such as deleting unwanted files on users' computers, restoring files that were unintentionally deleted, and configuring features. When combined with a rapid application development (RAD) tool such as FaceSpan, AppleScript can even help you create an entire application, complete with a user interface.

You also can use AppleScript to extract information from scriptable databases, such as FileMaker Pro, and to create Common Gateway Interfaces (CGIs) on Web servers.

First and foremost, AppleScript is useful as a tool for creating shortcuts for tasks such as finding a URL and opening the appropriate helper application, organizing files and folders, and controlling file sharing. The great thing about scripting is that it is both powerful and very helpful for even the most basic tasks.

What's New in AppleScript

Mac OS 9.1 includes version 1.5.5 of AppleScript, which builds on the inventiveness of previous versions and paves the way for AppleScript in Mac OS X. The latest version of AppleScript includes several improvements and new features, which are summarized as follows:

- *PowerPC-native code*—AppleScript is completely PowerPC-native and substantially faster than previous versions.

- *Revised dictionaries*—The scripting dictionaries for OS-level components such as the Finder have been streamlined and reorganized to make them easier to use.

- *Centralization of scripts*—You can store all your scripts in the Scripts folder within the System Folder; in fact, when dropped onto the System Folder, your scripts are automatically placed in that folder.

- *More scriptable components*—Several components of the Mac OS are now scriptable, including:
  - Appearance (Control Panel)
  - Apple Help Viewer (application)
  - Apple Menu Options (Control Panel)
  - Apple System Profiler (application)
  - Application Switcher (Extension)
  - ColorSync (Extension)
  - Desktop Printer Manager (application)
  - File Exchange (Control Panel)
  - File Sharing (Control Panel)
  - Keyboard (Control Panel)
  - Location Manager (Control Panel)
  - Network Setup Scripting (faceless application)
  - Memory (Control Panel)

14. AppleScript

- Mouse (Control Panel)
- Remote Access (Control Panel)
- Sherlock 2 (application)
- Startup Disk (Control Panel)
- USB Printer Sharing (Control Panel)
- Web Sharing (Control Panel)

- *Consolidated OSAXen*—Scripting extensions (also called scripting additions) from Apple, such as Beep, Choose Application, and New File, have been consolidated into a single OSAX called Standard Additions, which includes the following features:

  - *User interaction commands*—Select applications, files, folders, URLs, and dialogs.

  - *File commands*—Obtain information for files, folders, and disks.

  - *String commands*—Convert strings of text and numbers, find a particular string of text, and summarize a document.

  - *Clipboard commands*—Use the Clipboard, set the Clipboard, and retrieve Clipboard information.

  - *File read/write commands*—Read and write files, as well as go to the end of a file and set the end of a file.

  - *Scripting commands*—Load, store, and run scripts.

  - *Miscellaneous commands*—Insert date, change system volume, and generate a random number.

  - *Folder actions*—Attach an AppleScript to a folder so that the script is triggered whenever the folder is opened, closed, added to, deleted from, moved, or resized (i.e., enlarged or reduced). Also known as attachable Finder folders.

  - *Internet suite*—Add support for Common Gateway Interface (CGI) events and the ability to open Internet URLs.

- *Mac OS X support*—The Script Editor can use the scripting dictionaries of Mac OS X applications; scripts written under Mac OS 9.1 can be saved as Mac OS X applications that are executable without requiring the Classic environment.

- *AppleScript over TCP/IP*—Scriptable applications may be controlled on other computers via TCP/IP.

- *File status*—Obtain the status of a file to determine whether it is in use by the Mac OS or another application.

- *Large file support*—Files, folders and volumes over 2GB may be used using AppleScript.

- *Keychain support*—The keychain is scriptable to allow remote volumes to be mounted without requiring a password, provided that the volume access information is stored in the keychain.

- *Unicode support*—Improved support for converting Unicode text into international languages.

Be aware that AppleScript 1.5.5 is not backward compatible with earlier versions of the Mac OS and AppleScript. Scripts that work in Mac OS 9.1 and AppleScript 1.5.5 are not guaranteed to work with previous versions of the Mac OS.

AppleScript Components

Although Mac OS 9.1 has very few AppleScript components, you can append many scripting additions and components from the Mac OS 9.1 CD-ROM, Apple's Web site, and third-party developers. The basic components of AppleScript include:

- *AppleScript Extension*—Located in the System Folder; allows the Mac OS to interpret AppleEvents and AppleScripts.

- *Scripting Additions folder*—Located in the System Folder; contains scripting extensions, additions, and applications used by AppleScript to provide added functionality.

- *Scripts folder*—Located in the System Folder; serves as a central location for scripts.

- *Script Editor*—Located in the AppleScript subfolder in the Apple Extras folder; writes, edits, and records AppleScripts and other Open Scripting Architecture (OSA)-compliant scripts.

You can install additional scripting components—which we'll discuss later in this chapter—in various locations on your hard drive, but for the most part, they will automatically be placed in the Scripts and Scripting Additions folders.

How AppleScript Works

AppleScript is not just a scripting language; it is an object-oriented programming language that works by interpreting English-like commands into AppleEvents and passing them to the appropriate application or to the Mac OS. The AppleScript commands are interpreted by the AppleScript Extension, as well as any additions (OSAXen) that are installed on your computer. Basic scripts that rely on the standard suite of OSAXen work on any computer on which AppleScript has been fully installed. Scripts that rely on special OSAXen do not function properly (or at all) on computers that lack these OSAXen.

14. AppleScript

AppleScripts work in conjunction with portions of the Mac OS and applications that have been written to be AppleScript compatible. AppleScript compatibility has three levels:

- *Scriptable applications*—Applications that understand AppleScript commands.

- *Attachable applications*—Applications that contain elements such as buttons to which AppleScripts can be attached.

- *Recordable applications*—Applications that allow you to use the Record feature to create AppleScripts, rather than requiring you to write AppleScript code.

Although more and more applications, such as BBEdit 6, are now recordable, most AppleScripts are written manually for applications that are scriptable or scriptable and attachable.

Scripting the Mac OS

Many—but not all—elements of the Mac OS are scriptable, and many of the best applications for the Mac OS are scriptable in varying degrees. Examples of scripts that perform actions in the Finder and various Control Panels can be downloaded from the official AppleScript Web site (**www.apple.com/applescript/**). Several folders that contain sample scripts are shown in Figure 14.1.

Basic scripts can turn File Sharing on and off and select user-interface configuration preferences such as themes, fonts, and Desktop patterns. However, most users will want to explore the new folder action scripts mentioned previously. We'll look at these in detail later in the Immediate Solutions section of this chapter.

In addition to the Finder, which is scriptable, Table 14.1 lists the Control Panels and their scriptability in a standard installation of Mac OS 9.1.

We can assume for now that future releases of the Mac OS, including Mac OS X, will probably incorporate more scriptability.

Related solutions:	Found on page:
Configuring the Appearance	78
Allocating Application Memory	184
Configuring File Sharing and Program Linking	337
Sharing Files and Folders	339

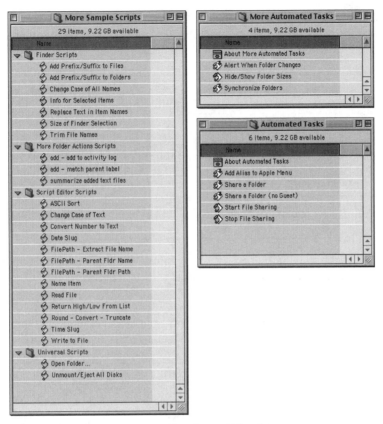

Figure 14.1 Sample AppleScripts for the Mac OS.

Table 14.1 Control Panels in Mac OS 9.1 and their scriptability.

Control Panel	Scriptable?
Appearance	Yes
Apple Menu Items	Yes
AppleTalk	Yes (via Network Setup Scripting Addition)
ColorSync	Yes (via ColorSync Extension)
Configuration Manager	No
Control Strip	No
Date & Time	No
DialAssist	No
Energy Saver	No
Extension Manager	No

(continued)

Table 14.1   Control Panels in Mac OS 9.1 and their scriptability *(continued)*.

Control Panel	Scriptable?
File Exchange	Yes
File Sharing	Yes
General Controls	No
Internet	No
Keyboard	Yes
Keychain Access	Yes (via Scripting Addition)
Launcher	No
Location Manager	Yes
Memory	Yes
Modem	No
Monitors	No
Mouse	Yes
Multiple Users	No
Numbers	No
QuickTime Settings	No
Remote Access	Yes
Software Update	No
Speech	Yes (via Scripting Addition)
Startup Disk	Yes
TCP/IP	Yes (via Network Setup Scripting Addition)
Text	No
USB Printer Sharing	Yes
Web Sharing	Yes

Scripting Applications

Many Mac OS 9.1-compatible applications are scriptable. The scriptable applications that are part of the default installation of Mac OS 9.1 include:

- Aladdin DropStuff
- Aladdin StuffIt Expander
- Apple Applet Runner
- Apple Verifier
- Disk Copy

- Disk First Aid
- FontSync
- Iomega Tools
- Microsoft Internet Explorer
- Microsoft Outlook Express
- Netscape Communicator
- QuickTime Player
- Sherlock 2

Of course, it's up to the individual software developer to decide whether to support AppleScript. But if you or your organization rely on AppleScript, choose products that are scriptable and let vendors know that AppleScript is a critical feature.

Alternatives to AppleScript

At the moment, Frontier from UserLand (**www.userland.com**) is the only alternative to AppleScript that is also OSA-compliant; Frontier is more a Web-based database solution than an alternative to AppleScript, however. FaceSpan (**www.facespan.com**), another product that uses AppleScript, is a robust application development environment that allows developers to place Mac-like interfaces, including dialog boxes and windows, on top of AppleScripts. FaceSpan is a great tool to have if you want to distribute AppleScript-based solutions to others, and if your users prefer a familiar user interface environment.

Several alternatives to Apple's Script Editor are also available. This editor is very basic when compared to programs such as Scripter from Main Event (**www.mainevent.com**). Scripter is a great choice because it goes well beyond the capabilities of Apple's Script Editor, especially in its capability to debug scripts. Another recommended tool is Script Debugger from Late Night Software (**www.latenightsw.com**). Script Debugger is an extensible tool that is also much more powerful than Script Editor.

Working with Script Editor

Script Editor is a very basic scripting tool that enables you to perform all the scripting tasks most beginner and intermediate users will need to get started. Advanced users, on the other hand, will probably want to consider a more sophisticated editor. Script Editor will allow you to perform the following tasks:

- View dictionaries
- Create, edit, and save scripts
- Do basic debugging

14. AppleScript

Figure 14.2   An AppleScript viewed in Script Editor.

Figure 14.2 shows a sample script, written to activate File Sharing and perform several steps along the way, as it appears in the Script Editor.

The Script Editor's interface is simple, and using it to edit a script is straightforward. The editor window is divided into two sections. In the top portion of the window, you can write a description of the script, or include whatever you like, such as instructions or background notes.

The lower portion of the window contains the script, as well as buttons for the following:

- Recording a script
- Stopping recording or playing back a script
- Running the current script
- Checking the syntax of the script

Working with Scripter

Scripter is much more powerful than Script Editor and has dozens of features—too many, in fact, to even begin to cover here. When comparing it to Script Editor, you'll quickly see that it is a comprehensive scripting tool, not just a script editor. For example, Figure 14.3 shows the same script that appeared in the previous figure opened in Scripter.

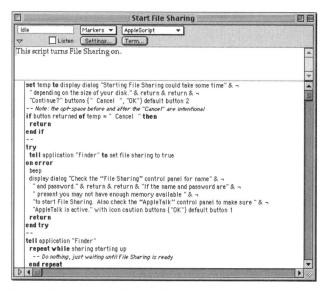

Figure 14.3   A sample script in Scripter.

Scripter performs all the same tasks as in Script Editor, but it also enables you to do the following:

- Debug scripts in detail

- Build custom scripting additions

- Build databases of coding shortcuts

- Customize your scripting environment with multiple palettes for shortcuts and assembly tools

- Perform complex search and replace

- Enact multiple undos

The demo version of Scripter (available from **www.mainevent.com**) is fully functional, except that it will not allow you to print or save scripts. However, you can try out its many features, including:

- *Application bar*—Adds quick access to your favorite scriptable applications, such as BBEdit.

- *Builder*—Builds scripting additions for an application (see Figure 14.4).

- *Tools palette*—Provides shortcuts to commonly used scripting tools and commands, such as commenting and searching scripts.

- *Collection*—Provides a central location for frequently used scripts (see Figure 14.5).

- *Command tool*—Quickly executes a brief command as a reference tool to help debug scripts (see Figure 14.6).

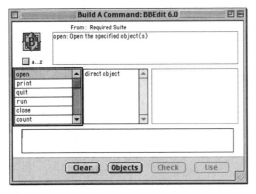

Figure 14.4   A builder for BBEdit in Scripter.

Figure 14.5   Use the Collection feature in Scripter to store your frequently used scripts for
quick reference or execution.

Figure 14.6   Scripter's Command tool.

Expanding AppleScript

AppleScript has the wonderful capability to provide a framework that allows programmers, amateur and professional alike, to create sophisticated forms of interapplication communication. Here are three useful resources for expanding
AppleScript that you can download from the Web.

Apple Data Detectors

Apple Data Detectors (**www.apple.com/applescript/data_detectors/**) is an AppleScript-based technology that recognizes certain types of data, such as URLs, and provides additional options to users when selected in the Finder or an application such as BBEdit. It is also a framework that allows developers to create different types of detectors—not just URL detectors—that can be available across applications and in the Finder.

Apple Data Detectors consists of a contextual menu and a Control Panel that allow you to designate the helper applications that should be used with the various types of data it can detect. Apple Data Detectors automatically installs Internet Address Detectors, a module that can detect several types of URLs, including the following:

- Email addresses
- Web addresses
- Usenet newsgroup addresses
- FTP addresses
- Host addresses

Apple Data Detectors is easy to install and works by allowing you to select text in an application and activate the contextual menu; then, it displays a set of options. For example, Figure 14.7 shows some text with three URLs, the first of which is designated to be opened with Netscape Navigator.

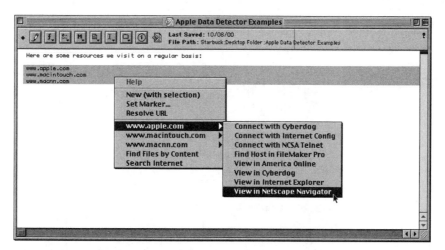

Figure 14.7   An example of how AppleScript and Apple Data Detectors work together to provide easy access to URLs.

Acme Contextual Menu Manager Widgets

Another cool AppleScript plug-in is Acme Contextual Menu Manager (CMM) Widgets from Acme Technologies (**www.acmetech.com**). Like Apple Data Detectors, Acme CMM Widgets provide several additional features to the Mac OS's beloved contextual menus. For example, Acme CMM Widgets provides several additional menu options under the Acme Widgets option. These options, shown in Figure 14.8, are very useful for Web developers and Webmasters.

OSA Menu Lite

OSA Menu Lite by Leonard Rosenthol (**www.lazerware.com**) is a program that adds a script menu to all elements of the Mac OS and all applications, even if they have their own script menu (as is the case with BBEdit). Figure 14.9 shows the OSA Menu as it appears when viewed while in the Finder.

If you rely on AppleScript in your daily work, you'll find this to be an excellent feature.

Additional Scripts

The best sources for more example scripts are the Mac OS 9.1 installation CD-ROM and the AppleScript Web site at **www.apple.com/applescript/scripts/scripts. 00.html**. These two resources offer enough scripts to keep you busy for months to come.

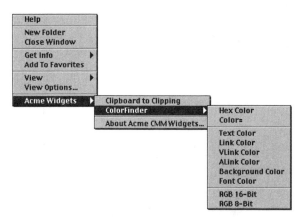

Figure 14.8   The new Contextual menu options added by Acme CMM Widgets.

Figure 14.9   The OSA Menu, an optional installation with Mac OS 9.1.

Additional Resources

Because AppleScript is a huge subject to attempt to cover in this book, we encourage you to explore the following resources for additional information:

- *Apple Computer's AppleScript Web site*—**www.apple.com/applescript/**

- *AppleScript Sourcebook Web site*—**http://oasis.bellevue.k12.wa.us/cheeseb/index.html**

- *Everything CD for Macintosh Scripting*— **www.isoproductions.com/cd/macscripting/**

- *MacScripting Mailing List*—**www.dartmouth.edu/info/macscript/mailinglist.html**

- *ScriptWeb Web site*—**www.scriptweb.com**

- Goodman, Danny. *Danny Goodman's AppleScript Handbook, Second Edition* (ToExcel Publishing), 1998.

- Wilde, Ethan. *AppleScript for the Internet: Visual QuickStart Guide* (Berkeley, CA: Peachpit Press), 1998.

14. AppleScript

Immediate Solutions

Identifying Scriptable Applications

Because not all applications and elements of the Mac OS are scriptable, identifying what is scriptable and what is not is one of the first tasks you should perform. Script Editor (or another editor, such as Scripter) offers several ways to identify scriptability in an application or in the Mac OS. Each of these methods entails opening the application's scripting dictionary, where the scripting commands are stored.

Opening the Dictionary Using Script Editor

The Script Editor can open a scripting dictionary in two ways. The first way is through the File menu, as follows:

1. Launch Script Editor and choose File|Open Dictionary.

2. Select an application or Mac OS component that appears in the Open dialog box.

3. The dictionary will open in Script Editor (see Figure 14.10).

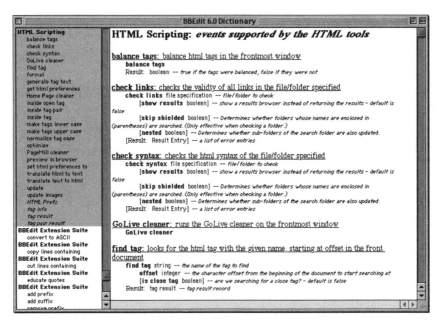

Figure 14.10   An example of a scripting dictionary, with several elements selected.

Only those items containing dictionaries will appear in the dialog window. All other applications that lack scriptability (and therefore, scripting dictionaries) will not even appear in the Open dialog window.

You can also drag and drop an application or OS component onto the Script Editor icon to determine whether it is scriptable. If it is scriptable, the dictionary will open in the Script Editor. If it is not, an information dialog box will open with an error message, such as the one shown in Figure 14.11.

Opening a Dictionary with Script Debugger

You can also use Script Debugger to open a scripting dictionary. Compared to Script Editor, Script Debugger does a much better job of displaying the information. To open a scripting dictionary:

1. Launch Script Debugger and choose File|Open Dictionary.

2. Select from the options presented in the Open Dictionary menu, such as items in the Scripting Additions folder, a specific application, or the scripting dictionary of an application currently running on your computer, as shown in Figure 14.12.

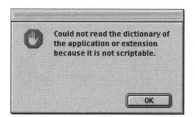

Figure 14.11   Unscriptable applications generate this error when dropped onto the Script Editor application icon.

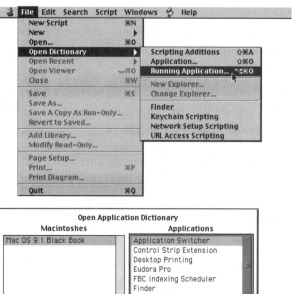

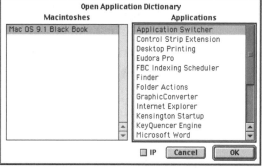

Figure 14.12   Script Debugger is a very utilitarian method of opening a scripting dictionary.

Recording Scripts

The best way to learn how AppleScript works is to create a script by recording a few simple Finder actions. Remember, the Finder is scriptable as well as recordable, so creating a Finder script is very easy. The following examples create a script that performs several actions on a folder in the Finder.

Recording in Script Editor

To record a script using Script Editor, follow these steps:

1. Open the Apple Extras folder on your hard drive and select View|As Icons, then move the window so that it is easily visible on the Desktop.

2. Launch Script Editor and click on the Record button that appears in the untitled script window, as in Figure 14.13.

3. Select the Apple Extras folder on the Desktop.

Figure 14.13   Preparing to record a script.

4. Choose View|As List.

5. Click on the Zoom box in the Apple Extras folder window.

6. Choose View|As Pop-up Window.

7. Press Command+W to close the pop-up window.

8. Return to the Script Editor by choosing it from the Applications menu or by clicking anywhere in the open script.

9. Click on the Stop button to stop recording.

Script Editor will automatically check the syntax of the script and display the results of your recording in the untitled window, shown in Figure 14.14.

Because not all actions are recordable in the Finder (or in any application, for that matter), some of your actions may not be recorded and will therefore not appear in your script. All actions in this example are recorded, however.

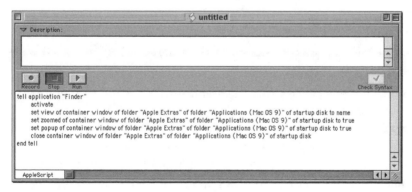

Figure 14.14   A newly recorded AppleScript.

Recording in Script Debugger

Script Debugger also records scripts, but uses different commands. To perform the same task as in the previous example, follow these steps:

1. Launch Script Debugger and choose Script|Record (or press Shift+Command+R).

2. Select the Apple Extras folder on the Desktop.

3. Choose View|As List.

4. Click on the Zoom box in the Apple Extras folder window.

5. Choose View|As Pop-up Window.

6. Press Command+W to close the pop-up window.

7. Return to Script Debugger and choose Script|Stop (or press Command+R). Figure 14.15 shows the results of the recording—a script code that is identical to the one produced by Script Editor.

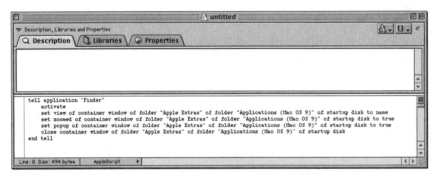

Figure 14.15   Recording a script in Scripter.

Understanding Scripts

AppleScripts can be very easy to understand—or they can be so complex that only a seasoned programmer can really comprehend them. As we mentioned earlier, the AppleScript Web site is a source for sample scripts (**www.apple.com/applescript/**). The sample scripts give a good overview of the basics of AppleScript usage, but the mechanics of a script rely on at least three things:

• The level of scriptability programmed into an application by its creators

• The scripting dictionary and documentation of its scripting commands

• Any scripting additions or Extensions that may be installed and can influence the scriptability of an application

For example, look at the result of the script we recorded in the example from the previous section:

```
tell application "Finder"
    activate
    set view of container window of folder "Apple Extras" of folder
    "Applications (Mac OS 9)" of startup disk to name
    set zoomed of container window of folder "Apple Extras" of folder
    "Applications (Mac OS 9)" of startup disk to true
    set popup of container window of folder "Apple Extras" of folder
    "Applications (Mac OS 9)" of startup disk to true
    close container window of folder "Apple Extras" of folder
    "Applications (Mac OS 9)" of startup disk
end tell
```

AppleScript is an *object-oriented language*, which means it uses commands (such as **open**, **close**, **change**, or **print**) to act upon objects (such as windows, selected words, or interface features). These commands are listed in the scripting dictionary, and the objects are grouped into logic units referred to as *object classes*. Commands and objects are described by using *expressions* (collections of values) and are capable of performing simple (*unary*) and complex (*binary*) operations, such as simple mathematical or algebraic calculations. In our example, the Finder is commanded to change the *value* (view as name) of certain *objects* (windows) and then perform other commands as well (close container window).

It's easy enough to learn to record basic scripts in AppleScript. Don't underestimate the capacity of AppleScript, however. It is a highly complex object-oriented programming language that is most powerful when utilized by experienced programmers, and is limited only by the software developers who choose to make their products scriptable.

Debugging Scripts

Because AppleScript is a programming language, you must ensure that your code is free of all errors before your scripts can be properly executed. Errors can result from a variety of causes, including:

- Bad syntax and inaccurate usage of commands
- Misplaced variables
- Typographical errors
- Circular logic

Fortunately, Script Editor, Scripter, and Script Debugger provide various levels of debugging to help us correct scripting errors. Debugging code can be as simple as fixing a typographical error in a script, or it can be as hideously complex as correcting a series of AppleScript commands that, for whatever reason, don't yield the correct result. This is where patience and programming skills come into play.

Debugging in Script Editor

Script Editor provides only a very basic level of code debugging and execution error reporting called *syntax checking*. To generate a test error to demonstrate how Script Editor reacts to errors, take these steps:

1. Make the Apple Extras folder a pop-up window by dragging it to the bottom of the screen, or by choosing View|As Pop-up Window. Because the folder is already a pop-up window, the script we recorded in the previous example will fail because it doesn't contain any IF-THEN logic to take into account the fact that the folder is already a pop-up window.

2. Open the script we just recorded.

3. Click on the Run button and Script Editor will generate an error like the one shown in Figure 14.16. Notice that Script Editor highlights the area of the script containing the coding error.

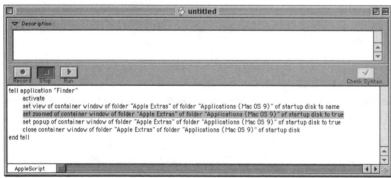

Figure 14.16   An execution error warning from Script Editor (top) and the problematic code automatically highlighted by Script Editor (bottom).

In addition to this warning, you can also view the Event Log, which logs both successful and unsuccessful scripting activities. To view the Event Log:

1. Run the script.

2. Choose Controls|Open Event Log, as shown in Figure 14.17.

Script Editor also has a basic syntax-checking feature. You can utilize this feature by following these steps:

1. Open the script we just recorded.

2. Change the first instance of the command **set** to a nonsensical term like **setter**.

3. Click on the Check Syntax button. Script Editor will generate an error like the one shown in Figure 14.18.

Finally, Script Editor has one other feature, the *Result window*, that you can implement to debug your scripts. To view the Result window:

1. Open any script.

2. Run the script.

3. Choose Controls|Show Result.

The Result window displays the result of successful scripts only. Reviewing the contents of the Result window can help you refine the steps in your script and optimize them accordingly (see Figure 4.19).

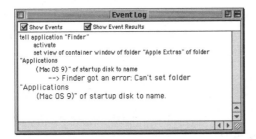

Figure 14.17   Errors are recorded in the Event Log.

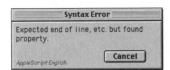

Figure 14.18   Script Editor's syntax-checking feature returns results like this.

Figure 14.19   The Result window.

Debugging with Script Debugger

When it comes to debugging, Script Debugger lives up to its name. It has all the capabilities of Script Editor and more, including our favorite feature: its capability to step through a script one line at a time, checking syntax and debugging along the way. To debug a script in Script Debugger:

1. Launch Script Debugger and enable the AppleScript debugger in the Scripting Settings section of the Edit|Preferences menu. You'll also need to choose Include Controls in the Script Editor Window Style section.

2. Open a script that contains a known error or performs an illegal operation, as in the previous section.

3. Choose Script|Step Over (or click the Step button in the editor window) to step through the script one line at a time, or choose Script|Step Out to automatically return to the Script Debugger editor after each step has been completed. Figure 14.20 shows the script window with a blue arrow beside the last line that was successfully executed.

4. When Script Debugger encounters an error, it returns as the foreground application and presents an error dialog box detailing the error. Moreover, it uses a red arrow to indicate the error in the editor window and highlights the line of code containing the error, as shown in Figure 14.21.

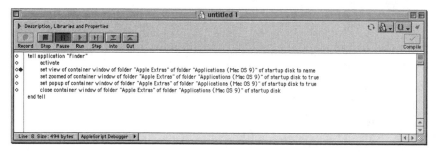

Figure 14.20   Script Debugger uses visual clues like this arrow to indicate good and bad lines of code.

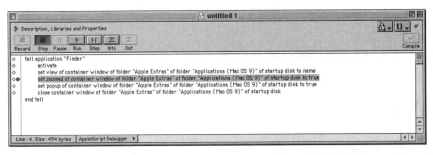

Figure 14.21 Script Debugger reports errors like this to help identify problematic code.

Saving Scripts

One of the coolest things about AppleScript is that you can create several different types of scripts from the same code base. In AppleScript 1.5.5, you can create the following types of scripts:

- *Text*—ASCII text files that other editors can open in their native dialect.
- *Compiled scripts*—Scripts from which the native dialect has been removed so that they are executed by AppleScript in a more AppleScript-native format; these scripts run only under a scripting editor or are called (i.e., referenced) by another script.
- *Classic Applet*—An application that will run on a computer with AppleScript.
- *Mac OS X Applet*—An application that will run on a computer with AppleScript and CarbonLib or Mac OS X.

Scripter and Script Debugger, however, do not allow you to save scripts in each of these formats.

To save a script in Script Editor, Scripter, or Script Debugger:

1. Open a script and choose File|Save As (Script Editor or Script Debugger) or File|Save As Run-Only (Scripter).

2. In the Save dialog box, select Application, Compiled Script, or Text.

For example, Figure 14.22 shows a script being saved as an application (i.e., Classic Applet).

14. AppleScript

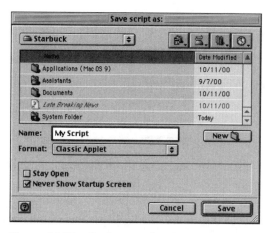

Figure 14.22   Saving a script as an application.

Creating Folder Actions

The ability to attach or associate a script with a particular folder is another of AppleScript's best features. The script is activated whenever the associated folder is:

- Opened

- Closed

- Added to

- Deleted from

- Moved or resized

Using the contextual menu, you can easily add and delete folder action scripts, and even add multiple folder actions to a single folder. To try this out, first locate an existing script to attach to the folder, or create a new script such as the following one, which simply beeps and displays a message whenever the folder is opened (see Figure 14.23 for the result of this script when activated by opening a folder associated with this script):

```
on opening folder this_folder
    tell application "Finder"
        activate
        set the folder_name to the name of this_folder
        beep
        display dialog "Greetings!" giving up after 30
    end tell
end opening folder
```

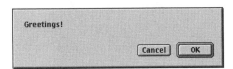

Figure 14.23   The result of our sample folder action script.

For inspiration in creating folder action scripts, check the Scripts folder in your System Folder for the following text scripts installed by Mac OS 9.1:

- add-duplicate to folders
- add-new item alert
- add-reject added items
- add-set view prefs to match
- close-close sub-folders
- mount/unmount server aliases
- move-align open sub-folders
- open-open items labeled 1
- open-show comments in dialog
- remove-retrieve items

Once you have selected or written a script and saved it as compiled script, follow these steps to attach the folder action:

1. Command+click on a folder to activate the contextual menu.
2. Choose Attach A Folder Action.
3. Locate the compiled script and select Open to open and attach the script.

For example, Figure 14.24 shows what this operation looks like using a folder called My Folder (top), and the folder as it appears once a folder action has been attached (bottom). Notice the small scroll that has been added to the standard folder icon as a visual clue that a folder action is attached.

The task of removing or editing the folder action is accomplished through the same steps as those for attaching a folder action, except for choosing the desired option from the contextual menu.

14. AppleScript

Figure 14.24   Attaching a folder action (top), and a folder with a folder action script
attached (bottom).

Chapter 15

Java

In Depth

This chapter introduces Java and Mac OS Runtime for Java. Java, created by Sun Microsystems, is a very important language because it is cross-platform and can be used over the Internet. Java has received more press and public review than any other computer language in history, and this attention has helped it evolve into an even safer and more robust language. The number of developers who have already switched to programming in Java is unprecedented. In fact, the simplicity of Java seems to be attracting those who wouldn't otherwise be programmers. As a result, a huge body of software is available for developers and users alike, with more to come in the next few years.

Introducing Java

Java is a cross-platform programming language, which makes it ideal for developing content that can be downloaded from the Web by a variety of browsers running on a variety of operating systems. A compiler changes Java code into *byte code* that is stored on a server. (Byte code is similar to machine code instructions for a computer chip.) Byte code can be assembled to form a specific type of Java program called an *applet*, which may then be used as part of a Web page. When a Web page contains a reference to an applet, the Web browser downloads the byte code and runs the Java program inside the Web page. To keep Java from doing any harm, special security restraints within the browser limit the applet's capabilities. This is known as running Java *in the sandbox*. Java also has a server-side functionality called *servlets*. These programs work in a manner similar to CGI and are created to replace Perl as the server language of choice.

Technically speaking, *Java* is an object-oriented programming language that is rendered cross-platform by the *Virtual Machine*, a program that runs Java applications on a specific operating system, in this case the Mac OS. Like any other program, the Virtual Machine had to be written differently for Unix, Windows, and the Macintosh. Nevertheless, it has a consistent interface for Java programs, as shown in Figure 15.1. Java will run on any platform, provided that a Virtual Machine exists for that platform. Other programming languages, such as C++, will also run on different platforms. However, a C++ program must be written with great care for the underlying operating system. Rewriting code for different operating systems, a process known as *porting*, requires a significant investment of time and effort because the programmers must know two operating systems.

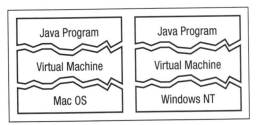

Figure 15.1   Java Virtual Machine, which takes care of the differences between platforms.

With Java, however, it's not necessary to rewrite a program for multiple operating systems. Moreover, the Virtual Machine takes care of running the Java application on each specific platform.

Although the Virtual Machine can be considered an operating system, it actually runs on top of the other operating systems as sort of a co-operating system. It's also often described as a *translator*, which may be illustrative but is not technically correct. Whereas many scripting languages use a program called a translator to communicate with the native operating system, Java is compiled into byte code designed for the Virtual Machine. Unlike a translator, the Virtual Machine has its own registers, instruction stack, and Garbage Collector. These differences, however, are relatively unimportant to anyone except computer programmers.

The major Internet browser companies embed Virtual Machines into their browsers, allowing Java programs to be run directly from Web pages. Programs that are run in this way are called *applets*, and they are under certain security restrictions intended to protect the user from malicious applets. These restrictions are important, and we'll discuss them fully later in this chapter.

Aside from the Virtual Machine, Java gives developers a large library of functionality that is referred to as the *Class Library*. Within it, developers find pieces of software that they can easily use to create programs. This library keeps them from reinventing the wheel. It also speeds up Internet delivery, because large program elements are already on your computer. The Class Library was created by taking a cross section of the functionality provided by programming libraries on major operating systems like the Mac, Windows, and Unix.

Another important Java concept is the *Just In Time Compiler (JITc)*; its function is illustrated in Figure 15.2. JITc optimizes Java code as it is running by compiling parts of the Java program into platform-specific code.

The final important concept of Java is the *Native Interface*, which allows Java programmers to issue commands to the Mac OS from within Java code (this function is especially important to the Mac for several reasons that we'll talk about in the following section). Allowing system calls from Java removes the capability to

15. Java

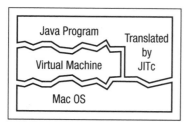

Figure 15.2   The Just In Time Compiler (JITc) translates cross-platform Java code into platform-specific code.

easily transfer Java applications from platform to platform, although not completely. The framework and user interface of a program are still primarily written in Java, with smaller parts of the program specific to the operating system.

Several competing standards for the Native Interface exist. The first edition of Java used a technique known as *native methods* to achieve the goals of the native interface. However, the native methods code was not very portable. Native methods written for one Virtual Machine would not work on another Virtual Machine, even if the machines were on the same platform. Netscape came out with a solution named *Java Raw Interface (JRI)*, and Microsoft released its own solution, *Raw Native Interface (RNI)*. But because RNI is Microsoft specific, code written with this interface is not portable. Sun assembled a committee, including Microsoft, that created a specification named *Java Native Interface (JNI)*. It is largely based on Microsoft's RNI, except that the code written with JNI is portable among Virtual Machines on the same platform. Although it participated in the creation of JNI, Microsoft continues to push developers to use RNI. Go figure.

Other features of Java include easy-to-use networking, connectivity to databases, and internationalization, which is the ability of a program to automatically display itself in a different way—or even in different languages—for users in other cultures. Each of these enterprise features represents a step toward a quantum leap in the current state of the Internet.

Mac OS Runtime for Java

Mac OS Runtime for Java (MRJ) is more than just an implementation of Java for the Mac OS. The Runtime environment provides a standalone Apple Applet Runner in addition to the Java Runtime Libraries that comprise Java applications and applets. The Apple Applet Runner program allows you to use applets without a Web browser. This is convenient for several reasons, the foremost being that it takes a relatively long time for the average Web browser to start.

An advantage of the Apple Applet Runner is that it is frequently updated. The MRJ Virtual Machine is capable of dynamically replacing your Web browser's internal

Virtual Machine. This means you don't have to wait for a new release of your Web browser to check out new applets that have been developed with the latest technology. Java Plug-In (sometimes called Java Activator) approximates this technology on other platforms; however, it requires applet distributors to rewrite their HTML files using plug-in syntax, rather than the applet tag.

MRJ includes several development tools that can turn your Mac into the premier development platform for Java. To access these features, you'll first need to download and install the MRJ *Software Development Kit (SDK)*. The components of the MRJ SDK are as follows:

- *JBindery*—Packages Java programs as Macintosh programs, which ensures that they'll be ready to run without any special preparations. JBindery helps developers come up with Macintosh "wrappers" for Java applications. In spite of Java's full class library of graphical interface tools, few Java applications are designed to integrate tightly with the systems they are delivered on, such as the Mac OS. JBindery doesn't remove the portability of Java code—it merely makes Java applications act like Macintosh applications.

- *JDirect*—Makes Macintosh functionality available to Java developers by way of an easy-to-use alternate to standard channels. JDirect allows Java code to directly call Macintosh Toolbox routines. Although customizing a Java applet for use on a specific platform using a tool like JDirect destroys the Java code's portability, it ultimately benefits developers by giving them access to the Mac platform. By placing a Java wrapper around the Macintosh system calls, JDirect makes it easy for developers to integrate those calls with their own Java code. Ultimately, JDirect encourages developers to create products for the Macintosh platform.

- *MRJ Toolkit*—If you want to write a Java program that has the grace of a good Macintosh program and is also portable, use the MRJ Toolkit. It provides techniques that help Java applications fulfill the *Human Interface Guidelines*, a book printed by Apple that describes exactly how every computer program should act. For example, it outlines that every program should have a File menu that allows the user to quit. The MRJ Toolkit also allows Java applications to respond to Apple Events so that these signals will be caught, and users will be more comfortable with familiar keyboard combinations. Because the toolkit is written in Java, it does not limit the developer to one platform.

Java vs. JavaScript

Many users remain somewhat confused about the differences between Java and JavaScript, as well as JScript—Microsoft's implementation of JavaScript—and ActiveX. Each of these technologies is used to add interactivity to Web pages, and for some of them, that's the only trait they have in common.

15. Java

As we discussed earlier in the chapter, Java is a cross-platform, object-oriented language that is ideal for use over the Internet by many different computer platforms. Similarly, JavaScript, created by Netscape, is a scripting language for browsers. It is interwoven with HTML within Web pages and is not compiled. JavaScript's sole concern is the browser, although its origins can be found in the syntax of Java. LiveWire, a server-side version of JavaScript, also has built-in database-access capabilities. LiveWire is the same as JavaScript, except that the objects deal with server activities rather than browser activities. LiveWire is similar to Active Server Pages, which is a very popular method of creating Web sites that interact with databases to create dynamic Web pages.

JScript, Microsoft's version of JavaScript, is nearly identical to JavaScript. Some differences, however, affect compatibility. Recent updates to JScript diverge from JavaScript by focusing on ActiveX objects (more about them in a moment). VBScript, another Microsoft scripting language, is based on Visual Basic instead of JavaScript. It is somewhat similar to JavaScript in syntax, but lacks the object model and handles user events in a different manner.

ActiveX is a scripting language based on a *component technology*—software that comes in pieces, or components, that are linked to form bigger applications. For the most part, these components have two functions: They are used to create applications, or they are embedded in a container (such as a Web page) and scripted with another language (in this case, JScript or VBScript). ActiveX components embedded in Web pages are inherently more dangerous than Java applets because ActiveX components have no security restrictions when they are run within a user's Web browser. Furthermore, ActiveX has no precautionary measures comparable to the byte code verifier, a Java Virtual Machine that checks the validity of downloaded code before running it.

Java Development Environments

Java developers are in great demand, second only to HTML developers and graphic designers. If you're a programmer for the Mac OS, consider exploring the various development environments that are available for use in the Mac OS. Development environments, also referred to as development tools, provide several features that are not available from text editors. These environments can automate programming tasks and present information in a way that makes it easier to understand and manipulate. Make it a point to try several tools before buying one; nearly all of the most popular development tools offer free demo versions that you can download. Although too many development tools exist to try to list all of them here, we've selected a few of the most popular ones for discussion, including the following:

- *Metrowerks CodeWarrior for Mac OS, Professional Edition*—CodeWarrior is a widely accepted programming environment that features many languages and built-in support for development across platforms and with many other types of devices. Robust and fairly intuitive, CodeWarrior is a good touchstone by which to measure other environments (**www.metrowerks.com**).

- *WebGain Visual Café*—Visual Café works on the Rapid Application Development (RAD) model, a new wave in software development that involves using pre-built components to assemble applications. You can "recycle" components written by other developers and never see the actual code (**www.webgain.com**).

- *GenieWorks SpotCheck*—SpotCheck's strategy for RAD is the opposite of VisualCafé's approach: Rather than hiding information from developers, SpotCheck provides more information by catching higher-level programming errors than most programming environments are capable of detecting. This speeds development by reducing compilation time and by preventing the developer from pursuing an erroneous line of thought. SpotCheck also provides fast options for common tasks, such as writing common loop structures (**www.genieworks.com**).

- *Zero G's InstallAnywhere Now!*—This installer program—which was voted one of the top 10 Java packages by the Java Report—allows you to create cross-platform installer programs in six steps. It is included free with the MRJ SDK (**www.zerog.com**).

Sample Applets

The following previews highlight some of the sample applets that are installed as part of Mac OS Runtime for Java:

- *Animator*—The Animator applet (see Figure 15.3) shows several animations of increasing complexity. The "coffee-bean" applet instructs developers on how to play sounds, display pictures, and double-buffer animations.

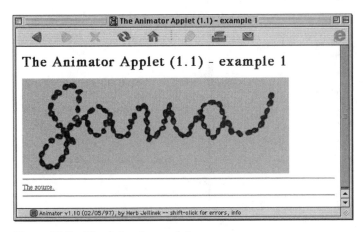

Figure 15.3   The Animator applet.

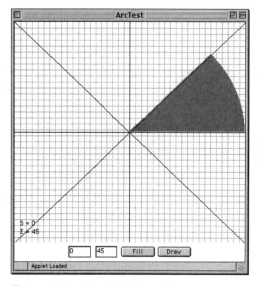

Figure 15.4   The ArcTest applet.

- *ArcTest*—The ArcTest applet, shown in Figure 15.4, displays an arc based on user input. This demonstration exposes Java's drawing primitives, which are very similar to those of OpenGL or Microsoft's DirectDraw. ArcTest is a good introduction to two-dimensional graphics for beginning developers.

- *Bar Chart*—The Bar Chart applet, shown in Figure 15.5, reads numbers from the HTML file in which it is embedded, and then generates a bar chart based on those numbers. Bar Chart is particularly useful for business-oriented Web sites.

- *Draw Test*—The Draw Test applet, shown in Figure 15.6, is a color sketchbook that shows beginning programmers how to handle events, such as mouse clicks and drags, within Java programs.

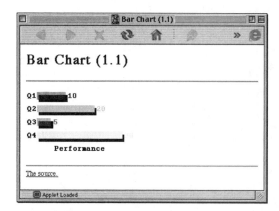

Figure 15.5   The Bar Chart applet.

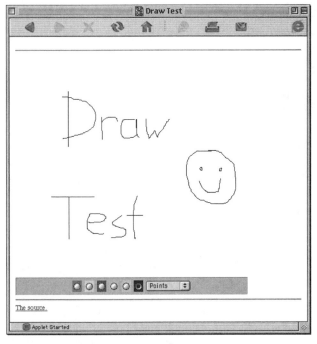

Figure 15.6   The Draw Test applet.

- *Lightweight Gauge*—The Lightweight Gauge applet (see Figure 15.7) is an example of how dynamic screen elements (the dancing bars) can be superimposed over a JPEG image file for a more interesting graphic presentation.

- *Sun Sphere*—The most sophisticated example applet, the Sun Sphere applet uses a database of date and time information to show the sunrise and sunset

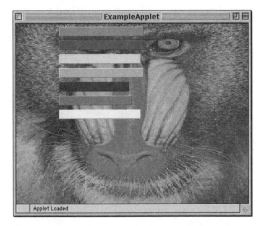

Figure 15.7   The Lightweight Gauge applet.

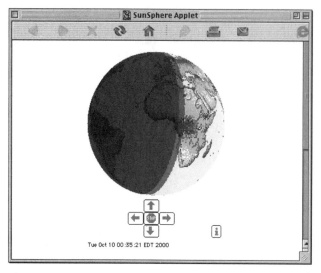

Figure 15.8   The Sun Sphere applet.

terminators for the current day, while rotating around the earth's axis (see Figure 15.8).

Launching Java Applets

The MRJ installation routine installed several example Java applets on your hard drive. These applets and the Apple Applet Runner are good examples of the capabilities of Java, and can be an invaluable aid for anyone who wants to learn Java programming. In addition to demonstrating Java's capabilities, these applets also include all the source code so you can see exactly how they were written. You can open an applet with the Apple Applet runner or a Java-enabled Web browser, such as Netscape Navigator or Microsoft Internet Explorer.

Additional Java Resources

Many online resources are available for exploring and developing Java applets. Too many exist for us to really do the subject justice, but here are some favorites that can at least get you started.

MRJ Sites

- **www.lists.apple.com/mrj.html**
- **www.apple.com/java/**

Frequently Asked Questions

- www.ping.be/beta9/MRJ-FAQ.html
- www.outlawcafe.org/MRJ-FAQ/

Other Java and Mac Development Web Sites

- http://devworld.apple.com/java/
- http://developer.apple.com/techpubs/macos8/mac8.htm
- http://java.sun.com/products/
- http://developer.javasoft.com/developer/jdchome.html
- www.javaworld.com
- www.ibm.com/developer/java/
- www.gamelan.com
- http://javaboutique.internet.com
- http://java.oreilly.com
- www.javacats.com
- www.teamjava.com
- www.javology.com/javology/
- www.javalobby.com
- www.sys-con.com/java/

Java Newsgroups

- alt.www.hotjava
- comp.compilers.tools.javacc
- comp.lang.java
- comp.lang.java.advocacy
- comp.lang.java.announce
- comp.lang.java.beans
- comp.lang.java.corba
- comp.lang.java.databases
- comp.lang.java.gui
- comp.lang.java.help
- comp.lang.java.machine
- comp.lang.java.misc

- **comp.lang.java.programmer**
- **comp.lang.java.security**
- **comp.lang.java.setup**
- **comp.lang.java.softwaretools**
- **comp.lang.javascript**

Immediate Solutions

Installing Mac OS Runtime for Java

Mac OS Runtime for Java (MRJ) is installed by default with OS 9.1. To verify this, look in your Extensions folder; if it contains the MRJ Libraries folder, then MRJ is definitely installed. Make sure that the MRJ Extensions are at least version 2.2.3 by highlighting one of the files in the MRJ Libraries folder and pressing Command+I to Get Info on the item. If you discover that the Extensions predate version 2.2.3, run the MRJ installer from the Mac OS 9.1 CD-ROM and perform a custom installation, as in Figure 15.9. After the installation is complete, your system should have a new folder entitled Mac OS Runtime for Java, and the appropriate files should have been added to the MRJ Libraries in the Extensions folder.

The Apple Extras folder should contain a folder called "Mac OS Runtime for Java," which contains the following:

- *About MRJ readme file*—Gives a general overview of Mac OS Runtime for Java.

- *License Agreement folder*—Contains a license agreement in the appropriate language.

- *Apple Applet Runner folder*—Contains the Apple Applet Runner and an Applets folder. (We will explore these in the following section.)

The MRJ Libraries folder, located in the Extensions folder, contains the following items that enable Java to run on the Mac OS:

Figure 15.9　Use the Mac OS 9.1 installation CD-ROM to reinstall Mac OS Runtime for Java.

15. Java

- *Lib folder*—This folder stores the properties files that house Java Preferences. Unlike Macintosh Preferences, these files are not regenerated—so don't delete them.

- *MRJ Symantec JITc*—The Just In Time Compiler for the Macintosh PowerPC platform, licensed from Symantec, is responsible for the performance of the Mac Java Virtual Machine.

- *MRJClasses folder*—This folder contains the JDKClasses.zip, MRJClasses.zip, and QTJava.zip files:

  - *JDKClasses.zip*—Houses the core Java class libraries.

  - *MRJClasses.zip*—Contains the specialized Java class libraries that allow Java files to use Macintosh resources, respond to Apple Events, and call Macintosh System Functions. These are the classes that make up JManager, JBindery, the Java Native Interface, and other helper classes, such as those that provide mapping between Mac and Java fonts.

  - *QTJava.zip*—Stores the class libraries that enable MRJ to execute QuickTime commands to play sound and movie files in the QuickTime format.

- *MRJLib*—This extension contains functions used by the Virtual Machine.

TIP: *By default, Mac OS 9.1 installs the Text Encoding converter, which MRJ relies upon to function. The MRJ installer can install the Text Encoding Converter as well.*

Using Apple Applet Runner

The Apple Applet Runner works like any other application for the Mac OS. To launch an applet, take these steps:

1. Launch the Apple Applet Runner application, located in the Mac OS Runtime for Java folder within the Apple Extras folder.

2. Choose an applet using one of the following methods:

   - Select an item from the Applets menu

   - File|Open Location (Command+N)

   - File|Open (Command+O)

3. Once the applet has been loaded, choose an option from the Applet menu (Suspend Applet or Resume Applet, for example); then close the applet or quit the Apple Applet Runner application.

You can also launch an applet by dragging and dropping the HTML file containing the applet onto the Applet Runner icon, or by double-clicking on the HTML file. (The latter option is applicable only if the applet's creator code is that of the Apple Applet Runner, in which case the applet will be automatically opened in the Apple Applet Runner instead of a Web browser or HTML editor, such as BBEdit.)

NOTE: *The File|Open Location option for loading an applet over the Web resembles the File|Open option of opening a local file, except that remote files are opened with security settings automatically on, as you will see in the following section.*

In addition, the Applets menu can be configured to remember frequently accessed URLs containing Java applets. This enables you to choose the URL from a menu, rather than retyping it (see Figure 15.10).

Little more is involved in running the Apple Applet Runner, except perhaps reviewing the Preferences for security and access permissions, as shown in Figure 15.11. The Apple Applet Runner security configuration options include:

- *Network Access*—Choose how your applet connects to the Internet:
  - *No Access*—No network access
  - *Applet Host*—Restricted network access
  - *Unrestricted*—Local or remote applets
- *Filesystem Access*—Determines how an applet accesses your hard disk:
  - *No File System*—No access permitted

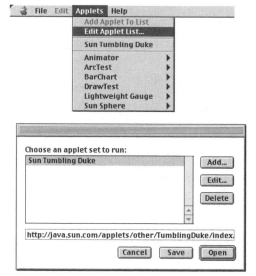

Figure 15.10   Customizing the Applets menu.

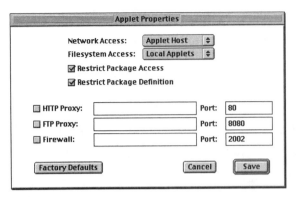

Figure 15.11   The Applet Properties dialog box allows you to restrict an applet's abilities.

- *Local Applets*—Permission granted to access the local hard disk only

- *Unrestricted*—No restrictions imposed

- *Restrict Package Access and Restrict Package Definition*—Controls how the applet interacts with the Java VM system and whether the applet can change your default Java classes.

- *Proxy access*—Configures the HTTP, FTP, and firewall proxies and ports if your computer is behind a firewall or accesses applets on non-standard ports.

Configuring Java Security

We've briefly mentioned the applet sandbox, which prohibits certain activities when code is loaded over a network. Now let's take a closer look at what goes on in the sandbox, the headquarters of Java security.

Whenever you load a Java class into the Virtual Machine, an internal object called the *ClassLoader* inspects the class. If it comes from an untrusted source (such as the Internet), the class will be placed under restrictions.

Major Restrictions Placed on Untrusted Code (the Sandbox)

Code from an untrusted source has the following major restrictions:

- You are not allowed to read or write files.

- You are not allowed to control threads that do not belong to a specific Java applet or class library.

- You cannot start any other processes.

- You cannot use native methods (which we discussed previously in the "Introducing Java" section).

- You cannot create network connections to any server except the one from which the applet was downloaded.

You can see in Figure 15.12 how Microsoft Internet Explorer allows you to choose how much of the sandbox you want in place. You can decide to give applets full network connectivity, if you want.

With these restrictions in place, it's safe to interact with executable content on the Web. However, these restrictions are very limiting. Fortunately, other security techniques allow you to trust code that you otherwise would throw in the sandbox.

Digital Signatures and the Trust Model

When describing security, computer consultants sometimes refer to the *trust model*. This is a security guideline that formally states the obvious: You can trust your own code, but not code that you download from a Web site. Most Java code falls somewhere in between. When security consultants say that code is *untrusted*, they aren't casting aspersions. Untrusted code is simply code whose safety cannot be verified. Trusted code has each of the following traits:

- *Authenticity*—The creator of the code can be reliably determined.
- *Integrity*—The code could not have been altered in transit.
- *Nonrepudiation*—The creator of the code cannot later deny having created it.

You can ensure the security of code by using *digital signatures*, a special way of processing a file so that no one can tamper with the code in any way without changing the file's signature. This assures the receiver that nobody has infected

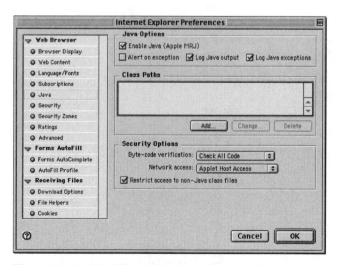

Figure 15.12   The Microsoft Internet Explorer Preferences dialog box, showing the Java preferences area.

the original file with a virus. Although a digital signature cannot eliminate the possibility that the original creator embedded a virus in the file, at least it can prove that the creator was the culprit.

Digital signatures are implemented through large organizations known as *Certificate Authorities*. You can see the ones that your browser supports by opening the security preferences in Internet Explorer (shown in Figure 15.13) and Netscape Navigator (shown in Figure 15.14). Using a digital signature can be equated to obtaining a co-signature from a Certificate Authority. In order to open a file bearing a digital signature, the digital signer's Certificate Authority must be listed in your browser's security preferences.

To learn more about a particular certificate, such as its expiration date, click on the Edit button. Don't attempt to edit the certificate—just use this window as a means of verifying its content (see Figure 15.15).

ActiveX also uses the trust model for security. When you go to a Web page that has an ActiveX control, a dialog box gives you the name of the signer of the code and asks if you want to trust that person. If anything goes wrong, you'll know exactly where to place the blame. With ActiveX, you have only two options: you can trust other people completely or not trust them at all. Java, on the other hand, allows you to use the trust model, but also allows partial trust by way of the Java Sandbox. It's the best of both worlds.

Related solutions:	See page:
Configuring the TCP/IP Control Panel	369
Locking Folders	470

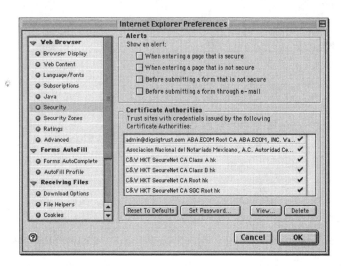

Figure 15.13   Microsoft Internet Explorer's Security preferences.

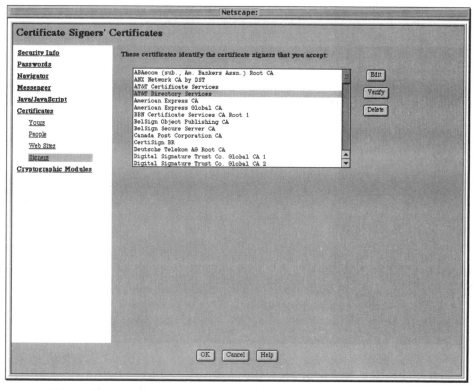

Figure 15.14   Netscape Navigator's Security Info settings.

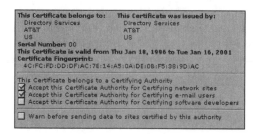

Figure 15.15   Editing a Certificate Authority in Netscape Navigator.

Inserting Applets in HTML Documents

Now that you've seen what applets can do, you can experiment with inserting Java applets into your own HTML documents using the many shareware and freeware applets available on the Web, especially navigational aids for browsing Web sites. You'll need some knowledge of HTML, however. If you just want to experiment, you can alter one of the pages from the example section.

The JAR File Format

Before we discuss the applet HTML tag, let's look at one more element that you'll encounter with applets, a *Java Archive (JAR)* file. A JAR file employs the Zip format created by PKWare. The benefits of using JAR files when working with applets include:

- Whereas operating systems have different naming conventions for files, no limit exists for the length of a file name within an archive.

- JAR allows you to compress files, which can reduce network transfer times and improve performance.

- Digital signatures are only possible on archive files, because they store information about the signature within the archive itself.

The MRJ SDK comes with a tool for creating JAR files. You can extract files from a JAR file with any commercial decompression utility that understands the Zip format, such as Aladdin's StuffIt Expander. Most modern browsers can implement JAR files.

Embedding Applets in Web Pages

The **<APPLET>** tag is the mechanism used to embed applets in Web pages. Suppose that the applet is in a file named Test.class, and we want the applet to be centered in a red page. The width of the applet is 200 pixels, and the height is also 200 pixels. Here is a sample:

```
<HTML>
<HEAD>
<TITLE>The First Applet</TITLE>
</HEAD>
<BODY BGCOLOR="#800000" TEXT="#FFFFFF">
<CENTER>
<H3> This is a Test Applet <H3>
<APPLET CODE=Test.class HEIGHT=200 WIDTH=200>
I can write stuff here that will only appear
if the applet doesn't work, or if Java applets
aren't supported by the browser.
```

```
</CENTER>
</BODY>
</HTML>
```

In the following example, we're still using Test.class; this time, however, we've stored Test.class in a different directory, and need to specify that its location has changed. We do this by using the **CODEBASE** attribute. Just to make things interesting, we'll say that it's actually located on a different computer, and rather than listing a different directory, it will be an entirely different URL:

```
<HTML>
<HEAD>
<TITLE>The First Applet</TITLE>
</HEAD>
<BODY BGCOLOR="#800000" TEXT="#FFFFFF">
<CENTER>
<H3> This is a Test Applet </H3>
<APPLET CODE=Test.class WIDTH=200 HEIGHT=200
CODEBASE=www.otherserver.com>
Notice that the height and width are in a
different order than they were last time.
It doesn't matter! They work either way.
BUT THEY ALWAYS HAVE TO BE PRESENT!
</CENTER>
</BODY>
</HTML>
```

If you read the code closely, you saw the comment about **HEIGHT** and **WIDTH**. Those two tags, along with **CODE**, are the only things that are required to be in every **<APPLET>** tag.

This time around, we've stored Test.class in a JAR file named codefiles.jar:

```
<HTML>
<HEAD>
<TITLE>The First Applet</TITLE>
</HEAD>
<BODY BGCOLOR="#800000" TEXT="#FFFFFF">
<CENTER>
<H3> This is a Test Applet </H3>
<APPLET CODE=Test.class WIDTH=200 HEIGHT=200
CODEBASE=www.otherserver.com
ARCHIVE=codefiles.jar>
</CENTER>
</BODY>
</HTML>
```

15. Java

Now that you know how to put a Java applet in a Web page, the next step is figuring out how to send information to the applet so that you can customize it to your own needs. The exact parameters required by each applet vary, depending on the developer.

If you're developing an applet for widespread distribution, make it as customizable as possible—but don't make it too complicated. In this example, we'll assume that the developer lets us customize the applet's background by sending in a color, and that there is a line of text that we can also customize. To see an example of this in practice, modify the HTML file of the BlinkingText example.

```
<HTML>
<HEAD>
<TITLE>The First Applet</TITLE>
</HEAD>
<BODY BGCOLOR="#800000" TEXT="#FFFFFF">
<CENTER>
<H3> This is a Test Applet </H3>
<APPLET CODE=Test.class WIDTH=200 HEIGHT=200
CODEBASE=www.otherserver.com
ARCHIVE=codefiles.jar>
<PARAM NAME=BGCOLOR VALUE="red">
<PARAM NAME=textstring VALUE="This is my line of text.">
</CENTER>
</BODY>
</HTML>
```

Chapter 16

System Security

In Depth

Security is the most important—and most neglected—issue facing computer users today. ADSL and cable modem users are targets for "backdoor" invasions. Coworkers with access to shared servers lack adequate virus protection. Unsecured Telnet sessions transfer login and password data in plain text over the Internet, where hackers "sniff" ports and record the data for later use. Face it: We're under attack. The good news is that Mac OS 9.1 and third-party products offer excellent features designed to protect your data, systems, and network.

Security Issues

A computer's vulnerability, like that of a person, depends on its situation. For example, a person working on a ship in the middle of the Atlantic is at a greater risk of drowning than someone working on a construction site in Arizona. Similarly, a computer that is not networked is not as vulnerable to hacking as a computer that is in an Ethernet environment. Nevertheless, that isolated computer may face serious problems if no data backup strategy exists when its hard drive fails. It's paramount that you analyze all of your computer's possible vulnerabilities and protect it with Mac OS 9.1's built-in security features as well as third-party security applications.

Keep in mind that security programs have limitations. The best security plan includes a mixture of physical devices and data protection.

Physical Security

Users commonly overlook the physical security of their computers. It's easy for users to forget that thieves find computers—particularly PowerBooks and iBooks—very appealing. The insurance industry is all too aware of this, however. Billions of dollars' worth of claims for stolen computer property are filed each year. Home computers are as much at risk as workplace computers; in fact, a thief is as likely to walk off with a computer as with your VCR.

Most Macintosh computers are equipped with a slot in the back that can connect to inexpensive security cables. Although they don't provide complete physical security, these cables at least make it more difficult to steal the computer. You can also set up other physical security options in your home or office, such as alarm systems and video surveillance devices; with the appropriate configuration, even a QuickCam video camera can serve in this capacity.

You can purchase physical devices that lock the floppy and CD-ROM drives, eliminating the possibility of bypassing software-based security programs (especially shareware or freeware programs) by booting from an alternate medium. If your funding is limited, try a simpler measure, such as removing your keyboard and mouse and locking them in a separate location.

Configuration Preservation

Most computers are one-person machines. Computers in a lab or cluster setting, on the other hand, are shared by a group of users. Without the appropriate security software, these machines can be accidentally or deliberately disabled. For example, a person may install a program that removes a necessary system Extension (such as TCP/IP) and then replace it with an incompatible TCP/IP stack. In this case, your goal (as administrator of these computers) is to preserve or restore a particular system configuration. Unfortunately, Mac OS 9.1 does not have a complete set of features that will enable you to meet this goal in its entirety. However, third-party security programs can help reduce or remove the risk of computer mangling.

Mac OS 9.1 Multiple Users

Because previous versions of the Mac OS provided little in the way of limiting access, administrators had to turn to programs like At Ease (discussed a little later in this chapter) to stop users from tampering with public computers. Multiple Users, a new option in Mac OS 9.1, makes it possible for you to restrict user access as you see fit. Multiple Users acknowledges that just because computers are shared doesn't mean that *control* of the computers is also shared.

With Multiple Users, you can configure many accessibility options, ranging from who can modify components of the system to who can use the CD-ROM drive. Accounts can be maintained on the local computer or retrieved from a server running Macintosh Manager. A user can select his or her login name from a list, type it, or even speak it, depending on options you set up; passwords can be typed or spoken as well. Access privileges fall under four categories:

- *Owner access*—Allows the user to have complete control over the computer. Owners can create, delete, and modify other users' accounts.

- *Normal access*—Permits the user to operate with almost complete access to the computer. Some limitations, such as whether this user can change his or her password or access other users' document folders, can be set.

- *Limited access*—Allows you to determine what programs a user can launch and where a user can save documents. The limited user may also have reduced access to the Finder.

• *Panels access*—Modifies the user's view of the Finder to a "panel" view. Although this is the most restricted type of access, it makes the computer very easy to use. The user only sees two panels: one panel for approved applications and the other for user documents.

Each person who shares the computer has a folder for document storage. Depending on access rights, users cannot look in each other's folders or make changes to them. When you think about the environment in the previous versions of Mac OS, you'll realize how useful personal document folders can be. In the past, documents could be deleted or modified by anyone sitting in front of the computer. With Multiple Users, documents remain safe and intact.

Multiple Users is a good first step in protecting your computer, but it has one drawback: The Multiple Users protection can be disabled by booting with Extensions off. Nevertheless, you can liken it to locking your car—many thieves will pass a locked car in search of easier targets.

NOTE: *You may be familiar with the options in the General Controls Control Panel that enabled you to protect the System and Applications folders. In Mac OS 9.1, the Folder Protection options in the General Controls Control Panel are visible but dimmed because this method of folder protection is no longer available. Apple recommends that you use the Multiple Users option to protect folders on your computer.*

Mac OS 9.1 Administrator Mode

You can take a few measures to protect some important settings from curious users. Several Control Panels, including AppleTalk, TCP/IP, and Modem, have an option called Administrator. When this option is enabled, you can lock particular settings within the Control Panel. When you save the settings and lock them with a password, a user can view—but cannot change—the settings. Of course, an experienced user simply has to delete the preference for any of these Control Panels, and this option is immediately disabled. To really protect settings, you need third-party software.

Apple Network Administrator Toolkit

This software application from Apple is a suite of network administrator tools that helps control computer configurations and aids in day-to-day maintenance. This suite includes At Ease for Workgroups, Apple Network Assistant, and Apple User and Group Manager.

At Ease controls basic system configuration and determines who can access the computer and what they can see and do while accessing it. At Ease requires an AppleShare server, which many lab or cluster environments already have. At Ease offers more protection than Multiple Users by prohibiting startup with Extensions off. You must either turn At Ease off or boot from another medium. The hard drive can also be locked in such a way that it is very difficult to format the disk even if you boot from another medium.

The Apple Network Assistant remotely accesses the computer and allows an administrator to control the computer, install or remove software, or display the user's screen on the other computers in the network. This tool does not require a server and is especially useful in a learning environment. The Network Assistant client is listed as an install option if you customize the Mac OS 9.1 system installation. It is not enabled by default.

The Apple User and Group Manager manages user accounts across AppleShare servers (this utility also requires an AppleShare server). If you manage more than one AppleShare server, then you may find this utility very useful.

MacPrefect

MacPrefect from Hi Resolution (**www.hi-resolution.com**) is a security program that locks down areas of the computer and prohibits making changes to protected areas. In fact, to bypass this security feature, you must launch the MacPrefect software and enter an appropriate password. MacPrefect enables you to hide certain Control Panels so that they are not visible from the Apple menu. A user who attempts to add or remove components from areas that you have locked receives an error message and is unable to complete the task. You can also limit printing options and installation of new software, as well as prevent users from pirating software by disabling the copy capability of certain files or folders. MacPrefect can be installed on a single machine or a cluster of computers as a method of protecting the hard drive; no server is required.

One final benefit of MacPrefect is that it cannot be bypassed. You cannot boot from another medium, such as a floppy or CD-ROM, and disable the security software. Therefore, unlike other security programs, MacPrefect cannot be disabled.

MacAdministrator

MacAdministrator, also from Hi Resolution, is an administrator tool that features unique login requirements for users. The environment can be customized to each user without compromising security. MacAdministrator also has the ability to run certain scripts at startup, login, logout, and shutdown that will prepare the computer for the next user. These scripts can empty the Trash, restore default screen resolutions and sound levels, clear browser caches, and perform many other tasks as well. Educational institutions have also tied the login feature of MacAdministrator to a Kerberos server in order to provide secure logins for users.

16. System Security

MacAdministrator and MacPrefect contain many of the same features, including launch control, folder protection, and limited access to system resources such as Extensions and Control Panels.

Assimilator

Assimilator is a shareware utility that is used to create an "image" of a hard drive. Creating this image takes a while, but when it's complete you can store it on a server and use it to restore a computer's original configuration. This utility is especially useful for creating images of computers with almost identical configurations. One drawback of Assimilator is that it has not been updated since early 1999. Although Assimilator is being used with Mac OS 9.1, compatibility issues will almost inevitably arise as the software ages and the operating system improves. Assimilator is available at **www.assimilator.com**.

Data Security

The security of the computer itself, as well as that of the system configuration, is of utmost importance. But you also need to protect your data from prying eyes and corruption, and have a data recovery method, just in case disaster strikes. In many ways, the OS and applications are expendable—you can always reinstall them. But documents that you or your users create are unique, vulnerable, and even confidential. Mac OS 9.1 includes excellent encryption options, and other companies also provide encryption software and hardware.

File and Folder Locking

You can protect files within the Mac OS by locking them. Within the General Information section of a file's Get Info window, you'll find an option that allows you to lock the file. After the file has been locked, you can open it, but you cannot make changes to it. In fact, you can't even use Save As to replace the existing file. If a locked file is dragged to the trash, the Empty Trash action cannot delete the locked file—you must unlock the file or hold down the Option key as you select the Empty Trash option. In spite of these limitations, a locked file is not safe, particularly not from the experienced hacker. No password protection exists for the Get Info window, where you can simply deselect the Lock option.

You can protect a folder from being deleted, moved, or renamed. If File Sharing is enabled, you can access the Sharing options from the Get Info window. Select the option that restricts folder actions such as moving, renaming, or deleting the folder. It even says "Locked." Figure 16.1 shows a locked folder. This provides at least some protection for folders—no option is available to lock them the way you can lock a file. Of course, someone who is at your computer can easily disable this option. For better protection, you need to invest in other software applications.

Figure 16.1   A locked folder.

Where Are You?

One minor method of file protection is to make the file invisible in the Finder. If a file has an attribute of *hidden*, you will not see the file while exploring in the Finder. However, if you're in an application that navigates the Finder file system, you will see the file listed. You can also search for and delete invisible files via Sherlock 2. You can set an attribute of *invisible* by using a file modification utility such as File Buddy or ResEdit. In both programs, you select File|Get Info and activate the *invisible* flag.

Mac OS 9.1 Encryption

For a long time, the only method of file protection built into the Mac OS was the ability to lock a file. No data protection of any kind existed until Apple included an encryption method in Mac OS 9.1. Finally, Mac users have a way to protect what's really important about a file—its contents.

Locking a file and encrypting it are two different functions. Locked files can usually be viewed, but not modified. Encrypted files cannot be viewed; they are encoded and cannot be deciphered without the appropriate key. Even if you could somehow crack open the file in a text editor, the contents would not make sense. Sensitive data can now be protected so that only authorized parties can view the information. Encrypted files can be recognized easily in the Finder by the small key over the icon; Figure 16.2 shows the same file without and with encryption.

Only users with the correct password can decrypt an encrypted file. If you forget the password, you can forget about opening the file. To make password management a little easier, add the passwords for encrypted files to your keychain with Keychain Access.

Keychain Access

Passwords are the most important—and the most frustrating—feature of a good security system. Just think about some of the different instances of password use in a day:

Figure 16.2   A file with and without encryption.

- Multiuser login
- Web sites
- Encrypted files
- Email
- File servers

Even as a professional, you may find it nerve-wracking to keep all the passwords straight. But Mac OS 9.1 includes a utility called Keychain Access that allows you to use one password that acts as a "key" to unlock and access other passwords on a keychain. Programs that support Keychain Access permit you to add password information to a keychain. When unlocked, the keychain will pass the correct password to the appropriate application.

You can have multiple keychains on the same machine. Keychains can also work with Multiple User configurations so that each person who is authorized to access a machine has a personal keychain. You can use your keychain on another machine by simply copying it from the Keychains folder in System Folder|Preferences.

Keychains are a powerful way of making security simple. Encourage your users to add passwords to their keychains, whenever possible and feasible, instead of writing the passwords down on paper or using the same password for all servers and systems. Keychain Access's only drawback is that not all programs support keychains. Most servers that support File Sharing allow keychains, as do many newer Internet applications such as the FTP client NetFinder. You can determine whether an application supports keychains in two ways:

- It will have a checkbox with the phrase Add To keychain.
- It will have icons for adding items to the keychain, as shown in Figure 16.3.

Other Encryption Methods

Mac OS 9.1 encryption isn't the only encryption method. Pretty Good Privacy (PGP) is an excellent encryption method that makes files unreadable without the appropriate key. PGP works in two parts, a public key and a private key. You can distribute the public key freely. A user who wants to send you information simply looks up your public key in the PGP database or asks you what your public key is, and then encrypts the information using this key. This information cannot be opened without the corresponding private key, which only you know and do not distribute.

Figure 16.3   The icons used for unlocking and adding items to a keychain.

Information about PGP could fill a book. Suffice it to say that you can download free versions of PGP from the MIT Web site at **http://bs.mit.edu:8001/pgp-form.html**, or you can purchase the commercial version, PGP Personal Privacy, at **http://store.mcafee.com**. Although the encryption utility included with Mac OS 9.1 is very effective when it comes to file encryption, it does not cover email. Some email programs such as Eudora and Outlook Express support PGP encryption. To learn more about email security, take a look at some the many question-and-answer documents on the Internet, such as those available at **www.pgpi.com**.

Back Up

If you faithfully back up your computer, you may never need to recover data. If you never back up, you're living dangerously. The risks are varied: Databases can become corrupted and unusable. A user can accidentally overwrite a file and need to recover the original. A hard drive can completely crash. In situations like these, a backup copy of the drive would save time restoring the configuration.

A backup program is a worthwhile investment in data protection. The Iomega drives include backup software. Retrospect, a backup program from the Dantz Corporation (**www.dantz.com**), can be configured to run automatically and is capable of backing up both Macintosh and Windows machines. It can also send messages to the system administrator when the backup program has started or finished, or if a particular tape or medium is needed. With high-capacity storage devices such as tape drives, you can pretty much put things back to normal following a data disaster.

Viruses

Someone is out to attack you, with the intention of causing problems with your computer or servers. It may be an innocuous saying that flashes on your screen, but does little else. It may eat away at your hard drive or memory. Or, it may attempt to completely destroy your configuration. Does this person know you? Probably not. It's just some strange individual who has learned how to write a malicious program called a *virus*. Multimillion-dollar companies exist solely to provide virus protection programs to computer users. You can find some degree of reassurance in the knowledge that the vast majority of computer viruses are written for DOS and Windows applications. Mac users have at least one benefit of being the minority platform—fewer viruses have been written to attack our computers. Nevertheless, the viruses out there are quite vicious, and virus-protection software should be included on every computer, no matter what the platform. And just like Typhoid Mary, you can be a virus carrier without experiencing the effects of the virus.

Macro and Email Viruses

In most cases, PC viruses do not affect Macintosh computers, and vice versa. However, macro viruses developed from the macro files for Microsoft Word and Excel cross platforms. Anyone who uses one or both of these applications is susceptible to the macro viruses. If you consider that they are the biggest-selling word-processor and spreadsheet applications for the Mac, then you can get an idea of the scope of the threat posed by these viruses. Fortunately, many virus-protection packages can remove and repair virus-infected files, and the Office 98 suite now allows you to block the automatic launching of macros. Make sure you take measures to protect your computer by using the latest virus protection software.

Today the most popular route of virus attack is through an email attachment. The subject heading of an email message may say "I love you" or "Resume," but the attachment includes a script that searches Outlook Express address books for more unsuspecting recipients, and then sends the virus-laden message on to them. The script may also damage the computer by deleting all image files, for example. The most dangerous characteristic of this type of virus is that it attacks servers and networks, as well as recipients. Mail servers become overloaded with all the "carrier" messages and, in some cases, even shut down. Although Mac users are not affected by the script, you may still receive the message. The best protection against this type of attack is to refrain from opening attachments unless you know who sent them and why. Some virus protection packages may scan email attachments, but the fact is that a virus can be released in the "wild" and propagate worldwide before virus-protection companies can even detect its presence.

WARNING! Just because you know the person who sent you the email doesn't mean that it's safe. Remember, a virus can invade your friend's email address book and send itself to you automatically.

AutoStart Worm

For several years, the macro viruses were the biggest virus concern of Mac users; true Macintosh viruses just weren't being written, and the few that existed were handled by a free virus-protection program called Disinfectant. (Disinfectant is no longer being updated because it could not address macro viruses.) All this changed with the discovery of the AutoStart Worm. This hidden file runs when QuickTime is set to AutoPlay CD-ROMs. The virus is then passed across the computer to different volumes—from floppies to Zip disks to remote volumes. In fact, one symptom of this virus is that the computer suddenly reboots when a disk is inserted. Another symptom is computer or network activity every 30 minutes. If your computer seems to be crashing frequently or just behaving strangely, you should run a virus-detection program and remove all viruses. You should also disable the QuickTime setting that automatically launches CD-ROM applications. If you don't already have the virus, these steps will give you a measure of protection.

The AutoStart virus has many variations, but several commercial virus-detection programs are capable of recognizing and removing the AutoStart Worm as well as other known viruses. Moreover, some virus-protection packages can monitor the system for virus-like activity in addition to detecting existing viruses.

Denial-of-Service Attacks

Most Mac users may not even care what a denial-of-service attack is until they try to access their favorite Web site only to find that the site is unavailable. Denial-of-service attacks involve the bombardment of a particular server with requests that overload the server until it can no longer function. These types of attacks usually involve the coordination of many unwitting computers by a determined hacker. Why is it worth mentioning in this book? Because it's possible that some Mac OS 9 machines could be used in these attacks. Mac OS 9.1 does not have this problem, but if you have users in your environment who are not running the latest version (Mac OS 9.1), you can download a patch that fixes this problem from Apple at ***http://asu.info.apple.com/swupdates.nsf/artnum/ n11560/***.

Kerberos

Kerberos is a method of authentication in a multiserver environment. It runs on a Unix server that has been designated a *trusted server*, meaning that a user can verify who he or she is by entering secure information to this server. The server then grants the user a ticket that can be used to access other servers that support Kerberos authentication. This reduces the need to log in so frequently to multiple servers, a common problem in multiserver environments. Kerberos, which was developed at MIT, requires a Kerberos server and client software to function.

MacLeland from Stanford is an excellent Kerberos client; however, you must edit the resource fork with ResEdit in order to use MacLeland at locations other than Stanford. MacLeland has the side benefit of locking the Mac and permitting the user to locally mount remote AFS volumes.

16. System Security

Immediate Solutions

Setting Up the Multiple User Environment

As a Mac user, you have a method of authentication built into the operating system. The Multiple User environment will allow you to create an account for each person who has access to the computer. Each user has his or her own document directory, and may have limitations on what can be launched during a user session. But you don't have to set up your computer as a shared workstation to benefit from Multiple Users—you can set yourself up as owner and enable Multiple Users. Once enabled, you will have to enter the appropriate password before you can use the computer. Follow these steps to set up the Multiple User environment:

1. If you have not defined the owner of your computer, go to Control Panels and open File Sharing. Designate an owner name, password, and (optionally) a computer name, then close File Sharing. Changes take effect immediately.

2. Open the Multiple Users Control Panel. You should see the owner name listed as shown in Figure 16.4.

3. Set Multiple User Accounts to On.

4. Click the Options button to set the login environment for the machine. Options available include a custom welcome message and voice verification login (see Figure 16.5). These options will affect everyone who uses your machine.

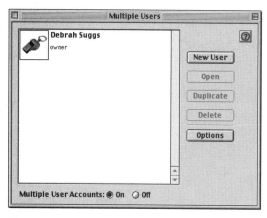

Figure 16.4   The Multiple Users Control Panel listing the owner.

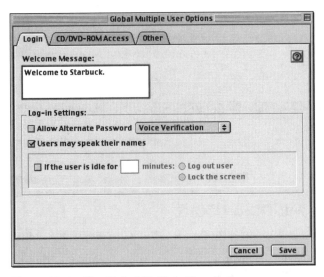

Figure 16.5   The Global Multiple User Options.

5. Click the CD/DVD-ROM Access tab to set limits on CDs and DVDs and what can be launched from them.

6. Click the Other tab to set parameters such as whether to allow guest access or whether you want to be notified if software is installed, as shown in Figure 16.6. You can also decide the login method for your machine: The users select a name from a list or manually type in their login.

7. When you have set your global options, click the Save button to save changes and close the Multiple Users Control Panel.

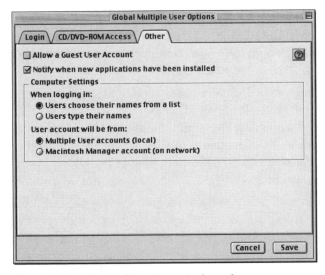

Figure 16.6   The Multiple Users login options.

After setting up the Multiple User environment, you'll see that a Logout option now appears in the Finder's Special menu. At the point that you enable Multiple Users, you are logged into the system. You can choose Logout to see how your machine will function under the new environment.

Related solution:	**Found on page:**
Configuring File Sharing and Program Linking	337

Adding Accounts to Multiple Users

Now that Multiple Users is activated, you can begin adding accounts. First, decide what kind of access you want each user to have:

- *Panels*—Most restrictive with little Finder access

- *Limited*—Very restrictive with a Finder interface

- *Normal*—Least restrictive

Keep in mind that the more restrictive accounts will require more work to set up. The following steps show you how to add accounts for Multiple Users:

1. Go to Control Panels|Multiple Users.

2. Click the New User button.

3. You will be given the option to set the user name, password, and level of user access (Normal, Limited, or Panels). Click the triangle beside Show Setup Details to see more options. The expanded window shown in Figure 16.7 will appear.

4. The availability of tabs in the expanded window will vary depending on the type of access you have chosen for the account. You can set the following parameters for the different levels of access:

   - *Normal access*—Users with Normal access can run all applications on the machine (note that, with this level of access, the Applications and Privileges tabs are unavailable). By default, these users can log in and change their passwords. You can also authorize them to manage other accounts. If you've enabled voice verification, they can speak a passphrase rather than type a password.

   - *Limited access*—Users with Limited access can run only the applications you designate in the Applications tab. They can access documents in their personal documents folder only—unless you allow them broader access via the User Info tab. In the Privileges tab, you can allot access to

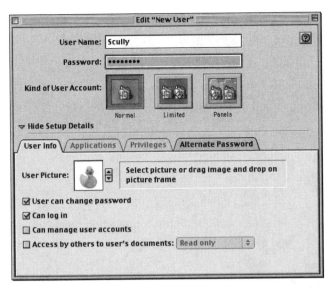

Figure 16.7 The New User window with Show Setup Details active.

the Chooser and printers as well as rights to run programs from a CD/DVD drive. Limited users enjoy a Finder interface when using the computer.

- *Panels access*—Users with Panels access can run only the applications you designate from the Applications tab. They can access only the documents available in their personal documents folder, set by you in the User Info tab. Access to the Chooser and CD/DVD drive can be restricted via the Privileges tab. The Panels interface, shown in Figure 16.8, is the most restrictive environment because users do not have access to the Finder.

5. For accounts with Limited or Panels access, click the Applications tab and identify the applications that the user should be permitted to use. You can limit the content of this list via the pop-up menu for Show. If the user will have access to most applications on the computer, you can choose Select All and turn off applications.

6. When you have set the account parameters, close the window. The account will then be created. If you're creating several accounts that will have the same access profile, click the Duplicate button to establish new accounts with the same rights. Close the Multiple Users Control Panel when you are finished.

After you log out, the system will create a new folder called Users that contains a subfolder for each of the new accounts. Each user will enjoy his or her own computing environment, including unique preferences and startup and shutdown items. You can place an alias on the desktop to direct the user to a personal documents folder.

16. System Security

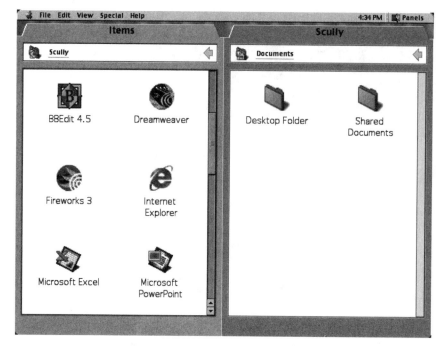

Figure 16.8   The Panels view.

Related solutions:	Found on page:
Sharing Files and Folders	339
Changing Passwords	346

Setting Up Voice Verification

You have the option of speaking a passphrase, rather than typing a password, when you log in. Voice verification, a feature of Multiple Users, is easy to enable. Be aware that it is not the most reliable method of authentication. You may be denied access if the environment is quieter or louder than when you created the passphrase. And in some cases, a user can gain access by imitating your voice. But it can be helpful for those with difficulties typing or who have difficulty remembering a password. To set up voice verification, take these steps:

1. Launch the Multiple Users Control Panel.

2. Click the Options button and enable Allow Alternate Password Voice Verification. Click Save to continue.

3. Open the account that will be using voice verification.

4. Click the Alternate Password tab and enable the option This User Will Use The Alternate Password.

5. Click the Create Voiceprint button. When prompted, enter the password for the account, and then click OK.

6. You will be prompted to enter the passphrase four times. The default phrase is "My voice is my password," but you can designate a new phrase. Click Continue and follow the steps for recording your phrase.

7. You'll be required to record the passphrase four times; the Mac OS keeps track of each recording. At the end of the process, you'll have a chance to try the voice print out to verify that it will work.

8. Close the account window and Multiple Users Control Panel. At the next login, you'll have to speak the phrase to access the computer.

If all attempts at voice verification fail, you'll be prompted to type the password.

Related solutions:	Found on page:
Configuring Speech Recognition	91
Changing Passwords	346

Choosing a Good Password

No matter how effective your security software is, it's only as good as your password. A good hacker can bypass your security measures if your password is predictable or not secure. Use the following suggestions to create a good password:

- Make sure that your password is not a common word; never use a word that is in the dictionary.

- Do not use your initials, your name, or a relative's name.

- Do not use your home address, telephone number, or any other personal information that can be retrieved easily.

- Make sure that the password is long. The recommended minimum length for a password is six characters. The more important the data, the longer the password should be. However, File Sharing may limit you to eight characters.

- Mix numbers with letters.

- Mix cases if you are on a case-sensitive system. Mac OS 9.1 is case-sensitive.

- Change your password at least every three to six months.

- Do not write your password down—memorize it.

- Do not share your password with anyone.

Related solutions:	Found on page:
Enabling Password Protection	219
Changing Passwords	346

Locking Files

You can take some basic steps to protect your files from being accidentally over-written. One option you can easily activate is locking a file. A knowledgeable Macintosh user can disable it, but—like leaving the front light on in a darkened house to scare away burglars—this option may deter some users. To lock a file, take these steps:

1. Click once on the file you want to lock.

2. Select File|Get Info and choose General Information.

3. Enable the option to lock the file.

When you open this file within a software application and attempt to make changes to the file or use the Save As option to overwrite it, you will receive an error message indicating that the file is read-only. You must save the file under a different name or go to Finder and unlock the file. Locked files that are placed in the Trash cannot be deleted by the Empty Trash command unless the files are unlocked or the user presses the Option key while emptying the trash.

Related solution:	Found on page:
Making a File Read-Only	146

Locking Folders

Technically, you cannot lock a folder in the same way that you can a file. However, you can lock a folder through the Sharing option without ever sharing the folder's contents. You should be aware that a knowledgeable Macintosh user could easily disable this setting while sitting at your computer. To lock a folder with File Sharing, take these steps:

1. Enable File Sharing.

2. Select the folder you want to lock.

3. Select File|Get Info and choose Sharing.

4. Enable the Can't Move, Rename, Or Delete This Item (Locked) option, as shown in Figure 16.9.

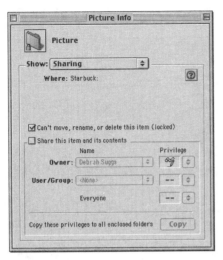

Figure 16.9   Locking a folder through the Sharing window.

5. Close the window to initiate the changes. The folder icon will now have a lock attached.

Related solution:	Found on page:
Configuring File Sharing and Program Linking	337

Enabling Administration Mode in Control Panels

Sections of several Control Panels, including AppleTalk, Internet, Modem, Remote Access, and TCP/IP, can be locked. When they are locked, you cannot make changes to the protected sections unless you initiate Administration mode by way of a password. Of course, the Mac OS is very open, and an experienced Mac user can simply remove the preference for the particular Control Panel to disable the locks. For the purposes of this section we will lock the TCP/IP Control Panel, but the instructions apply to any Control Panel with the User Mode option under the Edit menu. To enable Administration mode, take these steps:

1. Open the TCP/IP Control Panel.

2. Choose Edit|User Mode.

3. The User Mode window appears, as shown in Figure 16.10. You have three options: Basic, Advanced, and Administration. Choose the Administration option.

Figure 16.10   The User Mode window.

4. Click on the Set Password button, enter an appropriate password, and then retype it in the Verify field.

5. Click on OK to exit the User Mode window. The AppleTalk window will now be changed to allow you to lock certain portions of the Control Panel.

6. Click on the Lock button for any part of the Control Panel that you want to protect, as shown in Figure 16.11. The open lock icon will change to a closed lock.

7. Close the Control Panel and save the settings. No users will be able to make changes to the locked portions of the Control Panel.

8. To disable the security, open the AppleTalk Control Panel and select Edit|User Mode.

9. Select Administration and enter the administrator password when prompted, then click on OK.

10. Click on OK to return to the AppleTalk window. Now you can unlock the locked options. When you are finished, close the window and save the settings.

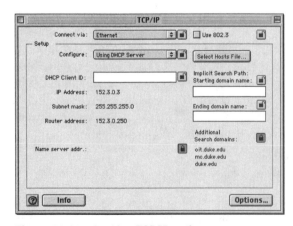

Figure 16.11   Locking TCP/IP options.

Related solution:	*Found on page:*
Configuring the TCP/IP Control Panel	369

Securing Documents within Applications

Some applications, including those in the Microsoft Office suite, allow you to password-protect a file. When you attempt to open a protected file, you will be prompted for a password. For the purposes of this example, we will use Microsoft Word 98 for Macintosh. Word 98 has several layers of protection that you can employ. Follow these steps:

1. Open an existing file, or create a new one, within Microsoft Word 98.

2. Select File|Save As.

3. Name the file and click on the Options button, as shown in Figure 16.12.

4. The Save options window will appear, as shown in Figure 16.13; the file sharing options are in the lower third of the window:

   - Click in the Read-Only Recommended checkbox if you want to lock the file against changes.

   - Enter a password in the field under Password To Open to force a user to enter a password; after the correct password is given, the user has complete access to the file.

   - Enter a password in the Password To Modify field to ensure that a user who doesn't know this password can view the file but not make changes to it.

   Figure 16.13 shows these options enabled.

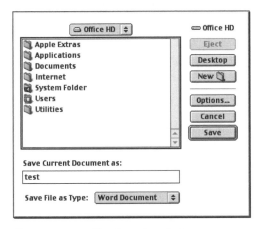

Figure 16.12   The Save As window.

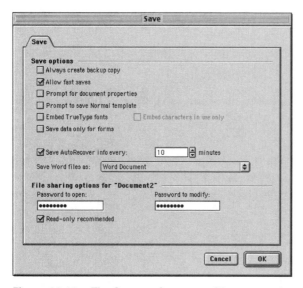

Figure 16.13   The Save preferences with password protection enabled.

5. When you've determined your settings, click on OK. If you entered passwords, you will be prompted to verify them. Now you can save the file.

This password protection applies only when the creator application (in this case, Microsoft Word) is used to open the file. You can open these files with another word processor, but the documents will be very difficult to read.

WARNING! If you save the file in another format such as text only, you will lose the password protection.

Using Virus Protection

If a user is complaining of strange computer activity or poor performance, running a virus check is one of the first actions you should take. If you haven't already installed anti-virus software, you can download a free version called Disinfectant. Although Disinfectant doesn't detect Microsoft Word macro viruses or Trojan Horse programs, it does detect several system viruses that are rather dangerous. It can also repair the files effectively.

TIP: A Trojan Horse program is a file that masquerades as a specific kind of program, but when run, actually performs an unexpected—and usually malicious—task. For example, when you launch "FontFinder"—which is really a Trojan Horse program—it makes the files on your hard drive inaccessible.

To really protect your hard drive, invest in a commercial virus-protection program. Several are available, but for the purposes of our example, we'll discuss Dr. Solomon's Virex (**www.mcafee.com**), one of the first commercial programs to address the AutoStart Worm. Figure 16.14 shows the main Virex application window.

Running just a few Virex options will clean your computer:

- *Diagnose for viruses*—This option doesn't repair infected files, but it operates faster than the Repair Infected Files option, and reports the viruses it finds.

- *Repair infected files*—This option runs slower than a scan, but can repair the files if it encounters viruses. Depending on the preferences chosen, it repairs the files with or without immediate notification and generates a report at the end of the process.

- *Automatically scan floppies*—For a long time, the floppy was the major source of virus infection. Today, files from the Internet are also major virus carriers. A good virus-protection program will automatically scan removable media such as floppies and Zip disks, as well as compressed files that you download.

- *Schedule virus scanning*—If you have a large hard drive, a virus scan can take several minutes. During that scan you should allow the program to run uninterrupted. A good virus-protection package will allow you to schedule virus scanning and repair. This is helpful because you are not interrupted and also don't have to remind yourself to perform a virus check. Virex can also be configured to retrieve the latest virus definition or DAT file from the Virex FTP server. Most DAT files are released once a month, usually at the first of the month.

In addition to these options, some programs will watch certain files and report the occurrence of questionable changes within the files' structure.

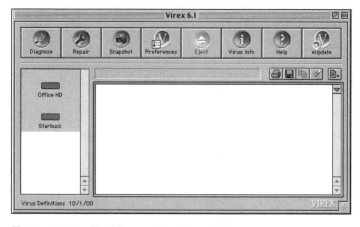

Figure 16.14   The Virex application window.

Screen-Saver Security

The Energy Saver Control Panel contains no option to prompt for a password when the system is "awakened" from sleep mode. If you want protection while your computer is inactive, you can download many free screen savers or purchase a commercial version. After Dark from Berkeley Systems (**www.berksys.com**) is a very popular screen-saver package. You can easily require a password to cancel the screen saver by following these instructions:

1. Launch the After Dark Control Panel.

2. Click on the Setup button. The window shown in Figure 16.15 will appear.

3. Select the Password section.

4. Determine if a password will be required during wakeup and/or startup.

5. Click on the Set Password button, and then enter and confirm your password. Click on OK twice to close the setup options.

6. Close the After Dark Control Panel.

TIP: *Did you notice that you can require a password at startup? If you want to use this as password protection when your computer is started, select this option. If a user cannot enter the appropriate password, the computer immediately goes into the screen saver program and cannot be accessed. This protection can be disabled during computer startup by holding down the Shift key.*

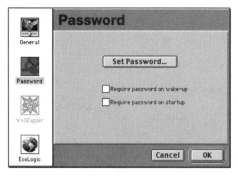

Figure 16.15   The Setup options in the After Dark screen saver.

Secure Internet Access

You're probably most vulnerable to security breaches when you access the Internet. Your information passes through several routers on its journey to a server or Web site; you need to take steps to protect the information you submit—or at least be warned that your connection is not secure. Most Web browsers include security options. For the purpose of this discussion, we'll look at the security options in Internet Explorer, the default Web browser of Mac OS 9.1.

To view the security options in Internet Explorer, follow these steps:

1. Launch Internet Explorer.
2. Go to Edit|Preferences.
3. Click on the arrow beside the Web Browser category on the left to produce more options.
4. Select Security to view the window, as shown in Figure 16.16.
5. Select the options you want active during a browsing session. By default, they may all be enabled. If you only want to be notified that you are entering an insecure site, for example, you can disable the option to show an alert when entering a page that is secure.
6. Select Security Zones to set levels of security for different zones of access. For example, local sites may be more trusted and can enjoy a lower level of security whereas sites you place in the Restricted Sites Zone need to have a very high level of security.
7. When you are finished, click OK to save preferences.

This window also contains information on Certificate Authorities; these are companies that issue secure certificates to users, usually for a fee. When a user submits information by using a certificate from a certifying authority, Internet Explorer accepts or trusts the information, provided that it comes from one of the companies on this list. You can disable, delete, or password protect any of the companies listed. A certificate can protect information that you submit over the Web.

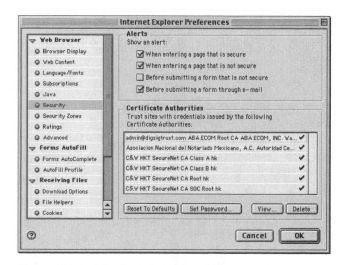

Figure 16.16   The Security options in Internet Explorer.

Controlling Cookies

When you use a Web browser, a text file, or *cookie*, is created that browsers and Web sites use to store information about you. For example, if you have a login and password that you use to read a popular newspaper via the Web, you can store that information in the cookie file so you don't have to enter it every time you read the news. Some Web sites use Java applets to load different images each time you access a Web site, and this information is also stored in the cookie file.

One of the Web community's great debates regards the use of cookies. Privacy is at the center of the controversy; some users dislike the fact that Web sites can use cookie information to target advertising banners. Although cookies are not inherently dangerous to your system and do not contain viruses, some users prefer to disable them—or at least know when a cookie is being placed on their system. You can disable cookies in several ways (these instructions are based on Internet Explorer's settings):

1. Launch Internet Explorer.
2. Go to Edit|Preferences.
3. Under the Receiving Files section heading, select Cookies.
4. The Cookie Settings window, as shown in Figure 16.17, lists servers that have placed cookies on your computer. You can delete any or all of these submissions.
5. Indicate how you want the browser to respond to cookies and click on OK.

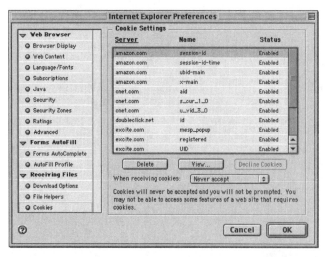

Figure 16.17   The Cookie Settings in Internet Explorer.

Creating and Adding Items to a Keychain

You can't use the same key to unlock your office or house or start your car—but wouldn't it be convenient if you could? Mac OS 9.1 enables you to open many locks with the same key by allowing you to store different passwords on a keychain. You can unlock the keychain with a single password, and then the keychain sends the appropriate passwords to different applications. To create and add items to a keychain, follow these steps:

1. Open the Keychain Access Control Panel.

2. If you've never created a keychain, you will be prompted to create a new one or open another keychain. You may need to open another keychain when you're working on a machine that has not set any keychains.

3. Click the Create button. You will be prompted to give the keychain a name and enter a password for the keychain twice. You can then click Create.

4. A window will appear with the name that you chose for the keychain. Its contents will be empty. At this point the keychain is unlocked.

5. You can now begin opening applications or servers that support Keychain Access. To determine whether a server or program supports Keychain Access, look for the Add To Keychain option or the buttons shown earlier in Figure 16.3. If the keychain option is present, you can use it to add keys to the keychain. Figure 16.18 shows a keychain with items attached.

In addition to passwords, Keychain Access also contains a host of built-in certificates. You can add new certificates as you receive them. However, you must verify their authenticity. The certificates included with Keychain Access have been verified as coming from the issuing site.

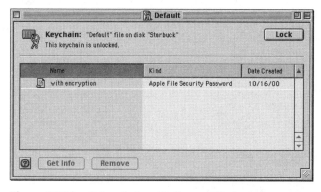

Figure 16.18   A keychain with items attached.

16. System Security

Related solution:	Found on page:
Changing Passwords	346

Setting Keychain Access Preferences

Keychain Access can make life easier, but it can also add or remove a layer of security depending on your choices for how it should function. By default, the keychain is locked at startup. However, you can modify these settings to reflect your own environment. Follow these steps to set keychain preferences:

1. Open the Keychain Access Control Panel (a Keychain Access Control Strip module is also available).

2. At the dialog box, enter the keychain password and click on Unlock.

3. Go to Edit|Default Settings. You must again enter the keychain password to proceed to the settings window.

4. Figure 16.19 shows the available Keychain Access settings. You can change the keychain password and tighten security by locking the keychain after a predetermined period of inactivity or when the computer goes to sleep. You can also loosen security by removing the warning message when the keychain is accessed.

5. Choose your options, then click Save and close the keychain window.

TIP: *Would you like the benefits of a keychain without the pesky password prompt? Jason Giles has written Keychain AutoUnlock, a utility that will unlock a keychain automatically at system startup or whenever the utility is run. Keychain AutoUnlock is available from **www.chaoticsoftware.com**.*

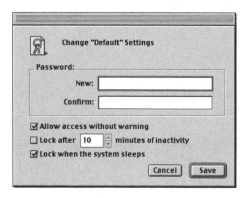

Figure 16.19   Keychain Access settings.

Using Mac OS 9.1 Encryption

For some users, security means more than just protecting a file. It means protecting the contents of the file from prying eyes no matter where it's located—on the local computer or in transit over a network. In the past, you had to use third-party utilities to encrypt a file; now Mac OS 9.1 includes encryption capabilities that allow you to protect what's most important about a document—its contents. Follow these steps to encrypt a document:

1. Create and save your document.

2. Select the document and choose File|Encrypt, or activate the contextual menu using the Control key and then select Encrypt. You can also drag the file over the icon for Apple File Security. Apple File Security is located in the Applications (Mac OS 9)|Security folder.

3. You will be prompted to enter a passphrase that will be used to decrypt the file later. Enter and confirm the phrase, and then click on Encrypt.

4 The icon of the file will now have a small key in its bottom left corner. This visual clue indicates that the file is encrypted.

5. To decrypt the file, simply open it and enter the password when prompted. You will need to encrypt the file again to protect it.

Generating a PGP Key

We could write an entire chapter on PGP (or Pretty Good Privacy). It is a versatile program that can generate public and private keys and encrypt files. If you'd like to learn more about the program, PGP includes an extensive Help section. For the purpose of this discussion, however, take the following steps to create your own PGP key:

1. Launch PGP.

2. You will be prompted to create a new key or locate an existing one. Choose to create a New Key File.

3. The Key Generation Wizard will launch. Click on Next to continue through the wizard.

4. Enter the name and email address that will be associated with this public key and click on Next.

5. Choose your key pair type. Two options are available: Diffie-Hellman/DSS and RSA. Diffie-Hellman/DSS will be understood by a greater number of email recipients. Select your key pair type and click on Next.

6. Select the size of the key. The larger the bit number, the greater the security and the slower the performance. A number between 1024 and 2048 bits should provide adequate security. Select the size or designate a custom number and click on Next.

7. You can set the key to expire after a certain date. The default option is Never. Set your option and click on Next.

8. Enter your passphrase for your key. This phrase should be confidential. PGP will rate the security of your passphrase as you type it. Confirm your passphrase and click on Next.

9. The wizard will begin generating a key. After the key is generated, you will have the option to put the public key on a server. This will make retrieving your public key easier for potential correspondents. This step is optional. Click on Next to go to the final screen where you can exit the wizard by clicking Done. You will see your key listed with those of other PGP users who have made their public keys available.

Now that you have a PGP key, you can use PGP to encrypt and decrypt mail as well as files on the computer. PGP will even encrypt files within supporting applications such as BBEdit and Outlook Express.

16. System Security

Chapter 17

Event and System Monitoring Tools

In Depth

As you're working on your computer, you experience a drag in system performance. Did you just send a long document to print? Is someone accessing your computer via file sharing? Are you running an application that periodically takes over system resources? Are you running multiple applications? How long has it been since you've defragmented your hard drive? Any of these variables could be the cause. Correctly identifying the culprit is the problem.

Monitoring System Performance

If you've noticed that your computer isn't as peppy as it should be, ask yourself a few questions: What applications are running? How are the applications configured? Is virtual memory active? Is your Mac connected to a network? Are unexpected services being used? Mac OS 9.1 includes some basic programs that tell you what applications are running, who is accessing the computer, and how the computer is configured. In this section, we'll discuss the monitoring utilities that are included with Mac OS 9.1. We'll cover third-party utilities that can perform some of these functions better in the section entitled "Choosing the Right Tools."

The Applications Menu

The Mac OS has frequently used graphical objects as menus. For example, the Help menu was located under a question mark—until Mac OS 8, when Apple wisely decided to replace the image with the word "Help." Unlike the Help menu, however, the Applications menu, located at the top right of the screen, remains something of a mystery to many users. Because it doesn't display the word "Applications," many users are unaware of its location and function. They launch huge applications such as Microsoft PowerPoint or Excel, and then close document windows without actually quitting the application. The number of running applications adds up, system performance slows, and soon memory errors are occurring.

In the past, frustrated system administrators have installed programs such as Tilery or GoMac to give users visual reminders of what applications were running. (We'll be discussing these applications later in this chapter.) Mac OS 9.1's updated Applications menu makes it easier for the user to keep track of his or her applications. You can still click on the Applications menu to see a list of running programs, and now you can also "tear off" the menu and place it on the Desktop by holding down the mouse in the Applications menu and dragging the menu outline to the Desktop. In this state, the menu, now called the *Application Switcher*, changes into a strip containing icon buttons and/or titles for each running program. You can simply click on the desired application to switch to it or to quit. Figure 17.1 shows the Applications menu placed on the Desktop.

By clicking on the Zoom box within the title bar, you can collapse the buttons to icons or expand the buttons to include the application title. Table 17.1 lists some shortcuts for changing the display icons in the Application Switcher. You can move the Application Switcher to any part of the Desktop by dragging its title bar. The Application Switcher stays in the foreground no matter what application is active, and remains there even after you restart your computer. Because the Application Switcher is AppleScriptable, you can write a script that designates the location and appearance of the Application Switcher, and then use the script to preserve your settings or the settings of another user. If you close the Application Switcher, however, the visual reminders of running applications will be lost. You will have to tear off the menu again for the visual reminder.

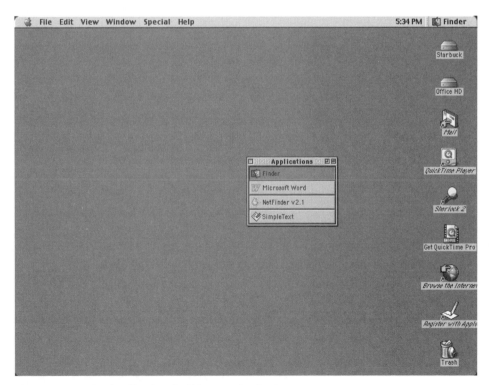

Figure 17.1   The Application Switcher on the Desktop.

Table 17.1   Shortcuts for the Application Switcher.

Action	Result
Click the Zoom box	Toggles between icons or icons and text
Option+click on the Zoom box	Toggles between large and small icons
Option+Shift+click on the Zoom box	Toggles between vertical and horizontal views
Delete Application Switcher preferences and restart	Restores the Application Switcher to its default settings

File Sharing Monitor

As we discussed earlier in this book, file sharing has many benefits. However, it can decrease your system performance, especially when someone is performing processor-intensive tasks such as copying a file to or from your computer. If you experience a sudden reduction in system performance, determine whether file sharing is active by checking the File Sharing Control Strip icon or opening the File Sharing Control Panel. If file sharing is active, use Activity Monitor to find out if someone else is accessing your computer. *Activity Monitor* is a subpanel of the File Sharing Control Panel that keeps track of who is connected to your computer, the level of activity, and what items are being used. If you're working on an extremely important document and need every bit of computer power, click on the Disconnect button located on the Activity Monitor tab in the File Sharing Control Panel to stop others from sharing your resources. You can detach users immediately, or give them a grace period during which they can detach themselves.

The Activity Monitor tab also identifies the access privileges of a user who is accessing your computer. For example, you may notice that someone logged on as *Guest* seems to be accessing files on the root of your hard drive. Unless you granted *Guest* complete access to your hard drive, you may be witnessing a security breach in progress. Someone may have changed your computer's file-sharing settings while you were away and is now grabbing all kinds of information without your permission. In other cases, you can verify whether a particular user was able to log in to your computer to copy information in a shared folder. Whatever the case, you can see quickly who is using your computer resources.

About This Computer

When you're experiencing memory errors, the About This Computer window should be one of the first steps in the troubleshooting process. About This Computer is located under the Apple menu, and can only be accessed within the Finder. About This Computer gives you accurate information about the general allocation of memory and how each application is utilizing that partition. The combined amount of built-in memory and virtual memory equal the total amount of available memory. About This Computer also indicates what applications are currently running on your computer.

When an application crashes due to a specific error, increasing the amount of memory allocated to that application is probably the first reaction of most knowledgeable Mac users. However, memory is not always the problem. If you later determine that the crash was due to a corrupted document or some other problem, be sure to change the application's memory allotment back to its original setting. Until you do, this allocated block of memory is unavailable to other programs. To avoid wasting memory, check About This Computer periodically to see whether a particular application was allocated more memory than it is actually using.

Software Update

In the past, many Mac OS users ran out-of-date software simply because they had no reliable way of learning that the program had been updated. News of updates may have come from a colleague or Web site. Although this is still true of some applications, you can at least keep your system components current with the Software Update Control Panel included with Mac OS 9.1. This built-in utility scans your system components and determines if any updates apply. It gives you the opportunity to download the files and apply the updates to your computer manually, or you can configure Software Update to do this for you automatically. Although you can schedule daily scans, weekly checks should keep system components up-to-date.

Choosing the Right Tools

The Mac OS provides adequate programs and menus for monitoring activities within the system. Sometimes, however, you need more information than these utilities can provide. The information is often there; you just need the right software to reach it. You can find tools that show open applications and reveal exactly how the memory is being distributed, tools that restart your computer in the event of a system or application crash, and tools that show you exactly what processes are running—even processes usually hidden within the System. Many of these programs are commercially available. You can download several of them from software archives, and some of these applications are free.

Application Monitoring

The detachable Applications menu is a handy method of viewing and switching among open applications, but you can purchase third-party programs that not only provide this view, but also allow you to easily retrieve important program information. In fact, until Mac OS 8.5 you had to use a third-party utility to view open applications as buttons on a task bar.

Tilery

Tilery is an application monitoring program that has been available for some time, and is still being updated with each new Mac OS release. Because Tilery is an application rather than a Control Panel or Extension, you must put an alias of the Tilery program in the Startup Items folder if you want it to launch whenever the computer is booted. Tilery displays open applications as buttons or bars, with or without the applications' names. Clicking on a Tilery button opens a contextual menu that gives you quick access to the Get Info window as well as information on the application's memory usage. Tilery also has an extensive online help system. Tilery differentiates itself from other programs of its kind by featuring *remembered tiles*. These tiles are actually buttons for programs that are not currently running (this feature is similar to the Launcher Control Panel). You can launch an application simply by clicking on its button within Tilery. Tilery is a shareware program that you can download from most software archives, including **www.macdownload.com**.

GoMac

GoMac is a Control Panel that gives the Mac OS a task bar similar to the one available in Windows 95/98. It displays a button for each running application in the GoMac task bar that appears across the bottom of the screen. GoMac also creates a Start Menu Items folder, located within the System Folder. This folder contains a list of the applications that appear when you click on the Start button located on the GoMac task bar. An extensive listing of Start Menu Items is automatically created when you install GoMac and restart your computer. However, you can add new items to the Start menu by dragging an icon over the Start menu button. An alias for the new item will be placed in the Start Menu Items folder.

GoMac also provides a QuickLaunch section for frequently accessed applications, and allows you to add Control Strip modules to the task bar. A calendar is also included in the date and time portion of the task bar.

Like Tilery, GoMac opens a shortcut menu when you click on an application's button within the task bar. The shortcut menu allows you to minimize, hide, and quit a running application. It also tells you how much memory the application is using.

Moreover, GoMac allows you to use Command+Tab to switch among open programs. GoMac is a shareware program that you can download from most software archives, including **www.macdownload.com**.

OneClick

OneClick from WestCode Software is a commercial program that enables you to see exactly what applications are running. It gives you extra functionality in managing open programs, including the ability to hide, show, and quit a selected application from the toolbars. OneClick has a task toolbar with buttons that represent the applications that are currently running; it also provides a launcher toolbar you can use to launch files, applications, and folders. OneClick's extensive scriptability makes it an excellent addition to your system. The OneClick Web site (**www.westcodesoft.com**) includes a large library of buttons that have useful scripts attached. You can also record and write scripts to reduce the steps you take in often-repeated tasks. You truly can do many system functions with just OneClick.

UpdateAgent

The Software Update Control Panel keeps the OS up to date, but what about the rest of your applications? Web sites such as **www.versiontracker.com** track application updates, but utilities like UpdateAgent will catalog your hard drive and download updates to your computer. UpdateAgent from Insider Software tracks software updates on Insider Software servers, and gives you the opportunity to download the update and apply it to your applications. UpdateAgent brings us a step closer to the dream of computer self-maintenance. You can find more information about UpdateAgent at **www.insidersoftware.com**.

Memory Monitoring

Although About This Computer provides adequate information about memory allocation, more information is available that can help you improve memory management or determine if you should restart the computer to defragment your memory. Perhaps an application has not completely released its memory, or so many applications have been launched that no large blocks of memory are available. Whatever the situation, applications exist that can uncover more information about what is going on with your computer's memory.

MATM

More About This Macintosh (MATM) is an application that you can launch at any time to report on the state of your computer's memory allocation. It shows the actual division of memory between System and Finder, as well as the blocks of available memory. The presence of several free blocks, rather than one large empty one, indicates fragmented memory. MATM warns you of fragmentation, and helps you determine which applications to quit in order to regain the most memory. MATM also provides volume and system information.

RAM Doubler

RAM Doubler is a commercial program that works at the system level to increase memory performance. Initial setup is simple—you simply move the slide bar to indicate how much additional performance you want RAM Doubler to generate, as shown in Figure 17.2. This program has the added benefit of comprehensive memory usage reports. You can compare how much memory is allocated versus how much memory an application is actually using, as well as determine how the memory in each application is being used, as shown in Figure 17.3. For more information about RAM Doubler, visit **www.connectix.com**.

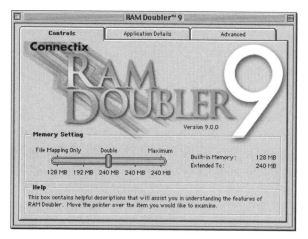

Figure 17.2   RAM Doubler memory adjustment.

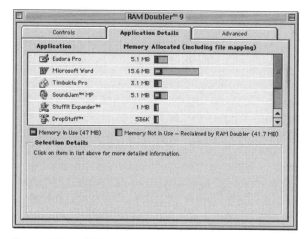

Figure 17.3   RAM Doubler memory usage information.

TIP: If you can afford it, you will find that investing in more physical RAM will give you the greatest system performance benefits.

System and Server Crashes

Although Macintosh computers are wonderful, they aren't perfect. Sometimes applications hang and the system crashes. Usually you have to restart the computer to restore it to working order. Rebooting is not an acceptable option, however, when dealing with mission-critical computers, such as a network server that users access to run applications or a company Web server that must stay up at all times. In many situations, crash messages may not be immediately visible because the server is located in a protected room, or the crash may occur after hours and force a server administrator to return to work to reboot the computer. The following utilities help predict a crash or automatically reboot in the event of one.

Norton CrashGuard

Symantec's Norton CrashGuard, a simple program included with Norton Utilities, helps prevent crashes and gives you a few more options in the event that a crash occurs. Norton CrashGuard requires almost no configuration. Simply install and run it—CrashGuard automatically watches for application instability. If it detects problems, CrashGuard displays an alert window where you can choose to quit the application, fix the application, or restart the computer. Quitting the application is the safest option. You should attempt to fix the application only if it contains unsaved work. If CrashGuard is successful, save the data under a different name to prevent corruption and then restart your computer. If you do not restart, you may cause an error that even CrashGuard cannot bypass. When crashes do occur, CrashGuard makes an entry in the log file. You can use this log file to diagnose problems on the computer.

Norton DiskLight

Symantec's Norton DiskLight is also a component of Norton Utilities. DiskLight is a Control Panel that provides a simple functionality: It displays a tiny icon in the corner of the screen that indicates what type of disk is processing information. The icon also indicates if data is being written to the disk and gives you the device's SCSI ID.

PowerKey

Although it doesn't have much to do with monitoring system performance, PowerKey products from Sophisticated Circuits provide excellent hardware and software solutions for many concerns, such as keeping your mission-critical machines running. For example, PowerKey Pro is a sophisticated power strip with an Apple Desktop Bus (ADB) port. You can plug your computer's power cords into this strip (including peripheral devices such as scanners and Zip drives), and then use an ADB cable to connect your computer to the PowerKey Pro ADB port. This connection makes it possible for you to start all your devices with one push of your power button. PowerKey also makes products that you can use to "call" your computer and, by a series of telephone rings, initiate the command to turn the computer on. If you need something simple, PowerKey Rebound! is a small device that plugs into the ADB port. It will check the computer to confirm activity and restart the computer if activity fails.

What makes the PowerKey Pro and PowerKey Rebound! software/hardware solution really practical is that the hardware can determine if the computer has crashed, and then send a signal to restart the computer. This is especially useful if

**17. Event and System
Monitoring Tools**

the crash occurs when you're out of the office. Sophisticated Circuits also sells Kick-off!, which does the same tasks as Rebound! but on a USB-compatible Macintosh. You can find more information about PowerKey products at **www.sophisticated.com**.

AutoBoot

AutoBoot is a shareware utility that performs a specific function: It restarts a Mac after a system crash or bomb. It doesn't detect application crashes or hangs (Keep It Up, discussed in a few sections, performs that task), but this utility is wonderful if you have a computer that must stay up and running in good order. When the system crashes, AutoBoot displays an alert message that a crash has occurred (it might also display a bomb). In most cases, enough system resources are available to cause AutoBoot to restart the computer (which helps eliminate cross-town trips back to work to restart the computer). When AutoBoot is activated, it keeps a log file so that you can determine the cause of the crash. Be aware, however, that this information may be lost in the restart; in this case, the log file gives the reason as "cause unknown." AutoBoot is available at most software archives.

Server Sentinel

Server Sentinel from Intelli Innovations is a shareware utility that tracks applications or processes running on a workstation or server. This utility will notify the appropriate party if the computer fails to respond to a predetermined task such as an HTTP call. Notification methods include paging, email, and even the launching of SoundJam, an MP3 player. Server Sentinel has an additional feature that makes it different from other monitoring utilities—it works in conjunction with PowerKey's hardware solutions to keep important machines up and running at all times. You can learn more about Server Sentinel at **www.intellisw.com/sentinel/**.

Keep It Up

Keep It Up is a shareware utility that you can configure to monitor certain applications for signs of activity. If, over a predetermined period time, a monitored application does not interact with the system because the application crashed or because you quit the application, Keep It Up restarts the application. If the program cannot be launched again, Keep It Up displays a warning dialog box and restarts the computer. You can configure Keep It Up to automatically disable itself during certain periods of the day and schedule automatic computer restarts. Keep It Up is available at most software archives.

MacsBug

MacsBug is a utility that provides detailed system information to programmers. An entire chapter could be written on MacsBug; much of what it does is outside the scope of this chapter. MacsBug gives you detailed information on what is happening in Mac OS 9.1; however, much of it will only make sense to developers and system engineers. If MacsBug is installed in the System Folder, the MacsBug window will appear when an application or the Mac OS crashes. You may also accidentally enter the MacsBug window if you should type the keystroke combination Command+Power. The window is completely text-based and includes a prompt for entering text-based commands. Common MacsBug commands will be covered in "Using MacsBug" in this chapter's Immediate Solutions section. MacsBug may be included on your system. If not, you can retrieve it from **www.apple.com**.

System Processes

Today, many work environments interact heavily within a network. You may be running multiple Internet and client applications simultaneously. Suppose that you are working on your computer when you notice that at regular intervals it seems to hang for several seconds. You may have a problem identifying which application is taking over system processes. Prime candidates are email programs checking for new mail, word processors performing an automatic save, or a client program interacting with its server. Utilities can help you determine exactly what is happening with the system. And if you provide support for other users, you may often hear complaints that a user's computer is out of memory when "nothing is running"—only to find the entire Microsoft Office suite in memory. This happens when users close document windows without quitting the applications. A utility exists that can provide help with this situation, too.

Peek-a-Boo

Peek-a-Boo is a shareware utility that monitors system processes and displays information about them. It is useful if you routinely experience a degradation in system performance and are unsure of the culprit application. Some client applications are notorious for polling the server at incredibly short intervals and monopolizing system resources while doing so. Peek-a-Boo provides great detail, including history graphs, about these applications, and even allows you to "kill" a process from within Peek-a-Boo. Kill commands the application to quit, allowing it to shut down properly. Peek-a-Boo also allows you to determine what processes are most and least important. Peek-a-Boo is available from **www.macdownload.com**.

Quit It

A user may experience memory errors when several applications are running simultaneously. This usually is the result of the user's closing a document window without quitting the program, hopping over to check email, and then launching another application. Quit It is a Control Panel that will quit "abandoned" applications after a predetermined period of time. It checks running applications and, if no document windows are open, issues a command to quit the application. Quit It is very useful in environments such as public access machines and kiosks where users commonly leave applications running. You can configure Quit It to ignore applications as well. Quit It is available from **www.katoemba.com**.

Okey Dokey Pro

Okey Dokey Pro is a free Control Panel that performs a very simple function: In dialog boxes that are left unattended, it accepts the default option and clears the window. You can configure Okey Dokey Pro to clear the dialog window after a certain period of time has elapsed, provide a countdown of the time remaining before Okey Dokey Pro will accept the default, and keep a log of missed dialogs. This program is invaluable for restarting crashed servers because it answers the dialog box's query about restarting the computer. However, Okey Dokey Pro has not been updated for a few years and is not compatible with the newer Navigation Services windows or system alerts that appear as small, yellow windows. Nevertheless, you may want to check this program out to see if it can meet your needs. After all, many developers have not updated their software's Save and Open windows to Navigation Services. Okey Dokey Pro is available from **_www.macdownload.com_**.

Immediate Solutions

Monitoring Applications in the Finder

Mac OS 9.1's Applications menu is a simple method of determining what applications are running. It is located in the top-right corner of the screen, but you can also detach it and display it on the Desktop. Follow these steps to detach the Applications menu:

1. Click on the Applications menu.

2. Click and drag the window out of the menu frame and wait for the outline of a box to appear on the Desktop.

3. Release the mouse in the location where you want the Application Switcher to appear.

4. Click on the Zoom box to reduce the Application Switcher to small buttons (see Table 17.1 earlier in the chapter for more shortcuts). Figure 17.4 shows the Application Switcher in large and small sizes.

Related solution:	*Found on page:*
Configuring the Application Switcher	86

Figure 17.4   Two sizes of the Application Switcher.

Monitoring Memory in About This Computer

About This Computer can help you sort out memory errors, identify what version of the OS a Mac is running, and determine whether your memory is allocated efficiently, how much memory is on the machine, and how much memory is free. To access About This Computer, follow these steps:

1. Go to the Applications menu and select Finder.

2. Select About This Computer from the Apple menu.

3. Look in the top-right corner of this window for operating system information.

4. Look under the Mac OS logo for built-in, virtual, and free memory information.

5. Control+click on an application to open a contextual menu that can reveal the location of the program on the computer and access Get Info information.

6. Double-click on an item in the About This Computer window to switch to the application.

Each open application is listed within the About This Computer window, and memory usage is represented by a boxed progress bar. The more the progress bar fills the box, the more allocated memory the application is using. Figure 17.5 shows the About This Computer window.

Related solutions:	Found on page:
Checking for Available Resources by Using About This Computer	43
Allocating Application Memory	184

Figure 17.5 The About This Computer window.

Using the File Sharing Activity Monitor

If file sharing is active and you suddenly notice a lot of hard drive activity on your computer—especially if you take a significant performance hit—someone may be accessing your computer. Mac OS 9.1 gives you several ways to determine if this is happening:

1. Go to Apple menu|Control Panels and select File Sharing.

2. Click on the Activity Monitor tab.

3. Look at the box listing connected users. If it's empty, no one is accessing your computer. If the box contains a list of users, check the Sharing Activity level to see if file sharing is responsible for the increased activity on your computer. Figure 17.6 shows the File Sharing Activity Monitor window.

TIP: *You can easily see if someone is accessing your computer from the Control Strip because the File Sharing icon adds the image of a person to the folder. You can click on the File Sharing button and see the connected users. Figure 17.7 shows the changed folder and menu that lists connected users.*

Related solution:	**Found on page:**
Configuring File Sharing and Program Linking	337

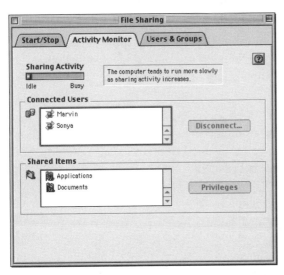

Figure 17.6   The File Sharing Activity Monitor window.

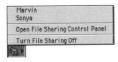

Figure 17.7   The File Sharing Control Strip showing attached users.

17. Event and System Monitoring Tools

Updating the System with Software Update

Imagine having a car that can notify you automatically of a recall notice. You wouldn't have to rely on the media or your dealer for the news. Software Update is Mac OS 9.1's version of that level of self-sufficiency. Software Update is a Control Panel that will analyze your system components and compare them to updates available at Apple. You have the option of downloading the files and immediately applying them to your OS. The Software Update Control Panel also has a scheduling option, and the option of automatically applying updates without waiting for your approval. To use the Software Update Control Panel, follow these steps:

1. Open the Software Update Control Panel (it is part of a standard Mac OS 9.1 installation).

2. Click on the Update Now button. A dialog box will indicate that the software update is about to begin and give you the option to cancel or continue. Click on Continue to proceed.

3. A progress bar indicates communication with the Apple servers. If any updates are found, they will be listed in a separate window, as shown in Figure 17.8. You can install the update or click Cancel to stop the process. Click Install to continue.

4. You may be asked to accept a license agreement for the software. After accepting the agreement, the update will be retrieved. Depending on what components were installed, you may need to restart your machine. You'll be notified when the process is finished.

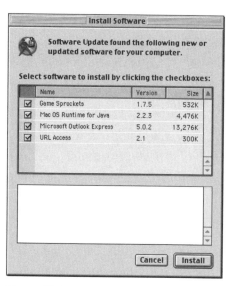

Figure 17.8   The results of a software check.

5. You can also configure Software Update to check for available updates on a regular schedule. Activate the option Update Software Automatically, and then determine the schedule by clicking on the Set Schedule button. You can set a time and day of the week for scheduled updates.

6. If you would like to apply updates automatically, disable the option Ask Me Before Downloading New Software.

7. Close the Control Panel to save your changes. Figure 17.9 shows the Software Update Control Panel configured to run and apply updates automatically.

Figure 17.9   The Software Update Control Panel.

Using Tilery

The Application Switcher in Mac OS 9.1 shows only open applications. Tilery, however, is a third-party application that goes beyond just listing the open applications. You can see how much memory the programs are using, create buttons to launch favorite programs, and easily access the Get Info window for a particular application. Follow these steps for using Tilery:

1. Launch the Tilery application (add the Tilery alias to your Startup Items folder if you want Tilery to launch automatically).

2. All open applications should appear as buttons on your Desktop, as shown in Figure 17.10. To change the style of these buttons go to Tiles|Tile Styles.

3. If you don't like the location of the tiles, go to Tiles|Tile Placement to set the location of the beginning tile, the orientation of the tiles, and the space between them.

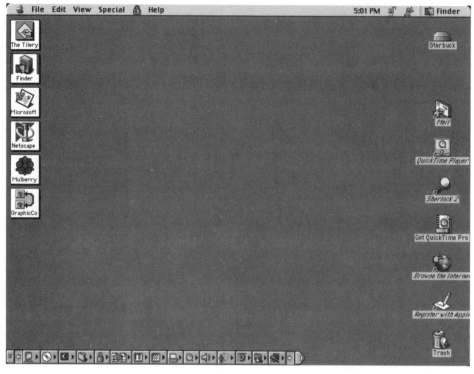

Figure 17.10   The Tilery buttons on the Desktop.

4. As you launch an application, you can configure Tilery to display a button for the program at all times—even when it's not running. Click on the application's Tilery button; when the menu appears, select Remember Tile (see Figure 17.11).

Figure 17.11   The Tilery button menu.

Using GoMac

GoMac is a wonderful third-party Control Panel that provides you with a task bar similar to the one in Windows 95/98 (actually, it mimics the Windows task bar very closely). Open applications will appear as buttons on the GoMac task bar, and sections of the task bar are available for Control Strip items and QuickLaunch applications. Clicking on an application's task bar button brings up the appropriate menu. GoMac's Start menu provides fast access to specified applications. GoMac also includes a clock and built-in calendar.

To install and use GoMac:

1. Run the GoMac installation program and then restart your computer.

2. A welcome screen for the GoMac Control Panel will give you some quick tips and remind you to pay for the product. GoMac will initiate the creation of a folder in the System Folder called Start Menu Items.

3. If GoMac has successfully loaded, a task bar with a button for each open application will appear at the bottom of the screen.

4. When GoMac is first installed, it initiates a search of the hard drive and uses the results to generate a Start menu. Usually, the Start menu contains folders for Microsoft Office, Internet applications, Programs (links to all applications on your computer), Documents, Drives, Recent, and Settings (links to several system components). You can add an item to the Start Menu Items folder by dragging an icon over the Start menu button. Figure 17.12 shows a sample Start menu.

5. Contextual menus can be activated by clicking and holding down the mouse button over different parts of the task bar (Figure 17.13 shows a sample task bar). Depending on where you click, you will get different menus:

   • Clicking the Start menu gives you access to most of your computer.

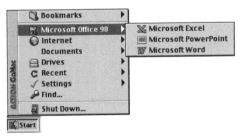

Figure 17.12   A GoMac sample Start menu.

Figure 17.13   The GoMac task bar.

- Clicking items in the QuickLaunch section located next to the Start menu brings up menu options for removing and opening the item, as well as Get Info options.

- Clicking open application buttons on the task bar will bring up a quit option, GoMac settings for the application, and QuickLaunch and hide options as well as memory information.

- Clicking an empty part of the task bar will bring up options to hide parts of the task bar and add modules to the control strip.

- Clicking the time will bring up a monthly calendar.

The GoMac program includes an ACTION Utilities Control Panel that controls many aspects of the task bar. Figure 17.14 shows the ACTION Utilities Control Panel setting for the Start menu.

Related solution:	Found on page:
Configuring ACTION GoMac	77

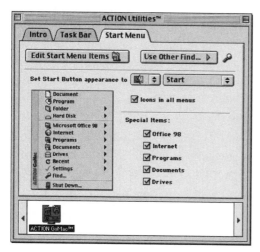

Figure 17.14   The ACTION Utilities Control Panel options for the Start menu.

Using MATM

The About This Computer (formerly About This Macintosh) window provides adequate information for the average user, but sometimes you need more information. MATM (More About This Macintosh) is an application that provides the same information as About This Computer and also expands on it. MATM can indicate that memory is fragmented and also provide volume and system information. Follow these steps for using MATM:

1. Launch MATM; the window shown in Figure 17.15 will appear.

2. MATM will warn you if memory fragmentation is present, and even suggest that you restart the computer to repair your memory.

In MATM, blue bars appear to the right of all open processes and applications. Red bars indicate a block of free memory. If the memory is fragmented, you may see more than one red bar.

Related solution:	Found on page:
Using MATM	44

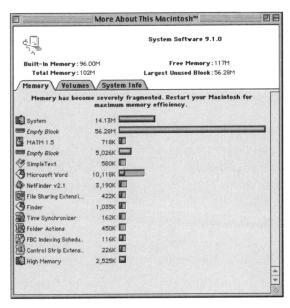

Figure 17.15   The MATM window.

Using Server Sentinel

Server Sentinel monitors several servers at once and notifies you if a server is not accessible. Several server configurations are built into Server Sentinel. All you need to do is select the type of server you want to monitor (such as AppleShare IP, Web, DNS, FTP, Telnet, SMTP, and so on) and enter the server's IP address. Server Sentinel also includes the Sentinel MicroServer, a small program that can be placed on client machines. Server Sentinel can then monitor these machines and notify you if the machine is inaccessible. Although Server Sentinel does not restart servers, it does ensure that you'll be the first to know if a server is down. Use these steps to set up Server Sentinel.

1. Launch Server Sentinel.

2. If the program is not registered, you will have an opportunity to register the program. Click on Not Yet if you are just evaluating the product.

3. Set your preferences for Server Sentinel. You can determine the frequency with which Server Sentinel checks your server, as well as how much of a delay in the server's response it should tolerate before determining a server failure. You can also enter your email address and include programs such as paging software that will work with Server Sentinel to notify you of server failure. Be sure to save your preferences.

4. You now have the option to add servers. In the Server tab, give your task a name and enter the IP address or host name and port, if known. Alternatively, locate your server from the list and supply an IP address or host name. The port will be added. For Web servers, you can enter the path to the process that needs to be monitored. Figure 17.16 shows an AppleShare IP server configuration.

5. In the accompanying tabs, indicate how you want to be notified in the event of a failure. The most straightforward method is via email, but with additional utilities you can be paged or have messages sent to PowerKey devices that will cause the server to be restarted. When the server is configured, click Save.

6. The server will appear in a list view (as shown in Figure 17.17). You can determine whether the configuration is correct by selecting the server and clicking the Check button. If communication is successful, you will see a status of Up and the time.

7. You can add workstations in your area to this list by running the Sentinel MicroServer on the client computer.

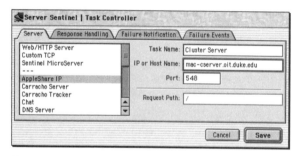

Figure 17.16   Creating a task in Server Sentinel.

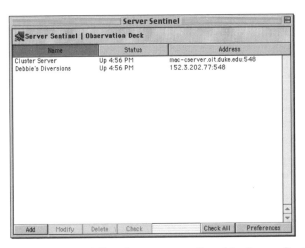

Figure 17.17   A list of servers monitored by Server Sentinel.

Using AutoBoot

AutoBoot, a program made up of a system Extension and a Control Panel, can restart your computer in the event of a system crash or bomb. This kind of utility is particularly useful for monitoring important computers and servers that must be up and running at all times. AutoBoot works in conjunction with Keep It Up to make sure that your computer or server is operational without forcing you to return to work just to reboot the system. To use AutoBoot:

1. Select the AutoBoot Control Panel and Extension, and drag them over the System Folder. Allow the System Folder to place the files.

2. Restart your computer.

3. Go to Apple menu|Control Panels and select AutoBoot (see Figure 17.18).

4. Set your options for AutoBoot (you can even indicate what should trigger AutoBoot to restart the computer and the length of the delay before the computer is restarted).

WARNING! You should not run AutoBoot and Norton CrashGuard at the same time.

If you are adventurous (or skeptical) and want to test AutoBoot, you can launch some of the applications included in AutoBoot's Bomb folder. This should generate a system error and cause the computer to restart.

17. Event and System Monitoring Tools

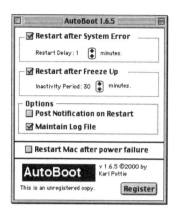

Figure 17.18   The AutoBoot Control Panel.

Using Keep It Up

Keep It Up, a companion product to AutoBoot, is a shareware utility that monitors a defined set of applications. If Keep It Up determines that a program is no longer running or functioning, it restarts the program after a predetermined period of time has elapsed. You can also configure Keep It Up to restart the computer on a regular schedule. Follow these steps to configure Keep It Up:

1. Launch Keep It Up (place an alias of Keep It Up in your Startup Items folder to automatically launch Keep It Up when your computer is restarted).

2. A KIU Startup Items folder will be created in the Preferences folder. In this folder, place aliases to the applications or documents (but not both) that you want Keep It Up to monitor. Make sure they are not duplicated in the Startup Items folder. Bear in mind that Keep It Up is activated only when an application quits, not when a document is closed.

3. Return to the Keep It Up program and go to File|Preferences. The window in Figure 17.19 will appear. The preferences are organized into different categories that you can access via the pop-up menu at the top of the window.

4. Under General Options, you can set a password for Keep It Up (optional). If you plan to use Web access for Keep It Up, you will need to set a password. You can require a password for Keep It Up changes or exits. Passwords for Keep It Up are not keychain compatible.

5. Under Restart Options, you can choose a clean or a forced restart. For a clean restart, Keep It Up will try to quit all applications before restarting, but may fail if an application displays a dialog box (Okey Dokey Pro may be useful in those instances). A forced restart is more brutal, but Keep It

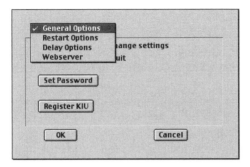

Figure 17.19 The Keep It Up Preferences window.

Up will try to quit the applications gracefully before forcing the restart. You can also disable the option to restart the computer altogether. However, if Keep It Up is on a server, you should leave this setting enabled.

6. Under Delay Options, determine how long Keep It Up should wait before attempting to relaunch applications that have quit. You can also set an interval between launches and decide how long Keep It Up should wait before restarting the machine.

7. Keep It Up also features a Web server function. You can remotely access Keep It Up on your computer via a Web browser and perform maintenance on the computer. If you would like to launch items remotely, including customized AppleScript applications, add them to the KIU WebLaunch Items folder located in the Preferences folder within the System Folder. You can even restart the computer from a remote location.

8. After you have set the desired options for Keep It Up, click on the OK button.

When Keep It Up is active, a small window appears that contains the Keep It Up icon. This is a visual reminder that the program is running.

Using MacsBug

MacsBug is a free developer's tool that debugs programming. It provides detailed technical information that is useful for fixing problems in software. You can obtain it from Apple's software archive at **www.apple.com**. For the average user, MacsBug is confusing, intimidating, and downright frightening compared to the simplicity of the graphical user interface. However, it enables you to document errors within an application or system process. You can then pass this information on to the developer.

You may see MacsBug on two occasions—when you have activated it accidentally, or when an application has crashed. When MacsBug is activated, the screen is filled with text information, and a prompt is available for entering commands. Table 17.2 shows the text-string commands that a non-programmer would use within MacsBug.

You can provide a software developer with information about a buggy application by using the **stdlog** command. Simply invoke MacsBug, type "stdlog", go back into the Finder, and then launch the problem application. When the application crashes, a log file is created with detailed information you can give to the developer.

Table 17.2   Useful MacsBug key commands.

Command	Result
Command+Power	Activates the MacsBug interface (often done accidentally).
Esc	Toggles between the Finder and MacsBug interfaces.
g	Returns the user to the Finder interface.
help	Displays MacsBug help information.
help miscellaneous	Provides list and results of common MacsBug commands.
ea	Restarts the current application.
es	Forces the running application to quit (you should restart after this command).
rs	Unmounts all volumes except the server and restarts the computer.
rb	Unmounts everything and restarts.
stdlog	Logs the current application's activity.

Using Peek-a-Boo

Peek-a-Boo is a shareware program that provides information on all processes running on your computer and how much of the system resources each process is using. Peek-a-Boo displays information that you normally cannot see. You can use this information to pinpoint troublesome programs. Follow these steps to use Peek-a-Boo as a diagnostic tool:

1. Launch the Peek-a-Boo application. Figure 17.20 shows an example window.

2. Watch the CPU% bar for the different processes.

3. If you think you have identified a problem application or process, select the process and go to Processes|CPU% History. A small window will appear, and eventually a graph indicating the activity history of the process will be drawn.

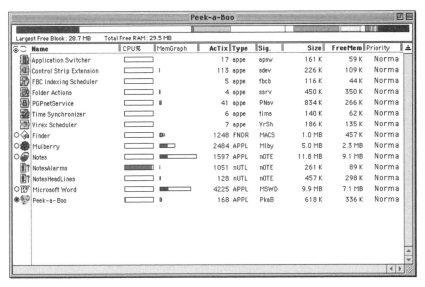

Figure 17.20   The Peek-a-Boo process monitoring window.

Using Quit It

You can use all kinds of monitoring utilities to keep a system operational, but you may find that users are the greatest threat to stable computing. Many users make the mistake of closing a document window without ever quitting the application. Soon the computer is out of memory. Quit It is a Control Panel that will detect when an application is running with no open windows and then issue a quit command to the program. To configure Quit It, follow these steps:

1. Drag the Quit It Control Panel over the System Folder to install Quit It. Then restart the computer.

2. Open the Quit It Control Panel (Figure 17.21).

3. The default configuration has Quit It enabled. You can determine the conditions under which Quit It should quit an application. If you are dealing with a single-user workstation, you may want to enable Confirm Quit or Confirm, Quit After Timeout so the user can stop the process. In a public or shared environment, you may want to select Quit After Timeout.

4. If you choose a timeout setting, indicate the amount of time that passes before the application is closed.

5. You can set other configuration options, including override options, and how the document window should be closed before an application is quit.

17. Event and System
Monitoring Tools

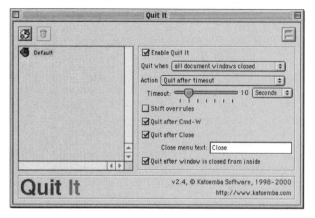

Figure 17.21   The Quit It Control Panel.

6. You can add additional applications that should be treated differently by Quit It. Simply click the Add button in the window and locate the application. You can then configure Quit It with the settings for that application.

7. If you want to disable Quit It without losing settings, click the button in the top right corner. If the bar is red, Quit It is disabled; if the bar is green, Quit It is active. Close the Quit It Control Panel to save your changes.

Chapter 18

Troubleshooting

In Depth

Even the most complex computer system needs occasional attention and maintenance. The Macintosh computer is no exception. The Mac OS is constantly under revision, and with each new release comes a new set of possible problems. The Macintosh platform underwent a major shift several years ago with the switch to the RISC (PowerPC) chip. When this happened, old software often did not run properly under the new processor chip. Gradually, software developers made the switch to the Power Macintosh platform, and today most software for the Macintosh requires that the computer have a PowerPC processor.

This chapter will not cover every troubleshooting situation in depth. In fact, entire books have been written on this subject. We'll give you tips to speed up the general troubleshooting process and cover some of the common situations you may face.

Steps in Troubleshooting

When you have a problem with your system, one of the most frustrating aspects is realizing that you've wasted a lot of time and energy trying to solve it—when in fact the solution was right under your nose. For example, while typing a document in a common word-processor program, a user noted that strange formatting changes occurred with nearly every keystroke. After a system upgrade and other hardware improvements, the problem persisted. Eventually the cause of the problem was determined: Her workstation chair that was too low, causing her hands to accidentally push the Control key while typing.

Whether you're dealing with a problem on your own computer or providing support for a user in your department, the following series of steps can help you understand the problem and narrow your scope of solutions.

Get the Details

If you're experiencing a problem with your computer, one of the first things you need to do is document the details of the problem. Ask yourself if you've installed any new software, made changes to the configuration of a Control Panel, or performed a system upgrade. Note the last time you successfully performed the task that now is failing. Document the operating system environment when the problem occurs. Pay attention to any system error messages; they often identify the problem for you. For example, suppose that Netscape Navigator seems to run out of memory after extensive Internet browsing. Determine exactly what versions of the Mac OS and Netscape Navigator you're using, as well as the amount of available memory and how long you were able to browse the Web before the failure occurred. If the problem seems to be widespread across multiple applications, try keeping a journal of error messages and crashes. You may be surprised to discover that a pattern really does exist. The Apple or Netscape Web sites may offer a well-documented explanation for this problem.

When dealing with a user who is experiencing computer problems, the most important thing you can do is listen carefully to the description of the problem. If you're thinking ahead of possible solutions, or of the next customer, then you're not listening. First let the user explain the problem, and then ask him or her key questions such as, "Did you change anything on the computer?" and "When was the last time you could perform this task?" If you have an unreliable memory, write down the information. When you have the details, you can begin to isolate the problem and look for solutions.

Duplicate the Problem

Using the information you have gathered, try to duplicate the problem yourself. In some cases, this may be easy. If the computer freezes when it boots, you should be able to verify the problem easily. Some problems may be more difficult to duplicate. For example, a user reports that everything on the computer seemed to crash at once. The computer was restarted, but the document that was open at the time of the crash was lost. In order to detect the action or system process that could be causing the problem, you may have to observe the user at work on the computer or ask the user to keep a diary. After you duplicate the problem, you can analyze the process that's causing it.

Some problems occur intermittently and cannot be witnessed very easily—which makes resolving them even more challenging. In these instances, the only way to diagnose the problem is to seek outside assistance by collaborating with others, hiring a consultant, or visiting an Apple-certified repair technician.

Check the Obvious

Suppose a user has trouble mounting the external SCSI Zip drive. Check the system to ensure that the necessary components are in place and that the physical connection is intact. For instance, the Zip drive's SCSI selector could be terminated when termination should have been disabled, an obvious problem.

Here's another example: A PowerMac G4 is turned on and makes a startup sound, but the monitor never displays an image. Check the obvious. Are the video cables securely connected? Can you hear the hard drive spinning? Will the computer boot from another system disk or CD-ROM? If you can boot from an external source, you may want to try some quick fixes such as running Disk First Aid, rebuilding the Desktop file, or running a virus check on the affected disk.

Checking the obvious—such as making sure everything is physically connected—before exploring the obscure can save a lot of time and effort.

Find the Cause

If all the obvious components are in place, you should begin the process of isolating the cause of the problem. Note every process that takes place before the problem occurs. Try a few general solutions and document their results. Don't try several solutions at once, such as disabling multiple Extensions, because the process of elimination requires that you try one solution at a time or you won't be able to pinpoint the *exact* cause of the problem. For example, you may try rebuilding the Desktop file. At this point, rather than zapping the PRAM, see if the problem continues.

Begin with general solutions, then narrow your approach. If you suspect an Extension conflict, enable only the Mac OS 9.1 Base Extensions or Mac OS 9.1 All Extension sets in the Extension Manager and see if the problem continues. If it does, try enabling a few extensions at a time until you can isolate the problem.

Repair the Problem

Now that you have a general idea of the cause of the problem—and that it does not have an obvious solution—you can suggest ways to repair it. In some cases, you can update software or device drivers if the manufacturer documents a known problem that is fixed by a software patch or minor upgrade. You can also rearrange the load order of Extensions by adding blank spaces to the beginnings of the file names to get them to load first, for example, to diagnose an Extension conflict. Whatever the solution, make sure that you document it for future reference. If you have the means, make the solution available to other users who may face the same situation.

Common Problems

Check out the Tech Info Library at **http://til.info.apple.com**. This database contains many documented problems and their solutions. Remember, however, that a small handful of solutions can help you resolve the majority of computer problems.

Sound but No Picture

A user presses the power button on a computer, but no booting activity occurs and nothing displays on screen. Determine how much of the power process is occurring, such as verifying that the power strip is plugged into the power socket and the surge protector is turned on and distributing power to other sources. Verify that a startup sound occurred (a computer may not make a startup sound if the volume is turned completely down or, in the case of the Cube, the speakers are not attached). If the CPU has an indicator light, see if it is glowing. If the indicator light is off, check the hardware connections, especially the keyboard. (The keyboard passes the signal to activate the computer; if the keyboard connection is loose, the signal will not reach the computer.)

If the indicator light is on, check the monitor light. Today's EnergyStar-compliant monitors usually display an amber-colored indicator light when the CPU is not emitting a video signal or when the system is in energy-saver mode. When a signal is received, the amber light changes to green. If this doesn't happen but the CPU indicator light is active, check the monitor connections. If you find a loose monitor cable and reconnect it, you may have to restart the system before the CPU and monitor can communicate.

If all connections are intact, restart the computer and listen for system activity. Lack of system activity may indicate a hardware problem. Try switching monitors; if the monitor works on another computer, the problem is localized to the CPU. If not, the monitor is the source of the problem. If the CPU is to blame, check the video card. Also, some older-model Macintoshes produce a startup sound, but no other system activity, when the battery is dead. If none of these options work, you should probably have an Apple-authorized repair shop look at the computer.

Finally, if you have switched monitors and the new monitor is not displaying images, it may not be capable of displaying at the same resolution and refresh rate as the previous monitor. The solution to this problem is to reboot with Extensions off (hold down the Shift key while restarting); and the computer will start up with the display at its lowest and slowest settings (usually 640×480). In the Preferences folder, locate the Monitors Preferences folder; then find the Monitors Preferences file within that folder. Trash the Monitors Preferences file, and then restart.

Related solution:	*Found on page:*
Configuring Monitors	68

Problems Getting Started

What do you do with a Macintosh that starts but cannot seem to progress to the Welcome screen? Examine the display icons for clues such as the Mac OS startup icon (a.k.a., the Happy Mac icon). If you see only a gray screen, determine whether any SCSI devices are attached to the computer. If so, turn off the computer and remove the SCSI cable from the back of the CPU; then restart the computer. If it

18. Troubleshooting

boots, examine the termination of the SCSI devices and ensure that their identifying numbers are unique. This may involve reattaching the devices one at a time and rebooting the computer after attaching each device.

If your computer displays an icon other than the Happy Mac, inspect the icon closely. The Sad Mac indicates that the computer performed an initial system check and discovered a problem. Try booting from the Mac OS 9.1 CD-ROM or a system disk. If you see the Sad Mac icon again, a hardware problem may be present. If the computer can boot from another disk, you may have a software problem, such as an incorrect system installation. (Users may cause this by copying a System Folder, rather than actually running the installation program.) You can run Disk First Aid, Norton Utilities, or TechTool Pro to fix the problem. Alternatively, you can reinstall the Mac OS.

A disk icon with a blinking question mark indicates that a bootable system cannot be located or used. Try booting with a system CD-ROM or floppy disk. If the computer boots without error, run Disk First Aid on the hard drive. Apple suggests that you run the program several times to be sure all the errors were fixed. Disk First Aid may initially say that it cannot repair the drive; however, it may be able to do so. For faster results, you may also want to run Norton Utilities or TechTool Pro. If the computer boots with an alternate system disk, but reports that the hard drive needs to be initialized, try running Disk First Aid. It may report that the disk cannot be repaired, but in many cases the computer will recognize the hard drive and allow you to boot from it. Take this opportunity to back up your data with an application like Dantz's Retrospect Express (**www.dantz.com**) before running a thorough diagnostic test. You may need to reinitialize the disk in order to fix it; if so, you can use the backup to restore the data to your disk.

Hanging During Startup

Your computer starts successfully, but cannot seem to finish the startup process. This may be due to an Extension conflict, a damaged Extension, or a corrupt preference file. If your computer freezes while booting, restart it with Extensions off to eliminate the possibility of an Extension conflict or damaged Extension; this will also verify that the computer is indeed capable of booting. If it cannot boot, you'll need to boot from a CD-ROM or floppy and then run Disk First Aid on your computer. If the computer can boot, try enabling the Mac OS 9.1 Base Extensions set in the Extensions Manager and restart. If the computer cannot boot, try booting from another medium and running Disk First Aid. If the computer can boot, begin enabling Extensions gradually; you'll probably restart the computer multiple times. Don't load huge batches of Extensions—it's difficult to pinpoint the conflict to a particular file. You may also want to observe where the booting process hangs. Extensions and Control Panels load in alphabetical order. If the computer stops suddenly, identify the last Extension icon that loaded successfully;

it may indicate the offending Extension. Many of these components do not exhibit an icon during the boot process, so don't assume that the icon frozen on the screen represents the culprit. Also, if a red X appears atop any of the Extension or Control Panel icons during startup, then that component did not load properly

If your computer seems to hang just before the end of the boot process, assess the contents of the Startup Items folder for a possible cause. You can disable items within this folder from the Extensions Manager.

Related solutions:	Found on page:
Starting the Computer	38
Monitoring Startup Progress	39
Disabling Extensions	39
Manipulating Load Order	42

Memory Trouble

When you launch an application, a system error message tells you that not enough memory is available. Begin your investigation in the About This Computer window. Locate the figure that indicates the largest free block of memory and compare it to the total memory used. If these figures added together do not equal your total memory, the memory is fragmented. Quitting other open applications may create a block large enough to accommodate the application you want to open. Restarting the computer will also clear memory fragmentation. Errors may occur when memory is not available for a process, such as sending an item to print, that is launched in the background. Quitting open applications should clear enough memory to enable the process.

You may need to adjust the amount of memory allocated to an application. While the application is closed, select it in the Finder, choose File|Get Info|Memory, and increase the preferred memory size. If an application suddenly quits because an error has occurred—usually identified by a numeric code—see if allocating more memory improves the application's performance.

If it's necessary to run several applications simultaneously—but you don't have enough built-in memory—open the Memory Control Panel and allocate hard drive space as Virtual Memory. (Virtual Memory is enabled by default.) Remember that increasing the Virtual Memory allocation reduces system performance because the hard drive memory partition is much slower than actual RAM. If you frequently run out of memory, consider a physical memory upgrade.

Related solutions:	Found on page:
Allocating Memory for RAM Disks	182
Allocating Application Memory	184

18. Troubleshooting

Printing Problems

A user reports a Mac that is unable to complete the boot process. You learn that a document was sent to a printer, but before it printed, the system crashed and the user was forced to restart the computer. Now, the computer hangs as soon as the printing software attempts to pick up where it left off. The most common solution is starting the computer with Extensions disabled and removing the document from the print queue. Large Xs will now appear through each of the Desktop printer icons, as shown in Figure 18.1. Double-click on the icon of the printer driver that was in use during the crash. Although printing software is disabled, you can still remove documents from the print queue.

Another common printing problem is that the printer cannot be found. To resolve this error, reselect the printer in the Chooser. If the printer is not listed in the Chooser, check the printer's indicator light and cabling to make sure that the printer is on and connected to the computer or network. If the printer is on and correctly connected, turn it off for 10 seconds, then turn it back on to reinitialize it. If you still cannot see the printer, you may need to turn both the printer and computer off and then restart them. You should then be able to choose the printer and print your document.

If you're experiencing memory errors when printing, you can increase the memory allocated to the Desktop Print Monitor by going to the Desktop Print Monitor application located in the Extensions folder. If you're sending a large and complex document to print, it's a good idea to quit all open applications so that the bulk of the computer's resources can be used to print the document.

Document Dilemmas

Suppose that a user has previously created and saved a file, but now cannot locate it. This is most often due to user error. Many applications default to the application's home folder the first time a file is saved. Users may not pay attention to the Save path, and select the Save option without switching to a documents folder. Mac OS 9.1 also provides an option for Favorite folders. Applications that support Mac OS 9.1's new Save and Open dialog boxes make it easier to locate files. You can also use the Find utility to search for the missing file by name, date created, date modified, kind, type, and even creator.

Figure 18.1   A disabled desktop printer icon.

Another common document problem occurs when a user double-clicks on a document, but the application that created it cannot be found. First verify that the application is installed on the computer. If it is not, you have several options:

- Install the missing application.

- Ask the person who supplied the document to save it in a lowest-common-denominator format such as Rich Text Format (for a word processor document) or TIFF (for an image).

- If you have an application similar to the missing one, translators that can open the document in question may be available. For example, if you have Microsoft Word 6 but receive a document from a colleague that was created in Word 97, the Microsoft Web site has a translator you can download that enables Word 6 to open Word 97/98 documents. You may also get better results if you launch the application first, then open the file in question.

If you double-click on the document and receive a message that the application cannot be found—although the application is indeed installed on your computer—rebuild the Desktop file. This corrects the file and document association problem. If you need to open the document immediately, try launching the application first, and then open the file from within the application.

Useful Tools

Whether you support only your own Macintosh computer or an entire organization's worth of Macs, you need a toolkit of troubleshooting software. Because the utilities included in Mac OS 9.1 are limited, you should invest in commercial software utilities that will help you effectively maintain and support the Macintosh computer. Many excellent programs are available for fixing various problems under Mac OS 9.1; we'll discuss the most popular ones.

Mac Help

The first place to look for basic troubleshooting information is the built-in assistance offered by the Mac OS itself, Mac Help. When the Finder is the front-most application, just look under the Help menu or select Command+? to activate Mac Help. Then select the subsection entitled "Preventing and Solving Problems" (see Figure 18.2). The advice is basic, but nevertheless this can be a good place to start.

Disk First Aid

Disk First Aid, a utility included with Mac OS 9.1, allows you to diagnose or repair many disk problems, including directory structures for HFS and HFS+ disks, catalogs, volume bit maps, and extent files. Figure 18.3 shows the Disk First Aid utility. Its options are very simple: Select a disk to examine and choose to Verify or

18. Troubleshooting

Figure 18.2 Look to Mac Help for the basics on troubleshooting your Mac.

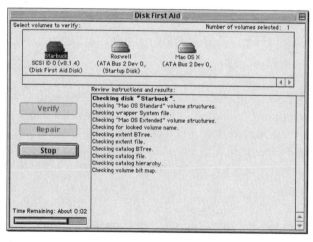

Figure 18.3 The Disk First Aid utility.

Repair the disk. Verify scans the disk and generates a report indicating what repairs are needed and whether Disk First Aid can repair them. Repair also scans the disk and generates a report; then it repairs the problem, if possible. Don't despair if Disk First Aid says it cannot repair a disk problem. Run the utility multiple times; it may actually be fixing the problems bit by bit. This option is even recommended by Apple.

Disk First Aid can also repair the startup disk while it is active. Provided that the Warn Me If Computer Was Shut Down Improperly option is checked in the General Controls Control Panel, Disk First Aid automatically scans the disk upon restart if you shut down or restarted your computer improperly. Although Disk First Aid lacks the features of commercial and shareware programs, it can repair many disk problems.

Drive Setup

The Drive Setup utility is another diagnostic tool from Apple. Although you may not think of Drive Setup as anything more than a tool for initializing and reformatting hard drives, it is, in fact, the ideal tool for troubleshooting drives that do not mount on startup. Shown in Figure 18.4, Drive Setup can scan SCSI and ATAPI interfaces for drives that are mountable by Mac OS 9.1. If a drive is supported by the Mac OS, you should be able to initialize, test, partition, mount, and eject the disk. If the drive is compatible with the Drive Setup utility, you will also be able to update the disk driver.

Software Update

A common solution for many software-related problems is to simply update or patch an application. But with so many applications on the market, it can be a hassle to find a company's Web site and download the correct update or patch. The Software Update Control Panel, shown in Figure 18.5, serves as a single point of contact for locating updates to all the components of the Mac OS.

Figure 18.4   The Drive Setup utility is a multipurpose tool for diagnosing disk-related problems.

Figure 18.5   Use the Software Update feature to keep the Mac OS up to date.

Software Update allows you to schedule automatic updates. This feature is more practical if your computer has a fast and permanent connection to the Internet rather than a dial-up connection.

Apple System Profiler

The Apple System Profiler is an information-gathering tool. As we've said before, you'll be in a much better position to repair a problem if you have sufficient information about your computer in its entirety. The Apple System Profiler, shown in Figure 18.6, collects information on all of your computer's essential hardware, including disks, RAM, processor(s), and network connections, as well as detailed information on disks, Control Panels, Extensions, and installed applications. Use this information to get the big picture when diagnosing a problem on your own computer, or ask your users to utilize the Apple System Profiler to generate a report that will help you diagnose their problem.

Norton Utilities

Norton Utilities from Symantec is one of the most recognized disk repair and maintenance programs available today. It can do much more than Disk First Aid, and has an excellent library of programs to help you recover data, improve disk performance, and protect against crashes. Figure 18.7 shows the main application interface for Norton Utilities.

Disk Doctor is the most well known utility in the Norton Utilities suite. For many users, disk protection is an afterthought. Suddenly strange things happen to their computers that Disk First Aid cannot fix. Almost in desperation, they run out and purchase Norton Utilities just to run Disk Doctor and repair their disks. Fortunately,

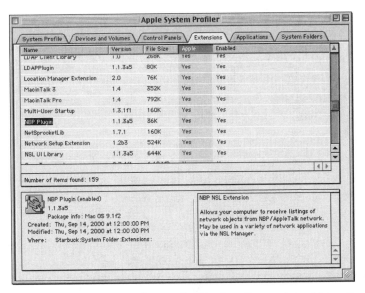

Figure 18.6   The Apple System Profiler is a thorough tool for gathering detailed
information about a computer.

Disk Doctor can usually save the day. Norton Utilities can do much more than fix
disks, however. Each of its elements is useful for troubleshooting. Some of the
most commonly used of the Norton Utilities are the following:

- *DiskDoctor*—The mainstay of the utilities, it repairs damaged disks and
  volumes. Visit **www.norton.com** for the latest version of Norton Utilities
  and information about Mac OS 9.1 compatibility issues.

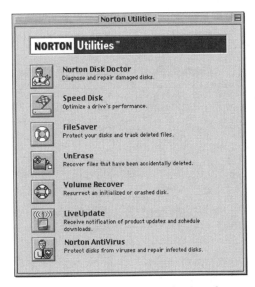

Figure 18.7   The Norton Utilities interface.

- *Speed Disk*—Defragments and optimizes the contents of disks.

- *FileSaver*—Catalogs disks and volumes and saves the information to a file. When you need to run UnErase, you have the best chance of data recovery if the volume has been cataloged by FileSaver.

- *UnErase*—Recovers files that have been deleted from the hard drive. UnErase works best with FileSaver.

- *Volume Recover*—A final-resort program for extremely corrupted or damaged disks. Avoid running this utility unless Norton Disk Doctor has suggested it.

- *System Info*—Tests your system and gives you information on its performance. You can use this information to determine whether your system is performing suboptimally or needs an upgrade.

Norton Utilities includes several other components that provide information about your system and allow you to check for updates to Norton Utilities. If you have Norton AntiVirus installed as well (it is a separate program, and is shown in Figure 18.8), it will be available in the Norton Utilities application, too, although it is

Figure 18.8 Norton AntiVirus is a companion product to Norton Utilities that is also a must-have utility for your troubleshooting toolkit.

not part of Norton Utilities, per se. Both Norton Utilities and Norton AntiVirus are valuable programs to include in your troubleshooting toolkit.

TechTool Pro

TechTool Pro from MicroMat is an extensive hardware and system testing utility. It can run a battery of tests on your computer and advise you of problems with your system. It also can test many of your hardware components, including your floppy drive, Zip drive, modem, mouse, and main system hardware. TechTool Pro has two interfaces to tailor the program to the needs of the user:

- *The Standard interface*—This interface has preconfigured the system testing so that even a beginner can check the computer (see Figure 18.9). If TechTool Pro finds a problem, it informs you and indicates whether it can make the repair. TechTool Pro can also tell you when hardware elements need to be repaired.

- *The Expert interface*—This interface is geared toward a knowledgeable user who wants to control the testing and even limit it to a particular device. For example, if a user is having trouble with a modem, you can test the modem only. TechTool Pro tests the integrity of the telephone line as well as the modem. It can conduct over 300 tests on the system and its many components.

TechTool Pro, which provides the same software functionality as Norton Utilities, has a long history of providing the extensive hardware testing that Norton Utilities lacks. TechTool Pro's strength is in its hardware testing programs and extensive information about the Mac OS. For this reason, TechTool Pro is an excellent

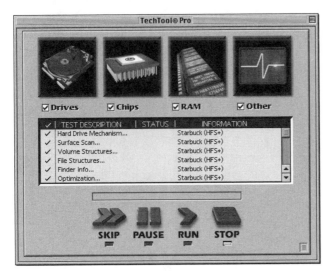

Figure 18.9   TechTool Pro's Standard interface, suitable for all user levels.

addition to your software library. TechTool, a freeware version of this software, is also available; it can perform some of the same functions.

Conflict Catcher

An Extension conflict is one of the most difficult problems to diagnose. Although Apple includes Extensions Manager in Mac OS 9.1, sometimes you need more help. Conflict Catcher, a commercial utility from Casady & Green (**www.casadyg.com**) may suit your needs. If you are encountering an Extension conflict, Conflict Catcher can do all the tedious work of restarting the computer and testing the Extensions. In addition to identifying the Extensions that don't seem to get along, it will also name the program that crashes your system. Conflict Catcher provides useful information about each Extension and Control Panel, including the version number, type of file, and even links to the company that developed the program. If your computer is configured to load many Extensions and Control Panels, consider adding Conflict Catcher to your software library.

Where to Get Help

You may know a lot about your system and how it functions, but at some point you'll encounter a situation where none of your "tricks" works. You need to know where to go to get help. An extensive listing of helpful resources is included in Appendix E, and as we mentioned earlier in this chapter, the Mac OS includes an excellent online Help Viewer. If you want an extensive resource of troubleshooting information for the Mac OS as well as many Macintosh models, you may want to consult *Sad Macs, Bombs, and Other Disasters* by Ted Landau. Many practical solutions, as well as in-depth information, are included in this volume. Ted also maintains a Web site at **www.macfixit.com** that provides troubleshooting information for the Macintosh computer and Mac OS.

Immediate Solutions

Resolving Startup Conflicts

If your computer cannot complete the booting process and has displayed the Happy Mac icon, a conflict probably exists between Extensions. It's also possible that your computer has a problem launching an application. Follow these steps to troubleshoot an Extension conflict:

1. Restart the computer while holding down the Shift key to disable all Extensions.

2. Go to Apple menu|Control Panels.

3. Open Extensions Manager, and click on the Selected Set pop-up menu to select the Mac OS 9.1 Base set, as shown in Figure 18.10.

4. Restart the computer. If the system will not boot properly, you have a problem with the basic Mac OS 9.1 installation. If the computer will boot with Extensions off, reboot and run Disk First Aid and perhaps rebuild the Desktop file. You may need to reinstall the operating system. If the computer will not boot with Extensions off, boot from the installation CD-ROM and reinstall the Mac OS.

5. If the computer will boot with the basic set of Mac OS 9.1 Extensions, launch the Extensions Manager and enable a few of the programs (perhaps

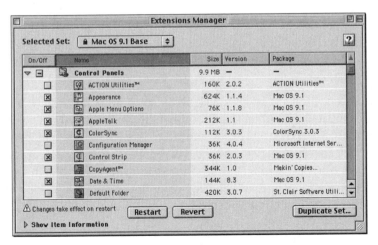

Figure 18.10   The Extensions Manager window with Mac OS 9.1 Base Extensions selected.

those that are closely related to each other, such as telecommunication software), and restart the computer. Repeat this process until you experience the conflict.

6. When you locate the Extension that is causing the problem, determine if it is needed. If it is, you may want to rearrange the order in which the Extension loads by changing its name (insert a number or space at the beginning of the file name to force it to load earlier; insert a tilde or bullet to force it to load later). Check also that the software has been updated to be compatible with Mac OS 9.1.

7. In some cases, you may find that you can enable all Extensions and no longer have a conflict. You should still observe the system closely to see if the problem reoccurs.

TIP: If you have a lot of Extensions, consider purchasing Conflict Catcher. It can automate much of the process of determining the source of an Extension conflict.

Fixing Corrupted Preferences

Suppose that a user is experiencing strange problems within an application. For example, the application crashes when a particular feature is activated, or a specific document cannot be opened. A corrupted preference file might be the cause, which can hamper the effective functioning of the application in question as well as that of an Extension or even the Finder itself. The best course of action is to delete the corrupted preference and allow the application to create a new one. Follow these steps for locating, deleting, and re-creating a preference file:

1. Quit the application that may have a corrupted preference and reboot with Extensions off.

2. Open the Preferences folder in the System Folder, or use Sherlock 2 to find the preference file by name or modification date.

3. Drag the preference file to the Trash. Because some applications (Netscape Navigator, for example) store entire folders of information in the Preferences folder, you may need to open additional folders to access the preference file. In these cases, make sure that you remove only the preference file. The application may store other important information in this folder that you don't want to lose (in a Web browser, for example, your bookmarks and emails are stored in this folder).

TIP: Some applications store their preferences within the same folder as the application itself. If the preference file is not stored in the Preferences folder, check in the application folder.

---

4. If the preference file you removed belonged to an application, you should be able to start the application and re-create the preference file. You may have to reconfigure some settings or enter the program's serial number.

5. If the preference file you removed belonged to the Finder or a system component, trash the preference file and restart the computer with Extensions on to re-create it. You can empty the Trash once the computer has been restarted a second time.

TIP: If the Finder, an Extension, or a Control Panel has a corrupted preference file, you'll achieve the best results by booting from another startup disk to completely purge the preference information from memory.

Rebuilding the Desktop File

If you have a computer that is not performing as well as it should, you may need to rebuild the Desktop file, a database that keeps track of associations between documents and the programs used to create them. This database can become rather convoluted if you have tens of thousands of files on your computer. One specific symptom of a corrupted Desktop file occurs when you double-click on a document associated with a specific program on your computer, but receive an error that the application that created the document could not be found. Networking problems are also associated with a corrupt Desktop file. Follow these steps to rebuild the Desktop file:

1. Restart the computer with Extensions off by holding down the Shift key.

2. When the startup screen appears that says the Extensions are off, release the Shift key and hold down the Option+Command keys until the dialog box shown in Figure 18.11 appears.

3. Release the keys and allow the computer to rebuild the Desktop file.

If you have purchased TechTool Pro, you can use this program to rebuild the Desktop file more efficiently. TechTool Pro completely removes the existing Desktop file and creates a new one. You can also perform this function with TechTool, the free utility from **www.micromat.com**.

Figure 18.11   Rebuilding the Desktop file.

Zapping the PRAM

Suppose you have an application that you must use every day. The program is poorly written, and in spite of your best efforts, it causes an application crash on a daily basis. As these crashes continue, your Parameter RAM (PRAM) can develop problems. Symptoms include poor system performance and trouble with basic system settings, such as the sound level. When this happens, zap the PRAM using these steps:

1. Restart your computer holding down these keys during startup: Command+Option+P+R.

2. Hold down the key combination described in Step 1 until the computer restarts itself a second time, rather than continuing with the normal startup process; the second restart indicates that the PRAM has been cleared. Some sources recommend holding down the key combination until the Mac has restarted several times, but Apple states that two starts should be adequate.

When you zap the PRAM, some basic system settings are reset to the factory defaults. For example, the system alert sound and highlight color will return to the original settings, and your AppleTalk port connection may default to the printer port.

TechTool and TechTool Pro have the capability to completely test and clear the PRAM; Figure 18.12 shows the options in TechTool Pro for this feature. If the PRAM is not cleared, some of the corruption can remain and continue to cause problems. If the keystroke combination given in this solution does not solve your problem, download TechTool from **www.micromat.com** or purchase TechTool Pro.

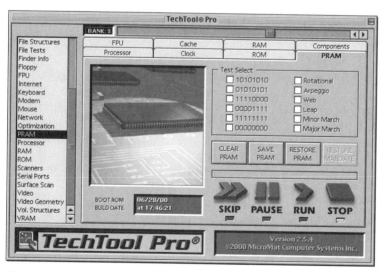

Figure 18.12   Using TechTool Pro to test and reset PRAM.

Fixing Common Printing Problems

Printing is often a critical task. A user who can't print may be upset (to put it mildly) if the problem is not solved. You can follow some common procedures to resolve the problem:

1. If you receive an error message that the document failed to print and are offered the option to print again, try printing again. Your document may print.

2. If you tried again to print and failed, cancel the print job and see if the printer is still visible within the Chooser. You may have lost your network connection and need to restore it, or the printer may no longer be visible on the network.

3. For locally attached printers, check your cables and make sure the correct serial or USB port is selected in the AppleTalk Control Panel.

4. If you still cannot print or if a networked printer is not visible on the network, turn the printer off and on.

5. If necessary, restart your own computer and the printer and then attempt to print again.

6. If you still cannot print, try removing the printer preference file, restarting the computer, and generating a new preference file for the preferred printer.

7. Check the indicator lights on the printer and verify that the printer does not have a hardware problem.

Identifying a Bad Battery

Imagine that you accidentally click on the time on the menu bar, and notice that you are living in the past—in the year 1956, to be precise. This is one of the most common symptoms of a failing motherboard battery. Symptoms similar to those indicative of a corrupted PRAM may also appear because the battery preserves the contents of the PRAM. When the battery begins to die, the PRAM settings are frequently lost. In extreme cases, your computer may not be able to boot.

Apple warns that replacing the battery could void your warranty on your computer, but your computer usually is no longer under warranty by the time the battery dies. If you want to replace your battery on your own, Charles D. Phillips's Web site **www.academ.com/info/macintosh/** provides instructions for replacing the battery in most Macintosh models.

18. Troubleshooting

Using Disk First Aid

Described earlier in this chapter, Disk First Aid is a utility written by Apple that provides some disk repair options. Because Disk First Aid, which is very easy to run, has been written to perform the task of disk repair, you should be able to teach users to run this utility. Disk First Aid is usually found in the Utilities folder. To use Disk First Aid, follow these steps:

1. Launch Disk First Aid.

2. All data volumes, including hard drives, CD-ROMs, floppies, and removable media such as Zip disks, will appear.

3. Select the disk that needs repair. In previous versions of Disk First Aid, you booted from another system disk to repair the startup volume. Mac OS 9.1 now allows you to repair the primary volume while its system is active, but not while other applications are running.

4. Select Verify or Repair (some people who are nervous about doing a repair immediately run Verify to assess the disk's problems). Verify only checks the volume for problems and creates a report. Repair identifies the problems and attempts to fix them.

5. If Disk First Aid reports that it cannot fix the volume, run Disk First Aid again and again. Although it may continue to report that it cannot fix the disk, in some cases it is actually fixing the problem incrementally.

If Disk First Aid really cannot repair your volume, invest in a commercial utility, such as Norton Utilities from Symantec or TechTool Pro from MicroMat, that specializes in disk repair.

Using Norton Utilities Disk Doctor

If a user experiences strange errors and you've tried all the free solutions, such as Desktop rebuilds and Disk First Aid, you may want to run Norton Utilities.

Norton Utilities includes an excellent disk repair program called Disk Doctor. Although Disk Doctor takes longer to run than Apple's Disk First Aid, it does a careful examination of the system, including the disk media and volume structure, at a basic level, and analyzes every file on the system for errors and problems. Follow these steps to run Disk Doctor:

1. Launch Norton Utilities and click on the Disk Doctor icon, or launch the Disk Doctor application directly.

2. Select the volume that you want to analyze.

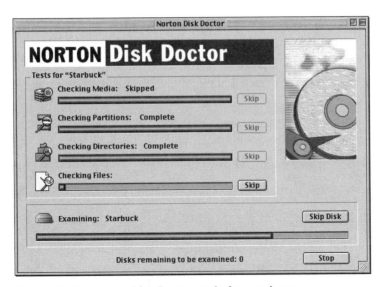

Figure 18.13   Norton Disk Doctor analyzing a volume.

3. Disk Doctor proceeds through a series of tests and programs (see Figure 18.13). If it encounters an error, it will alert you.

4. When the volume has been repaired, Disk Doctor generates a detailed report that you may want to keep if this volume has a history of similar problems.

5. If Disk Doctor cannot repair the volume, the disk may be in extremely poor condition. At this point Disk Doctor may recommend using Volume Recover to recover the data to another volume. Do this only if Disk Doctor recommends it.

Using Norton Utilities UnErase

In a multiuser environment, one of the most common problems is the accidental deletion of an important file, folder, or application. Here is your chance to be a hero! Norton Utilities includes a program named UnErase that can recover files that have been deleted. Remember that when a file is deleted, only the "directory" information is gone. The file itself is still on the hard drive and will remain there until the space is needed for writing new data. Logic dictates that the more free space you have on your disk, the longer the deleted files will remain there. If you have nearly filled the hard drive, run UnErase as soon as possible to recover the files. Follow these instructions to run UnErase:

1. Launch Norton Utilities. Then click on the UnErase button, or launch UnErase from the Finder.

18. Troubleshooting

2. If File Sharing is enabled, you will be advised to disable it so that UnErase can run effectively.

3. A window appears in which you can select the volume that contains the information you want to recover. Choose the volume and click on the Search button.

4. UnErase scans the drive and presents you with a list of the files it located and their chances of being recovered.

5. Select the file you want to recover and click on the Recover button (see Figure 18.14).

Figure 18.14   Recovering a deleted file using UnErase.

Using TechTool Pro

The difference between TechTool and TechTool Pro is in the scope of their capabilities. TechTool is limited to only a few functions, such as rebuilding the Desktop file and zapping the PRAM. TechTool Pro has over 300 tests for hardware as well as software that can be performed on your system. TechTool Pro is also capable of performing disk repair. Both TechTool and TechTool Pro are known for their hardware testing capabilities. For the purposes of this example, we'll look at what TechTool Pro can do. To use it, take these steps:

1. Launch TechTool Pro.

2. The Standard Interface, which is the default interface setting for TechTool Pro, will appear. TechTool Pro has already selected the appropriate tests that will give you a general overview of the condition of your computer. If you are not familiar with TechTool Pro, use this interface to ensure that the appropriate tests are run.

3. By removing the checkmarks next to system categories, or those next to individual tests, you can choose to test only a part of your system. Decide what system categories to check, what tests to disable, or leave the settings as they are.

4. When you're ready to begin, click on the Run button. You can pause or stop the testing if necessary.

5. As each test is finished, the status of the item being tested indicates whether it passed or failed. When the battery of tests is complete, TechTool Pro generates a report of test results.

6. You can switch to the Expert Interface by selecting Interface|Expert. The window changes and allows you to manually determine what tests should be run, such as the RAM test shown in Figure 18.15.

7. You can select a category from the list at the right, or use the scroll bar to select a category from the window tabs. Choose a category and the test you want to run.

8. Click on the Run button to start the test.

9. TechTool Pro runs the diagnostics and generates a report. In some cases, TechTool Pro repairs the problem. For hardware problems, TechTool Pro generates a report and indicates if a trip to the computer shop is necessary.

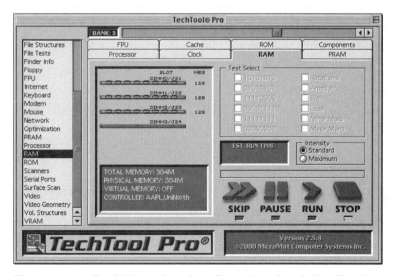

Figure 18.15   The RAM section of the Expert Interface in TechTool Pro.

18. Troubleshooting

Appendix A

Shortcuts and Tricks

Sometimes you just want the facts or, as this appendix is entitled, the shortcuts. This section covers some of the hints and tricks that you should know as you support Macintosh computers. You may even find some gems that have not been covered previously in this book.

Starting the Computer

Use some of these tricks and diagnostic tools to help your system start properly.

Power Key vs. CPU Power Button

The most common and proper method for turning on your Macintosh is to press the power key on the keyboard. This sends a signal to the computer to turn on and begin loading the system.

If you press the keyboard power button and nothing happens, you may want to confirm the model. Some models, such as the 6100, have a button located on the front of the computer. In fact, a limited number of Macs, including the early models (such as the Classic, the Centris, and the Quadra 610) up to the 6100 Power Macintosh, cannot be started from the keyboard. This is also true for some Performa models.

Newer Macintosh computers with USB keyboards present a few problems. Because some USB keyboards won't start the computer, you may need to push the power button on the CPU to start up. If your Apple monitor includes a USB port, you can plug the USB keyboard into the monitor and start the entire system from the monitor power button. Be aware that the Apple Pro keyboard, a revamped USB keyboard, does not provide a power button. If you use this keyboard, you must start the computer from the CPU or monitor, depending on your configuration.

Zapping the PRAM

If your computer has been crashing and you've had to improperly restart it or shut it down multiple times, then you may want to clear the PRAM. The PRAM contains some very basic system configurations, including the display bit depth, system sound, and the date and time. System crashes affect the PRAM, causing the system to malfunction even more and, consequently, perpetuating this circle of trouble. Zapping the PRAM sets everything back to normal (and returns some settings to the factory default).

To zap the PRAM, restart the computer while holding down the Option+Command+ P+R keys. When the computer reaches the point where the welcome screen should appear, the computer will restart. Some Mac gurus recommend that you let the computer restart this way a second or third time, and then release the keys and let the system boot normally.

After you have zapped the PRAM, some system settings may change. Most of these are of minor significance, such as system volume or highlight color. However, one change is particularly important: In newer computers that support network booting (such as the iMac and G4 series), the PRAM may select a network disk as the startup disk. This will cause a short delay in booting the computer. Go to the Startup Disk Control Panel and select your hard drive to resolve this problem.

TechTool, an excellent freeware utility, can zap the PRAM effectively so that you don't have to scramble for the keystroke combination.

Startup Screens

The first image you see on your screen after turning your Macintosh on is usually the small computer. The second image welcomes you to the Macintosh. This second screen is the *startup screen*. It has changed over the various versions of the Macintosh OS to the simple yet elegant version you see today. However, you can display an alternate image in its place. You can locate these alternate startup screens in two ways:

- You can download ready-made startup screens from most shareware sites.

- You can create your own startup screens:

    1. Determine what image you want to use as a startup screen.

    2. Save the image in PICT format, with an ID of zero.

    If you have Graphic Converter, you can save files as a startup screen. Other imaging programs also have this capability. If you're adventurous, you can use ResEdit to change the resource ID to zero.

After you have the file with the correct resource ID, you can finish the process by renaming the file *StartupScreen* and placing it in the System folder. The next time your system launches, the new image will be the startup screen.

One note of caution: Some startup screens can wreak havoc. You'll know immediately if your alternate startup screen is a troublemaker because your system will hang and you will be unable to boot. The only solution is to remove the startup screen from the System folder. You'll have to restart the computer and boot from another disk, such as a CD-ROM or floppy disk with Mac OS 9.1 installed. You can then remove the offending file and boot the computer normally.

Starting with Extensions Off

You can start your system with only the basic system components loaded by starting with Extensions off. You may want to do this when you install new software or when your system cannot boot normally.

To start the computer with Extensions off, turn on or restart the computer as you normally would, but hold down the Shift key until the welcome screen appears. In addition to the normal image, it should say "Extensions Off." Then release the Shift key (if you've installed a startup screen, you can alternatively release the Shift key when the startup screen appears).

Although your system will be very limited at this point, you can begin your search for Extension conflicts. To start the process of elimination, start your computer next with only the basic Mac OS 9.1 Extensions loaded. This will help determine if the system itself is the problem or if you are dealing with a problem third-party driver.

Calling the Extensions Manager

What if you forget to press the Shift key while restarting to disable Extensions? You still have a second chance. As long as Extensions have not begun loading, you can hold down the spacebar until the Extensions Manager Control Panel is launched. You can disable one, several, or all of the Extensions and then allow the system to continue booting.

Rebuilding the Desktop File

The hidden Desktop file tracks documents and applications and how they are related to each other. Occasionally, this information becomes garbled—files take longer to open or lose their distinctive icons. One of the most recognizable symptoms of Desktop file problems is the appearance of an error message, indicating that the application that created the document cannot be found when you double-click on a file that should open with the correct application.

For problems like these, as well as generally poor system performance, try rebuilding the Desktop file. For the best results, restart the computer with Extensions off (hold down the Shift key). After the welcome screen indicates that

Extensions are disabled, release the Shift key and press the Command+Option keys. Continue holding them down until you are asked if you want to rebuild the Desktop file; this will occur for each of your volumes or disk partitions. You should rebuild at least your hard drive partitions.

After you have rebuilt the Desktop file with the Extensions disabled, restart the computer. When this has concluded, your computer should be ready to work.

You may also want to use TechTool to rebuild the Desktop file. It completely removes the Desktop folder and re-creates it, thus eliminating the possibility that corrupted data could survive the standard method for rebuilding the Desktop file.

Startup Items

Do you use the same programs every time you start your computer? If so, you may want to put aliases of these programs in your Startup Items folder. The contents of the Startup Items folder will launch in alphabetical order, but you can control this by using numbers or special characters to alter the launch sequence. If you expect to quit some of these applications during your computer session, place them near the end of the list. When you exit the application, it will free up valuable memory. On the other hand, quitting the first applications that launched often causes fragmented memory.

Disk and File Management

Use the following tricks, shortcuts, and diagnostic tools for handling files, folders, and disks.

Changing an Icon

Occasionally, you may not like a file's icon. For example, you've been editing an application configuration file in a particular word processor. When you saved the file, it assumed the icon of the word processor instead of matching the other files associated with the application. It's easy to change it to the correct or favored icon. First, locate the icon that you want to associate with the file, click on it once, and select File|Get Info (Command +I). Click once on the icon that appears in this window, and then press Command+C to copy the icon. Close the Get Info window and click once on the icon you wish to change. Again select File|Get Info (Command+I) and click on the icon within this window. This time, press Command+V to paste the new icon.

Deleting a File

To delete a file, drag it to the Trash. Then go to the Special menu and select Empty Trash to delete everything in the Trash can. To recover files that you have deleted, you will need to use disk utility software such as Norton Utilities.

If you don't like dragging files to the Trash, you can select the file and use the keystroke combination Command+Delete to move the file to the Trash. You can also access the contextual menu by clicking on the file while holding the Control key.

You can delete a whole range of files by using the Sherlock 2 utility. Simply search for the files that you want to delete (for example, every file that contains the words "backup copy" in the file name). You can then drag the files directly from the results window to the Trash.

Copying with Drag and Drop

Dragging and dropping a file onto another partition or volume will result in an automatic copy. However, when you click on a folder or file and drag it to a location on the same volume, the file will be moved rather than copied. To force the system to copy the file, hold down the Option key while you are dragging. When you release the mouse, the system will copy the file rather than move it. You can even do this within the same window (the duplicate file will have the word "copy" after the file name).

Disabling the Trash Warning

Have you been annoyed by the dialog box that tells you how much trash you have and asks if you're sure you want to delete it? Although it's nice to know how much disk space you'll recover and you may appreciate a chance to cancel the Empty Trash command, most power users hate the delay this dialog box causes. You can easily disable this warning. Simply click once on the Trash icon, then press Command+I for the Get Info window. At the bottom of the window, remove the check from the box next to the Warn Before Emptying option.

Determining File or Folder Size

Knowing the size of files and folders helps you perform housecleaning functions on your hard drive. The simplest method for obtaining this information is the Get Info window. Click once on the icon of the file or folder, and then press Command+I or select File|Get Info. You should see the file size in this window.

You can also see file size by viewing the contents of a window as a list rather than viewing by icon. If the folder size doesn't display, you can turn it on by going to the View menu and selecting View Options. Enable the option to calculate folder sizes. After you click on OK and close this window, you should see folder sizes listed. Be careful with this option because it does affect system performance (information will be slower to display in the Finder windows); you may want to enable it only for short periods.

Repairing a Damaged Disk

It's distressing to insert a Zip disk and be told that your Mac doesn't recognize the disk. You'll be offered the option to eject or initialize the disk, but don't panic and format the disk. This dialog box may be an indication that your disk needs repair. Simply launch Disk First Aid, then insert the Zip disk (or any removable medium that needs repair). You can attempt to fix the disk and at least recover the data.

If this warning does appear, you may want to exercise caution with the medium in question. Move the data to a secure medium and then format the disk. Even then, the disk may not be reliable and probably should be discarded.

The Finder

Most Macintosh users spend their time in applications rather than in the Finder. In applications, they perform tasks like reading email, composing documents, or browsing the Web. But the driving force behind this productivity is the Finder. Here are some tips for using the Finder.

Organizing Columns in Views

Mac OS 9.1 allows you to control columns in the List view in much the same way as spreadsheet applications. You can rearrange the columns and change their width. Simply move your cursor to the headers that label the columns. To move a column, click on the header and drag it where you want it (the cursor changes to the shape of a hand). To control the width, move the cursor to the end of the header where the columns meet. The cursor will change to a resize cursor that you can drag to the left or right to adjust column width.

Hiding the Desktop

If you want to see only application windows, you can activate a setting that hides the Finder or Desktop whenever it is not active. Go to the General Controls Control Panel, deactivate the Show Desktop When In Background option, and close the window. Some users enable this accidentally and report it as a problem. To see the Finder again, you can go to the Applications menu and select Finder or go back to the General Controls window and reactivate the Show Desktop When In Background option.

Labeling Files

You can use file labeling to add pretty colors to icons, or to organize files according to importance, subject matter, or level of completion. Simply edit the file labels to reflect your organizational method. Go to the Edit menu and select Preferences. Select the Label tab and edit the text. You can also change the label colors from here.

To apply a label to a file or folder, select it and go to the File|Label menu or click and hold down Control to activate the contextual menu. Choose your label—it's that easy. You can display file views by labels as well and search by label within the Sherlock 2 utility.

Indexing with Sherlock 2

Mac OS 9.1 enables you to search files by content. To expedite this process, index the volumes that you'll be searching. You can arrange automatic scheduling and manual indexing through the Sherlock 2 Utility. Select Find|Index Volumes to set your options and conduct searches.

Scrolling without Scroll Bars

One of the coolest things you can do in Mac OS 9.1 is see the window's hidden contents without scrolling. Click anywhere in the window while holding down the Command key. Your cursor becomes a grabbing hand and you can move the window contents in realtime (you don't have to wait until the display redraws the window).

Aliases

Aliases are found throughout the Mac OS. Even installation programs create aliases to give you easy access to the installed program.

Creating an Alias

Use an alias to access a frequently needed folder from multiple locations or to provide access to a program without duplicating it. Simply click once on the item that needs an alias and select File|Make Alias (Command+M). An icon will appear with an italic typeface and the word "alias" appended to the file name. You can move the alias to any location. If you have a particular location in mind, click once on the original, hold down the Option+Command keys, and drag the icon to its destination folder. When you release the mouse, an alias with exactly the same name as the original will appear in the destination folder. This second method is preferable because you don't have to edit the file name to remove the word "alias."

Finding the Original

Many software installations automatically place aliases on the Desktop or in the Apple menu. If you want to find the program that originated the alias, go to File|Show Original (Command+R). The Finder will locate the original application. This option is also available in a contextual menu by holding the Control key as you click on the alias.

Selecting a New Original

If you have an alias on the Desktop or in the Apple menu that should now point to a new original (perhaps you've upgraded the software in a new folder), Mac OS 9.1 allows you to point the alias to a new application. Click once on the alias and go to File|Get Info (Command+I). Select General Information and click the Select New Original button at the bottom of the window. Then use the browser window to redirect the alias to a new original.

Memory Management

Use these tips for improving your system performance with effective memory management.

Increasing an Application's Memory Allocation

If you find that an application seems to be malfunctioning regularly, one of your first actions should be allocating more memory to the program. Make sure that the program is not running, and then click once on the application icon. Go to File|Get Info and select Memory. Manually increase the preferred memory size. Use your judgment on how much additional memory to allocate.

Virtual Memory

Virtual memory is enabled by default; this helps decrease the memory needs of some applications. However, some programs—usually games—don't behave well with virtual memory. To disable virtual memory, go to the Memory Control Panel. Locate the virtual memory section and click the Off radio button. You can also go to the Memory Control Panel and increase the virtual memory allocation. Both actions require you to restart the computer to use the new settings. But remember—the larger the virtual memory partition, the more performance is affected. If you find that your installed memory is not enough, try installing additional RAM instead of increasing virtual memory.

Disk Cache

Some system functions or commands are enacted more frequently than others. The disk cache keeps a record of as many of these commands as possible so that the system won't have to retrieve this command information from the hard drive. Interaction with the hard drive is always slower than interaction with memory. In Mac OS 9.1, the disk cache is automatically set using the calculation of 32KB per 1MB of memory. You can customize this to a larger size, but a smaller cache will affect system performance.

Determining Available Memory

As you are working, you may need to know how much memory is available and whether you can launch another application. Switch to the Finder and select About This Computer from the Apple menu. You will see the memory allocation for each application that is running, as well as the system allocation. Occasionally, programs "leak" memory or use it to the point that it cannot be reallocated, even when you quit the application. Utilities such as More About This Macintosh (MATM) will show fragmented memory blocks. In most cases, only a system restart will restore all memory.

Printing

Printing tips could cover a whole chapter (in fact, they do, in Chapter 8). Here are a few ideas you can use when printing.

Switching Printers

When you changed printers in previous versions of the Mac OS, you had to go through the Chooser. Then, System 7.5 introduced Desktop Printing. This places the icon of a printer on the Desktop each time you select a new printer within the Chooser. The icon allows you to switch printers on the fly. If you already have the printer icon on the Desktop, you can make it your default printer by clicking on the icon and accessing the Print menu. This menu appears only when you select a printer icon. Choose the Set Default Printer option (this option is also available when you press the Control key as you click the printer icon). The default printer icon will have a heavy black border.

You can also drag a document to any Desktop printer icon. The application that created the document will launch and send the document to the printer you selected. Then, it will automatically exit.

Faster Printing

If the quality of the printing is not important, you can increase your printing speed by choosing a black-and-white scheme rather than grayscale.

Windows Compatibility

As a Mac user, use these tips to work with PC users. After all, we are in the minority in the computer world.

Formatting a Disk for Windows

You can use a PC-formatted floppy disk on both Macintosh- and Windows-based systems. You can even purchase PC-formatted disks and use them on the Mac.

However, you cannot use Macintosh disks on Windows systems without special utilities. To format a disk for the PC, simply insert it in the drive and select Erase Disk from the File menu. Choose DOS 1.4 MB instead of the Macintosh format. When the process is completed, you can use the disk on almost any system, including Sun computers.

Universal File Formats

When you're creating files that will be exchanged with other users who may not have the same word processor or version of the software, save the file in Rich Text Format. Most applications can translate this type of file format, which preserves special features such as bold and italic formatting and font type. If you want users to view your file exactly the way you intended, from the graphics to the alignment, then you may want to purchase Adobe Acrobat, which allows you to save files in Portable Document Format (PDF). Files that are saved as PDFs can be viewed by anyone using the free Adobe Acrobat Reader. If you are low on funds and have simple needs, try PrintToPDF. It's a shareware utility that creates simple PDF files.

Networking

Although not everyone has an Ethernet network, broadband access at home as well as in the office is becoming more of a reality. Here are some tips for accessing and navigating the network.

Accessing a Server

Accessing a server is as simple as double-clicking on the Network Browser, which saves many steps compared to server access from the Chooser. If you access a server on a regular basis, use the Network Browser to add the server to your Favorites list for easy access even from the Open and Save dialog boxes. Items in the Favorites list are accessible from the Favorites option in the Apple menu.

Organizing Favorites

You can place anything in the Favorites folder. After all, the items in Favorites are only aliases. You can include links to server volumes, shared disks, or files and applications on your hard drive. Eventually, however, this list is likely to become quite long—that's when you need to organize your Favorites folder. Open the folder by selecting Apple menu|Favorites or by opening the System Folder and locating the Favorites folder (the Favorites item in the Apple menu is itself an alias). When the window is open, you can create new subfolders to organize your items (perhaps by servers or by application).

Custom AppleTalk Configurations

The Location Manager allows you to save and use multiple AppleTalk configurations, which makes it easier for you to change your network settings depending on your environment or needs. When you configure your AppleTalk Control Panel for network access, the settings are saved to a default configuration. To create a new configuration file, go to the File menu and choose Configurations. Duplicate the current configuration, then modify and rename it appropriately. You can have several configurations, including sets for Ethernet and infrared.

Custom Remote Access Configurations

If you access multiple Internet service providers (ISPs) or must try several numbers to establish a connection, you can save this information in the Remote Access Control Panel. Duplicate the current configuration, make changes to it, and then give it a distinctive name. The Location Manager enables you to switch between configurations and work with the different files. If you have the Remote Access Control Strip module, you can switch configuration sets quickly and easily.

Creating a Remote Access Script

If you connect to an Internet service provider by using a command line prompt, you can record your keystrokes and save them to a script. Initiate the connection; when the terminal window appears, choose the Settings button. You can elect to save the connect script when the terminal window closes. When it's completed, you can change the settings in the Protocol tab from Use Terminal Window to Use Connect Script and locate the file you just created, making connecting to an ISP a little easier.

Internet

The Internet contains a vast storehouse of information. Use the following shortcuts and diagnostic tools to facilitate your Internet surfing.

Internet Control Panel

The Internet Control Panel is a wonderful extension of Mac OS 9.1. It allows you to store common Internet settings such as your email address and server, SMTP gateway address, and news server address. Many Internet and Web applications, including email clients and Web browsers, can retrieve your settings from the Internet Control Panel so that you don't have to keep entering the same information in different applications.

Internet Clippings

Mac OS 9.1 continues to support the text-clipping feature. Select text in an application such as SimpleText that supports text-clipping, and drag the text to the Desktop. A small file housing the contents of the selection then appears on the Desktop. Mac OS 9.1 also features intelligent clipping. If you clip and drag text that contains an email address, the icon will change to indicate its contents. Special icons exist for text that contains Internet clippings, such as Web page addresses, newsgroups, email addresses, and FTP sites.

Using Sherlock 2 to Search the Internet

The Sherlock 2 application can search the Internet. You could perform Web searches by going to different Web portals, but Sherlock 2 can search multiple sites in a single search. Results are ranked according to relevance. Sherlock 2 can search online phone directories and shopping sites, too.

Troubleshooting

In a perfect world, our computers would always start, would never hang while booting, and would never crash. Unfortunately, things can go wrong at any moment during a computer session. Use the following shortcuts and diagnosis tools to help you cope with mishaps.

Computer Will Not Turn On

If you press the power button on the keyboard but the indicator light on the CPU does not turn on, make sure the power strip and outlet are active. Check the keyboard connections and all power cords. Try using the power button on the CPU to turn on the computer. If not, you may have a hardware problem.

Monitor Will Not Display an Image

If the computer has begun to boot but you cannot see an image on the monitor, make sure the monitor power button has been depressed. Check the power cables as well as the monitor connection to the computer. If necessary, wait until enough time has lapsed for the computer to boot, then push the power button on the keyboard to bring up the Shutdown dialog window. Pressing the R key at this point will restart the computer. Be aware that some monitors will not display an image if they were not turned on before the computer. Restarting should display the image; however, if all else fails, switch monitors to rule out hardware problems.

Computer Will Not Boot

If you see any icon other than the smiling computer, you have computer problems. A disk with a blinking question mark indicates the computer cannot locate the Mac OS. Try inserting a boot disk or CD-ROM to see if the computer can boot by another medium.

A sad or sick Mac icon or a different startup sound such as a car crash or beeping sound usually indicates hardware problems. You can try using a boot disk to determine if the problem is associated with the hard drive or the components on the motherboard.

Computer Will Not Load Compact Disc

If you are using an iMac with the traditional CD-ROM drive (not a slot-loading drive), you may occasionally find that the CD-ROM drive will not boot the computer or mount CD-ROMs. This usually occurs after the computer crashes while a CD-ROM is in the drive, or after a user has ejected the CD manually using a paper clip in the bypass hole located on the front of the drive. In the wake of these occurrences, the computer believes a compact disc is still in the drive and will not recognize the disc that you have inserted. The solution is to shut the computer down, then restart. The disc should then be recognized.

Computer Cannot See the Network

If you cannot see AppleTalk zones in the Network Browser or Chooser, make sure that AppleTalk is active (assuming that the network is up and supports AppleTalk). You can verify that AppleTalk is active by looking at the Chooser or the AppleTalk Control Panel. If AppleTalk is active, go to the AppleTalk Control Panel and confirm that Ethernet is the chosen protocol. If it is, but no zones are available, try rebuilding the Desktop file. If you still cannot access the network, you may need to reinstall the network software. In some cases, you can access the Internet even though you cannot see AppleTalk zones. This is normal for home Ethernet users. For those in an environment that supports AppleTalk, however, you may need to reinstall the networking software to be fully functional.

General System Crankiness

If your applications seem to freeze or take too long to launch, or if icons seem to switch to generic images, you should rebuild the Desktop file. It will improve system performance and speed up application launching.

A Hanging Application

If you still have mouse movement but cannot select other options within the application or switch to the Finder, then you may have an application that is no longer responding or functioning. Make sure that adequate time has passed—some database clients must interact with the server, which can take some time. If you feel the application has stopped responding, use the Option+Command+Escape keystroke combination to force the program to quit. After forcing an application to quit, you should restart the computer to avoid a system crash.

System Freezes or Crashes

Lack of mouse movement or the appearance of a dialog box containing a system bomb or restart prompt are serious indications of a system crash. Restart the computer if you are given the opportunity to do so. If the system freezes, you will have to restart using the Reset button. If your Mac doesn't have a Reset button, press Control+Command+the keyboard power button to restart the computer. If you have a USB keyboard, you can try pressing Command+Shift+the power button. Be aware that this key combination does not always work. You can also attempt to access the system debugger by pressing the Command+Power keys. Type "RS" to restart the system or "G FINDR" to quit the Finder.

Shortcut Key Combinations

Use the keystroke combinations shown in Tables A.1 and A.2 to reduce the need to reach for a mouse and to speed up productivity.

Table A.1   Shortcut key combinations and results during startup.

Keystroke Combination	Result
Shift	Loads system with Extensions off
Option+Command+P+R	Resets PRAM
Shift+Option+Command+Delete	Forces a boot from another SCSI device
Command	Disables virtual memory
Option	Closes all Finder windows
C	Forces a boot from a System CD
Spacebar	Opens the Extensions Manager
Option+Command	Rebuilds the Desktop file

Table A.2   Post-startup shortcut key combinations and results.

Keystroke Combination	Result
Command+O	Opens a file or folder
Command+W	Closes a window
Command+N	Creates a new folder within the Finder
Control+click on icon	Brings up a contextual menu
Command+Z	Undoes previous action

(continued)

Table A.2   Post-startup shortcut key combinations and results *(continued)*.

Keystroke Combination	Result
Command+P	Prints
Command+X	Cuts
Command+C	Copies
Command+V	Pastes
Command+Q	Quits
Command+S	Saves
Command+A	Selects all
Command+I	Gets info
Command+M	Makes an alias
Command+F	Launches Sherlock 2
Command+E	Ejects disk
Command+Y	Puts away
Command+?	Launches Help
Option+close box	Closes all open windows in Finder
Command+window title	Displays path to folder
Command+Delete	Moves item to the Trash
Command+.	Cancels a command
Command+Option+Escape	Forces an application to quit
Control+Command+Power	Forces a computer restart (ADB keyboard)
Command+Shift+Power	Forces a computer restart (USB keyboard)
Command+Shift+3	Captures a PICT file of the desktop
Command+Shift+4	Manually selects a PICT file area
Command+Shift+Capslock+4	Captures a PICT file of the currently active window

Appendix B

Administrative Features and Tools

The Mac OS has been network-ready from the very start, and we're lucky that so many administrative tools are available to help us manage groups of networked computers. Over the past decade, we've used many administrative tools to administer small, medium, and very large groups of computers, and have found the following tools and features of Mac OS 9.1 to be the most useful. We'll point out what you can do in Mac OS 9.1 to make your users' computers more secure, and then touch on several utilities and programs to make your job as easy as possible.

Mac OS 9.1 Administrative Features

Mac OS 9.1 has several built-in features that system administrators can use to prevent unwanted tampering by users and would-be saboteurs. The configuration features found in the General Controls, Simple Finder, Multiple Users, AppleTalk, and TCP/IP Control Panels allow you to provide basic levels of protection for several aspects of a computer.

General Controls

The General Controls Control Panel, shown in Figure B.1, allows you to select an option that will help you administer a Macintosh. Although it isn't a particularly earth-shattering administrative feature, the Check Disk option can be useful for many environments and helps prevent file and disk corruption in the event of power outages and system crashes. In previous versions of the Mac OS, the General Controls Control Panel had several additional options that were useful for administering Macs, including folder protection options for the System Folder and Applications folder, which prevented users from deleting files and installing unwanted software, and the shut down warning.

The shut down warning, which simply displayed a warning dialog box to users when the computer was improperly restarted, has been replaced in Mac OS 9.1 with the new Check Disk feature. When the computer is restarted, Check Disk runs Disk

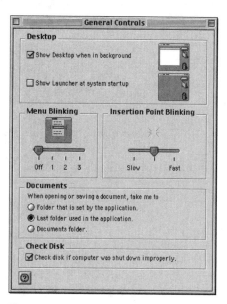

Figure B.1   The Check Disk option in the General Controls Control Panel offers some basic administrative assistance.

First Aid to search for and repair possible errors in the file system. Check Disk performs these tasks before loading any system Extensions or the Mac OS itself.

Simple Finder

The Simple Finder option, shown in Figure B.2, provides only the essential Finder features and commands to users. Ideally, the Simple Finder will decrease the number of questions and user-interface issues presented by novice users, especially in a computer lab environment. This option works by hiding menu options and disabling their respective features.

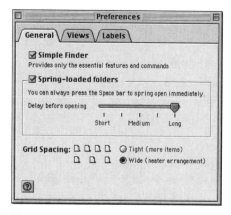

Figure B.2   The Simple Finder option.

To activate the Simple Finder:

1. Choose Edit|Preferences in the Finder.

2. Select the General tab.

3. Check the Simple Finder option and close the window.

The biggest difference between the Finder and the Simple Finder is the absence of menu options and keyboard-command equivalents, such as using Command+Delete to throw a selected item into the Trash, as well as the ability to create pop-up windows. Figure B.3 shows how checking the Simple Finder option affects the File and View menus.

Multiple Users

The ultimate way to limit a user's access to the computer's various resources is to enable and configure Multiple Users, which is discussed in Chapter 16. Multiple Users allows you to create three levels of access for up to 40 users and one guest:

- *Normal*—Least restrictions

- *Limited*—Moderate restrictions

- *Panels*—Most restrictions

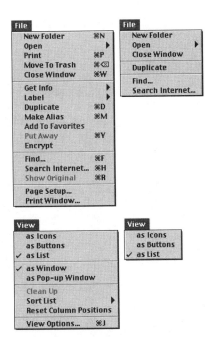

Figure B.3   The Simple Finder limits the options in menus, including the File (top) and View (bottom) menus.

You can configure each user's access privileges individually, such as allowing users to share documents and access the same applications and folders. For example, Figure B.4 shows a user named kbell who has been given Panels access, which restricts access to files, folders, applications, and the System Folder, as well as the full contents of the Apple menu.

To configure Multiple Users, access the Multiple Users Control Panel, enable the Multiple Users Accounts feature, and configure user accounts as necessary. You do not need to restart the computer to begin using Multiple Users.

AppleTalk Password Protection

When a user working in a networked environment unexpectedly takes his or her computer off the network, trouble usually ensues. This is especially true if the computer in question is hosting a printer or some other networked device that is accessible to other users over AppleTalk. You can prevent users from disabling certain AppleTalk features by following these steps:

1. Open the AppleTalk Control Panel and choose Edit|User Mode.

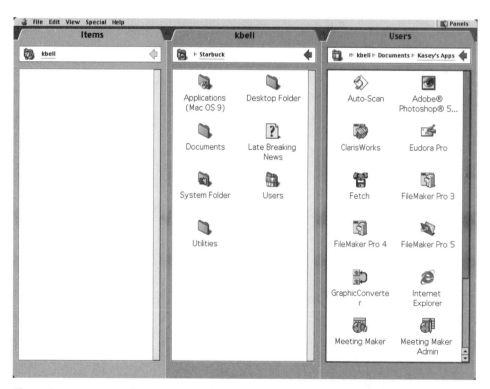

Figure B.4   The Multiple Users feature enables you to allocate access privileges to your computer.

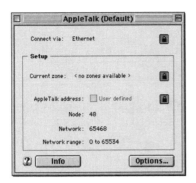

Figure B.5   While in Administration mode, you can selectively lock certain parts of the
AppleTalk Control Panel.

2. Choose Administration and enter an administrative password.

3. Lock down the desired options, as shown in Figure B.5. Toggle between
   locked and unlocked by clicking on the Padlock icon.

4. Quit AppleTalk, saving the changes when prompted to do so.

Users cannot re-enter Administration mode without first entering the password.
They can, however, switch between Basic and Advanced modes, and turn off
AppleTalk.

TCP/IP Password Protection

The TCP/IP Control Panel works just like the AppleTalk Control Panel to guard
certain features via password protection. It uses a different administrative password than does the AppleTalk Control Panel, although you may set them to be
the same. To configure the TCP/IP Control Panel, take these steps:

1. Open the TCP/IP Control Panel and choose Edit|User Mode.

2. Choose Administration and enter an administrative password.

3. Lock down the appropriate options.

4. Quit TCP/IP, saving the changes when prompted to do so.

As with the AppleTalk Control Panel, users will not be able to re-enter Administration mode without first entering the password, but they will be able to switch
between Basic and Advanced modes, as well as turn TCP/IP off entirely. Figure
B.6 shows the TCP/IP options that may be locked.

*WARNING! By simply replacing—rather than editing—the TCP/IP or AppleTalk Preferences file, users
can bypass the password security feature.*

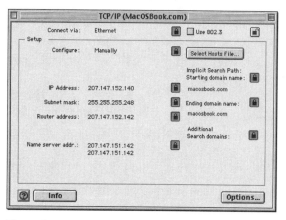

Figure B.6   The TCP/IP Control Panel with features locked down using an administrative password.

Apple Network Administrator Toolkit

The Apple Network Administrator Toolkit (ANAT), a collection of three applications from Apple, assists in the management of networked Macintosh computers (and is very popular in educational settings). These applications provide a very wide array of options, which is why the ANAT is expensive (about $400 for a 10-user license). It may be the only tool you'll need to administer a large number of computers. The three ANAT tools are:

- Network Assistant
- At Ease for Workgroups
- User and Group Manager

These three applications have more than one hundred options and benefits among them—so many, in fact, that we couldn't cover even a fraction of them here. Instead, we'll review each in the following sections, list their features, and discuss why you would want to use them on your network.

Network Assistant

The Network Assistant provides essential levels of control over clients joined in an AppleTalk or TCP/IP network. It allows you to perform the following tasks on client machines from a central Network Assistant server:

- Check software versions.
- Compare the differences in software versions, including applications, Control Panels, Extensions, fonts, shutdown items, and startup items, between the Network Assistant server and clients.

- Search client hard drives.

- Obtain system software information.

- Copy items between client and server.

- Open an application on a client from the server.

- Restart a client immediately or after allowing the client to save open documents.

- Share a client screen or the server screen with one of the clients.

- Lock a client screen after presenting it with a message.

- Observe a client screen.

- Control a client screen.

- Announce or talk with a client.

- Copy or delete items on a hard disk to or from a client.

- Change system settings, TCP/IP address, or Internet settings.

- Empty a client's Trash, rebuild the Desktop, or rename the client.

Network Assistant has a good user interface and is easy to use. It allows you to create up to 20 lists of clients with up to 250 clients in each list, and perform actions on one or more clients in a list or lists. For example, to remotely control the screen of a client computer, you would follow these steps:

1. Launch Network Assistant.

2. Open a list of clients.

3. Choose the client from the list, as shown in Figure B.7, and click the Control button in the menu bar.

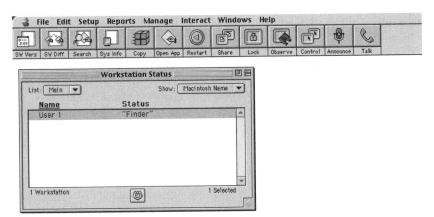

Figure B.7   Selecting a Network Assistant client using the Network Client administration tool.

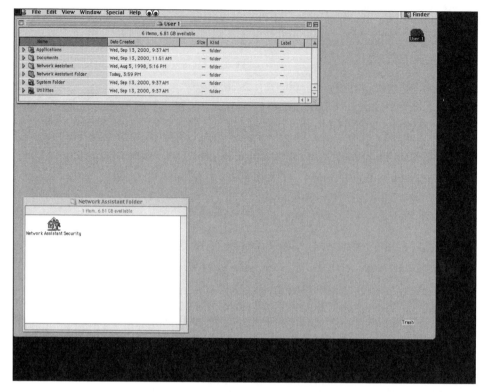

Figure B.8   One of the many tasks you can perform on a Network Assistant client is to control the computer's screen and mouse.

4. If the administrator's screen size is larger than the client screen, as in Figure B.8, black space will occupy the right and bottom regions of your screen, and the client's Desktop pattern or picture will not be transmitted (to save bandwidth and make your remote control session speedier).

At Ease for Workgroups

At Ease for Workgroups is a comprehensive client/server application that allows you to protect several thousand clients and prevent users from changing, adding, or deleting information from a computer without your permission or knowledge. You can assign several different levels of administrative privileges to allow other administrators to manage users and groups. The types of users are:

- *Administrator*—Full access
- *Teacher*—Full or limited access
- *Student*—Limited access
- *Guardian*—Limited access

At Ease administrators have the ability to control just about any kind of resource on a client computer, including:

- Documents
- Folders
- Applications
- Entire hard drives
- AppleTalk servers
- Printers
- Access to removable media
- System Folder contents

In addition to creating administrative rights and client access restrictions, At Ease also provides services that are useful in educational settings, such as classrooms and training clusters, that allow you to do the following:

- Access documents over the Internet.
- Use drop boxes to distribute information or submit documents.
- Manage Web browser preferences and bookmarks.
- Assign helper applications for use in conjunction with a Web browser.
- Set up multiple configurations, making it easy to manage different classes using one cluster of computers.
- Limit the amount of space available on a hard drive for personal use.
- Restrict login capabilities by date and time.
- Log usage.

User and Group Manager

The User and Group Manager is a simple application that allows you to perform administrative tasks on the following types of servers:

- AppleShare (version 3 or later)
- AppleShare IP
- At Ease for Workgroups (version 4 or later)
- First Class

The actions you can take with the User and Group Manager are limited in comparison to the other two applications that constitute the Apple Network Administrator Toolkit. The User and Group Manager actions include:

- Adding users and groups.

- Deleting users and groups.

- Modifying existing users and groups.

- Comparing groups of users.

- Exporting user and group information among different types of servers, as well as among similar servers.

- Importing and exporting lists of users and groups as ASCII text.

These are just a few of the features and applications that give administrators the ability to manage their computing environments. Many, many more freeware and commercial software tools for performing administrative tasks (such as managing inventory, distributing applications, and supporting users) are available. The following applications are the ones we use every day to support our users and manage their computers.

Timbuktu Pro

Timbuktu Pro from Netopia (**www.netopia.com**) is an essential tool for anyone who administers remote servers, such as co-located Web servers or file servers located in remote buildings or computer rooms. It can be equally valuable for providing support in computer clusters, training rooms, and for general remote technical support. Timbuktu costs about $50 per seat, doesn't require a server, and provides many services, including:

- Screen sharing

- Remote control

- File transfer

- Intercom

- File synchronizing

- AppleScript support

- Conferencing capabilities

The best thing about Timbuktu is that it is cross-platform compatible—you can use it to support Windows computers as well as Macintoshes. Timbuktu supports the following operating systems:

- Mac OS (Timbuktu Pro)

- Windows 95/98 (Timbuktu Pro)

- Windows NT/2000 (Timbuktu Pro NT)

Timbuktu is easy to install, very secure (it provides robust password encryption), and requires few system resources. To run Timbuktu, you'll need the following:

- Mac OS 7.5 or higher

- 68040 or PowerPC processor

- 8MB of physical RAM (total)

- AppleTalk, TCP/IP, or modem connection

The two most popular features provided by Timbuktu are remote control and file exchange. To remotely control another computer (either a Mac or a Windows machine), install Timbuktu and follow these steps:

1. Launch Timbuktu and choose File|New to open a new connection, called a Control connection.

2. Choose a connection method (address book, modem, AppleTalk, or TCP/IP).

3. Enter a username and password, if requested. The remote computer will open in a framed window, as shown in Figure B.9.

Figure B.9   A remote control connection using Timbuktu.

To exchange files with the same computer, once a control connection has been established:

1. Choose Service|Exchange.

2. A username and password will not be required, provided you have opened a Control connection and not closed out of it before opening the exchange connection. Figure B.10 shows an example of an Exchange connection.

In addition to Control and Exchange connections, you may also open the following types of connections:

- Observation (view only)

- Chat (text exchange)

- Notify (when a client becomes available)

- Intercom (voice exchange)

- Invitation (to open a connection)

If you manage multiple computers, Timbuktu is an essential tool that is well worth the cost.

netOctopus

Another essential tool for administering networked Macs (and PCs) is netOctopus (also from Netopia), a program that allows administrators to perform three major functions:

- Install software

- Configure client settings

- Inventory computers on your network

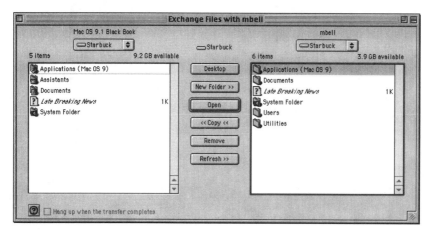

Figure B.10   A Timbuktu file exchange connection.

The netOctopus client is installed on computers as a series of Extensions that enable the netOctopus administrative application to select the computer (as in Figure B.11), log in, and perform tasks such as inventorying the computer's hardware and operating system information (as in Figure B.12), as well as every last application and utility. You can easily generate reports and save them as tab-delimited documents that can be imported into a spreadsheet for analysis and comparison. For example, you might want to assess your computers for the slowest processor or the least amount of RAM in order to easily target those in need of upgrades or replacement.

Retrospect

No Mac administrator should be without Dantz's Retrospect, the leading client/server backup program for the Mac OS. After all, what good is a well-administered network of computers if they aren't backed up on a regular basis? Dantz provides several options for backing up one or more Mac or Windows computers, including:

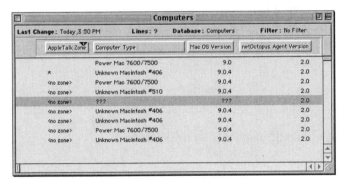

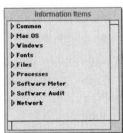

Figure B.11   Selecting a computer for administration via netOctopus.

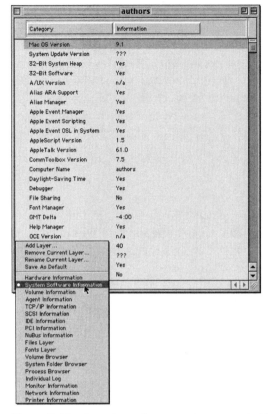

Figure B.12   Inventory of a computer generated by netOctopus.

- *Retrospect*—Back up a server
- *Retrospect Express*—Personal backup
- *Retrospect Network Backup Kit*—Back up a server plus a 10-user license

Retrospect is capable of backing up most Mac OS or Windows clients to a wide array of storage devices (over 150, according to Dantz). These devices include file servers, CD-ROMs, tape, and removable drives from ADIC, DEC, Exabyte, HP, Quantum, Seagate, and Sony. A few of Retrospect's features include the following:

- Full or incremental backup
- Automated or on-demand backup of the server itself or a remote client
- Quick, one-step restoration of a remote volume
- Archiving client data
- Data encryption

The approach we've always taken to backing up our computers with Retrospect follows this pattern:

- One full backup per week.

- Incremental backups every day, excluding Web browser cache files and other files that aren't necessary for the restoration of a client (see Figure B.13).

- Four archived sets of backups, which make it possible for us to restore a client to its original state for any of the previous 30 days.

Although it isn't necessary to back up a client hard drive in its entirety, it certainly isn't a bad idea if users are allowed to install their own software and customize their computers. If, however, you want to back up only the Documents folder, for example, and feel comfortable reinstalling the OS and any applications manually, a more limited backup is acceptable. Remember that you and your users need to first understand what is being backed up and what is not.

Client configuration is performed in two steps. First, load the client software, assign an activator code to each client, and select a few client configuration options (see Figure B.14). Next, open the Retrospect Client Preferences Control Panel on the client workstation (shown in Figure B.15) and make all necessary customizations, such as waiting for the next scheduled backup before shutting down the computer or notification if the computer isn't backed up on schedule.

Retrospect Express is a limited version of Retrospect. About 90 percent of the user interface and configuration options are the same, however, so if you're comfortable with Retrospect, the personal version will be just as easy to use.

Appendix B
Administrative Features
and Tools

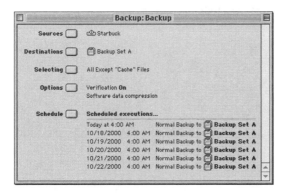

Figure B.13   A Retrospect script that excludes files that contain the word "Cache" from being backed up.

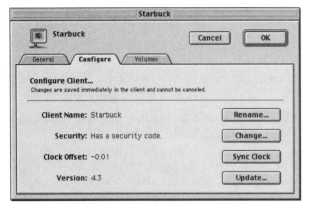

Figure B.14   Selecting the client volumes that will be backed up (note that some types of volumes, such as audio CD-ROMs, are excluded by default).

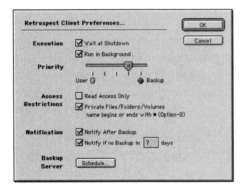

Figure B.15   The Retrospect Client Preferences Control Panel.

Appendix C

Mac OS Changes and Enhancements

The Mac OS has undergone many changes over the years, and the future of the Mac OS appears to be even more exciting. Mac OS 9.1 incorporates many significant changes over earlier versions of the OS; future versions will have even more impressive features while retaining backward-compatibility to most applications that will run under Mac OS 8 and higher. Because the beta version of Mac OS X (Developer Preview 4) was released about the time this book went to press, we aren't exactly sure what will be included in a final release. However, it has been in alpha and beta long enough so that we have a good idea of what it will bring in terms of features and underlying technology. Table C.1 illustrates the major components of the Mac OS and how they were (or will be) implemented in three major versions of the OS: System 7, Mac OS 9.1, and Mac OS X.

The following sections describe these versions in greater detail. They will give you a better idea of the historical significance of Mac OS 9.1 and of what lies ahead.

Table C.1   The major features of the Mac OS.

Feature	System 7.x	Mac OS 9.x	Mac OS X
File System	HFS	HFS, HFS+	UFS, HFS+
Tasking	Cooperative multitasking	Multithreaded, cooperative multitasking	Preemptive multitasking
Processor	Single 68K processor	Limited PPC multiprocessor	Symmetric multiprocessor PPC G4
Memory protection	No	No	Yes
Virtual memory	Optional	Optional	Mandatory
Networking	MacTCP, AppleTalk, TCP/IP	Open Transport, AppleTalk, TCP/IP	Berkeley Sockets, AppleTalk, TCP/IP
Graphics	QuickDraw	QuickDraw, ColorSync, QuickDraw 3D, QuickTime, OpenGL	Quartz, QuickTime, PDF, OpenGL

(continued)

Table C.1   The major features of the Mac OS *(continued)*.

Feature	System 7.x	Mac OS 9.x	Mac OS X
File sharing	File Sharing	File Sharing, personal Web sharing	File Sharing, Apache Web server, NFS
Java	n/a	MRJ	Tightly integrated
Users	Single user	Limited multiuser	Fully multiuser

Pre-System 7

Prior to System 7, several versions of operating systems ran on the first Apple computers (Apple I, II, II+, IIe, III) and the Lisa. When the first Macintosh was released in January 1984 (remember the famous Super Bowl commercial?), Apple introduced System 1.0. It (the original Macintosh) was able to run many versions of the operating system, up through the first releases of System 7. Each version of the OS fixed bugs, added features, and increased performance and stability. These versions include the following:

- System 1.0
- System 1.1
- System 2.0
- System 2.0.1
- System 5.0
- System 5.1
- System 6.0

- System 6.0.1
- System 6.0.2
- System 6.0.3
- System 6.0.4
- System 6.0.5
- System 6.0.7
- System 6.0.8

The next family of the Mac OS introduced even more features.

System 7

No other major version of the Mac OS has had as many version changes as System 7 (which eventually stopped with Mac OS 7.6.1). This is probably because System 7 introduced several important features that required updating and patching to keep pace with advances in hardware, such as the move by users from monochrome to color monitors and the migration from the 68000 family of processors to the PowerPC processor. New features such as virtual memory, increased physical memory addressing, multi-gigabyte storage space, PowerPC native code, Open Transport networking, and multithreading required numerous updates to the OS, producing the following versions:

- System 7.0
- System 7.0.1
- System 7.1
- System 7.1 P
- System 7.1.1
- System 7.1.2
- System 7.1.2 P

- System 7.5
- System 7.5.1
- System 7.5.2
- System 7.5.3
- System 7.5.5
- System 7.6
- System 7.6.1

Mac OS 8

When Mac OS 8 and 8.1 arrived, things started to look a lot simpler when it came to versions of the OS. Still, many changes were under the hood, including the multithreaded and PowerPC-native Finder, improved Open Transport networking, the new Apple Platinum appearance, Web sharing, Java, and updated versions of QuickTime, QuickDraw, and many other peripheral OS components. Mac OS 8.5, on the other hand, updated numerous features and incorporated several new additions, including:

- AppleGuide Help in HTML and new Help menu items
- Application Switcher
- Control Strip 2.0
- Date & Time Control Panel rewrite synchronizing and time server capabilities
- Desktop printer browser
- Disk-cache improvements
- Feature-rich content
- File Exchange Control Panel replacing Mac OS Easy Open and PC Exchange
- File sharing
- Font smoothing (anti-aliasing)
- General Controls
- Icons in Window title bars
- Internet Control Panel integrating Internet Config 2.0 capabilities
- JPEG files that are dropped onto the System folder are redirected to the Desktop Pictures folder
- Keyboard
- Launcher
- List View enhancements

- Modem
- Monitor Calibration rewrite
- Monitors and Sounds rewrite
- More PPC-native code
- Mouse
- Multiple scroll bar options (double scroll and proportional thumbs)
- Network Browser for file server and TCP/IP services
- New Find command powered by V-Twin engine allowing you to find-by-content, search the Internet, index a local drive, and use script
- New Get Info window
- New icons for files and folders
- New navigational services (Open/Save dialogs)
- Numbers
- Open Transport 2.0 supporting SNMP and better DHCP
- PPC-Native AppleScript 1.3 with more scriptable applications
- Personal Web server update
- PowerBook/Energy Saver replacing several PB Control Panels
- QuickDraw rewrite
- QuickTime settings
- Remote Access Control Panel/Apple Remote Access 3.1 replacing OT/PPP and ARA 2.1
- Revised sizable and scriptable Applications menu supporting tear-off menus
- Revised Location Manager Control Panel
- Revised Memory Control Panel
- Revised Monitors & Sound Control Panel
- Unicode and European character support by LaserWriter 8
- User-interface themes and sounds
- Virtual memory improvements

Mac OS 9

Mac OS 9 and 9.1 further refine the Mac OS to make more user interface improvements, added features, increased stability, and faster overall speed. There are over 100 improvements since Mac OS 8.x, but the main improvements are found in the following components and features:

- Alias Manager
- Apple File Security
- Apple Menu Options
- Apple System Profiler
- AppleScript
- AppleShare
- AppleShare Client
- CarbonLib
- ColorSync
- Control Strip Extension
- Desktop Printer Utility
- Drive Setup
- Energy Saver
- Enhanced speech recognition
- File Exchange 3.0.4
- File Sharing over TCP/IP
- File Synchronization
- File support (up to 2TB)
- Finder
- FireWire support
- FontSync
- Foreign File Access
- Game Sprockets
- General Controls
- Help engine
- Image Capture
- Iomega Driver and Tools
- Keyboard
- Language Encodings
- Language Kit support
- Mac Manager support
- Memory Manager
- Multiple Users

- Net Boot support
- Network Assistant client support
- Network Browser
- Open Transport
- OpenGL support
- Palm Desktop and HotSync support
- PowerPC Enabler
- Process Manager
- Resource Manager
- Script Editor
- Sherlock and Sherlock 2
- Software Update and Scheduler
- Sound
- Startup Disk
- Text Encoding Converter
- Trackpad
- URL Access
- USB Printer Sharing
- USB Software Locator
- USB support

Mac OS X

The future of Mac OS X is actually now, with the impending release of Mac OS X in early 2001. Mac OS X will bring all the features of a modern OS to the Mac platform, such as the following:

- Memory protection
- Preemptive multitasking
- Symmetric multiprocessing
- Robust virtual memory

To take advantage of these features, Apple culled through the more than 8,000 Application Programming Interfaces (APIs) that are found in Mac OS 8 and 9 and discarded those that would prevent applications and the OS from enabling these kinds of features, including 68K code. The remaining PowerPC-native APIs (a.k.a.

Carbon APIs) are placed atop the Mach kernel, which provides a hardware abstraction layer to most physical devices, such as the processor, RAM, SCSI, and IDE devices, and schedules the tasks the processor must handle. The result is serious protection against system freezes and crashes and a rock-solid OS that will be backward-compatible with most applications that currently run under Mac OS 9.1. The biggest improvement in Mac OS X in terms of hardware support will be support for symmetrical multiprocessing on the latest dual-processor G4 models.

**Appendix C
Mac OS Changes
and Enhancements**

Appendix D

Mac OS Error Codes

The numeric error codes returned by the Mac OS can be cryptic, frustrating, and sometimes not helpful at all. Most of you have probably encountered a few of the more common errors, such as Type 11, bus, or FPU. Usually you can't do anything about the errors because they result from programming mistakes within an application or the Mac OS. However, knowing a little about what caused the error can go a long way in helping you make decisions on how to correct the problem. You'll also want to try using MacsBug, Apple's system-level debugger, for assistance with solving errors that are difficult to diagnose. See **http://developer.apple.com/tools/ debuggers/MacsBug/** for more information and the latest release.

The following error codes were compiled by Caerwyn Pearce and exported directly from his shareware program, SysErrors. This useful program, which is included on this book's accompanying CD-ROM, is a great resource for understanding error codes, and we graciously thank Caerwyn for permission to include it in this book. We encourage you to check it out and register your copy with Caerwyn.

Mac OS System Errors

You may encounter the error codes shown in Table D.1 while using the Mac OS, using a debugger such as MacsBug, or in an application. Programmers will be familiar with many of these errors, but they can help anyone to better understand what caused the error in Mac OS, and, hopefully, fix it.

Table D.1 Mac OS error codes.

Code	System Error	Description
1	dsBusError	bus error
2	dsAddressErr	address error
3	dsIllInstErr	illegal instruction error
4	dsZeroDivErr	zero divide error

(continued)

Table D.1   Mac OS error codes *(continued)*.

Code	System Error	Description
5	dsChkErr	check trap error
6	dsOvflowErr	overflow trap error
7	dsPrivErr	privilege violation error
8	dsTraceErr	trace mode error
9	dsLineAErr	line 1010 trap error (A-line)
10	dsLineFErr	line 1111 trap error
10	dsLineFErr	line 1111 trap error (F-line)
11	dsMiscErr	miscellaneous hardware exception error
12	dsCoreErr	unimplemented core routine error
13	dsIrqErr	uninstalled interrupt error
14	dsIOCoreErr	IO Core Error
15	dsLoadErr	Segment Loader Error
16	dsFPErr	Floating point error
17	dsNoPackErr	package 0 not present [List Manager]
18	dsNoPk1	package 1 not present [Reserved by Apple]
19	dsNoPk2	package 2 not present [Disk Initialization]
20	dsNoPk3	package 3 not present [Standard File]
21	dsNoPk4	package 4 not present [Floating-Point Arithmetic]
22	dsNoPk5	package 5 not present [Transcendental Functions]
23	dsNoPk6	package 6 not present [International Utilities]
24	dsNoPk7	package 7 not present [Binary/Decimal Conversion]
25	dsMemFullErr	out of memory!
26	dsBadLaunch	can't launch file
27	dsFSErr	file system map has been trashed
28	dsStknHeap	stack has moved into application heap
30	dsReinsert	request user to reinsert offline volume
31	dsNotThe1	not the disk I wanted (obsolete)
33	negZcbFreeErr	ZcbFree has gone negative
40	dsGreeting	welcome to Macintosh greeting
41	dsFinderErr	can't load the Finder error
42	dsBadStartupDisk	unable to mount boot volume (sad Mac only)
42	shutDownAlert	handled like a shutdown error

(continued)

Table D.1   Mac OS error codes *(continued)*.

Code	System Error	Description
43	dsSystemFileErr	can't find System file to open (sad Mac only)
51	dsBadSlotInt	unserviceable slot interrupt
81	dsBadSANEopcode	bad opcode given to SANE Pack4
83	dsBadPatchHeader	SetTrapAddress saw the "come-from" header
84	menuPrgErr	happens when a menu is purged
85	dsMBarNFnd	SysErr—cannot find MBDF
86	dsHMenuFindErr	SysErr—recursively defined HMenus
87	dsWDEFnFnd	Could not load WDEF
88	dsCDEFnFnd	Could not load CDEF
89	dsMDEFnFnd	Could not load MDEF
90	dsNoFPU	"FPU instruction executed, but machine has no FPU"
98	dsNoPatch	Can't patch for particular Model Mac
99	dsBadPatch	Can't load patch resource
101	dsParityErr	memory parity error
102	dsOldSystem	System is too old for this ROM
103	ds32BitMode	booting in 32-bit on a 24-bit sys
104	dsNeedToWrite	need to write new boot BootBlocks blocks
105	dsNotEnough RAMToBoot	need at least 1.5MB of RAM to boot 7.0
106	dsBufPtrTooLow	bufPtr moved too far during boot
20000	dsShutDown OrRestart	user choice between ShutDown and Restart
20001	dsSwitchOff	user choice between OrRestart Switch off or Restart
20002	dsForcedQuit	"allow the user to ExitToShell, return if Cancel"
20003	dsRemoveDisk	request user to remove disk from manual eject drive
20004	dsDirtyDisk	request user to return a manually ejected dirty disk
20010	dsSCSIWarn	Portable SCSI adapter warning
20109	dsShutDown OrResume	allow user to return to Finder or ShutDown
32767	dsSysErr	general system error (catch-all used in DSAT)

Post-MacsBug System Errors

System errors (shown in Table D.2) are used after MacsBug is loaded to put up dialogs, because they shouldn't cause MacsBug to stop; negative numbers add to an existing dialog without putting up a whole new dialog.

Table D.2   Post-MacsBug error codes.

Code	System Error	Description
-10	dsMacsBugInstalled	say "MacsBug Installed"
-11	dsDisassemblerInstalled	say "Disassembler Installed"
-12	dsHD20Installed	say "HD20 Startup"
-13	dsExtensionsDisabled	say "Extensions Disabled"
General System		
1	evtNotEnb	event not enabled at PostEvent
0	noErr	0 for success
-1	qErr	queue element not found during deletion
-2	vTypErr	invalid queue element
-3	corErr	core routine number out of range
-4	unimpErr	unimplemented core routine
-5	SlpTypeErr	invalid queue element
-8	seNoDB	no debugger installed to handle debugger command
Color Manager		
-9	iTabPurgErr	from Color2Index/ITabMatch
-10	noColMatch	
-11	qAllocErr	from MakeITable
-12	tblAllocErr	
-13	overRun	
-14	noRoomErr	
-15	seOutOfRange	from SetEntry
-16	seProtErr	
-17	i2CRangeErr	
-18	gdBadDev	
-19	reRangeErr	
-20	seInvRequest	
-21	seNoMemErr	

(continued)

Table D.2   Post-MacsBug error codes *(continued).*

Code	System Error	Description
I/O System		
-17	controlErr	Driver can't respond to Control call
-18	statusErr	Driver can't respond to Status call
-19	readErr	Driver can't respond to Read call
-20	writErr	Driver can't respond to Write call
-21	badUnitErr	Driver ref num doesn't match unit table
-22	unitEmptyErr	Driver ref num specifies NIL handle in unit table
-23	openErr	"Requested read/write permission doesn't match driver's open permission, or Attempt to open RAM SerD failed"
-24	closErr	Close failed
-25	dRemovErr	tried to remove an open driver
-26	dInstErr	DrvrInstall couldn't find driver in resources
-27	abortErr	IO call aborted by KillIO
-27	iIOAbortErr	IO abort error (Printing Manager)
-28	notOpenErr	Couldn't rd/wr/ctl/sts because driver not opened
-29	unitTblFullErr	unit table has no more entries
-30	dceExtErr	dce extension error
File System		
-33	dirFulErr	Directory full
-34	dskFulErr	disk full
-35	nsvErr	no such volume
-36	ioErr	I/O error (bummers)
-37	bdNamErr	there may be no bad names in the final system!
-38	fnOpnErr	File not open
-39	eofErr	End of file
-40	posErr	tried to position to before start of file (r/w)
-41	mFulErr	memory full (open) or file won't fit (load)
-42	tmfoErr	too many files open
-43	fnfErr	File not found
-44	wPrErr	diskette is write protected
-45	fLckdErr	file is locked
-46	vLckdErr	volume is locked

(continued)

Table D.2   Post-MacsBug error codes *(continued)*.

Code	System Error	Description
-47	fBsyErr	File is busy (delete)
-48	dupFNErr	duplicate file name (rename)
-49	opWrErr	file already open with write permission
-50	paramErr	error in user parameter list
-51	rfNumErr	refnum error
-52	gfpErr	get file position error
-53	volOffLinErr	volume not on line error (was Ejected)
-54	permErr	permissions error (on file open)
-55	volOnLinErr	drive volume already online at MountVol
-56	nsDrvErr	no such drive (tried to mount a bad drive num)
-57	noMacDskErr	not a Mac diskette (sig bytes are wrong)
-58	extFSErr	volume in question belongs to an external fs
-59	fsRnErr	file system internal error: during rename the old entry was deleted but could not be restored
-60	badMDBErr	bad master directory block
-61	wrPermErr	write permissions error

Font Manager

Code	System Error	Description
-64	fontDecError	error during font declaration
-65	fontNotDeclared	font not declared
-66	fontSubErr	font substitution occurred
-32615	fontNotOutlineErr	bitmap font passed to routine that does outlines only

Disk

Code	System Error	Description
-64	lastDskErr	I/O System Errors
-64	noDriveErr	drive not installed
-65	offLinErr	r/w requested for an offline drive
-66	noNybErr	couldn't find 5 nibbles in 200 tries
-67	noAdrMkErr	couldn't find valid addr mark
-68	dataVerErr	read verify compare failed
-69	badCksmErr	addr mark checksum didn't check
-70	badBtSlpErr	bad addr mark bit slip nibbles
-71	noDtaMkErr	couldn't find a data mark header
-72	badDCksum	bad data mark checksum
-73	badDBtSlp	bad data mark bit slip nibbles

(continued)

Table D.2 Post-MacsBug error codes *(continued)*.

Code	System Error	Description
-74	wrUnderrun	write underrun occurred
-75	cantStepErr	step handshake failed
-76	tk0BadErr	track 0 detect doesn't change
-77	initIWMErr	unable to initialize IWM
-78	twoSideErr	tried to read 2nd side on a 1-sided drive
-79	spdAdjErr	unable to correctly adjust disk speed
-80	seekErr	track number wrong on address mark
-81	sectNFErr	sector number never found on a track
-82	fmt1Err	can't find sector 0 after track format
-83	fmt2Err	can't get enough sync
-84	verErr	track failed to verify
-84	firstDskErr	I/O System Errors
Serial Ports, PRAM/Clock		
-85	clkRdErr	unable to read same clock value twice
-86	clkWrErr	time written did not verify
-87	prWrErr	parameter RAM written didn't read-verify
-88	prInitErr	InitUtil found the parameter RAM uninitialized
-89	rcvrErr	"SCC receiver error (framing, parity, OR)"
-90	breakRecd	Break received (SCC)
AppleTalk		
-91	ddpSktErr	error in socket number
-92	ddpLenErr	data length too big
-93	noBridgeErr	no network bridge for non-local send
-94	lapProtErr	error in attaching/detaching protocol
-95	excessCollsns	excessive collisions on write
-96	portNotPwr	serial port not currently powered
-97	portInUse	driver Open error code (port is in use)
-98	portNotCf	driver Open error code (parameter RAM not configured for this connection)
Speech Manager		
-240	noSynthFound	
-241	synthOpenFailed	
-242	synthNotReady	

(continued)

Table D.2   Post-MacsBug error codes (continued).

Code	System Error	Description
-243	bufTooSmall	
-244	voiceNotFound	
-245	incompatibleVoice	
-246	badDictFormat	
-247	badInputText	

Scrap Manager

Code	System Error	Description
-100	noScrapErr	No scrap exists error
-102	noTypeErr	No object of that type in scrap

Memory Manager

Code	System Error	Description
-99	memROZErr	hard error in ROZ
-99	memROZError	hard error in ROZ
-99	memROZWarn	soft error in ROZ
-108	memFullErr	Not enough room in heap zone
-108	iMemFullErr	Not enough room in heap zone (Printing Error)
-109	nilHandleErr	Master Pointer was NIL in HandleZone or other
-110	memAdrErr	"address was odd, or out of range"
-111	memWZErr	WhichZone failed (applied to free block)
-112	memPurErr	trying to purge a locked or non-purgeable block
-113	memAZErr	Address in zone check failed
-114	memPCErr	Pointer Check failed
-115	memBCErr	Block Check failed
-116	memSCErr	Size Check failed
-117	memLockedErr	trying to move a locked block (MoveHHi)

HFS

Code	System Error	Description
-120	dirNFErr	Directory not found
-121	tmwdoErr	No free WDCB available
-122	badMovErr	Move into offspring error
-123	wrgVolTypErr	Wrong volume type error: not supported for MFS
-124	volGoneErr	Server volume has been disconnected
-127	fsDSIntErr	Internal file system error
-1300	fidNotFound	no file thread exists
-1301	fidExists	file id already exists
-1302	notAFileErr	directory specified

(continued)

Table D.2 Post-MacsBug error codes *(continued)*.

Code	System Error	Description
-1303	diffVolErr	files on different volumes
-1304	catChangedErr	catalog has been modified
-1305	desktopDamagedErr	desktop database files are corrupted
-1306	sameFileErr	can't exchange a file with itself
-1307	badFidErr	file id is dangling or doesn't match file number
-1308	notARemountErr	when _Mount allows only remounts and doesn't get one
-1309	fileBoundsErr	file's EOF offset mark or size is too big
-1310	fsDataTooBigErr	file or volume is too big for system
Menu Manager		
-126	dsMBarNFnd	system error code for MBDF not found
-127	dsHMenuFindErr	could not find HMenu's parent in MenuKey
-128	userCanceledErr	user canceled the operation
HFS FileID		
-130	fidNotFound	no file thread exists
-131	fidNotAFile	directory specified
-132	fidExists	file id already exists
Color Quickdraw		
-125	updPixMemErr	insufficient memory to update a pixmap
-145	noMemForPictPlaybackErr	
-147	rgnOverflowErr	"Region accumulation failed, rgn may be corrupt"
-147	rgnTooBigError	"Region accumulation failed, rgn may be corrupt"
-148	pixMapTooBigErr	passed pixelmap is too large
-149	nsStackErr	not enough stack space for the necessary buffers
-149	insufficientStackErr	not enough stack space for the necessary buffers
-150	cMatchErr	Color2Index failed to find an index
-151	cTempMemErr	failed to allocate memory for temporary structures
-152	cNoMemErr	failed to allocate memory for structure
-153	cRangeErr	range error on colorTable request
-154	cProtectErr	colorTable entry protection violation
-155	cDevErr	invalid type of graphics device
-156	cResErr	invalid resolution for MakeITable
-157	cDepthErr	invalid pixel depth
-158	cParmErr	invalid parameter

(continued)

Table D.2   Post-MacsBug error codes *(continued)*.

Code	System Error	Description
-500	rgnTooBigErr	region too big error
-1000	noMaskFoundErr	Icon Utilities Error
-11000	pictInfoVersionErr	wrong version of the PictInfo structure
-11001	pictInfoIDErr	the internal consistency check for the PictInfoID is wrong
-11002	pictInfoVerbErr	the passed verb was invalid
-11003	cantLoadPickMethodErr	unable to load the custom pick proc
-11004	colorsRequestedErr	the number of colors requested was illegal
-11005	pictureDataErr	the picture data was invalid
Resource Manager		
-185	badExtResource	extended resource has a bad format
-186	CantDecompress	resource bent (the bends) can't decompress a compressed resource
-188	resourceInMemory	Resource already in memory
-189	writingPastEnd	Writing past end of file
-190	inputOutOfBounds	Offset of Count out of bounds
-192	resNotFound	Resource not found
-193	resFNotFound	Resource file not found
-194	addResFailed	AddResource failed
-195	addRefFailed	AddReference failed
-196	rmvResFailed	RmveResource failed
-197	rmvRefFailed	RmveReference failed
-198	resAttrErr	attribute inconsistent with operation
-199	mapReadErr	map inconsistent with operation
Sound Manager		
-200	noHardwareErr	No hardware support for the specified synthesizer
-201	notEnoughHardwareErr	No more channels for the specified synth
-203	queueFull	No more room in queue
-204	resProblem	Problem loading resource
-205	badChannel	Invalid channel queue length
-206	badFormat	Handle to 'snd' resource was invalid
-207	notEnoughBufferSpace	could not allocate enough memory
-208	badFileFormat	"was not type AIFF or was of bad format, corrupt"

(continued)

Table D.2   Post-MacsBug error codes *(continued)*.

Code	System Error	Description
-209	channelBusy	the Channel is being used for a PFD already
-210	buffersTooSmall	cannot operate in the memory allowed
-211	channelNotBusy	
-212	noMoreRealTime	not enough CPU cycles left to add another task
-220	siNoSoundInHardware	no Sound Input hardware
-221	siBadSoundInDevice	invalid index passed to Sound In Get Indexed Device
-222	siNoBufferSpecified	nil buffer passed to synchronous SPBRecord
-223	siInvalidCompression	invalid compression type
-224	siHardDriveTooSlow	hard drive too slow to record to disk
-225	siInvalidSampleRate	invalid sample rate
-226	siInvalidSampleSize	invalid sample size
-227	siDeviceBusyErr	input device already in use
-228	siBadDeviceName	input device could not be opened
-229	siBadRefNum	invalid input device reference number
-230	siInputDeviceErr	input device hardware failure
-231	siUnknownInfoType	driver returned invalid info type selector
-232	siUnknownQuality	invalid quality selector returned by driver

Midi Manager

Code	System Error	Description
-250	midiNoClientErr	no client with that ID found
-251	midiNoPortErr	no port with that ID found
-252	midiTooManyPortsErr	too many ports already installed in system
-253	midiTooManyConsErr	too many connections made
-254	midiVConnectErr	pending virtual connection created
-255	midiVConnectMade	pending virtual connection resolved
-256	midiVConnectRmvd	pending virtual connection removed
-257	midiNoConErr	no connection exists between specified ports
-258	midiWriteErr	couldn't write to all connected ports
-259	midiNameLenErr	name supplied is longer than 31 characters
-260	midiDupIDErr	duplicate client ID
-261	midiInvalidCmdErr	command not supported for port type

Notification Manager

Code	System Error	Description
-299	nmTypErr	Wrong queue type

(continued)

**Appendix D
Mac Os Error Codes**

Table D.2   Post-MacsBug error codes *(continued)*.

Code	System Error	Description
Start Manager		
-290	smSDMInitErr	SDM could not be initialized
-291	smSRTInitErr	Slot Resource Table could not be initialized
-292	smPRAMInitErr	Slot Resource Table could not be initialized
-293	smPriInitErr	Cards could not be initialized
-300	smEmptySlot	No card in slot
-301	smCRCFail	CRC check failed for declaration data
-302	smFormatErr	FHeader Format is not Apple's
-303	smRevisionErr	Wrong revision level
-304	smNoDir	Directory offset is Nil
-305	smDisabledSlot	This Slot is disabled
-305	smLWTstBad	This Slot is disabled (Old mnemonic)
-306	smNosInfoArray	No sInfoArray. Memory Mgr error
-307	smResrvErr	Fatal reserved error. Reserved field <> 0
-308	smUnExBusErr	Unexpected BusError
-309	smBLFieldBad	ByteLanes field was bad
-310	smFHBlockRdErr	Error occurred during _sGetFHeader
-311	smFHBlkDispErr	Error occurred during _sDisposePtr (Dispose of FHeader block)
-312	smDisposePErr	DisposePointer error
-313	smNoBoardsRsrc	No Board sResource
-314	smGetPRErr	Error occurred during _sGetPRAMRec (See SIMStatus)
-315	smNoBoardId	No Board Id
-316	smIntStatVErr	The InitStatusV field was negative after primary or secondary init
-317	smIntTblVErr	An error occurred while trying to initialize the Slot Resource Table
-318	smNoJmpTbl	SDM jump table could not be created
-319	smBadBoardId	"BoardId was wrong, re-init the PRAM record"
-320	smBusErrTO	BusError time out
-330	smBadRefId	Reference Id not found in List
-331	smBadsList	Bad sList: Id1<Id2<Id3 . . . format is not followed
-332	smReservedErr	Reserved field not zero
-333	smCodeRevErr	Code revision is wrong

(continued)

Table D.2 Post-MacsBug error codes *(continued)*.

Code	System Error	Description
-334	smCPUErr	Code revision is wrong
-335	smsPointerNil	"LPointer is nil From sOffsetData. If this error occurs, check sInfo rec for more information"
-336	smNilsBlockErr	Nil sBlock error (Don't allocate and try to use a nil sBlock)
-337	smSlotOOBErr	Slot out of bounds error
-338	smSelOOBErr	Selector out of bounds error
-339	smNewPErr	_NewPtr error
-340	smBlkMoveErr	_BlockMove error
-341	smCkStatusErr	Status of slot = fail
-342	smGetDrvrNamErr	Error occurred during _sGetDrvrName
-343	smDisDrvrNamErr	Error occurred during _sDisDrvrName
-344	smNoMoresRsrcs	No more sResources
-345	smsGetDrvrErr	Error occurred during _sGetDriver
-346	smBadsPtrErr	Bad pointer was passed to sCalcsPointer
-347	smByteLanesErr	NumByteLanes was determined to be zero
-348	smOffsetErr	"Offset was too big (temporary error, should be fixed)"
-349	smNoGoodOpens	No opens were successful in the loop
-350	smSRTOvrFlErr	SRT overflow
-351	smRecNotFnd	Record not found in the SRT
Device Manager		
-360	slotNumErr	invalid slot # error
-400	gcrOnMFMErr	gcr format on high density media error
Edition Manager		
-450	editionMgrInitErr	edition manager not inited by this app
-451	badSectionErr	not a valid SectionRecord
-452	notRegisteredSectionErr	not a registered SectionRecord
-453	badEditionFileErr	edition file is corrupt
-454	badSubPartErr	cannot use sub parts in this release
-460	multiplePublisherWrn	A Publisher is already registered for that container
-461	containerNotFoundWrn	couldn't find editionContainer now
-462	containerAlreadyOpenWrn	container already opened by this section
-463	notThePublisherWrn	different publisher was first registered for that container

(continued)

Table D.2   Post-MacsBug error codes (continued).

Code	System Error	Description
SCSI Manager		
-470	scsiBadPBErr	invalid field(s) in the parameter block
-471	scsiOverrunErr	attempted to transfer too many bytes
-472	scsiTransferErr	write flag conflicts with data transfer phase
-473	scsiBusTOErr	bus error during transfer
-474	scsiSelectTOErr	scsiSelTO exceeded (selection failed)
-475	scsiTimeOutErr	scsiReqTO exceeded
-476	scsiBusResetErr	"the bus was reset, so your request was aborted"
-477	scsiBadStatus	non-zero (not Good) status returned
-478	scsiNoStatusErr	device did not go through a status phase
-479	scsiLinkFailErr	linked command never executed
-489	scsiUnimpVctErr	unimplemented routine was called
Debugger SysErrs		
-490	userBreak	user debugger break
-491	strUserBreak	user debugger break display string on stack
-492	exUserBreak	user debugger break execute commands on stack
TextEdit		
-501	teScrapSizeErr	scrap item too big for text-edit record
O/S		
-502	hwParamrErr	bad selector for _HWPriv
Process Manager		
-600	procNotFound	no eligible process with specified descriptor
-601	memFragErr	not enough room to launch app w/spec requirements
-602	appModeErr	"memory mode is 32-bit, but app not 32-bit clean"
-603	protocolErr	app made module calls in improper order
-604	hardwareConfigErr	hardware configuration not correct for call
-605	appMemFullErr	application SIZE not big enough for launch
-606	appIsDaemon	"app is BG-only, and launch flags disallow this"
-607	bufferIsSmall	error returns from Post and Accept
-608	noOutstandingHLE	
-609	connectionInvalid	
-610	noUserInteractionAllowed	no user interaction allowed

(continued)

Table D.2   Post-MacsBug error codes *(continued)*.

Code	System Error	Description
Memory Dispatch		
-620	notEnoughMemoryErr	insufficient physical memory
-621	notHeldErr	specified range of memory is not held
-622	cannotMakeContiguousErr	cannot make specified range contiguous
-623	notLockedErr	specified range of memory is not locked
-624	interruptsMaskedErr	don't call with interrupts masked
-625	cannotDeferErr	unable to defer additional functions
-626	noMMUErr	no MMU present
Database Access		
-800	rcDBNull	
-801	rcDBValue	
-802	rcDBError	
-803	rcDBBadType	
-804	rcDBBreak	
-805	rcDBExec	
-806	rcDBBadSessID	
-807	rcDBBadSessNum	bad session number for DBGetConnInfo
-808	rcDBBadDDEV	bad ddev specified on DBInit
-809	rcDBAsyncNotSupp	ddev does not support async calls
-810	rcDBBadAsyncPB	tried to kill a bad pb
-811	rcDBNoHandler	no app handler for specified data type
-812	rcDBWrongVersion	incompatible versions
-813	rcDBPackNotInited	attempt to call other routine before InitDBPack
Help Manager		
-850	hmHelpDisabled	"Show Balloons mode off, call to routine ignored"
-851	hmResNotFound	
-852	hmMemFullErr	
-853	hmBalloonAborted	if mouse was moving or mouse wasn't in window port rect
-854	hmBadHelpData	from HMShow MenuBalloon if menu and item is same as last time
-854	hmSameAsLastBalloon	from HMShow MenuBalloon if menu and item is same as last time

(continued)

Table D.2   Post-MacsBug error codes (continued).

Code	System Error	Description
-855	hmHelpManager	HMGetHelp MenuHandle if help menu not set up
-856	hmBadSelector	
-857	hmSkippedBalloon	Helpmsg specified a skip balloon
-858	hmWrongVersion	Help mgr resource was the wrong version
-859	hmUnknownHelpType	Help msg record contained a bad type
-860	hmCouldNotLoadPackage	
-861	hmOperationUnsupported	Bad method passed to HMShowBalloon
-862	hmNoBalloonUp	No balloon visible when HMRemove Balloon called
-863	hmCloseViewActive	CloseView active when HMRemove Balloon called
PPC Toolbox		
-900	notInitErr	PPCToolBox not initialized
-902	nameTypeErr	Invalid or inappropriate locationKind Selector in locationName
-903	noPortErr	Unable to open port or bad portRefNum
-904	noGlobalsErr	"The system is hosed, better re-boot"
-905	localOnlyErr	Network activity is currently disabled
-906	destPortErr	Port does not exist at destination
-907	sessTableErr	"Out of session tables, try again later"
-908	noSessionErr	Invalid session reference number
-909	badReqErr	bad parameter or invalid state for operation
-910	portNameExistsErr	port is already open (perhaps another app)
-911	noUserNameErr	user name unknown on destination machine
-912	userRejectErr	Destination rejected the session request
-913	noMachineNameErr	user hasn't named his Macintosh in the Network Setup Control Panel
-914	noToolboxNameErr	"A system resource is missing, not too likely"
-915	noResponseErr	unable to contact destination
-916	portClosedErr	port was closed
-917	sessClosedErr	session was closed
-919	badPortNameErr	PPCPortRec malformed
-922	noDefaultUserErr	user hasn't typed in owner's name in Network Setup Control Panel
-923	notLoggedInErr	The default userRefNum does not yet exist
-924	noUserRefErr	unable to create a new userRefNum

(continued)

Table D.2   Post-MacsBug error codes *(continued).*

Code	System Error	Description
-925	networkErr	"An error has occurred in the network, not too likely"
-926	noInformErr	PPCStart failed: dest didn't have inform pending
-927	authFailErr	unable to authenticate user at destination
-928	noUserRecErr	Invalid user reference number
-930	badServiceMethodErr	"illegal service type, or not supported"
-931	badLocNameErr	location name malformed
-932	guestNotAllowedErr	destination port requires authentication
AppleTalk NBP		
-1024	nbpBuffOvr	Buffer overflow in LookupName
-1025	nbpNoConfirm	Name not confirmed on ConfirmName
-1026	nbpConfDiff	Name confirmed at different socket
-1027	nbpDuplicate	Duplicate name exists already
-1028	nbpNotFound	Name not found on remove
-1029	nbpNISErr	Error trying to open the NIS
AppleTalk ASP		
-1066	aspBadVersNum	Server cannot support this ASP version
-1067	aspBufTooSmall	Buffer too small
-1068	aspNoMoreSess	No more sessions on server
-1069	aspNoServers	No servers at that address
-1070	aspParamErr	Parameter error
-1071	aspServerBusy	Server cannot open another session
-1072	aspSessClosed	Session closed
-1073	aspSizeErr	Command block too big
-1074	aspTooMany	Too many clients (server error)
-1075	aspNoAck	No ack on attention request (server err)
AppleTalk ATP		
-1096	reqFailed	SendRequest failed: retry count exceeded
-1097	tooManyReqs	Too many concurrent requests
-1098	tooManySkts	Too many concurrent responding-sockets
-1099	badATPSkt	Bad ATP-responding socket
-1100	badBuffNum	Bad response buffer number specified
-1101	noRelErr	No release received
-1102	cbNotFound	Control Block (TCB or RspCB) not found

(continued)

**Appendix D
Mac Os Error Codes**

Table D.2   Post-MacsBug error codes *(continued)*.

Code	System Error	Description
-1103	noSendResp	AddResponse issued without SendResponse
-1104	noDataArea	No data area for request to MPP
-1105	reqAborted	SendRequest aborted by RelTCB
-3101	buf2SmallErr	Buffer too small error
-3102	noMPPErr	No MPP error
-3103	ckSumErr	Check sum error
-3104	extractErr	Extraction error
-3105	readQErr	Read queue error
-3106	atpLenErr	ATP length error
-3107	atpBadRsp	ATP bad response error
-3108	recNotFnd	Record not found
-3109	sktClosedErr	Socket closed error

AppleTalk ADSP driver control ioResults

Code	System Error	Description
-1273	errOpenDenied	open connection request was denied
-1274	errDSPQueueSize	send or receive queue is too small
-1275	errFwdReset	read terminated by forward reset
-1276	errAttention	attention message too long
-1277	errOpening	open connection request was denied
-1278	errState	Bad connection state for this operation
-1279	errAborted	control call was aborted
-1280	errRefNum	bad connection refNum

Print Manager w/LaserWriter

Code	System Error	Description
-4096	???	No free Connect Control Blocks available
-4097	???	Bad connection reference number
-4098	???	Request already active
-4099	???	Write request too big
-4100	???	Connection just closed
-4101	???	"Printer not found, or closed"

File Manager Extensions

Code	System Error	Description
-5000	accessDenied	Incorrect access for this file/folder
-5006	DenyConflict	Permission/Deny mode conflicts with the current mode in which this fork is already open
-5015	NoMoreLocks	Byte range locking failure from Server

(continued)

Table D.2   Post-MacsBug error codes *(continued)*.

Code	System Error	Description
-5020	RangeNotLocked	Attempt to unlock an already unlocked range
-5021	RangeOverlap	Attempt to lock some of an already locked range
AppleTalk AFP		
-5000	afpAccessDenied	AFP access denied
-5001	afpAuthContinue	AFP authorization continue
-5002	afpBadUAM	AFP bad UAM
-5003	afpBadVersNum	AFP bad version number
-5004	afpBitmapErr	AFP bit map error
-5005	afpCantMove	AFP can't move error
-5006	afpDenyConflict	AFP deny conflict
-5007	afpDirNotEmpty	AFP dir not empty
-5008	afpDiskFull	AFP disk full
-5009	afpEofError	AFP End-of-File error
-5010	afpFileBusy	AFP file busy
-5011	afpFlatVo	AFP flat volume
-5012	afpItemNotFound	AFP item not found
-5013	afpLockErr	AFP lock error
-5014	afpMiscErr	AFP misc error
-5015	afpNoMoreLocks	AFP no more locks
-5016	afpNoServer	AFP no server
-5017	afpObjectExists	AFP object already exists
-5018	afpObjectNotFound	AFP object not found
-5019	afpParmErr	AFP parm error
-5020	afpRangeNotLocked	AFP range not locked
-5021	afpRangeOverlap	AFP range overlap
-5022	afpSessClosed	AFP session closed
-5023	afpUserNotAuth	AFP user not authorized
-5024	afpCallNotSupported	AFP call not supported
-5025	afpObjectTypeErr	AFP object type error
-5026	afpTooManyFilesOpen	AFP too many files open
-5027	afpServerGoingDown	AFP server going down
-5028	afpCantRename	AFP can't rename
-5029	afpDirNotFound	AFP directory not found

(continued)

Table D.2   Post-MacsBug error codes *(continued)*.

Code	System Error	Description
-5030	afpIconTypeError	AFP icon type error
-5031	afpVolLocked	Volume is Read-Only
-5032	afpObjectLocked	Object is M/R/D/W inhibited
-5033	afpContainsSharedErr	folder being shared has a shared folder
-5034	afpIDNotFound	
-5035	afpIDExists	
-5036	afpDiffVolErr	
-5037	afpCatalogChanged	
-5038	afpSameObjectErr	
-5039	afpBadIDErr	
-5040	afpPwdSameErr	someone tried to change his or her password to the same password on a mandatory password change
-5041	afpPwdTooShortErr	the password being set is too short: there is a minimum length that must be met or exceeded
-5042	afpPwdExpiredErr	the password being used is too old: this requires the user to change the password before login can continue
-5043	afpInsideSharedErr	folder being shared is inside a shared folder
-5044	afpInsideTrashErr	folder being shared is in the trash folder
-5060	afpBadDirIDType	
-5061	afpCantMountMoreSrvre	
-5062	afpAlreadyMounted	
-5063	afpSameNodeErr	
SysEnvirons		
-5500	envNotPresent	SysEnvirons trap not present (returned by glue)
-5501	envBadVers	Version non-positive
-5502	envVersTooBig	Version bigger than call can handle
Gestalt		
-5550	gestaltUnknownErr	Gestalt doesn't know the answer
-5551	gestaltUndefSelectorErr	Undefined code was passed to Gestalt
-5552	gestaltDupSelectorErr	Tried to add entry that already existed
-5553	gestaltLocationErr	Gestalt function ptr wasn't in sysheap
LaserWriter Driver		
-8132	????	Manual Feed time out
-8133	????	General PostScript Error

(continued)

Table D.2 Post-MacsBug error codes *(continued)*.

Code	System Error	Description
-8150	????	No LaserWriter chosen
-8151	????	Version mismatch between LaserPrep dictionaries
-8150	????	No LaserPrep dictionary installed
-8160	????	Zoom scale factor out of range

Thread Manager

-617	threadTooManyReqsErr	
-618	threadNotFoundErr	
-619	threadProtocolErr	

Power Manager

-13000	pmBusyErr	Pmgr never ready to start handshake
-13001	pmReplyTOErr	Timed out waiting for reply
-13002	pmSendStartErr	"During send, pmgr did not start hs"
-13003	pmSendEndErr	"During send, pmgr did not finish hs"
-13004	pmRecvStartErr	"During receive, pmgr did not start hs"
-13005	pmRecvEndErr	during receive pmgr did not finish hs configured for this connection

MacTCP

-23000	ipBadLapErr	Bad network configuration
-23001	ipBadCnfgErr	Bad IP configuration error
-23002	ipNoCnfgErr	Missing IP or LAP configuration error
-23003	ipLoadErr	Error in MacTCP load
-23004	ipBadAddr	Error in getting address
-23005	connectionClosing	Connection in closing
-23006	invalidLength	
-23007	connectionExists	Request conflicts with existing connection
-23008	connectionDoesntExist	Connection does not exist
-23009	insufficientResources	Insufficient rsrcs to perform request
-23010	invalidStreamPtr	
-23011	streamAlreadyOpen	
-23012	connectionTerminated	
-23013	invalidBufPtr	
-23014	invalidRDS	
-23014	invalidWDS	

(continued)

Table D.2 Post-MacsBug error codes *(continued)*.

Code	System Error	Description
-23015	openFailed	
-23016	commandTimeout	
-23017	duplicateSocket	
-23030	ipOpenProtErr	"Can't open new protocol, table full"
-23031	ipCloseProtErr	Can't find protocol to close
-23032	ipDontFragErr	Packet too large to send w/o fragmenting
-23033	ipDestDeadErr	Destination not responding
-23034	ipBadWDSErr	Error in WDS format
-23035	icmpEchoTimeoutErr	ICMP echo timed-out
-23036	ipNoFragMemErr	No memory to send fragmented pkt
-23037	ipRouteErr	Can't route packet off-net
-23041	nameSyntaxErr	
-23042	cacheFault	
-23043	noResultProc	
-23044	noNameServer	
-23045	authNameErr	
-23046	noAnsErr	
-23047	dnrErr	
-23048	outOfMemory	
Internal File System		
1	chNoBuf	no free cache buffers (all in use)
2	chInUse	requested block in use
3	chnotfound	requested block not found
4	chNotInUse	block being released was not in use
16	fxRangeErr	file position beyond mapped range
17	fxOvFlErr	extents file overflow
32	btnotfound	record not found
33	btexists	record already exists
34	btnospace	no available space
35	btnoFit	record doesn't fit in node
36	btbadNode	bad node detected
37	btbadHdr	bad BTree header record detected
48	cmnotfound	CNode not found

(continued)

Table D.2 Post-MacsBug error codes (continued).

Code	System Error	Description
49	cmexists	CNode already exists
50	cmnotempty	directory CNode not empty (valence = 0)
51	cmRootCN	invalid reference to root CNode
52	cmbadnews	detected bad catalog structure
53	cmFThdDirErr	thread belongs to a directory not a file
54	cmFThdGone	file thread doesn't exist
64	dsBadRotate	bad BTree rotate

Slot Declaration ROM Manager

1	siInitSDTblErr	slot int dispatch table couldn't be initialized
2	siInitVBLQsErr	VBLqueues for all slots couldn't be initialized
3	siInitSPTblErr	slot priority table could not be initialized
10	sdmJTInitErr	SDM Jump Table could not be initialized
11	sdmInitErr	SDM could not be initialized
12	sdmSRTInitErr	Slot Resource Table could not be initialized
13	sdmPRAMInitErr	Slot PRAM could not be initialized
14	sdmPriInitErr	Cards could not be initialized

HD20 Driver

16	wrtHsLw	HSHK low before starting
17	wrtHSLwTO	Timeout waiting for HSHK to go low
19	wrtHSHighTO	Timeout waiting for HSHK to go high
32	rdHsHi	HSHK high before starting
33	rdSyncTO	Timeout waiting for sync ($AA) bye
34	rdGroupTO	Timeout waiting for group
36	rdHoffSyncTO	Timeout waiting for sync after holdoff
37	rdHsHiTO	Timeout waiting for HSHK high
38	rdChksumErr	Checksum error on response packet
48	invalidResp	First byte in response packet was wrong
49	sqncNumErr	Sequence number in response packet was wrong
50	dNumberErr	Drive number in response packet was wrong
64	noResp	No response packet ever received

SCSI Manager (obscure)

2	scCommErr	Communications error (operations timeout)
3	scArbNBErr	Arbitration failed during SCSIGet—Bus busy

(continued)

Table D.2   Post-MacsBug error codes *(continued)*.

Code	System Error	Description
4	scBadparmsErr	Bad parameter or TIB opcode
5	scPhaseErr	SCSI bus not in correct phase for operation
6	scCompareErr	SCSI Manager busy with another operation when SCSIGet was called
7	scMgrBusyErr	SCSI Manager busy with another operation when SCSIGet was called
8	scSequenceErr	"Attempted operation is out of sequence—e.g., calling SCSISelect before doing SCSIGet"
9	scBusTOErr	Bus timeout before data ready on SCSIRBlind and SCSIWBlind
10	scComplPhaseErr	SCSIComplete failed—bus not in Status phase

Primary or Secondary Init Code

The following errors are for primary or secondary init code. The errors are logged in the vendor status field of the sInfo record. Normally, the vendor error is not Apple's concern, but a special error is needed to patch secondary inits.

Table D.3   Primary and secondary error codes.

Code	System Error	Description
-32768	svTempDisable	Temporarily disables card but runs primary init
-32640	svDisabled	Reserve -32640 to -32768 for Apple temp disables
Dictionary Manager		
-410	notBTree	The file is not a dictionary
-413	btNoSpace	Can't allocate disk space
-414	btDupRecErr	Record already exists
-415	btRecNotFnd	Record cannot be found
-416	btKeyLenErr	Maximum key length is too long or equal to zero
-417	btKeyAttrErr	There is no such key attribute
-20000	unknownInsertModeErr	There is no such insert mode
-20001	recordDataTooBigErr	The record data is bigger than buffer size (1024 bytes)
-20002	invalidIndexErr	The recordIndex parameter is not valid
AppleEvent Manager		
-1700	errAECoercionFail	bad parameter data or unable to coerce the data supplied
-1701	errAEDescNotFound	

(continued)

Table D.3   Primary and secondary error codes *(continued).*

Code	System Error	Description
-1702	errAECorruptData	
-1703	errAEWrongDataType	
-1704	errAENotAEDesc	
-1705	errAEBadListItem	the specified list item does not exist
-1706	errAENewerVersion	need newer version of the AppleEvent manager
-1707	errAENotAppleEvent	the event is not in AppleEvent format
-1708	errAEEventNotHandled	the AppleEvent was not handled by any handler
-1709	errAEReplyNotValid	AEResetTimer was passed an invalid reply parameter
-1710	errAEUnknown SendMode	mode wasn't NoReply, WaitReply, or QueueReply, or Interaction level is unknown
-1711	errAEWaitCanceled	in AESend the user cancelled out of wait loop for reply or receipt
-1712	errAETimeout	the AppleEvent timed out
-1713	errAENoUserInteraction	no user interaction is allowed
-1714	errAENotASpecialFunction	there is no special function for/with this keyword
-1715	errAEParamMissed	a required parameter was not accessed
-1716	errAEUnknownAddressType	the target address type is not known
-1717	errAEHandlerNotFound	no handler in the dispatch tables fits the parameters to AEGetEventHandler or AEGetCoercionHandler
-1718	errAEReplyNotArrived	the contents of the reply you are accessing have not arrived yet
-1719	errAEIllegalIndex	index is out of range in a put operation

OSL Error Codes

Code	System Error	Description
-1720	errAEImpossibleRange	A range like 3rd to 2nd or 1st to all
-1721	errAEWrongNumberArgs	Logical op kAENOT used with other than one term
-1723	errAEAccessorNotFound	Accessor proc matching wantClass and containerType or wildcards not found
-1725	errAENoSuchLogical	Something other than AND, OR, or NOT
-1726	errAEBadTestKey	Test is neither type LogicalDescriptor nor type CompDescriptor
-1727	errAENotAnObjSpec	Param to AEResolve not of type 'obj '
-1728	errAENoSuchObject	e.g. Specifier asked for the 3rd but only two exist, for example—basically this indicates a runtime resolution error

(continued)

Table D.3   Primary and secondary error codes *(continued).*

Code	System Error	Description
-1729	errAENegativeCount	CountProc returned negative value
-1730	errAEEmptyListContainer	Attempt to pass empty list as container to accessor
-1731	errAEUnknown ObjectType	available only in version 1.0.1 or greater
-1732	errAERecordingIs AlreadyOn	available only in version 1.0.1 or greater
OSA API Errors		
-1750	errOSASystemError	
-1751	errOSAInvalidID	
-1752	errOSABadStorageType	
-1753	errOSAScriptError	
-1754	errOSABadSelector	
-1756	errOSASourceNotAvailable	
-1757	errOSANoSuchDialect	
-1758	errOSADataFormatObsolete	
-1759	errOSADataFormatTooNew	
-1761	errOSAComponent Mismatch	Parameters are from 2 different components
-1762	errOSACantOpen Component	Can't connect to scripting system with that ID
-10000	errAEEventFailed	
-10001	errAETypeError	
-10002	errAEBadKeyForm	
-10003	errAENotModifiable	
-10004	errAEPrivilegeError	
-10005	errAEReadDenied	
-10006	errAEWriteDenied	
-10007	errAEIndexTooLarge	
-10008	errAENotAnElement	
-10009	errAECantSupplyType	
-10010	errAECantHandleClass	
-10011	errAEInTransaction	
-10012	errAENoSuchTransaction	
-10013	errAENoUserSelection	
-10014	errAENotASingleObject	
-10015	errAECantUndo	
-10016	errAELocalOnly	

(continued)

Table D.3 Primary and secondary error codes *(continued)*.

Code	System Error	Description
QuickTime		
-2000	couldNotResolveDataRef	
-2001	badImageDescription	
-2002	badPublicMovieAtom	
-2003	cantFindHandler	
-2004	cantOpenHandler	
-2005	badComponentType	
-2006	noMediaHandler	
-2007	noDataHandler	
-2008	invalidMedia	
-2009	invalidTrack	
-2010	invalidMovie	
-2011	invalidSampleTable	
-2012	invalidDataRef	
-2013	invalidHandler	
-2014	invalidDuration	
-2015	invalidTime	
-2016	cantPutPublicMovieAtom	
-2017	badEditList	
-2018	mediaTypesDontMatch	
-2019	progressProcAborted	
-2020	movieToolboxUninitialized	
-2020	noRecordOfApp	
-2021	wfFileNotFound	
-2022	cantCreateSingleForkFile	happens when file already exists
-2023	invalidEditState	
-2024	nonMatchingEditState	
-2025	staleEditState	
-2026	userDataItemNotFound	
-2027	maxSizeToGrowTooSmall	
-2028	badTrackIndex	
-2029	trackIDNotFound	
-2030	trackNotInMovie	

(continued)

Table D.3   Primary and secondary error codes *(continued)*.

Code	System Error	Description
-2031	timeNotInTrack	
-2032	timeNotInMedia	
-2033	badEditIndex	
-2034	internalQuickTimeError	
-2035	cantEnableTrack	
-2036	invalidRect	
-2037	invalidSampleNum	
-2038	invalidChunkNum	
-2039	invalidSampleDescIndex	
-2040	invalidChunkCache	
-2041	invalidSampleDescription	
-2042	dataNotOpenForRead	
-2043	dataNotOpenForWrite	
-2044	dataAlreadyOpenForWrite	
-2045	dataAlreadyClosed	
-2046	endOfDataReached	
-2047	dataNoDataRef	
-2048	noMovieFound	
-2049	invalidDataRefContainer	
-2050	badDataRefIndex	
-2051	noDefaultDataRef	
-2052	couldNotUseAnExistingSample	
-2053	featureUnsupported	
-2054	noVideoTrackInMovieErr	QT for Windows error
-2055	noSoundTrackInMovie Err	QT for Windows error
-2056	soundSupportNot AvailableErr	QT for Windows error
-2057	unsupportedAuxiliaryImportData	
-2058	auxiliaryExportDataUnavailable	
-2059	samplesAlreadyInMediaErr	
-2062	movieTextNotFoundErr	
-2201	digiUnimpErr	feature unimplemented
-2202	qtParamErr	"bad input parameter (out of range, etc.)"
-2203	matrixErr	bad matrix digitizer did nothing

(continued)

Table D.3   Primary and secondary error codes *(continued).*

Code	System Error	Description
-2204	notExactMatrixErr	warning of bad matrix digitizer did its best
-2205	noMoreKeyColorsErr	all key indexes in use
-2206	notExactSizeErr	Can't do exact size requested
-2207	badDepthErr	Can't digitize into this depth
-2208	noDMAErr	Can't do DMA digitizing (i.e., can't go to requested dest)
-2209	badCallOrderErr	Usually due to a status call being called prior to being set up first
-8960	codecEr	
-8961	noCodecErr	
-8962	codecUnimpErr	
-8963	codecSizeErr	
-8964	codecScreenBufErr	
-8965	codecImageBufErr	
-8966	codecSpoolErr	
-8967	codecAbortErr	
-8968	codecWouldOffscreenErr	
-8969	codecBadDataErr	
-8970	codecDataVersErr	
-8971	scTypeNotFoundErr	codecExtension Not FoundErr
-8972	codecConditionErr	
-8973	codecOpenErr	
-8974	codecCantWhenErr	
-8975	codecCantQueueErr	
-8976	codecNothingToBlitErr	
-9400	noDeviceForChannel	
-9401	grabTimeComplete	
-9402	cantDoThatInCurrentMode	
-9403	notEnoughMemoryToGrab	
-9404	notEnoughDiskSpaceToGrab	
-9405	couldntGetRequiredComponent	
-9406	badSGChannel	
-9407	seqGrabInfoNotAvailable	
-9408	deviceCantMeetRequest	

(continued)

Table D.3   Primary and secondary error codes *(continued).*

Code	System Error	Description
-9994	badControllerHeight	
-9995	editingNotAllowed	
-9996	controllerBoundsNotExact	
-9997	cannotSetWidthOfAttachedController	
-9998	controllerHasFixedHeight	
-9999	cannotMoveAttachedController	
Display Manager		
-6220	kDMGenErr	Unexpected Error
-6221	kDMMirroringOnAlready	Returned by all calls that need mirroring to be off to do their thing
-6222	kDMWrongNumber OfDisplays	Can only handle 2 displays for now
-6223	kDMMirroringBlocked	DMBlock Mirroring() has been called
-6224	kDMCantBlock	Mirroring is already on can't Block now (call DMUnMirror() first)
-6225	kDMMirroringNotOn	Returned by all calls that need mirroring to be on to do their thing
-6226	kSysSWTooOld	Missing critical pieces of system software
-6227	kDMSWNotInitializedErr	Required software not initialized (e.g., windowmanager or display mgr).
-6228	kDMDriverNotDisplayMgrAwareErr	Video Driver does not support display manager
-6229	kDMDisplayNotFoundErr	Could not find item (will someday remove)
-6229	kDMNotFoundErr	Could not find item
-6230	kDMDisplayAlreadyInstalledErr	Attempt to add an already installed display
-6231	kDMMainDisplayCannotMoveErr	Trying to move main display (or a display mirrored to it)
-6231	kDMNoDeviceTableclothErr	Obsolete
Colour Sync		
-4200	cmElementTagNotFound	
-4201	cmIndexRangeErr	Index out of range
-4202	cmCantDeleteElement	
-4203	cmFatalProfileErr	
-4204	cmInvalidProfile	A Profile must contain a 'cs1' tag to be valid
-4205	cmInvalidProfileLocation	Operation not supported for this profile location
-4206	cmInvalidSearch	Bad Search Handle
-4207	cmSearchError	

(continued)

Table D.3 Primary and secondary error codes *(continued)*.

Code	System Error	Description
-4208	cmErrIncompatibleProfile	
-4209	cmInvalidColorSpace	Profile colorspace does not match bitmap type
-4210	cmInvalidSrcMap	Source pix/bit map was invalid
-4211	cmInvalidDstMap	Destination pix/bit map was invalid
-4212	cmNoGDevicesError	Begin/End Matching—no gdevices available
-4213	cmInvalidProfile Comment	Bad profile comment during drawpicture
-4214	cmRangeOverFlow	One or more output color value overflows in color conversion

Colour Picker

Code	System Error	Description
-4000	invalidPickerType	
-4001	requiredFlagsDontMatch	
-4002	pickerResourceError	
-4003	cantLoadPicker	
-4004	cantCreatePickerWindow	
-4005	cantLoadPackage	
-4006	pickerCantLive	
-4007	colorSyncNotInstalled	
-4008	badProfileError	
-4009	noHelpForItem	

Translation Manager

Code	System Error	Description
-3025	invalidTranslationPathErr	Source type to destination type not a valid path
-3026	couldNotParse SourceFileErr	Source document does not contain source type
-3030	noTranslationPathErr	
-3031	badTranslationSpecErr	
-3032	noPrefAppErr	

Component Manager

Code	System Error	Description
-3000	invalidComponentID	
-3001	validInstancesExist	
-3002	componentNotCaptured	
-3003	componentDontRegister	

Apple Guide

Code	System Error	Description
-2900	kAGErrUnknownEvent	
-2901	kAGErrCantStartup	

(continued)

Table D.3 Primary and secondary error codes (continued).

Code	System Error	Description
-2902	kAGErrNoAccWin	
-2903	kAGErrNoPreWin	
-2904	kAGErrNoSequence	
-2905	kAGErrNotOopsSequence	
-2906	kAGErrReserved06	
-2907	kAGErrNoPanel	
-2908	kAGErrContentNotFound	
-2909	kAGErrMissingString	
-2910	kAGErrInfoNotAvail	
-2911	kAGErrEventNotAvailable	
-2912	kAGErrCannotMakeCoach	
-2913	kAGErrSessionIDsNotMatch	
-2914	kAGErrMissingDatabaseSpec	
-2925	kAGErrItemNotFound	
-2926	kAGErrBalloonResourceNotFound	
-2927	kAGErrChalkResourceNotFound	
-2928	kAGErrChdvResourceNotFound	
-2929	kAGErrAlreadyShowing	
-2930	kAGErrBalloonResourceSkip	
-2931	kAGErrItemNotVisible	
-2932	kAGErrReserved32	
-2933	kAGErrNotFrontProcess	
-2934	kAGErrMacroResourceNotFound	
-2951	kAGErrAppleGuideNotAvailable	
-2952	kAGErrCannotInitCoach	
-2953	kAGErrCannotInitContext	
-2954	kAGErrCannotOpenAliasFile	
-2955	kAGErrNoAliasResource	
-2956	kAGErrDatabaseNotAvailable	
-2957	kAGErrDatabaseNotOpen	
-2958	kAGErrMissingAppInfoHdl	
-2959	kAGErrMissingContextObject	

(continued)

Table D.3   Primary and secondary error codes *(continued)*.

Code	System Error	Description
-2960	kAGErrInvalidRefNum	
-2961	kAGErrDatabaseOpen	
-2962	kAGErrInsufficientMemory	

Code Fragment Manager

Code	System Error	Description
0	fragNoErr	
-2800	fragContextNotFound	contextID was not valid
-2801	fragConnection IDNotFound	connectionID was not valid
-2802	fragSymbolNotFound	symbol was not found in connection
-2803	fragSectionNotFound	section was not found
-2804	fragLibNotFound	library name not found in Frag registry
-2805	fragDupRegLibName	registered name already in use
-2806	fragFormatUnknown	fragment container format unknown
-2807	fragHadUnresolveds	"loaded fragment had 'hard' unresolved imports"
-2808	fragUnused1	unused
-2809	fragNoMem	out of memory for internal bookkeeping
-2810	fragNoAddrSpace	out of memory in user's address space for loadable section
-2811	fragNoContextIDs	no more context ids
-2812	fragObjectInitSeqErr	order error during user initialization function invocation
-2813	fragImportTooOld	import library was too old and therefore incompatible
-2814	fragImportTooNew	import library was too new and therefore incompatible
-2815	fragInitLoop	circularity detected in mandatory initialization order
-2816	fragInitRtnUsageErr	boot library has initialization routine
-2817	fragLibConnErr	error connecting to library (error occurred in sub prepare)
-2818	fragMgrInitErr	error in initialization of this manager
-2819	fragConstErr	internal inconsistency
-2820	fragCorruptErr	fragment container corrupted (known format)
-2821	fragUserInitProcErr	user initialization routine did not return noErr
-2822	fragAppNotFound	no application found in cfrg (for Process Manager)
-2823	fragArchError	fragment targeted for an unacceptable architecture
-2824	fragInvalid FragmentUsage	an application fragment or accelerated resource has no entry point or termination routine
-2899	fragLastErrCode	last reserved error code number

(continued)

Table D.3   Primary and secondary error codes *(continued)*.

Code	System Error	Description
Script Manager		
-2720	errASCantConsiderAndIgnore	Runtime
-2721	errASCantCompareMoreThan32k	Runtime
-2760	errASTerminologyNestingTooDeep	Parser/Compiler error
-2761	errASIllegalFormalParameter	Parser/Compiler error
-2762	errASParameterNotForEvent	Parser/Compiler error
-2763	errASNoResultReturned	Parser/Compiler error
Dialect-specific script errors		
-2780		-2780 thru -2799 is reserved for dialect specific error codes
-2799		Error codes from different dialects may overlap
-2780	errASInconsistentNames	English
Text Services Manager		
0	tsmComponentNoErr	component result no error
-2500	tsmUnsupScriptLanguageErr	
-2501	tsmInputMethodNotFoundErr	
-2502	tsmNotAnAppErr	not an application error
-2503	tsmAlreadyRegisteredErr	want to register again error
-2504	tsmNeverRegisteredErr	app never registered error (not TSM-aware)
-2505	tsmInvalidDocIDErr	invalid TSM documentation id
-2506	tsmTSMDocBusyErr	document is still active
-2507	tsmDocNotActiveErr	document is *NOT* active
-2508	tsmNoOpenTSErr	no open text service
-2509	tsmCantOpenComponentErr	can't open the component
-2510	tsmTextServiceNotFoundErr	no text service found
-2511	tsmDocumentOpenErr	there are open documents
-2512	tsmUseInputWindowErr	not TSM aware because we are using input window
-2513	tsmTSHasNoMenuErr	the text service has no menu
-2514	tsmTSNotOpenErr	text service is not open
-2515	tsmComponentAlreadyOpenErr	text service already opened for the document
-2516	tsmInputMethodIsOldErr	returned by Get DefaultInputMethod
-2517	tsmScriptHasNoIMErr	script has no input method or is using old IM
-2518	tsmUnsupportedTypeErr	unsupported interface type error
-2519	tsmUnknownErr	any other errors

(continued)

Table D.3   Primary and secondary error codes *(continued)*.

Code	System Error	Description
Drag Manager		
-1800	errOffsetInvalid	
-1801	errOffsetIsOutsideOfView	
-1810	errTopOfDocument	
-1811	errTopOfBody	
-1812	errEndOfDocument	
-1813	errEndOfBody	
-1850	badDragRefErr	unknown drag reference
-1851	badDragItemErr	unknown drag item reference
-1852	badDragFlavorErr	unknown flavor type
-1853	duplicateFlavorErr	flavor type already exists
-1854	cantGetFlavorErr	error while trying to get flavor data
-1855	duplicateHandlerErr	handler already exists
-1856	handlerNotFoundErr	handler not found
-1857	dragNotAcceptedErr	drag was not accepted by receiver
Telephony Manager (ISDN)		
-1001	isdnError	
-1002	isdnBadBufferLength	
-1003	isdnBadNetBufferLength	
-1004	isdnBadBufferSpecified	
-1005	isdnBadNetBufferSpecified	
-1006	isdnBadcsCode	
-1007	isdnCannotLoadLocalRPTask	
-1008	isdnCannotLoadNetworkRPTask	
-1009	isdnCardNotRunning	
-1010	isdnCANotInValidState	
Telephony Manager		
-1	telGenericError	
0	telNoErr	
8	telNoTools	no telephone tools found in extension folder
-10001	telBadTermErr	invalid TELHandle or handle not found
-10002	telBadDNErr	TELDNHandle not found or invalid
-10003	telBadCAErr	TELCAHandle not found or invalid

(continued)

Table D.3   Primary and secondary error codes *(continued).*

Code	System Error	Description
-10004	telBadHandErr	bad handle specified
-10005	telBadProcErr	bad msgProc specified
-10006	telCAUnavail	a CA is not available
-10007	telNoMemErr	no memory to allocate handle
-10008	telNoOpenErr	unable to open terminal
-10010	telBadHTypeErr	bad hook type specified
-10011	telHTypeNotSupp	hook type not supported by this tool
-10012	telBadLevelErr	bad volume level setting
-10013	telBadVTypeErr	bad volume type error
-10014	telVTypeNotSupp	volume type not supported by this tool
-10015	telBadAPattErr	bad alerting pattern specified
-10016	telAPattNotSupp	alerting pattern not supported by tool
-10017	telBadIndex	bad index specified
-10018	telIndexNotSupp	index not supported by this tool
-10019	telBadStateErr	bad device state specified
-10020	telStateNotSupp	device state not supported by tool
-10021	telBadIntExt	bad internal external error
-10022	telIntExtNotSupp	internal external type not supported by this tool
-10023	telBadDNDType	bad DND type specified
-10024	telDNDTypeNotSupp	DND type is not supported by this tool
-10030	telFeatNotSub	feature not subscribed
-10031	telFeatNotAvail	feature subscribed but not available
-10032	telFeatActive	feature already active
-10033	telFeatNotSupp	feature program call not supported by this tool
-10040	telConfLimitErr	limit specified is too high for this configuration
-10041	telConfNoLimit	no limit was specified but required
-10042	telConfErr	conference was not prepared
-10043	telConfRej	conference request was rejected
-10044	telTransferErr	transfer not prepared
-10045	telTransferRej	transfer request rejected
-10046	telCBErr	call back feature not set previously
-10047	telConfLimitExceeded	attempt to exceed switch conference limits
-10050	telBadDNType	DN type invalid

(continued)

Table D.3   Primary and secondary error codes *(continued)*.

Code	System Error	Description
-10051	telBadPageID	bad page ID specified
-10052	telBadIntercomID	bad intercom ID specified
-10053	telBadFeatureID	bad feature ID specified
-10054	telBadFwdType	bad fwdType specified
-10055	telBadPickupGroupID	bad pickup group ID specified
-10056	telBadParkID	bad park id specified
-10057	telBadSelect	unable to select or deselect DN
-10058	telBadBearerType	bad bearerType specified
-10059	telBadRate	bad rate specified
-10060	telDNTypeNotSupp	DN type not supported by tool
-10061	telFwdTypeNotSupp	forward type not supported by tool
-10062	telBadDisplayMode	bad display mode specified
-10063	telDisplayModeNotSupp	display mode not supported by tool
-10064	telNoCallbackRef	no call back reference was specified but is required
-10070	telAlreadyOpen	terminal already open
-10071	telStillNeeded	terminal driver still needed by someone else
-10072	telTermNotOpen	terminal not opened via TELOpenTerm
-10080	telCANotAcceptable	"CA not 'acceptable'"
-10081	telCANotRejectable	"CA not 'rejectable'"
-10082	telCANotDeflectable	"CA not 'deflectable'"
-10090	telPBErr	parameter block error bad format
-10091	telBadFunction	bad msgCode specified
-10101	telNoTools	unable to find any telephone tools
-10102	telNoSuchTool	unable to find tool with name specified
-10103	telUnknownErr	unable to set config
-10106	telNoCommFolder	Communications/Extensions *f* not found
-10107	telInitFailed	initialization failed
-10108	telBadCodeResource	code resource not found
-10109	telDeviceNotFound	device not found
-10110	telBadProcID	invalid procID
-10111	telValidateFailed	telValidate failed
-10112	telAutoAnsNotOn	autoAnswer in not turned on
-10113	telDetAlreadyOn	detection is already turned on

(continued)

Table D.3   Primary and secondary error codes *(continued)*.

Code	System Error	Description
-10114	telBadSWErr	Software not installed properly
-10115	telBadSampleRate	incompatible sample rate
-10116	telNotEnoughdspBW	not enough real-time for allocation
NameRegistry		
-2536	nrLockedErr	
-2537	nrNotEnoughMemoryErr	
-2538	nrInvalidNodeErr	
-2539	nrNotFoundErr	
-2540	nrNotCreatedErr	
-2541	nrNameErr	
-2542	nrNotSlotDeviceErr	
-2543	nrDataTruncatedErr	
-2544	nrPowerErr	
-2545	nrPowerSwitchAbortErr	
-2546	nrTypeMismatchErr	
-2547	nrNotModifiedErr	
-2548	nrOverrunErr	
-2549	nrResultCodeBase	
-2550	nrPathNotFound	a path component lookup failed
-2551	nrPathBufferTooSmall	buffer for path is too small
Mixed Mode Manager		
-2526	mmInternalError	
1010	dsBadLibrary	Bad shared library
1011	dsMixedModeFailure	Internal Mixed Mode Failure
ENET Errors		
-92	eLenErr	Length error ddpLenErr
-91	eMultiErr	Multicast address error ddpSktErr
SQL Errors		
-4	SQL_NO_TOTAL	
-2	SQL_INVALID_HANDLE	"Function failed due to an invalid handle, indicates a programming error"
-1	SQL_ERROR	Function failed
0	SQL_SUCCESS	"Function completed successfully, no additional information is available"

(continued)

Table D.3   Primary and secondary error codes *(continued)*.

Code	System Error	Description
1	SQL_SUCCESS_WITH_INFO	"Function completed successfully, possibly with a nonfatal error"
2	SQL_STILL_EXECUTING	A function that was started asynchronously is still executing
99	SQL_NEED_DATA	"While processing a statement, the driver determined that the application needs to send parameter data values"
100	SQL_NO_DATA_FOUND	All rows from the result have been fetched
OT/PPP (Preliminary)		
-7102		OT/PPP did not load properly at system startup
-7103		OT/PPP could not set up a port
-7104		OT/PPP is out of memory
-7105		The requested action is not supported
-7106		One or more resources are missing from OT/PPP's installed files
-7107		"The 'Remote Access Connections' file is not compatible with the installed version of OT/PPP"
-7108		An action requiring a connection was requested when there was no connection
-7109		The connection attempt or established connection was terminated by the user
-7110		The user name is unknown
-7111		The password is invalid
-7112		An unexpected error with no useful information has occurred
-7113		One or more of the installed OT/PPP files is damaged
-7114		The requested action could not be performed because OT/PPP was busy
-7115		The OT/PPP logical port is in an unknown state
-7116		The OT/PPP logical port is in an invalid state
-7117		The OT/PPP logical port has detected an invalid serial protocol
-7118		Login is disabled for the given user
-7120		The server administrator requires the user to enter a password
-7122		OT/PPP could not initialize Open Transport

(continued)

**Appendix D
Mac Os Error Codes**

Table D.3   Primary and secondary error codes *(continued)*.

Code	System Error	Description
-7123		The requested action could not be performed because OT/PPP is not fully initialized yet
-7124		TCP/IP is inactive and cannot be loaded
-7125		TCP/IP is not yet configured
-7126		PPP is not selected as the TCP/IP interface in the current TCP/IP configuration
-7128		The requested PPP protocol was rejected by the PPP peer
-7129		PPP authentication failed
-7130		PPP negotiation failed
-7131		PPP was disconnected locally
-7132		The PPP peer disconnected unexpectedly
-7133		The PPP peer is not responding
-7134		The OT/PPP log file is not open
-7135		The OT/PPP log file is already open
-7136		The OT/PPP log entry could not be retrieved
-7138		OT/PPP cannot locate the active System folder
-7139		OT/PPP cannot locate its preferences folder
-7140		There is a pre-existing file using an OT/PPP type or creator
-7141		There is a pre-existing folder using an OT/PPP folder name and location
-7142		"The 'Remote Access Connections' file is not open"
-7144		An unknown PPP control protocol type was received
-7145		PPP received a packet with an invalid length
-7146		PPP received a negotiable option with an invalid value
-7147		PPP received a negotiable option with invalid flags
-7148		PPP ran out of memory while negotiating with the peer
-7152		PPP encountered an error with no useful information
-7153		PPP is in an invalid state
-7163		The user canceled the password entry dialog
-7164		The user did not respond to the password entry dialog in time
-7165		An unknown Open Transport serial port was referenced

(continued)

Table D.3 Primary and secondary error codes *(continued).*

Code	System Error	Description
-7166		The OT/PPP logical port is not configured
-7167		No AppleTalk services endpoints are available
-7168		The modem script ASK or manual dialing dialog was canceled by the user

CTB Terminal

-1	tmGenericError	
0	tmNoErr	
1	tmNotSent	
2	tmEnvironsChanged	
7	tmNotSupported	
8	tmNoTools	
11	tmUnknownError	

CTB Connection

-1	cmGenericError	
0	cmNoErr	
1	cmRejected	
2	cmFailed	
3	cmTimeOut	
4	cmNotOpen	
5	cmNotClosed	
6	cmNoRequestPending	
7	cmNotSupported	
8	cmNoTools	
9	cmUserCancel	
11	cmUnknownError	

CTB File Transfer

-1	ftGenericError	
0	ftNoErr	
1	ftRejected	
2	ftFailed	
3	ftTimeOut	
4	ftTooManyRetry	
5	ftNotEnoughDSpace	

(continued)

Table D.3   Primary and secondary error codes *(continued)*.

Code	System Error	Description
6	ftRemoteCancel	
7	ftWrongFormat	
8	ftNoTools	
9	ftUserCancel	
10	ftNotSupported	
11	ftUnknownError	

Appendix E

Additional Resources

We've covered a lot of information in this book, but we may not have addressed some issues. An occasion may occur when this book may not be able to answer your question. This appendix provides information and resources where you can find additional help.

Online Help

One of the most useful, yet ignored, sources of assistance is the Mac OS online help. Help Center, the new online help found in Mac OS 9.1, has an interface that resembles a simple Web browser (the browser is called Help Viewer). Topics are arranged by category with links to other related documents. The online help is divided into at least three main categories: AppleScript, Mac, and QuickTime assistance (see Figure E.1). You may also see other help categories listed, such as DVD player, based on other hardware or software you have installed on your system. You can access system assistance directly by selecting Mac Help from the Help menu.

AppleGuide, the previous version of online help, is still supported in Mac OS 9.1 and is still used by developers. AppleGuide was well organized and could help even the most naïve computer user perform system tasks. Step-by-step instructions told you what to do and helpful screen hints were provided, such as a red marker circling an object or special highlighting within a menu. The AppleGuide window also stayed in the foreground, unlike other application windows, allowing you to continue following the steps without bringing the window to the front. Is the AppleGuide still included with the system? Not really. Many software applications did take advantage of AppleGuide and wrote their own help modules in this format. For this reason, the engine is still included in Mac OS 9.1. You may also be able to invoke AppleGuide within specific Control Panels. However, AppleGuide is no longer the default help method of OS 9.1.

One other help tool included with Mac OS 9.1 is Balloon Help. If you have a question about a menu option or button and a short definition will suffice, you can enable

Figure E.1   The Help Center.

Balloon Help by selecting it from the Help menu. When Balloon Help is active, you will see small balloons containing text that appear next to balloon-sensitive items. For example, if you enable Balloon Help within the Finder and move the mouse over the Edit menu, the following text will appear within a balloon: "Edit menu—Use this menu to undo an action, work with text and graphics, or set Finder preferences". Not all applications support Balloon Help and you may only be able to keep it active for a minute or two before it begins to irritate you. But in a pinch, it can help define a button or clarify a menu option, eliminating the necessity of launching the entire Help Center application. Figure E.2 shows Balloon Help active in the Apple Menu Options Control Panel.

TIP: *We could be cruel and let you suffer through the balloons a little longer, but we will put you out of your misery. To turn off Balloon Help, select Hide Balloons from the Help menu. (This menu option changes depending on the state of Balloon Help, allowing you to hide balloons when they are active or show balloons when they are inactive.)*

One final note about online help: Most applications—including Microsoft software programs—place their versions of online help under the Help menu. Microsoft has its own help method, as do many other packages. However, you may see the odd application that places its help files in a different location, such

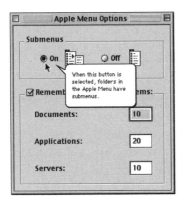

Figure E.2   Balloon Help active in the Apple Menu Options Control Panel.

as under the Apple menu or within the About This Application window. You may even find that help is a totally separate application that you will need to launch. Before you begin using a software application, locate its help documentation. Then use it; you might save valuable time.

Web Sites

The Internet contains a lot of good information. Whether it is the Tech Info library from Apple or the Info-mac shareware archives at MIT, sites are available that can answer your question or provide software to fix your problem. The one downside of the Web (and it's a big one) is that you may not know the reliability of the site. When was the last time it was updated? How knowledgeable is the author? Is this legal? We'll list some of the best sites available and a description of their contents. However, links die daily and we can't guarantee that these addresses will still be active. If you should find that the information listed is not at the address provided, use your favorite Web search engine to see if the site has relocated or if another Web page can meet your needs. Also, while we've tried to list a wide variety of sites, you'll find that many of these pages contain links to other great Macintosh sites.

Apple

All of these sites are supported and maintained by Apple Computer:

- **http://til.info.apple.com**—The Technical Information Library for Apple. This site is constantly changing to include new and old technical information for Mac computers. If you provide support for Macs you should bookmark this site.

- **http://support.info.apple.com/info.apple.com/manuals/manuals.taf**— The Product Manual Archive. You can locate and browse the user manual for many Apple products from this site (if you don't enter a search string, the results will list all manuals available online).

- **http://support.info.apple.com/info.apple.com/te/te.taf**—AppleCare Product Support. This site is an excellent starting point for several categories of support pages, including the Apple Spec database, Printers & Imaging, and basic troubleshooting.

- **http://asu.info.apple.com**—Apple Software Downloads. This is a software archive site containing software utilities and updates for Macintosh computers as well as some PC files. Archives of older Macintosh operating systems are also available to download freely.

- **http://mirror.apple.com**—The Apple Mirror software site. Mirrors of popular software archives are contained here on a very fast server.

- **www.apple.com/documents/publications.html**—Apple Online Publications. This page includes links to online publications both by and relating to Apple computing.

- **www.macsoftware.apple.com**—Macintosh Products Guide. This is a searchable database of over 18,000 hardware and software products for the Macintosh.

- **www.apple.com/developer/**—Apple Developer Connection. The Web site devoted to Macintosh developers.

- **www.apple.com/powerbook/**—Apple's resource page for PowerBook users.

- **www.apple.com/applescript/**—Apple's online resource for AppleScript programmers. This site contains links to online manuals as well as AppleScript tutorials.

- **http://store.apple.com**—Apple's online store. You can purchase hardware and software for personal, professional, or educational purposes.

News and Publications

If you want to find out what's happening in the world of Macintosh, consult these sites:

- **www.macsurfer.com**—*MacSurfer*. This site provides an overview of several popular Macintosh news pages on a daily basis. It's a site you should bookmark.

- **www.tidbits.com**—*Tidbits*. This is one of the original and best online Macintosh magazines.

- **www.macintouch.com**—*MacInTouch*. This is Ric Ford's Macintosh site. (Ric Ford is a Macintosh guru.) You can find reliable technical information and late-breaking information as well as links for other Macintosh sites.

- **www.zdnet.com/zdnn/mac/**—*ZDNet Apple/Mac.* Ziff Davis, the publishers of *MacWorld,* have an online site that includes news and information, software, help, and even investing information.

- **www.macaddict.com**—*MacAddict.* This is the online version of this popular Macintosh magazine.

- **www.macnn.com**—*Macintosh News Network.* This is an excellent site for tips, information, and sneak previews of upcoming software releases.

- **www.maccentral.com**—*MacCentral.* Check this site for reviews and tips for Macintosh software and hardware.

- **macworld.zdnet.com**—*Macworld.* This is the online version of the popular *Macworld* magazine.

- **macweek.zdnet.com**—*MacWEEK.* This is an online Macintosh magazine.

- **www.mactech.com**—MacTech. The MacTech site contains technical and developer information.

- **www.machome.com**—*MacHome.* The online version of the *MacHome* magazine is geared toward the home user, but its news information is updated hourly, which is beneficial to any Mac user.

- **http://mactoday.com**—Mac Today. This site is geared toward graphic designers who use the Macintosh.

- **www.mosr.com**—Mac OS Rumors. This site is not always right, but it is accurate a fair amount of time and is a good place to check if you are interested in the bleeding edge of Mac information.

- **www.applelinks.com**—The Ultimate Macintosh Resource. Look here for news, analysis, and resources for the Mac.

- **http://dealmac.com**—Macintosh Deals. This site locates the best deals on Macintosh systems, hardware, and software.

- **www.macledge.com**—MacGamer's Ledge. If you are a gamer, this site can help you find the latest information on games for the Macintosh.

- **www.appleturns.com**—As the Apple Turns. If you are looking for a little levity in your Macintosh reading, this site is for you. It features speculation, guesswork, and fabrication regarding the world of Macintosh.

Software

These addresses link to Macintosh software archives, including freeware, shareware, and demo software:

- **http://hyperarchive.lcs.mit.edu/HyperArchive.html**—A search facility for the Info-Mac software archive. This is one of the oldest and best software archives on the Internet.

- **http://download.cnet.com** and **http://shareware.cnet.com**—CNet software archive. This is a huge repository of software maintained by CNet.

- **www.macdownload.com**—Ziff Davis Macintosh software archive. This is a searchable Macintosh software archive.

- **www.tucows.com**—Tucows. This is a comprehensive Internet software archive.

- **www.macwindows.com**—MacWindows. This is a great site for Mac and Windows compatibility.

- **www.pixelfoundry.com**—The Pixel Foundry. This is a great graphics design archive and includes Kai's power tips and tricks.

- **www.insanely-great.com**—Insanely Great Mac. This is a diverse Web page with software downloads, reviews, and links to other great Mac sites.

- **http://mc04.equinox.net/informinit**—The Mac Pruning Pages and InformINIT. This is an excellent resource for finding out exactly the function of an extension or Control Panel.

- **www.powerbook.org/army/CSM/csm.html**—CSM Collection. This is a collection of control strip additions (it's also a PowerBook resource).

- **www.versiontracker.com**—VersionTracker. This is an excellent tool to keep you up-to-date on the latest versions of popular utilities.

- **www.kaleidoscope.net/greg/**—Greg's Shareware. Greg Landweber has written several Macintosh utilities including Aaron and Kaleidoscope, Control Panels that allowed the Mac user interface to be customized.

Hardware

These sites are geared to hardware solutions (although software may be referenced):

- **www.xlr8yourmac.com**—Accelerate Your Mac. Use this site as a reference for hardware information and tips to increase Mac performance.

- **www.everymac.com**—Every Mac. This detailed Web site contains information on every Macintosh and Mac compatible in the world.

- **www.macspeedzone.com**—MacSpeedZone. This site is *the* resource for CPU clock speeds as well as upcoming chip information.

- **www.ogrady.com**—O'Grady's PowerPage. This Web site is devoted to information about the Macintosh PowerBook.

iMac

These links provide information about the iMac, Apple's consumer Internet computer:

- **www.iMac2Day.com**—iMac2Day. This site provides information about the iMac computer, including USB peripherals.

- **www.theimac.com**—The iMac. This site provides information about the iMac.

Repair

Use these sites to help repair some common Macintosh problems:

- **www.macfixit.com**—MacFixIt. This is an excellent resource for fixing problems—both hardware and software related—on your Macintosh.

- **www.academ.com/info/macintosh/**—The Macintosh Battery Web Page. This site provides complete information and directions to handle almost any battery problem that you may encounter.

Mailing Lists

Mailing lists are excellent sources of information, and they have an advantage over Web pages. You don't have to visit a page to get information; it's delivered to your email account. Mailing lists also provide you the opportunity to get help from other knowledgeable Mac users (many of whom live for the opportunity to either help a user in need or show off their superior knowledge):

- **http://support.info.apple.com/support/supportoptions/lists.html**—This Web page allows you to subscribe to several mailing lists sponsored by Apple.

- **info-mac-on@roundtuit.com**—Subscribe to the Info-Mac digest. Send a message to **info-mac-on@roundtuit.com** and in the body of the message type "subscribe-info-mac".

- **Majordomo@cc.gatech.edu**—Mac Wizards (post questions for difficult problems and receive an answer in about a day). Send an email to **Majordomo@cc.gatech.edu** and in the body of the message type "subscribe mac-wizard *YOUR NAME*".

- **LISTSERV@LISTSERV.UTA.EDU**—IO MUG (a worldwide Mac Users Group). Send a message to **listserv@listserv.uta.edu** and in the body of the message type "subscribe IO-MUG *YOUR NAME*".

- **lyris@clio.lyris.net**—MAC-L (a mailing list for discussing Mac issues and information). Send a message to **lyris@clio.lyris.net** and in the body of the message type "subscribe Mac-L *YOUR NAME*".

- **majordomo@r8ix.com**—MacTalk (a mailing list geared toward advanced topics; "newbies" are discouraged). Go to **www.r8ix.com/lists.html** or send a message to **majordomo@r8ix.com** and in the body of the message type "subscribe MacTalk *YOUR NAME*".

- **http://emod.starnine.com/list-maintenance/Address-List-Editor.html**—Mailing lists for Macintosh Webmasters who use WebSTAR software to run Macintosh Web servers.

- **www.lists.apple.com**—This site has an index of many mailing lists either run by Apple or discussing Apple hardware or software. There are literally hundreds of mailing lists that may discuss a topic of interest to you.

Newsgroups

Newsgroups are discussion boards. Users post messages, which are freely viewable by other newsgroup users. Most of these newsgroups are in a hierarchy that is accepted by most news servers. The **comp** area of Usenet (the name of the collection of these newsgroups) is devoted to computing discussions. These groups discuss Macintosh issues, both software- and hardware-related. You must use special software applications called *newsreaders* to view these groups and your ISP must have access to or maintain its own news server. You can download newsreaders from software archives. The newsgroups are:

- **comp.binaries.mac**—Macintosh software encoded in binary (moderated).

- **comp.sources.mac**—Software for the Mac (moderated).

- **comp.sys.mac.advocacy**—The Macintosh computer, compared to other platforms.

- **comp.sys.mac.announce**—Announcements for Mac users (moderated).

- **comp.sys.mac.apps**—Macintosh applications.

- **comp.sys.mac.comm**—Macintosh communications.

- **comp.sys.mac.databases**—Macintosh database systems.

- **comp.sys.mac.digest**—Macintosh information and uses, but no programs (moderated).

- **comp.sys.mac.games**—Games on the Macintosh (a large hierarchy exists within the **mac.games** newsgroups).

- **comp.sys.mac.graphics**—Macintosh graphics issues.

- **comp.sys.mac.hardware**—Macintosh hardware issues (a hierarchy exists within the **mac.hardware** group that discusses particular hardware issues).

- **comp.sys.mac.hypercard**—Macintosh Hypercard information and discussion.

- **comp.sys.mac.misc**—General discussions about the Mac.
- **comp.sys.mac.portables**—Discussion about Mac portables.
- **comp.sys.mac.printing**—Mac printing issues.
- **comp.sys.mac.programmer**—Apple programming (a large hierarchy exists under **mac.programmer** to discuss programming specifics).
- **comp.sys.mac.scitech**—Scientific and technical Macintosh uses.
- **comp.sys.mac.system**—Macintosh system software.
- **comp.sys.mac.wanted**—Items wanted for the Mac.
- **misc.forsale.computers.mac**—Macintosh-related computer items for sale.

User Groups

User groups are groups of people who join together to discuss a particular application, platform, or function (such as Web servers). Hundreds of Mac user groups (MUGs) exist; they usually abbreviate their names to the acronym *MUG (the star being replaced by their geographical location). For example, one of the more famous Mac user groups is the Los Angeles Mac Users Group (LAMUG).

If you would like to locate a user group near you, go to **www.apple.com/usergroups/** for a listing of Mac users groups. If you don't find one for your area, maybe you should consider starting one.

Glossary

32-bit addressing—Allows a Mac to utilize more than 8MB of memory. This option must be checked within the Memory Control Panel for System 7.5.3 or earlier in order to efficiently use large memory blocks.

accelerator—Additional hardware that is installed when the existing software cannot perform particular functions at an acceptable speed. Graphic and float-point accelerators are the most common.

access privileges—The permissions a user is given to access a particular server, folder, or file.

ADB—(Apple Desktop Bus) The port on the Macintosh that is used to connect peripheral devices such as a keyboard or mouse.

Adobe Acrobat Reader—A free utility from Adobe that will view PDF files.

Adobe Type Manager—A commercial utility from Adobe that smoothes screen text.

AIFF—A window sound file format that is one of the most flexible formats found on the Internet.

Airport—A wireless technology supported by Apple that includes a base station that communicates with clients via specially installed hardware.

alias—A small file that references or points to an original file.

allow—To give access or rights (usually to a server).

analog—Data transmission format that uses wave (WAV) files.

animated GIF—A GIF file that contains a series of images that cause the GIF to appear as if it is moving and changing.

anonymous FTP—The ability to log on to a file archive server without an account.

anti-aliasing—The effect of removing jagged edges from images and fonts.

Appearance Control Panel—The Control Panel that manages the look and sound of the desktop interface.

Apple Computer Corp.—The company responsible for the Mac OS and the Macintosh computer.

Apple File Security—The file encryption software included with Mac OS 9.1.

Apple menu—A menu, represented by a small colorful apple, that can be customized by the user. Applications or aliases placed in the Apple menu will execute when selected and folders will show items.

AppleCD Audio Player—The desk accessory that controls audio CDs, including song order and volume.

AppleEvents—Interapplication communication on the same computer so that programs can exchange information.

AppleGuide—A component of the online help program that is activated by certain links. It takes the user step-by-step through various system tasks.

AppleScript—The scripting and programming utility included with the Mac OS that allows you to control functions within the system and certain applications.

AppleShare—Networking services included in the Mac OS that allow you to access other Macintosh computers, printers, and servers.

AppleTalk—A networking protocol developed and included in the Macintosh operating system.

AppleVision—Product description for the better Apple monitors.

Application—A file that when launched enables the user or computer to do a task.

Applications menu—The menu located in the top-right corner of the screen. The Applications menu lists all running applications and allows the user to hide particular programs. In Mac OS 9.1, the Applications menu can be torn off and dragged to any part of the Desktop.

Application switcher—The term for an Applications menu that has been torn from the menu bar and placed on the Desktop.

ARA—(Apple Remote Access) The modem software that allows a Macintosh to access other Macintosh computers remotely.

ASCII—(American Standard Code for Information Interchange) The standard character set for plain text files.

Assistants—Programs included with Mac OS 9.1 that automate the system and Internet configuration.

AVI—(Audio Video Interleave) An audio and video compression format for the Windows operating system.

background application—An application that launches and runs in the background without interfering with applications running in the foreground.

backwards compatibility—An application's ability to manage data from a previous version of the software.

Balloon Help—The component of the online Help application that provides quick descriptions of particular icons or menus in the format of speech balloons.

bandwidth—The number of packets of data that can pass through a network simultaneously.

base directory—A Web server's default directory; also called the root directory.

BBEdit—A text editor from Bare Bones Software that includes HTML and programming components.

binary—The primary building block for the storage of data; data is represented as a series of ones and zeros.

BinHex—A method of encoding files, especially mail attachments. Used most often with Macintosh files.

bitmap—A method of representing an image or font by filling squares or pixels. This often results in an image or font with jagged edges. This was the format used in the early days of computing for images as well as printing until PostScript was released.

Bookmarks—Netscape Navigator term for a list of sites that a user either frequently visits or wants to remember as a reference. Internet Explorer refers to this list as *Favorites*.

browser cache—The amount of hard disk space reserved for storing images, text, and visited links when using a Web browser. Caching is used to decrease the time it takes to load a Web page.

buffer—A portion of memory reserved for storing data.

Glossary

buttons—A preference within the Mac OS that changes the icons to buttons, allowing one-click launching or opening of documents, applications, or media.

CarbonLib—The library that allows developers to write software compatible with Mac OS 8, 9, and X with minimal effort.

CD-R—A compact disc on which data can be written if the user has the appropriate drive.

CD-ROM—A compact disc that can store large amounts of data and is read-only, thus protecting the contents from inappropriate changes. Most software is released on CD-ROM.

cdevs—A Control Panel device. This is the creator code for a file.

CGI—(Common Gateway Interface) A standard for sending data from a Web server to another application.

Chooser—A utility found under the Apple menu that allows a user to access other computers or printers.

CISC—(Complex Instruction Set Computer) A chip that stores a large variety of complex instructions. This format of processing is found in the Motorola 68040 and Intel X86 and Pentium chips.

clean install—The act of installing a new system folder rather than updating an existing one. If a user is having problems attempting to update a system, you may want to perform a clean installation of the operating system.

client—A computer that requests information or services from another computer, usually a server.

client/server—The relationship between computers that are requesting services of each other.

clipboard—The temporary buffer that stores information that has been copied or cut and saves it until new information is placed on the clipboard or the computer is turned off or restarted.

clipping—A file containing information that has been selected and dragged to a different location. The user can then drag the icon of the clipping into a new document or application. Not all applications support clippings.

close box—The small box on the top-left corner of a window in Mac OS 9.1 that will close the window.

CMYK—(Cyan Magenta Yellow Black) The system used by printers to produce color output. The K in black was used so as not to confuse users with the B in RGB (which stands for blue).

collapse box—The small box in the top right corner of a window that hides the window contents and displays only the title bar.

Color Picker—Launched when a user selects Other from a color listing menu. Color Picker contains several ways to choose custom colors.

ColorSync—The software used by Apple to match the color on a monitor screen with the color output of a printer. Because the two systems use different methods for color reproduction, the results often do not match. ColorSync helps reduce color conflict.

Command key—The key located next to the space bar on most Macintosh keyboards, denoted by the ⌘ and ⌘ symbols and used heavily in keyboard shortcut combinations (example: Command+Q = quit).

comments—Additional information about a file or folder that is entered and accessed by selecting Get Info from the File menu while the user is operating within the Finder.

compression—The method or algorithm of reorganizing the data bit structure of a file to shrink its size. This is used to save disk space or reduce file transmission.

computer name—The name a computer will broadcast over an AppleTalk network. It is entered in the File Sharing Control Panel.

Conseil Europeen pour la Recherche Nucleaire (CERN)—The European Laboratory for Particle Physics where the World Wide Web was developed.

contextual menu—A menu that is accessed by holding down the Control key and clicking the mouse. Depending upon the application or view, the menu may have different options. Not all applications support contextual menus.

Control Panels—A collection of customizable Extensions that control the function or look of the system.

Control Strip—A small strip, usually located at the bottom of the screen, that contains buttons for quick access to different applications. Most of the buttons access Control Panels. If the strip is not visible, the user may need to go to the Control Strip Control Panel to make it visible.

convergence—The overlapping of red, green, and blue signals to produce a sharp image. If convergence is off, monitor output appears blurred or the user may see rainbow effects around the edges of images on the screen.

Crayon Picker—A method of selecting colors via crayon images. Crayon picker is found when the user accesses the color picker application by electing to choose a color.

creator code—A four-digit identification that indicates what application created the file. This code can be used while conducting searches with the Sherlock 2 utility.

cursor—A graphical representation on screen, usually in the shape of an arrow, that indicates the active selection point. The cursor can also be in the shape of a watch, counting hand, or insertion point.

daemon—An application that lies dormant until the conditions are met that cause it to execute or become active.

data fork—The part of a file that contains the file's contents. Depending upon the file type, the data fork can be read on multiple platforms.

decompression—The act of removing compression information, allowing the file to expand to its original state and size.

dedicated server—A computer reserved for specific server applications. A dedicated server should not double as a workstation.

defragmentation—The act of repairing and optimizing a disk by rearranging the files to remove the gaps between files.

degauss—The act of correcting monitor screen distortions caused by magnetic interference from other devices, including monitors placed too close together, left on for a long period of time, or moved while powered up. Newer monitors degauss automatically when they are turned off and on while older monitors have a switch in the back usually located next to the power button.

desk accessories—Utilities included in the Mac OS that perform simple system functions. Examples of desk accessories are the Calculator, Stickies, or Scrapbook. Desk accessories are usually found on the Apple menu.

Desktop—The background area where hard drives, removable media, and the Trash can are displayed, as well as any other icons the user places on it. The Finder is responsible for displaying the Desktop and its contents.

Desktop printing—The method of placing printer icons on the Desktop and allowing the user to access the printer immediately for print job information as well as switch to other printers that have been selected in the Chooser.

disk cache—A portion of RAM allocated to store frequently used commands, information, or functions. In Mac OS 9.1, the disk cache is set in the Memory Control Panel.

Disk First Aid—An Apple utility that performs checks on media including hard drives, Zip disks, and floppies. Disk First Aid can repair many problems with disks, but there are problems that are beyond its capability. In those cases, a third-party utility such as TechTool Pro or Norton's Disk Doctor may be able to fix the problem.

DHCP—(Dynamic Host Configuration Protocol) The method by which a server automatically grants an IP number to a requesting client so the client can access the Internet.

DNS—(Domain Name System) A system whereby Internet addresses can have user-friendly names instead of a number sequence (example: 123.45.67.89 could now be my.computer.domain.com).

DOS—(Disk Operating System) The familiar name for the command-line operating system used to operate PCs. There are various versions of DOS, including MS-DOS, PC-DOS, and others.

dotted octet—The naming convention for IP numbers represented by four groups of numbers containing one, two, or three numbers.

double scroll arrows—A window feature in Mac OS 9.1 that can place an up and down scroll arrow together at the bottom of a scroll bar pane.

drag and drop—The ability to select an object, drag it, and drop it onto a new location such as a new folder or disk.

drag lock—The ability to view hidden areas of the window by holding down the Control key, grabbing an area of the window, and moving the entire pane.

Drive Setup—A utility released by Apple for formatting and partitioning hard drives. Later versions of Drive Setup include the ability to format a disk with the Macintosh Extended or Standard format.

drivers—Programs that run in the system and enable the computer to perform functions as well as talk to peripheral devices such as printers, scanners, and external drives.

droplets—Mini-applications created in AppleScript that perform certain functions.

DVD-ROM—The next generation in removable optical disc media. DVD-ROMs can hold more than double the capacity of a CD-ROM.

Dynamic Data Exchange—The communication protocol in a client/server model. This is often used in the Windows operating system.

Easy Access Control Panel—A Control Panel that contains options for customizing the Mac OS for users with special needs.

Easy Open Control Panel—Also known as Mac OS Easy Open. In OS 8.5, this Control Panel was combined with PC Exchange to form the File Exchange Control Panel.

Glossary

email—The generic term for the electronic exchange of messages.

email address—The unique address that allows electronic messages to be sent from one computer to another.

Empty Trash—Found under the Special menu. When selected, this command empties the contents of the Trash can. Files within the Trash can are not deleted until Empty Trash is selected.

emulator—An application that runs one environment on top of another. Macs utilize emulator programs to run Windows, DOS, and Unix.

Energy Saver Control Panel—The Control Panel that configures when the computer will put the system to sleep. Energy Saver also has settings for scheduling routine shut down and start up of the system.

Erase Disk—Found under the Special menu. When selected, this command will reformat whatever media is selected.

Ethernet—Local area network that transfers data via network protocols, including NetBEUI, IPX/SPX, AppleTalk, and TCP/IP.

Eudora—A popular Internet email package that utilizes the POP and IMAP protocols.

extended Desktop—A method of increasing Desktop space by using two monitors instead of one. This feature requires additional hardware to be installed.

Extensions—Programs that increase the functionality or repair or improve parts of the Mac OS.

Extensions Manager Control Panel—A Control Panel that manages the loading and unloading of Control Panels, Extensions, and startup and shutdown items.

FAT—(File Allocation Table) The database on a PC disk that keeps information on all files saved on the disk.

Favorites—In Mac OS 9.1, the list of commonly accessed servers and Web sites. This term is also used in Internet Explorer for remembered Web sites.

Fetch—The Macintosh FTP tool from Dartmouth that allows users to retrieve from and place files on file archives.

File Exchange Control Panel—The Control Panel that controls file translation and Extension mapping.

file sharing—Allows other Macintosh computers to access the user's computer. File sharing is activated from the File Sharing Control Panel and can use both AppleTalk and TCP/IP protocols.

Glossary

Find By Content—A feature of the Sherlock 2 utility included in Mac OS 9.1 that allows the searching of file contents. Find By Content can also index drives for routine searching.

Finder—The part of the system that opens and closes windows, displays the Desktop, and keeps a directory of the files on a disk.

FireWire—A new high-speed serial bus that supports the transfer of large amounts of data. FireWire supports a wide range of devices including digital video cameras and hard drives.

firewall—The act of defending a network or computer from outside hackers. Firewalls can also refer to a configuration to limit a user's access to the Internet from within a network.

floppy diskette—Refers to the three and one quarter inch diskettes. Floppy diskettes can be double or high density.

folder—An item used to organize files and data. Folders take up no drive space, but act as containers and dividers for other files.

fonts—A set of images representing letters in a character set.

FontSync—Software included with Mac OS 9.1 that allows you to synchronize the fonts in a document with the fonts on the computer where the document will be printed.

Force Quit—The act of forcing an application that has ceased to respond to shut down.

form—A Web page with fields that allow a user to input information to the server.

fragmentation—Gaps in a drive's storage system. Fragmentation is caused by saving, changing, and deleting files.

frames—Web pages that are written to display several HTML files at once.

freeware—Software that is available without charge. Freeware is usually found at public file archive sites such as **www.macdownload.com**.

FTP—(File Transfer Protocol) The method used for transferring files over the Internet.

Game Sprocket—Technology created for developers to make game development easier for the Mac.

gateway—A device that connects networks using different protocols.

Glossary

Geometry—The section of the Monitors Control Panel that controls advanced features of AppleVision monitors.

Get Info—Provides information about a selected object, including the size, date created and modified, and path.

GIF—(Graphics Interchange Format) The image compression method developed by CompuServe; denoted by the .GIF extension.

Gopher—A document retrieval system that has been largely superseded by the World Wide Web.

graphing calculator—A desk accessory included with Mac OS 9.1 that visually displays mathematical formulas and equations.

grid spacing—The ability to activate an invisible grid within Finder. Grid spacing grabs icons and places them in the appropriate space if the icon is moved.

Groups—A part of the File Sharing Control Panel that allows the creation of lists of approved users. The lists can then be selected when sharing an item.

GUI—(Graphical User Interface) This commonly refers to any operating system that utilizes images rather than a command line prompt.

hackers—People who attempt unauthorized and often illegal access to a server or system.

header—Information in an email message that includes the path of the message and special identifiers. Much of this information is hidden unless the user activates the option to view full headers.

Help Viewer—The online help system included with Mac OS 9.1. The Help Viewer now has a browser-like interface rather than relying completely on AppleGuide.

hierarchical submenus—Menus that will branch out from a menu selection and can often go for several layers. The Apple menu supports submenus.

home page—The main or index page at a Web site. Other pages at the site are accessed via links from the home page.

host—A machine that contains services it makes available to other computers.

hot swappable—The ability to switch hardware while the system is enabled. Several Apple PowerBooks have hot swappable CD and floppy drives. USB and FireWire devices are hot swappable.

Hot Sync—A feature of Mac OS 9 that allows the exchange of data between a Palm device and Mac OS 9.1.

HTML—(Hypertext Markup Language) The language used to write hypertext documents that can be displayed by Web browsers.

HTTP—(Hypertext Transfer Protocol) The method for transferring Web documents between servers and clients.

hub—A device that connects computers to a network.

hyperlink—Area of text within an HTML document that will access another document when clicked or selected.

icon—A graphic used to represent a file or document.

Image Capture Control Panel—A Control Panel in Mac OS 9.1 that allows you to download images from digital USB cameras.

image map—A graphic within a Web page with areas assigned to hyperlinks. When such an area is clicked, the user will be taken to another Web page.

IMAP—(Internet Message Access Protocol) Email protocol that allows a client to access mail stored on a server. IMAP differs from POP in that messages are stored on a server instead of locally.

inactive window—A window that is visible but in the background.

index—A file containing information about all the files on a volume. Indexing is used heavily in the Sherlock 2 utility when searching files by content.

infrared—A specialized technology that utilizes a frequency below visible light to transfer information.

INITs—Refers to Extensions and Control Panels that load within the system.

insertion point—The cursor commonly seen in word processing programs. It is sometimes referred to as the "I" bar because of its shape.

Internet—A collection of networks connected by routers. The Internet is made up of several layers.

Internet Control Panel—The Control Panel that houses user Internet preferences such as email address, SMTP server, and news host.

Internet Explorer—The Web browser released by Microsoft.

Internet Setup Utility—A program included with Mac OS 9.1 that asks basic questions of a user and uses the information gathered to configure the computer for Internet and network access.

Glossary

intranet—A private network accessible only by authorized users. An intranet may provide services similar to those found on the Internet to its users. Users may be segregated or disconnected from the Internet.

IP—(Internet Protocol) The Session layer of the TCP/IP protocol that routes data from its source to its destination.

IP address—The unique number assigned to a computer that is on the Internet. An IP address allows the computer to access other Internet services.

IP name—The user-friendly name that is bundled with the IP number.

IPX—(Internetwork Packet Exchange) A protocol used by Novell to provide clients with access to a server.

IrDA—(Infrared Data Association) The trade association that governs the industry standards for infrared data transmission.

IRTalk—The AppleTalk infrared data transmission protocol.

ISP—(Internet service provider) A company that provides Internet access to customers, usually for a fee.

Java applet—A portion of a World Wide Web document that performs simple Java actions. Most browsers restrict what Java applets can do for security reasons.

JavaScript—A programming language developed by Sun Microsystems that allows Web browsers to handle complex operations.

Jaz Drive—A removable media drive manufactured by Iomega that can handle cartridges in one and two gigabyte sizes.

JPEG—(Joint Photographic Experts Group). An algorithm that compresses images. It is the graphic format of choice for detailed grayscale or color images such as photographs. It is not the best format for cartoon or black-and-white images (GIF is a better option).

Kaleidoscope—A third-party utility that provides a way to change the look of the Mac OS. Some kaleidoscope themes will work with Mac OS 9.1.

Key Caps—A desk accessory that provides a keyboard-like interface for seeing all characters in a font set.

keychain—A feature of Mac OS 9.1 that allows multiple logins and passwords to be stored under a single password.

L2 cache—A protected area of memory that increases the system performance.

label—An option that allows you to assign a color and organizational name to an icon. The label names and colors can be customized.

LAN—(local area network) A small network of computers.

LaserWriter Bridge—An Apple utility that allows a computer with a locally attached LaserWriter to still run the AppleTalk protocol.

Launcher Control Panel—A Control Panel that contains buttons for single-click launching of programs. The launcher window can be customized by the user.

LocalTalk—An implementation of AppleTalk that allows Macintosh computers and printers to communicate.

Location Manager Control Panel—A Control Panel that allows a user to keep different network configurations based upon his or her location. Examples would include a profile for work using an assigned IP address and remote access at home using an Internet service provider.

locked file—A file that has the Lock option enabled from the Get Info window.

low level format—A type of format that completely wipes all data from a disk. A low level format also takes much longer than a standard format.

Mac clone—A computer that is capable of running the Mac OS but is not a Macintosh computer.

Mac OS Extended—The file format released with Mac OS 8.1 that increases the allocation bits to allow accurate representation of file size.

Mac OS Standard—The file allocation format on Macintosh disks prior to Mac OS 8.1. It allocated fewer bits and resulted in larger files and wasted disk space.

MacBinary—A method of file compression that results in a smaller file size than other compression methods.

Macintosh—The name given for the computer models released from the Apple Corporation.

Macintosh Manager—A software utility installed on a Macintosh server that can work in conjunction with Multiple Users to manage Macintosh clients over the network.

MacsBug—A debugging utility that allows the user to accurately determine what caused a system or application crash.

MacTCP—The classic TCP/IP Control Panel that can be configured for Internet access.

Glossary

marquee selection—The term used to describe the box that appears within Finder when the mouse button is held down to perform a click and drag function. Within certain applications such as Photoshop, the selection box appears to move in a marquee fashion.

memory—The colloquial term for RAM. Memory is measured in megabytes.

memory allocation—The amount of memory an application is allowed to use. The allocation amount can be changed in the Get Info window.

Memory Manager Control Panel—The Control Panel that controls disk cache and virtual memory options as well as the size of a RAM disk.

memory protection—A system that prevents one failed process from corrupting an entire system. This will be a feature of Mac OS X.

Menu Blinking—When selected within the General Controls Control Panel, this option causes a menu item to flash several times to indicate that the command has been chosen.

microkernel—An operating system with smaller components that provides flexibility.

MIME—(Multipurpose Internet Mail Extensions) A method of encoding email attachments.

MkLinux—A Macintosh-compatible version of Linux.

Monitor Calibration Assistant—A utility that will correctly configure and calibrate certain monitor models, including the AppleVision brand.

Mouse Keys—This option, set with the Easy Access Control Panel, allows the mouse to be controlled by keys rather than by physically dragging the mouse.

Motorola—The manufacturer of the RISC processor used in Power Macintosh computers.

MP3—A method of audio file compression that produces FM radio quality audio files using drastically reduced file sizes.

MPEG—(Motion Picture Experts Group) An organization, as well as a video and audio file format.

MRJ—(Macintosh Runtime for Java) A component of the operating system that allows the execution of Java applets and applications.

multimedia—Files and applications that contain elements of media including sound and graphics.

Glossary

Multiple Users Control Panel—A Control Panel that allows the Macintosh computer to be shared among multiple users. User accounts can have varying levels of access to the computer.

multitasking—The ability of the operating system to run and work with several applications at once.

native applications—Used to refer to applications that contain code specifically written for the Power Macintosh.

navigational services—The Open and Save dialog boxes in Mac OS 9.1. These include server access and a favorites list.

NetBoot—The environment created between a client and a Mac OS X server that allows the client to retrieve the system and applications from the server rather than the internal hard drive. Also known as Net Boot.

Netscape Communicator—The Web browser from Netscape Corp.

network—The generic term used to refer to computers that are connected together and that communicate with each other.

Network Assistant—The administrative software program that can remotely manage Macintosh computers. The client software is included with Mac OS 9.1 but must be managed by a central desktop with the management software installed.

Network Browser—The utility included in Mac OS 9.1 that allows users to browse the network in the same way that they browse their hard drive. Users can connect to servers from within the browser as well as keep a list of favorite servers.

network identity—A method for giving network devices unique names including IP numbers and Ethernet numbers.

NeXT—The computer developed by the NeXT Corporation that ran the OpenStep operating system. The OpenStep technology was purchased by Apple and developed as part of the Mac OS X operating system.

newsgroup—A discussion forum on Usenet where messages are posted and accessed.

NIC—(Network Interface Card) The card that allows a computer to connect to a network. NICs usually run the Ethernet protocol.

node—A computer or device on a network.

Norton Utilities—A third-party disk management utility from Symantec that can perform disk defragmentation and recover deleted files.

Glossary

Novell—The makers of NetWare, a popular server operating system.

NTP Time Servers—(Network Time Protocol Time Servers) Publicly accessible servers that can be used to keep the system clock accurate. The servers are selected in the Date and Time Control Panel.

OLE—(Object Linking and Embedding) Utilized heavily with Microsoft products, it allows applications to share and link information with documents.

Open Transport—The networking protocol currently used by Mac OS 9.1. Open Transport includes Ethernet and modem connectivity functions.

OpenGL—The programming interface developed by Sun and Apple that enhances video and game playing on the Macintosh.

OpenStep—The operating system purchased by Apple and incorporated into the Rhapsody operating system.

OS/2—The 32-bit operating system released from IBM. OS/2, also called Warp, is no longer in production.

Owner Name—The setting within the File Sharing Control Panel that determines the owner login account.

packet—A unit of data that is transferred across a network.

panels—A level of access on a shared Macintosh that limits access to the Finder, which is viewed as large folders or "panels." It is the most restrictive type of multiple user setting.

Pantone—A commercial color indexing system that allows the precise reproduction of particular colors. Pantone is used in the printing process.

PC coprocessor card—A third-party card that allows a Macintosh computer to simultaneously run a PC operating system such as Linux, Windows, and DOS.

PC disk—A diskette that has been formatted for a PC.

PC Exchange—The portion of the File Exchange Control Panel that allows PC disks to be mounted within the Mac OS desktop.

PCI card—(Peripheral Component Interconnect) A hardware device that plugs into the PCI slot on mobile computers. Common PCI cards are modem and Ethernet devices.

PDD files—Printer description documents that contain information about certain printers. Without the correct PDD file, the user cannot take advantage of the special functions of the printer.

PDF File—(Portable Document Format) Files that have been created using Adobe Acrobat. They can be viewed using Adobe Acrobat Reader.

PICT—An Apple graphics format that can be opened by most image editing applications as well as by SimpleText.

plain text—Files that contain only ASCII characters.

platform—The type of operating system that runs upon a computer.

plug-in—Special applications that run within a Web browser and allow special functions, including streaming video and QuickTime movies, to run.

POP—(Post Office Protocol) An email protocol that keeps mail on a server until the user accesses the mail via a POP email client. Mail is moved to the local machine and managed unless the user chooses to keep a copy on the server.

pop-up menu—A menu whose contents are viewable only if the user clicks on the menu.

PostScript—A technology developed by Adobe that radically improved printing. Prior to PostScript, printed images and especially fonts contained jagged edges. PostScript enables the smooth printing of text as well as images.

Power Macintosh—The line of Macintosh computers using the RISC processor (also known as the PowerPC chip).

PowerBook—The line of portable computers from Apple.

PowerPC—Computers that use a RISC processor.

PPP—(Point to Point Protocol) Network protocol used over a modem line that allows the computer to behave as if it was connected to the Internet.

PRAM—(Parameter RAM) An area of memory in a Macintosh that stores system information, including the desktop pattern, screen resolution, and system alert sound, when the computer is not running.

pre-emptive multitasking—A method of multitasking wherein a component of the operating system determines the amount of access to the processor. Pre-emptive multitasking will be a feature of Mac OS X and is not currently implemented in Mac OS 9.1.

preferences—Files stored within the System Folder that contain settings for an application.

print queue—The holding space that lines up print jobs in order of print submission. The print jobs stay within the queue until the printer is ready to print the file.

Glossary

print spooling—The act of preparing and submitting a file to a printer device for printing.

PrintMonitor—The utility that is used to monitor the progress of print jobs. If the system is using desktop printing, then PrintMonitor is disabled.

Program Linking—A setting within the File Sharing Control Panel that allows other Macintosh computers to run applications from the host machine.

proportional scroll box—The tab within a scroll bar that changes size depending upon how much of the contents of the window are visible. Proportional scroll boxes or "thumb tabs" are a new feature of Mac OS 9.1.

protocol—A standard for the transmission of data over a network.

proxy server—A server that is configured to allow computers not on a particular network to access protected servers and information.

Put Away—The menu option under the File menu within the Finder that will dismount and eject a disk.

QuickDraw—The technology used by the Mac OS to draw the graphical user interface.

QuickTime—Apple's standard for video.

QuickTime VR—A function of QuickTime that allows a series of still images to be interfaced into a seamless picture creating the illusion of three-dimensional imaging.

RAM—(Random Access Memory) The hardware within the computer that stores the operating system as well as any information that is launched or input. This storage is temporary and the data input must be transferred to a storage device to be kept permanently.

RAM disk—A portion of the RAM set aside as a storage device. RAM disks are used most commonly on mobile computers to increase battery life.

recalibrate—A method for correcting and optimizing the color display of high-quality monitors.

remote access—A method used to access a server while not directly connected to it. Remote access most commonly refers to dialup access.

removable media—Any of the various storage media that are not installed and stored within the CPU. Removable media includes diskettes, Zip disks, Jaz disks, CD-ROMs, DVD-ROMs, and removable hard drives.

repeater—An unintelligent device that repeats any network signal it intercepts.

ResEdit—A utility used to edit the programming information in a file or application.

resize handle—The small box located at the bottom left of a window that allows the user to drag the window to the desired size.

resolution—The number of pixels displayed in an inch of screen area. The more pixels on the screen, the higher the resolution is—the Desktop is larger and icons become smaller.

resource fork—The part of a file that contains information relevant only to the Mac OS, such as the creator type and icon.

restart—The act of bringing the Mac OS down and relaunching it. Restart could also be called a warm reboot.

RGB—(Red Green Blue) The color system that is used for screen color reproduction.

RISC—(Reduced Instruction Set Computer) A processor that contains limited system instructions, allowing for faster computing with a cooler chip. RISC processors are used in the Power Macintosh and PowerPC computers.

router—A device that forwards network traffic between networks.

Scrapbook—A desk accessory that stores any information pasted into it, including text, images, and sound files.

script—A file that contains instructions for a system or application. When executed, the instructions within the script are performed.

Script Editor—The utility included with Mac OS 9.1 that allows you to create, write, and edit AppleScripts.

scroll arrow—Small tabs at the bottom of a scroll bar containing triangles that allow the navigation of a window when all of the content cannot be seen.

SCSI—(Small Computer System Interface) A small chain of devices that contain a unique number between zero and seven. SCSI devices include hard drives, scanners, Zip drives, and external hard drives.

SCSI ID conflict—A situation involving the devices on a SCSI chain where two devices have been assigned the same number.

search engine—A Web site that allows a user to search the Internet. These sites use different methods for searching and cataloging the World Wide Web.

Glossary

server—A computer that provides information or applications to clients running on other computers.

shared folder—A folder that has been configured to allow other computers on the network to access the contents of the folder.

shared libraries—Common code libraries shared by multiple applications, allowing programs to utilize the code without re-creating it.

shareware—Software that has been written by developers and released with the request for a nominal fee. Shareware programs either rely on the honor system or put limits within the application until the software has been purchased.

Sherlock 2—The search utility included with Mac OS 9.1 that can search volumes, file contents, and the Internet.

Show Original—A menu option within Finder under the File menu that shows the original document or file for an alias. The alias must be selected to run this menu option.

Simple Finder—A setting within the Finder preferences that displays only the basic menus in the Finder.

Simple Player—A sound and video playback utility.

SimpleText—The text editing application included on all Mac OS systems as well as installer programs. Files saved in SimpleText are in plain text format.

size box—The small box located at the bottom right of a window that allows the user to drag the window to the desired size.

sleep mode—The act of ceasing the activity of the system without shutting it down entirely. Sleep mode is used most often on mobile computers.

SLIP—(Serial Line Interface Protocol) A networking protocol used over modem connections.

Slow Keys—A setting in the Easy Access Control Panel that decreases the sensitivity of the keyboard, causing the computer to take longer to register a keystroke. This eliminates repeating characters for users with special needs.

SMTP gateway—(Simple Mail Transfer Protocol) A machine that processes email to be delivered to other mail systems.

sneakernet—Colloquial term that refers to the act of manually handing a file on diskette to another user.

SNMP—(Simple Network Management Protocol) The network management protocol included with Mac OS 9.1 that manages network devices in a simplified way.

SoftPC—The emulation software from Insignia that allows a user to run DOS from within the Mac OS.

Software Update Control Panel—The Control Panel included with Mac OS 9.1 that allows you to manually or automatically download and apply the latest system software updates.

speech—The ability of the Macintosh to speak or read information back to the user. With additional software, the user can speak commands to the computer.

Speech Manager Control Panel—The Control Panel that manages the settings for the Macintosh's speech abilities.

spring-loaded folders—A system function initiated during the act of moving or copying a file within Finder. During the dragging process, when the mouse is held over a folder or storage device for a small length of time, the folder will spontaneously open and the process can continue until the end of the hierarchy has been reached.

SSL—(Secure Sockets Layer) The protocol designed for the secure transfer of information between the client and server.

startup disk—The device selected to boot the computer.

Startup Disk Control Panel—The Control Panel that allows you to determine what device will be the startup disk.

Startup Items—Files or aliases that are placed in the Startup Items folder. These items launch when the system is started.

Stationary—A file format used for creating templates.

Stickies—A desk accessory that is a utility for storing text information in small colored windows. Information stored in Stickies is kept even when the application has been closed.

Sticky Keys—A setting in the Easy Access Control Panel that increases the sensitivity of the keyboard.

streaming—A method of distributing video and audio so that the user can begin listening to and viewing the file contents while the file is still downloading. Streaming is also used for live Web events so that the user maintains a constant connection with the multimedia server.

StuffIt—A utility from Aladdin software that can compress files so that the file is reduced in size.

StuffIt Expander—A free utility from Aladdin Software that decompresses files compressed with StuffIt, as well as those compressed using MacBinary, BinHex, and Compact Pro.

subnet mask—Used to identify the portion of the IP number that corresponds to the network address. Subnet masks are also determined by the class of the IP address.

suffix mapping—The act of programming the File Exchange Control Panel to open certain applications when files with a particular extension are opened.

SuperDisk—A USB drive from Imation that supports both traditional floppy disks and 120MB Superdisks.

SuperDrive—The floppy drive installed in most Macintosh and Mac clone computers. SuperDrives are characterized by their ability to eject a diskette without the use of an eject button.

syntax—The structure of the spelling and grammar in a scripting language. Proper syntax is required in order for the programming language to understand the request of the programmer.

System—The file that contains the resources necessary to run the computer and other applications.

System Folder—The folder on a startup disk that contains the information for launching the operating system as well as Extensions, preferences, fonts, and other components of the operating system.

system heap—An area of RAM set aside for components such as fonts and desk accessories.

system requirements—A list of system specifications that must be met before an application or program will run on a particular computer.

tags—Text enclosed in brackets in an HTML file that gives instructions to the browser for handling and displaying the file.

TCP/IP—(Transmission Control Protocol/Internet Protocol) The protocol used on Ethernet networks to transport and encapsulate data packets.

tear-away menu—A special function of the Applications menu that allows the user to drag it from the top-right corner to any location on the Desktop. The menu then becomes known as the Application Switcher.

TechTool—A commercial disk management utility from Micromat that can repair disks that are beyond the capability of Disk First Aid.

Telnet—An application that accesses a remote server and initiates a terminal connection.

templates—Specialized files that are saved with certain data intact but are protected so that the user is prompted to choose a different name for the file.

themes—A set of system appearance configurations. Mac OS 9.1 contains several ready-made themes, but additional themes can be created and saved.

TIFF—(Tagged Image File Format) An image file format commonly used on Windows computers.

Timbuktu—Commercial software that allows one computer to control another computer remotely.

title bar—The top portion of a window that contains the title of the disk or folder.

Token Ring—A local area network developed by IBM.

trackpad—A pointing device that moves the cursor around the screen by gliding a finger over the surface. Most PowerBooks contain a trackpad.

Trash—The container on the desktop that stores items dragged to it until they are removed or deleted.

TrueType—A font technology developed by Apple as an alternative to PostScript fonts.

Unix—A powerful and flexible operating system that includes the ability to be a server plus protected memory and a very stable environment.

URL—(Uniform Resource Locator) Used to specify the location of an object on the World Wide Web.

USB—(Universal Serial Bus) An interface or port that provides a method for connecting external devices to the Macintosh computer. USB differs from SCSI in that devices can be connected to USB ports while the system is still active. Newer Macintosh computers utilize USB ports for the keyboard and mouse as well as other peripheral devices as they become available.

USB Printer Sharing Control Panel—The Control Panel included with Mac OS 9.1 that allows you to share USB printers over a network.

Usenet—An organization of discussion areas organized into newsgroups. Messages are posted to Usenet groups and are available for anyone to read who has the appropriate software.

Glossary

User Mode—A menu option in certain Extensions, such as the TCP/IP Control Panel, that determines the type of information revealed in the Control Panel settings and whether the user can modify the information shown.

video mirroring—The act of displaying the same image or desktop on a computer with two monitors attached.

Video Player—A desk accessory that will display video and television images. Additional hardware must be installed to use this utility.

views—Different methods of displaying the information in a window. Folder contents can be viewed by such methods as by icon or list.

virtual memory—A part of the hard drive that is reserved as memory. It is often necessary to enable virtual memory for the system to function efficiently, although some programs such as game applications may generate errors when virtual memory is activated.

Virtual PC—Emulation software from Connectix that allows the Mac OS to run any application that will run on a CISC chip within the operating system in an application window.

volume—An area of a storage device that has been partitioned.

VRAM—(Video Random Access Memory) Memory allocated for the video operations of the system. Expanded VRAM allows a user to display thousands or millions of colors in multiple resolutions.

WAN—(wide area network) A large network that can contain smaller local area networks.

WAV—An audio file type used most often in the Windows operating system.

Web—Colloquial term used to describe the World Wide Web.

Web browser—An application used to retrieve content and information from the World Wide Web.

Web sharing—A function of the Mac OS that allows a user to set up a computer as a Web server.

Windows 95, 98, NT 4, 2000, Me—GUI operating systems developed and released by Microsoft. MS Windows and its different variations are the most popular operating systems running on computers today.

Windows NT/2000 Server—An installation of Windows that provides server access and applications for remote clients.

Glossary

WindowShade—The action of decreasing a window so that only the title bar is shown. This action can occur by either clicking the collapse box or double-clicking on the title bar.

WorldScript—Unifies script-specific behavior as defined by tables in the system resources.

WWW—(World Wide Web) The term for the network of computers sharing information via the HTTP protocol.

Zip drive—An external disk drive that uses 100MB to 250MB disks. Zip drives are manufactured by Iomega and can be installed internally or connected externally using SCSI or USB.

zones—The logical grouping of computers into small networks. AppleTalk zones are often determined by routers on the network.

zoom box—The small box in the top right of a window that expands the window to display as much of the contents as possible.

Glossary

Index

A

About This Computer, 43, 120–121, 486–487, 495–496
   memory, 162–163, 174–176, 489, 545
About This Macintosh. *See* About This Computer.
Accelerator cards, 107
Access privileges
   Multiple Users, in, 455–456, 466–467
   sharing files and folders, 339–342
Acme Contextual Menu Manager (CMM) Widgets, 416
Acrobat file, 248
ACTION Files, 102–104
ACTION GoMac, 57–58, 77–78, 502
Active Server Pages, 436
ActiveX, 435–436, 448
Activity Monitor, 486, 496–497
Administrator mode, 456, 471–472
Adobe Acrobat, 230, 546
Adobe Photoshop, 166, 202, 258, 263, 264, 269, 285, 319
Adobe PostScript, 229
ADSL (Asymmetric Digital Subscriber Line), 200, 325, 350, 354–355
After Dark, 476
AIFF, 263
Airport, 112, 127, 198, 353–354, 355, 370–371
Airport security, getting computers through, 209
Aladdin Systems, Inc., 299, 314, 410
Alarm system (PowerBook), 209
Aliases
   applications, launching, 25
   creating and using, 156–157, 543
   cursor with right arrow, 10–11
   double-clicking, 25
   finding the original, 543

   icons, 8–9, 100
   selecting new original, 544
   Startup Items folder, 35, 540
   Tilery program, 487–488, 499
Alpha software applications, 51
America Online, 280, 348
Analog telephone lines, 201
Anarchie, 348
Anderson, Glen, 379
Animator applet, 437–438
Anonymous FTP, 382
AntiVirus, Norton, 524
Apache Web server, 377, 378
AppDisk, 183
Appearance
   configuration options, 56, 79
   custom appearances, 11–12
   defined, 16
   themes, 16, 79
Appearance Control Panel, 78–82
   navigational services, 62
   theme views, changing, 16–17
Appearance Manager, 11
Apple
   beta version, 109
   DVD Software, 112
   menu. *See* Apple menu.
   microphone, 257
   updates, 109
Apple Applet Runner, 410, 434, 440, 444–446
Apple Attachment Unit Interface (AAUI) port, 351
Apple Data Detectors, 415
Apple DVD Player, 257, 289–291
Apple File Exchange, 297
Apple Internet Mail Server (AIMS), 379
Apple IR File Exchange, 200
Apple IrDA protocol, 200
Apple menu. *See also* Menus.

P

Q

Coriolis Creative Professional Press Titles

Illustrator® 9 Visual Insight

By T. Michael Clark

ISBN: 1-57610-749-3 • $24.99 U.S. • $37.99 CANADA • 256 pages • Available Now

Illustrator® 9 Visual Insight helps you quickly grasp this powerful illustration software to create eye-catching illustrations. Learn the basic features and drawing techniques of Illustrator using layers, masks, filters, and actions, and create illustration for the Web. Then use those basics in real-world projects, such as product brochures, posters, and Web-site interfaces.

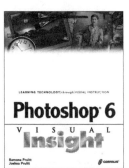

Photoshop® 6 Visual Insight

By Ramona Pruitt and Joshua Pruitt

ISBN: 1-57610-747-7 • $29.99 U.S. • $44.99 CANADA • 416 pages • Available Now

Learn Photoshop®'s basic features, including layering, masks, and paths, as well as intermediate functions, such as Web graphics, filters, and actions. In addition, this book teaches the most useful Photoshop techniques and allows readers to use these in real-world projects, such as repairing images, eliminating red eye, creating type effects, developing Web elements, and more.

Illustrator® 9 f/x and Design

By Sherry London

ISBN: 1-57610-750-7 • $49.99 U.S. • $74.99 CANADA • 560 pages with CD-ROM • Available Now

Provides new information and projects on styles and effects, how to integrate with Web products, as well as other enhanced features. With real-world projects, readers learn firsthand how to create intricate illustrations and compositing techniques. Readers also learn how to work seamlessly between Illustrator® and Photoshop®.

Flash™ ActionScript f/x and Design

By Bill Sanders

ISBN: 1-57610-821-X • $44.99 U.S. • $67.99 CANADA • 344 pages with CD-ROM • Available Now

Get the most out of Flash™ 5 using ActionScript. ActionScript for Flash 5 is a quantum leap from previous versions of this scripting language for Flash. Using ActionScript, the developer can add interactive functionality like never before. All major concepts in ActionScript for Flash 5—including the actions operators, functions, properties, and the many new objects and their methods—are covered. Also included is an Example Glossary for a quick lookup and a CD-ROM with the source files (FLA), the SWF files, and Flash 5 trial version software to test.

THE CORIOLIS GROUP, LLC   Telephone: 480.483.0192 • Toll-free: 800.410.0192 • In Canada: 905.477.0722 • www.coriolis.com
Coriolis books are also available at bookstores and computer stores nationwide.